Hope's Promise

Hope's Promise

Religion and Acculturation in the Southern
Backcountry

S. Scott Rohrer

THE UNIVERSITY OF ALABAMA PRESS
TUSCALOOSA

The University of Alabama Press
Tuscaloosa, Alabama 35487-0380

∞

The paper on which this book is printed meets the minimum requirements of
American National Standard for Information Science–Permanence of Paper for Printed
Library Materials, ANSI Z39.48-1984.

Library of Congress Cataloging-in-Publication Data

Rohrer, S. Scott, 1957–
  Hope's promise : religion and acculturation in the Southern backcountry / S. Scott Rohrer.
    p. cm. — (Religion and American culture)
  Includes bibliographical references and index.
  ISBN 0-8173-1435-0 (cloth : alk. paper)
  1. Moravians—North Carolina—Forsyth County—History. 2. British Americans—
North Carolina—Forsyth County—History. 3. Acculturation—North Carolina—Forsyth
County—History. 4. Ethnicity—North Carolina—Forsyth County—History. 5. Forsyth
County (N.C.)—Ethnic relations. 6. Forsyth County (N.C.)—Religious life and customs. 7. Evangelicalism—Social aspects—North Carolina—Forsyth County—History.
8. Christian communities—North Carolina—Forsyth County—History. 9. Frontier and
pioneer life—North Carolina—Forsyth County. I. Title. II. Religion and American culture (Tuscaloosa, Ala.)
  F262.F7R64 2005
  975.6'6700882846—dc22

                                                          2004008812

For Anne and Josh

Contents

Illustrations

Tables

Acknowledgments

This book has been a challenge to write on several levels. I would first like to thank those who provided so much encouragement and support over the past ten years during the many ups and downs of the research and writing process.

John B. Boles graciously agreed to read the completed manuscript, helped smooth out the writing, and steered me to the University of Alabama Press. John Stagg, my dissertation adviser at the University of Virginia, has been unflagging in his support of my work and endlessly patient with my numerous questions and concerns. His help was no small thing: John is editor of *The Papers of James Madison* and is an authority on, among other things, the War of 1812. A study on a small religious community in backcountry Carolina could not have been further removed from his research interests. Yet his enthusiasm for my work was genuine and long lasting. I benefited greatly from his extensive knowledge of social history and the early national period. I also learned a great deal from other members of Virginia's venerable History Department, most notably Stephen Innes and Peter Onuf. The first hesitant manifestations of this book appeared in their seminar classes, and they helped shape my work at an early stage.

A summary of the book was published in the summer 2001 issue of the *Journal of the Early Republic,* and I thank the editors for allowing me to use this material. Christine Leigh Heyrman and the anonymous readers of my article greatly clarified my arguments, astutely challenged many of my assumptions, and pushed me to take my analysis to another level. The final version has benefited immeasurably from their vigorous critiques. I also benefited greatly from the input of panelists and participants at two conferences. In 1997, I presented a paper on Hope at a conference of the Omohundro Institute of Early American History and Culture. I thank commentator Philip D. Morgan for his excellent suggestions in his critique, and I thank those audience members who urged me to integrate my work on religious acculturation with outside economic and political forces.

The symposium on German Moravians in the Atlantic world, held in April 2002 at Wake Forest University, played a far bigger role in the completion of this book than its organizers probably realized. I began rewriting my dissertation in earnest in late summer of 2001—and was promptly thrown off track by the events of September 11. Besides being a national tragedy, the terrorist attacks in New York and Washington forced me to work long and tiring hours at the Washington magazine where I work. The symposium succeeded in refocusing my efforts on the manuscript and in convincing me that my approach was the correct one. I returned from Winston-Salem, North Carolina, re-energized and determined to finish the manuscript by the end of 2003. I especially thank Marianne Wokeck for her encouragement, advice, and support. She took a great interest in my work and helped provide me with the confidence to finish. She also suggested using Hope as the title of the book. I also thank Michele Gillespie, Robert Beachy, and Randal Hall of Wake Forest for their encouragement and help.

Parts of chapter 1 appeared in the *North Carolina Historical Review* in 2002, and I am grateful to Anne Miller and her staff for permission to use this material. Aaron Spencer Fogleman played an especially important role in improving this section of the manuscript, and I thank him for his assistance. Quite simply, Aaron has proved to be the most perceptive critic of my work yet.

My debts to previous scholars of Moravianism, including Elisabeth W. Sommer, should be apparent. I gratefully acknowledge their excellent work and thank them for the support they have given mine. Daniel B. Thorp has written the finest study on Wachovia's founding, and I have relied greatly on his research throughout. I had the good fortune to meet Jon F. Sensbach in 1989 while working as a consultant at Old Salem Inc., and he has proved to be both a friend and a mentor since those days.

The research would not have been possible without the support of my friends at Old Salem and in the Moravian Church. I thank the staff of the Moravian Archives in Winston-Salem for making their impressive collections available to me. The archives staff—C. Daniel Crews, Richard Starbuck, and Grace Robinson—handled my ceaseless requests with patience and good humor. I also owe a large thanks to the staff of the Moravian Archives in Bethlehem, Pennsylvania, led by Vernon Nelson. It was in this congenial setting where I learned to read archaic German script, and it was there where I researched the northern origins of the *Landgemeinen*. The staff of Old Salem and the Museum of Early Southern Decorative Arts (MESDA) were exceedingly generous in making their collections available to me. Brad Rauschenberg, director of research, allowed me to copy vital biographical records that made the demographic study possible; the librarians were gracious in lending me books; and Jennifer Bean Bower assisted in providing illustrations. Other staff members, John Larson in particular, provided much other help as well, including lodging for a last-minute research trip to the archives.

Financial assistance on the graduate level aided the research. The North Caroliniana Society awarded me an Archie K. Davis fellowship in 1996 to support my research in North Carolina. The Society of Cincinnati provided a generous grant, and Virginia's History Department provided timely support along the way.

I owe a debt of gratitude to other friends, colleagues, and family members. Steve Manson, a childhood friend from New Jersey who has put up with me way too many years, converted the dissertation to Microsoft Word. This sleight of hand saved me from countless hours of retyping. I also thank my colleagues and friends at *National Journal* magazine—including Charles Green, Marge DuMond, Monica Sullivan, and Marty Davis—who have tolerated my love of history and taught me so much about good writing and editing. Jodie Morris took time out of her busy schedule at the magazine to produce two of the maps that appear in this book.

Last but not least, I thank the two most important people in my life—my wife, Anne, and son, Josh, who have supported me through all the highs and lows of writing this book. Anne, a talented wordsmith at the *Washington Post,* helped prepare the manuscript for publication, and Josh, a bright and inquisitive high school student, kept me on my toes with his probing questions about history that ranged from the bubonic plague of the medieval period to German military strategy in World War II. Their faith in me and in this book never wavered. And it is to them whom I dedicate this work, with love and gratitude.

A Note about Translations

The Moravians kept voluminous records, and many of these records have been translated into English. I have availed myself of these translations when available. Church records after 1845 were mostly in English. In the notes, I was the translator on those primary sources listed in German. I also relied on my own translations for the Land Arbeiter Conferenz, except where indicated (I am grateful to Frances Cumnock for her help with the Land Arbeiter Conferenz minutes).

Introduction

Hope's promise could be found in a remote corner of a remote community of an emerging evangelical world along the southern frontier. Hope, the settlement, was tucked among the hills of Piedmont North Carolina. Its founders—tobacco farmers and fishermen from Maryland—selected the site in 1772, partly for its promise as a farming community. Along the fertile banks of Muddy Creek, they would build their houses and establish their working farms of 175 acres and up. Hope, the congregation, represented something far more important to its founders than good soil and a bountiful supply of water. Here, in this backcountry haven, Hope's members would worship the Savior and raise their children in God's ways. As a sign of their commitment, the settlers built a small meetinghouse at the center of their community and a bridge over the river so that all interested hearers could reach this house of God.

Hope's promise represented something else, however, something deeper. These English speakers—former members of the Anglican Church who hailed from Carrollton Manor in Frederick County, Maryland, and who numbered about seventy-five souls in 1772—had chosen to live in an enclave of German-speaking evangelicals belonging to a German-based sect known formally as the Renewed Unitas Fratrum (Unity of Brethren) and informally as the Moravian Church. Small and obscure as it was, Hope was thus something quite interesting: an Anglo-American congregation of evangelicals residing in a predominately German-speaking enclave located along a predominately English-speaking frontier. These Anglo-Americans were the ultimate minority—a minority within a minority.

The Marylanders' seemingly unusual decision to live among German-speaking Moravians hints at the complexity of what was happening along the southern frontier in the eighteenth century. From Maryland to Georgia, the population of the southern backcountry was exploding in midcentury as thousands of settlers migrated from Pennsylvania and other northern colonies. North

Carolina alone watched its white population swell from 40,000 in 1740 to 175,000 in 1770. These newcomers to the southern backcountry were, in the words of Charles Woodmason, an Anglican missionary, from "all Sects and Denominations—A mix'd Medley from all countries and the Off Scouring of America." And they were, indeed, a diverse group: English, Scots and Scots-Irish, Welsh, Dutch, and German, among others. Their religious backgrounds were equally diverse: Separate Baptist, Presbyterian, Methodist, Quaker, Moravian, Dunker, and Lutheran.[1]

Other missionaries saw the migration in a more positive light than did Charles Woodmason. For them, the huge influx of people constituted an opportunity to spread their evangelical belief that one can achieve eternal life by undergoing a "new birth." The missionaries' optimism was well placed. As at Hope, the massive migration to the southern frontier was bringing people anxious to find not only land but God.[2] The overall migration was so large that it outran the ability of established churches and sects to supply ministers. Evangelical missionaries, ranging from the Moravians to the Baptists, traveled on horseback throughout the backcountry to fill the void, and they routinely drew crowds of people from diverse ethnic and religious backgrounds. Their work among both the churched and unchurched laid the groundwork for the growth and eventual dominance of evangelism throughout the South in the antebellum period.[3]

The intense rivalries among evangelical sects and their feuding leaders are well known and documented. Theologians argued passionately, and sometimes violently, over everything from baptism to conversion. Their followers, meanwhile, aggressively sought to win converts to Christ and to reform a world they saw as corrupt and godless. Their efforts often unleashed a flood of hostility from those at the receiving end of their proselytizing—the unsaved and the gentry.[4] Beneath all this divisiveness, though, evangelism was producing a different kind of tremor on the southern social landscape. By creating an evangelical culture centered on the new birth, this religious movement was influencing the very way that people from different ethnicities interacted. In open fields and at informal gatherings among the curious and the devout, communities of believers were forming. These communities were based not on ethnicity or nationality or sectarian loyalties, but on a commitment to Jesus Christ and the new birth. Within these communities of believers, peoples in a polyglot South met and mingled, creating social bonds that often transcended ethnicity and sectarian differences: English with German, Baptist with Presbyterian, "commoner" with gentry, and (within limits that grew stricter over time) white with black.[5]

Hope's Promise tells the story of one such community in the evangelical world: the Moravian colony in North Carolina called Wachovia, of which Hope was a member. This book, covering the years 1750 to 1860, peers into the inner workings of these communities of believers in an effort to answer far larger questions about religion, identity, ethnicity, and cultural development. By examining one outpost in an evangelical world that stretched in the 1750s from the northern colonies to Georgia, this study seeks to understand the ability of the new birth to mold a common identity among diverse groups of people. More specifically, it seeks to understand how an evangelical culture influenced the acculturation of ethnic groups in the southern backcountry. The settlement of Hope—the most obscure of the obscure—serves as the central metaphor in a complex story of religion and acculturation. Hope's promise, as should be abundantly evident in the following pages, represents the flowering of the evangelical dream of creating a community of believers based on Jesus Christ and not ethnicity or nationality.

The Moravians came to North Carolina in 1753. They founded der Wachau, or Wachovia, on a 98,895-acre tract that the brethren had purchased from Lord Granville, the last of the colony's original proprietors. The church leadership, based in Herrnhut, Saxony, envisioned Wachovia as a religious enclave where its followers could worship free of the persecution religious sects still faced in Europe. It also intended that this Moravian colony be a viable commercial enterprise. In the fertile soils of the southern backcountry, Wachovia was to be an economically diverse community mixing crafts and farming that would generate income to help support a Moravian missionary movement with global ambitions.[6]

The Unitas Fratrum had a long history behind it by the time it launched its colony in North Carolina. Followers of reformer John Hus founded the Moravian movement in Lititz, Moravia, in the mid-fifteenth century and preached a radical social doctrine. Disillusioned with a Catholic Church they saw as corrupt, they wanted to emulate the early primitive Christians by renouncing all worldly wealth and living a life of simple piety, based on a belief in Jesus Christ. Granted asylum in Moravia by a sympathetic archbishop, the brethren established a settlement in Lititz and proceeded to gain an impressive following by the early sixteenth century in Moravia and neighboring Bohemia. Membership totaled more than two hundred thousand on the eve of the Counter-

Reformation.[7] The Unity became so large that it became a threat to the Roman Catholic Church; in the early seventeenth century, Hapsburg emperor Ferdinand III spearheaded a Catholic attack on Protestantism that saw the brethren, now known as the Unitas Fratrum (or Unity of Brethren), forced underground during the Counter-Reformation. The Moravian congregations in Bohemia and Moravia disappeared as their members scattered to avoid persecution. Jan Amos Comenius, the last independent bishop of the ancient Unity, kept the episcopal succession—and the seed of faith—alive. Comenius found asylum in England. There, he recorded the Unity's beliefs in a document he titled *Ratio Disciplinas,* a document that Count Nicholas von Zinzendorf and his Moravian followers discovered in the eighteenth century.[8]

In 1722, carpenter Christian David led a small group of refugees from Moravia to Zinzendorf's estate at Berthelsdorf, seeking asylum.[9] The refugees' choice was an understandable one. Zinzendorf, who was born in 1700 and died in 1760, was a committed Pietist who would presumably be sympathetic to their plight. The count's maternal grandmother, Henriette Catherine von Gerstorff, raised Nicholas after his father died in 1700. From the outset, she exposed her young charge to the latest teachings from Halle, the center of German Pietism in the eighteenth century. Philipp Jakob Spener, the main pietist leader in Halle, became Nicholas's godfather, and other Pietists routinely stopped at the Gerstorff castle for lodging and companionship. In 1710, Nicholas's mother and grandmother sent him to Halle for his education. When Christian David's tiny band arrived in 1722 at the count's estate, Zinzendorf took them under his wing. Other emigrés followed until the settlement's population had reached two hundred by 1727. Zinzendorf eventually took charge of the settlement and compiled a set of regulations on civil life called "Manorial Injunctions and Prohibitions." He drew up a second document called the "Brotherly Union and Compact" that dealt with religious practices. The community, named Herrnhut, selected twelve elders with spiritual oversight of religious life. On August 13, 1727, the settlement held a communion service. Moravian Church historians mark this date as the rebirth of the Unity.

Zinzendorf guided the Unity during his lifetime and espoused "heart religion," where religion was to be a matter of feeling, not reasoning. He expressed an intense, almost mystical, devotion to Jesus Christ that went beyond what more mainstream Pietists and evangelicals preached.[10] For Zinzendorf, Jesus was the center of everything. "The Savior is our God," he liked to say. "Through him we know the Father and the Holy Spirit."[11] A critical component of his plan for Moravianism was his ecumenical vision. He wanted to

NICOLAUS LUDOVICUS COMES
A ZINZENDORF.

Count Nicholas von Zinzendorf, the leader of the Moravian Church in the eighteenth century, established the Diaspora in an effort to revitalize Christendom by spurring an awakening among individual hearers. *Collection of the Wachovia Historical Society, Winston-Salem, North Carolina; courtesy of Old Salem Inc., Winston-Salem, North Carolina.*

carry the message of Christ's salvation to all parts of the globe—"heathen" and Christian alike—and, in 1727, the Moravians began sending missionaries to continental Europe, Greenland, Africa, the Caribbean, South America, and North America for work among blacks, Indians, and whites. Besides trying to Christianize the "heathen," Zinzendorf established his "Diaspora": the Moravian missionaries' effort to win over Christians of other faiths to heart religion. The goal was a very pietistic one. Moravian missionaries sought to awaken spiritually dead worshippers of other faiths. Zinzendorf hoped to minimize doctrinal differences between Protestant denominations and create a Christian church family that, while having different worshipping styles, would be united in the figure of Jesus Christ. The count's highest hopes for this ecumenical vision were in America and specifically Pennsylvania. On the Monocasy Creek north of Philadelphia, the Unity purchased five hundred acres for a *Pilgergemeine*—a congregation town that would focus on missionary work. In 1741, Zinzendorf arrived to oversee the development of Bethlehem.[12] Within twelve years, the Unity cast its eye southward as well because of the need to find a refuge for members of two European congregations and to generate income for a debt-laden Unity.[13]

The large tract the brethren bought in central North Carolina was chosen carefully to meet their spiritual and worldly goals. The site was relatively empty but not isolated. Thus, the Moravian colony would have some distance from neighbors while not being too far from markets. The land itself was beautiful— well wooded and watered among rolling hills. Located at the three forks of Muddy Creek, the tract "has countless springs, and numerous fine creeks. . . . There is much beautiful meadow land," Bishop Augustus Gottlieb Spangenberg recorded in his diary.[14]

Church authorities in Bethlehem handpicked ten men to establish a base on the North Carolina frontier.[15] This vanguard left Bethlehem on October 8, 1753, and founded a small village called Bethabara, the house of passage. The Unity established two other villages (Bethania in 1759 and Salem, Wachovia's capital, in 1766) known as *Ortsgemeinen,* or congregation towns, where church leaders restricted residency to full-time church members and expected inhabitants to devote their lives to Jesus and the church. In practice, this meant that the church owned the land and tightly controlled the economy and residents' social lives. Here, in these congregation towns, the Unity would realize its dream of creating communities of the truly devout that would set an example for others to emulate. Christian love would be the bond that united inhabitants.[16]

But there was another side to this religious mission. The mandate to revitalize Christianity by introducing inhabitants to the new birth resulted in the formation of Moravian societies, where interested hearers could participate in Moravian congregational life without having to become full members of the Unity. A second settlement type grew up around these societies: *Landgemeinen,* or farm congregations, that consisted of full and partial members. Under the

Diaspora, Moravian missionaries in the northern colonies offered Christians of all faiths a chance to worship with the Moravians and learn of Christ's liberating power while remaining members of their home churches. In the 1760s and early 1770s, largely in response to this missionary outreach, nearly three hundred society members from northern colonies founded three *Landgemeinen* settlements (Friedberg, Friedland, and Hope) in southern Wachovia. In the *Landgemeinen,* diverse groups of German- and English-speaking settlers from a variety of religious backgrounds did not live in compact towns but on dispersed family farms with less oversight from church authorities. By 1800, Wachovia's population totaled some twelve hundred pilgrims, 88 percent of whom were German speakers from Lutheran, Reformed, and Moravian traditions. The remaining 12 percent were Anglo-Americans, Scots-Irish, Irish, and others from western Europe, the Caribbean, the northern states, and elsewhere.[17] Living side by side in six distinct settlements under different rules, yet sharing a common belief in the power of the new birth, Wachovia's inhabitants created one of the most sophisticated and enduring religious communities in early America.[18]

It is within Wachovia's borders, amid a complex ethnic and religious landscape, that we can so clearly see how an evangelical culture influenced social development and the interaction of diverse groups of evangelicals. As the Moravian experience demonstrates, assimilation among evangelicals was multi-layered and worked in three stages.[19] In the first stage, evangelism—because of its ability to create a community of believers centered on the new birth—helped create the conditions that made intermixing between various ethnic groups possible. These individuals met and mingled in and outside of the meetinghouse and came to share a close bond from having undergone a rigorous conversion. This common experience enabled the reborn to overcome ethnic and social differences, leading to close friendships and often intermarriage. Thus, the conversion experience and religious life fostered an intermixing that produced swift and decisive cultural change beginning in the first generation. This, however, was not traditional "assimilation," where a minority group absorbed the ways of the dominant cultural group. Instead, different cultural groups coalesced around a shared evangelical religion to produce a new "ethnicity" that was an amalgam of their respective cultures. Ethnicity, in this case, did not mean a sense of peoplehood defined by language, customs, place, and a shared ancestry. It was, instead, a sense of peoplehood defined by religion. Such a phenomenon was not unique to evangelism; certain other religions such as Mormonism could produce the same results. In the 1940s, soci-

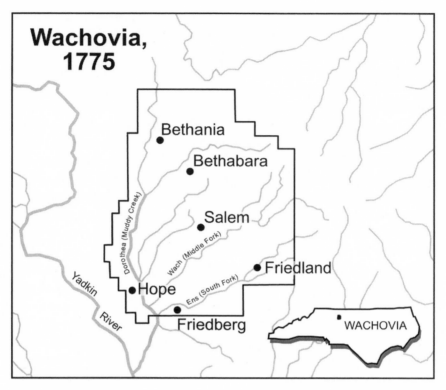

Map by Jodie Morris.

ologist Ruby Jo Reeves Kennedy coined a phrase for the impact of religion on acculturation—a "triple melting pot." That is, nationality groups merged through intermarriage and acculturation into their larger respective religious backgrounds.[20]

While this new ethnicity was being created, evangelical religion was helping to drive a second stage of acculturation. Evangelicals, unlike many Anabaptist and utopian sects, were never recluses from the world. They actively sought to convert the unconverted and to reform a corrupt world they saw around them. This mandate meant that evangelicals were engaging the outside world on several fronts, from the frontier store to the meetinghouse. Such an engagement led to extensive intermixing with outsiders in the economic, religious, and political spheres, an engagement that changed the evangelical in profound ways. It meant, in the case of the Moravians, that the brethren were drawing closer to their southern and American neighbors, and this growing closeness was occurring at the same time the brethren were creating creole families and forming multiethnic congregations. The first two stages overlapped, and they combined to produce a third stage of assimilation, which in the case of Wachovia began about 1830. The separate cultural and religious ingredients from the first two stages mixed together to produce something quite unique: an Anglo-German culture that was drawing ever closer to American and southern society. In this third stage, acculturation accelerated under the impact of intermixing, and the brethren became even more "American" and "southern." The use of the German language declined, and the nature of religious commitment shifted. Yet the impact of the first stage remained critical, and the commitment to heart religion remained strong. The brethrens' world of the 1830s and beyond was very much an Anglo-German one whose foundation remained evangelical religion. In this religious "melting pot," Wachovia became an amalgam of cultures whose key ingredient was evangelism.

Part One of *Hope's Promise*—three chapters in all—shows in detail how this new ethnicity arose during the first stage of acculturation. The story begins not in Europe but in the northern colonies, where Moravian missionaries attracted a large and diverse following among German and English speakers. Chapter 1 explores the origins of Wachovia's founders. It focuses on those brethren from Maryland, Pennsylvania, and Maine who founded the North Carolina *Landgemeinen*. These settlers were the most ethnically and religiously complex in Wachovia, and they played a huge—if not decisive—role in driving change within southern Moravianism. The opening chapter shows how Diaspora members began to form a Moravian identity before coming to Wachovia, and it explains why these pilgrims migrated to North Carolina. Chapter 2 concentrates on the heart of the evangelical experience—the new birth. It demonstrates how evangelicals regardless of ethnicity came to share a bond as reborn Christians. The chapter also shows how religious life, and strife, contributed to the acculturation process. Chapter 3 looks at the Anglo-German world that emerged from all this internal intermixing. By peering into the workings of Moravian families, the chapter reveals that Anglo-Americans and German speakers successfully merged their two respective cultures into a new ethnicity based on heart religion.

Chapters 4 and 5 deal with the second stage of the assimilation process—the Moravians' encounters with the outside world. Chapter 4 looks at the Revolutionary era and its impact on Wachovia. The American war for independence forced North Carolina's Moravians to take sides and to get involved with the political issues of the day. The tremendous stresses of war helped forge a sense of nationalism among Moravians of all ethnicities, and the war accelerated the process by which the brethren saw themselves as "American." Chapter 5 examines a closely related development—how North Carolina's brethren began to see themselves as "southern." The Moravians participated fully in the regional and national economies, and through this participation, they began absorbing the ways of their neighbors. Acculturation in the economic realm was nowhere more evident than in the brethrens' attitudes toward slavery and religion. The Moravians became willing, and in some ways eager, participants in slavery. By holding slaves, they identified even closer with their fellow southerners.

The concluding chapter looks at the third stage of assimilation through the eyes of a twenty-eight-year-old German-speaking Dane who arrived in Wachovia in 1834 to become pastor to the congregation at Bethania. The Reverend George Frederic Bahnson was very much an outsider who was somewhat taken aback by what he found in his new home: a community that was very southern, American, and evangelical. The first two stages had produced a thorough assimilation into American and southern life. The use of German was on the wane, and North Carolina's Moravians were becoming both more mainstream and more like other southern evangelicals. Yet in 1860, the brethren still followed heart religion, and elements of their German culture endured.

The story is important in several particulars. *Hope's Promise* is one of the first studies on evangelism to explore in such detail the effect of an evangelical culture on ethnicity and social development. Historians have recognized that evangelism attracted a diverse following, but few have examined how the new birth itself influenced the acculturation of ethnic groups on the community level. Instead, the political implications of evangelism continue to fascinate historians. This fascination takes two forms: one school of historians seeks to understand how evangelical religion contributed to the rise of individualism and democracy in the early Republic, and a second school debates how evangelicals tried to reform—or not reform—American society. For historian Rhys Isaac, the radicalism of evangelicals produced a cultural clash in Virginia as the Baptists confronted the gentry with a spirited challenge to their worldly lifestyle centered on tobacco, horse racing, gambling, and drinking.[21] For Nathan O. Hatch, evangelism helped democratize American society by giving power to ordinary people.[22] Countless other historians have likened the explosive growth of the Baptists and Methodists in the early nineteenth century to an invasion, with circuit-riding evangelicals putting older, supposedly more mainstream churches on the defensive in a cultural war.[23] Certainly, such scholarship has proved fruitful, illuminating the tensions in southern society and the inherent radicalism of evangelical religion. But this paradigm of political/cultural conflict continues to dominate historians' understanding of evangelism, with new works merely arguing over the radicalism of evangelism.[24]

Hope's Promise, by contrast, explores another side of evangelism and its cultural importance—the role of religion as unifier and not as divider. In backcountry settlements such as Hope, North Carolina—obscure places that have been little studied and little understood—evangelicals from different ethnicities and backgrounds coalesced around the new birth to form sophisticated communities of believers.[25] As places where the unsaved learned how to become one with Jesus Christ, these communities stood at the center of the evangelical experience. The sinner did not walk alone in this spiritual journey but with hundreds of other pilgrims. Seekers forged tight bonds on religious and social levels, and they created relationships that had momentous consequences for their communities, for the acculturation of various ethnic groups, and ultimately for the South.

Evangelism's ability to unify disparate groups and influence acculturation becomes clearer when this religious movement is compared with others in pre–Civil War America. In broader studies of American religion, historians have shown how religion and ethnicity reinforced each other, with religion serving as an important tool in enabling immigrant culture to survive in a new land. Steven M. Nolt offers one of the most recent examples of this genre. In his book, *Foreigners in Their Own Land,* he demonstrates how Pennsylvania's Germans managed to keep a distinctive identity in the early Republic. For these Lutheran and Reformed Germans, *avoiding* evangelism became a way to maintain their ethnic identity.[26] Religion and ethnicity, in other words, were closely intertwined, with religion being used as a bulwark to defend traditional ethnicity and a sense of peoplehood. Evangelism worked differently: for its adherents, evangelism was not a means to protect ethnicity. Developing a heart religion concerned them; ethnicity itself did not.

Because evangelism attracted people from diverse backgrounds, historians' transatlantic view of cultural change has its limitations for understanding how assimilation proceeded among evangelical groups in early America. In the transatlantic paradigm, historians typically track an ethnic religious group, such as a community of Scots-Irish Presbyterians or Russian Mennonites, from its Old World roots to America in an effort to understand how the group gradually accommodated (or did not accommodate) to its New World environment.[27] Such an approach has its parallels in Moravian studies as well. Most works present North Carolina's Moravians as a "German" religious group that confronted an alien environment in the New World. Historian Jerry Lee Surratt, for one, argues that Salem declined from a strict, Old World–style Christian community in the 1770s to an Americanized secular town by the Civil War. The model developed by Ferdinand Tonnies heavily influenced Surratt's interpretation of this decline; *Gemeinschaft,* or community, seeks to preserve itself through isolation from *Gesellschaft,* or society and association. Under this model, community involved the old, warm personal way of village life; society involved the more modern, impersonal urban life. The village, in other words, was a warm and caring place that disappeared under the onslaught of modernization. In Surratt's study, outside "American" forces undermined Salem's purity as *Gemeinschaft* gave way to *Gesellschaft.*[28]

A close variation of this view is that the Moravians lost their Germanness and religious distinctiveness after encountering American individualism in the countryside. Assimilation, in other words, was generational; those brethren born into the American landscape became Americanized and somewhat estranged from their elders, who adhered to an older view of what community should be.[29] For historian Elisabeth W. Sommer, the change was more than generational; Salem itself came of age during the Revolutionary period, with American notions of freedom penetrating the central *Ortsgemeine* and changing how youths looked at authority and their German connection. Inevitably, German and American brethren on opposite sides of the Atlantic Ocean grew apart.[30]

Historian Daniel B. Thorp offers one of the most sophisticated views of Moravian assimilation. He argues that the brethren and their leaders sought to selectively adapt to their American environment while retaining their core values. In an article on Moravian assimilation, he describes how the clash between a religious movement and the backcountry environment resulted in the Moravians modifying their agricultural practices and settlement plans.[31] More broadly, in his book *The Moravian Community,* Thorp describes how Wachovia in its early years both resisted and embraced change: "While Wachovia's residents did seek to protect many elements of their community from outside influences, they also made a deliberate and sustained effort to get along with their neighbors and to integrate themselves into the legal, political, and economic systems around them."[32] The theoretical foundation of his thesis rests on the work of

Fredrik Barth, a Norwegian anthropologist. For Barth, groups maintain their distinctiveness in a multiethnic society not by isolating themselves, but by "maintaining peaceful, regulated contact across clearly defined cultural boundaries." Barth's model, and Thorp's interpretation of it, makes the implicit assumption that these groups were relatively cohesive and somewhat monolithic as they confronted an "outside" world "across clearly defined" borders.[33]

All of these views—including Thorp's sophisticated version—miss the layered complexity of what was really happening. For starters, the Moravians were not a traditional "German" immigrant community that traveled en masse from the Old World to the New. They were an ecumenical group, consisting of congregations scattered throughout the Western Hemisphere. In America, the Diaspora's aggressive missionary efforts among Christians meant that the movement from the 1740s on was attracting not only English-speaking Anglicans, Methodists, and Presbyterians but also German-American Lutheran and Reformed settlers in various stages of assimilation. In Wachovia's case, such "nontraditional" members outnumbered the supposedly "traditional" Moravians who did come to North Carolina from Germany by way of Bethlehem at the behest of church leadership. Indeed, the migration to the North Carolina *Landgemeinen* was far larger than historians have recognized. Wachovia quite quickly created a creole population of Anglo-American and German speakers in various stages of assimilation who lived among Danes, Scots, Irish, and others. As the three-stage assimilation model demonstrates, cultural and religious change came simultaneously from within Wachovia and from without, thanks to intermixing among ethnically diverse Moravians and among outsiders. In meetinghouses and farm fields, encounters between the saved helped shift the social and religious landscape in numerous ways. Change, of course, was not generational involving a Germanic group slowly shedding its Old World ways—it began almost immediately with the earliest arrivals to Wachovia. Nor was change declensional. From the outset, the first generation of brethren struggled to maintain their piety while immersing themselves in their American surroundings.

The Moravians may seem like an odd choice for a case study involving evangelism. The Renewed Unitas Fratrum of the eighteenth century, after all, had its roots in German Pietism—the reform movement that sought to revitalize religious life in western Europe and elsewhere by leading people to a new birth. Count Zinzendorf, the brethrens' revered leader in the eighteenth century, was a Pietist and a Lutheran who espoused doctrines that often left theologians from other faiths puzzled and suspicious. Many historians and laypersons, as a result, perceive the Unity as another quirky German sectarian group that espoused a strange brand of religion. Although the Unity today remains a worldwide church, it has faded into relative obscurity, and this obscurity has contributed to the contemporary belief that the Moravians were minor players in the eighteenth- and nineteenth-century evangelical world who were not representative of anything.[34]

Scholars of Moravianism, ironically, have contributed to these misperceptions by focusing on only one aspect of the brethrens' complex movement—the congregation town. These towns were small, restricted, and somewhat insular. Religious practices were far more stringent within their borders, and the towns' ethnic makeup was mainly German. The countless studies on the *Ortsgemeinen* have left scholars of early America with the impression that the Moravians lived mostly in these tightly controlled congregation towns and were thus overwhelmingly German and somewhat utopian.[35]

In reality, more than 50 percent of Wachovia's population lived outside of the congregation towns, and the largest settlement well into the antebellum period was not Salem, the capital, but the farm congregation of Friedberg. When the full Moravian movement is taken into account, a quite different view of the brethren emerges that shows they were distinctive in some ways *and* typical in others. Wachovia's population was not at all unique—it was a true "mix'd Medley" that reflected the makeup of the southern backcountry. Indeed, in a description of Wachovia in 1765, Anglican itinerant Charles Woodmason astutely noted that the Moravians "receive to their Community Persons of all Nations, Religion and Language."[36] Wachovia's openness and diversity were not unique in the Moravian world, either. In the Unity's northern province, membership was equally diverse and complex, with Zinzendorf's Diaspora attracting a large and vibrant society movement made up of members from many different faiths and ethnicities. The Unity also had long experience evangelizing among Anglo speakers, launching congregations in England, the very heart of Anglicanism.[37]

The evangelical world, of course, was not a monolithic one. Its leaders fiercely debated baptism, conversion, confessionalism, revivalism, and other key doctrines.[38] And its followers could be as prejudiced toward other ethnic groups as any American or European of the early modern period. Yet, despite these differences, evangelism did constitute a coherent movement, albeit one with many branches. Evangelism was characterized by biblicism; individual and experiential conversion; energetic activism; and the strong belief that Jesus Christ and his work was at the center of Christianity. Evangelical followers of all faiths who underwent an emotional new birth came to share a belief in religious renewal and the power of the "new light"—that the spirit of God dwelled within the reborn. When the movement is seen in this way, it becomes clear that evangelism was a broadly encompassing reform movement in America and western Europe whose ranks included the Moravians, Pietists, some Anglicans, Methodists, Baptists, revivalists, and others. It also becomes clear that the brethren not only occupied one corner of this evangelical world but also were a prominent part of the movement. Seen as small and quirky today, the Moravians in the eighteenth century constituted the largest and most important pietist group in the Western Hemisphere. The brethren were extremely active in the backcountry and elsewhere, and their missionaries consistently attracted large, interethnic crowds from all denominations. Within the evangelical world, the brethren earned the admiration of its many friends and the wrath of its enemies. Moravian ranks included powerful members of the nobility in Germany and some of the most energetic and ubiquitous missionaries in the Christian world. Contemporaries did not see the brethren as inconsequential; they saw them as allies or threats, depending on their viewpoint.[39] The Moravians, as historians of Methodism have documented, greatly influenced the development of the Methodist Church and its religious practices, ranging from the lovefeast and "classes" to the use of circuit riders.[40] In North Carolina, Wachovia's Moravians in 1753 shared with southern evangelicals a core belief in the new birth and a strong missionary impulse; in 1850, the two groups had even more in common as Wachovia's residents became more southern and as they immersed themselves ever deeper in the evangelical world. Both groups changed, and both became more alike, over the 110 years of this study.

Although no one group—not even the Baptists or Methodists—can claim to be truly "representative," Wachovia makes for an excellent place to study evangelical culture and acculturation because of its great ethnic diversity. It was here in this southern outpost where communities of different faiths and ethnicities formed around the new-birth experience. Wachovia contained clearly defined borders with an array of settlement types that make comparisons between different groups both possible and illuminating. The excellent Moravian Church records, when combined with traditional courthouse records, allow us to look at religious life in detail that is difficult elsewhere.

Using a series of case studies, *Hope's Promise* seeks to recapture the lives of a fascinating group of evangelicals. The brethrens' experience indicates that where evangelical religion was a significant force among the laity, communities of different ethnicities were interacting, adapting, and changing—usually in far-reaching ways. In at least one outpost of the Lord, German and English came together as one.

Hope's Promise

PART ONE
Coming Together

Creating an Anglo-German World

In the backwoods of colonial North Carolina, the brethren cobbled together a cohesive community out of many disparate parts. Their glue was an evangelical religion centered on the new birth. The brethrens' task of forging a Moravian identity actually began years earlier, in places as disparate as Carrollton Manor, Maryland, and Broadbay, Maine. There, English and German speakers learned of the Lord and his mysterious ways. They learned enough that they came south to a place called der Wachau, where they founded three settlements outside of the church-run congregation towns and began life anew. Under the new-birth experience, the Moravians created an ethnicity centered on heart religion. The process of acculturation began quickly, and so did a complex series of changes.

I

Prelude
The Northern Years

The Peddycoards' journey to heart religion began not in a pew but behind a plow. Nathan Peddycoard moved his family to Carrollton Manor, Maryland, in the early 1750s from Prince George's County, where he had run a tavern. Religion, however, did not draw the Peddycoards to Carrollton; land did. Apparently tired of tavern life and a money-losing business, Nathan wanted the chance to farm. Once settled at Carrollton, Nathan and his sons began working the fields on the small tract that he rented from the wealthy Carroll clan of Annapolis. The former tavern keeper grew tobacco—some years, as much as 2,918 pounds—that allowed him to pay his rent and to trade on the transatlantic market. He also grew another highly marketable crop—hemp, the tall asiatic herb whose fiber was used to make rope.[1]

For Nathan, these were good years. Besides tobacco, he grew a trio of grains (wheat, rye, and oats) and built up herds of cattle, sheep, swine, and horses. His family farm prospered, with his estate reaching a modest but respectable value of 111 pounds at his death in 1759.[2] Nathan's focus during the 1750s, not surprisingly, remained firmly on the plow. Members of the Anglican Church, the Peddycoards paid little attention to spiritual matters. Building a successful farm consumed them; religion did not.[3]

The Peddycoards were hardly unique in their indifference to religion. Carrollton Manor was populated by tenants who focused on affairs of the world and not of the Lord. As his death approached, Nathan very likely had no inkling that this was about to all change—and that the agents of this change would be a relatively small, foreign-speaking sect from Saxony, Germany. Invited to preach on the manor by the Carrolls' steward, the Moravians confidently entered this English-speaking world and thus set off a complex chain of events that culminated in the founding of the Hope settlement in North Carolina in 1772.[4]

The encounter between German missionary and English tenant was one rich with irony and significance. That the Moravians were at Carrollton at all says a great deal about the brethrens' dream of reforming Christianity. And that they were so successful says even more about the power of the evangelical message. It was at Carrollton that the "unsaved" were awakened to Jesus Christ, became active in Moravian societies, and began to formulate a close identity with an evangelical religion whose roots were in Germany.

Such encounters between unsaved and missionary were repeated across the North among a diverse group of English- and German-speaking colonists. In all places, the awakened underwent a life-changing new birth that reoriented their lives toward Jesus Christ and the church. For many new members, evangelism became so important to them that they moved several times to be closer to their home congregation. The acculturation process, however, was an incomplete one during the pre-Revolutionary years and was filled with pitfalls. Nearly three hundred members of the society movement—mostly from Carrollton Manor; southeastern Pennsylvania; and Broadbay, Maine—decided to migrate to Wachovia in the 1760s and early 1770s, a migration that led to the founding of Hope, Friedberg, and Friedland. A general dissatisfaction with life in the North helped drive this migration: land prices were rising. And land shortages were becoming more common. But religious factors loomed even larger: several congregations—most notably at Carrollton and at Broadbay—faced severe internal problems. A unique Moravian community, meanwhile, was taking shape in the North Carolina backcountry that served as a beacon to those society members unhappy with their lot in Maryland and the North. Land beckoned, and to the Peddycoards' astonishment, so did God.

Carrollton Manor and the Formation of a Moravian Congregation

For Nathan Peddycoard, deciding to give up his inn may have been the easy part. Deciding where to go was likely harder, given the great range of options in early America at midcentury. To name just two, the fertile Shenandoah ran just to the south and the North Carolina backcountry beyond that, where a two-hundred-acre farm could be had quite cheaply. The Peddycoards, however, chose not to buy land on any of these frontiers but to rent a small tract on a manor owned by a politically unpopular Catholic family. That the Peddycoards made this decision said a great deal about the perceived virtues of Carrollton Manor.

The manor, located in the heart of Monocacy Valley in western Maryland, was part of the substantial Carroll family empire amassed by the founding patriarch, Charles the Settler, who relentlessly accumulated money, slaves, and property after emigrating from Ireland in the late seventeenth century. Charles owned several estates throughout the colony, including Doohoragen Manor at Elk Ridge and Poplar Island on the Chesapeake Bay.

Carrollton Manor was one of the family's largest holdings and one of its most lucrative. It was the Settler's son, Charles of Annapolis, who inherited the manor in the 1730s and who decided to develop the 12,553-acre tract not by deploying slave labor, but by using tenants to farm individual tracts of about one hundred acres. That way, the Carrolls would see their lands developed and improved without the family having to undergo the massive expense that acquiring and maintaining a large slave force involved. Charles recruited tenants from as far away as his native Ireland and from Germany, but he found most of his renters from eastern Maryland. As a recent chronicler of the Carroll family concluded, Charles's strategy proved to be "enormously successful," with the son negotiating nearly two hundred leases and putting more than nineteen thousand acres into production throughout the Carroll holdings.[5]

Carrollton Manor was plenty enticing to the Peddycoards and others despite the supposed drawbacks of renting. With its fertile and well-watered lands, the manor was ideal for the planting of grains and tobacco. One contemporary praised the county's "good clay soil" that gave "an excellent account of the seed entrusted to it." The manor's land itself was neither flat nor hilly but gently rolling.[6] The manor, which encompassed twenty square miles, ran along the Monocacy River south to the Potomac River, where it spread out in opposite directions in a shape that resembled an inverted T.[7]

The Peddycoards were English, as were most of Carrollton's inhabitants of two hundred people. The manor, in fact, constituted an English-speaking enclave in the populous German county of Frederick. In the years before 1773, German speakers constituted less than 10 percent of the manor's population, whereas the county itself was about 50 percent German.[8] German speakers flocked to Frederick County from southeastern Pennsylvania in the 1730s because of the land deals offered by Maryland's proprietor Charles Calvert and the growing scarcity of land in Pennsylvania and because of the rising prices that accompanied this shortage. By 1755, the county had grown into the third largest in the province, with a population of 13,969.[9]

Most Carrollton tenants, including the Peddycoards, were Anglicans, but a recent historian of the manor found none of their names on the All Saints Parish register. Other faiths did little better. The Quaker community north of the manor had stagnated, and few tenants—possibly as few as two—were Friends.[10] Most of the tenants who affiliated with the Moravians later recalled having spent childhoods in a religious wilderness. Mary Padget, for one, told a church chronicler that, as a child, "she did not get the least learning or any instruction in the Christian faith . . . but had grown up in the greatest ignorance and stupidity."[11] Such was the religious milieu that the Moravians encountered as they entered the area in 1758: an ethnically diverse population of German and English speakers who had had little or no exposure to evangelical religion. Culturally, the area was a complex mix between the Chesapeake, with its slave-oriented tobacco plantations, and the grain-based family farms of Pennsylvania. Carrollton reflected both environments. The Peddycoards, quite typically, owned a slave, grew tobacco, and cultivated several grains on a family farm of about one hundred acres.

The Peddycoards had never heard of the Moravians when the brethren first began appearing at the manor and in Frederick County in the late 1750s. That they got to hear the brethren preach at all on the manor was largely due to the efforts of one man—the Carrolls' longtime steward at Carrollton, Joseph Johnson. Johnson's job was straightforward: to oversee the manor for the Carrolls. He collected rents and enforced the leases, among other things. It was a job that Johnson performed fairly capably, holding the post until his death in 1781. At his passing, Charles Carroll, son of Charles Carroll of Annapolis, praised his old steward as an "honest man," although he added that Johnson was "too indolent and indulgent to the tenants, at our expense."[12] Johnson, unlike the Peddycoards, had been exposed to evangelical religion. Raised in England, he was "awakened" there, according to a Moravian account of the manor congregation's founding, but "afterwards lost this received Grace by being enamored with this World." Like the Peddycoards, Johnson had been raised Anglican but was no longer active in that church. Johnson became "stirred up again by reading Mr. [George] Whitefield's evangelical sermons" and began to worry anew about the salvation of his family and servants. Unsure what to do, the steward talked with a member of the congregation that the Moravians had founded in northern Frederick County that became known as Graceham. Johnson informed George Gump, who lived about three miles from his house, of his worries for himself and for others, and he asked the brethren to send missionaries to the manor. He also later offered the use of his house for preaching. The Moravians accepted the invitation to come preach. But because the pastor at Graceham, J. M. Zahn, spoke only German, they first had to find English-speaking missionaries who could successfully converse with Carrollton's tenants. Bethlehem found no shortage of candidates, sending in these early years more than ten missionaries, including Bishop Augustus Gottlieb Spangenberg, Richard Utley (who would later pastor to the fledgling Hope congregation in North Carolina), and the ubiquitous George Soelle (who would later pastor to the congregations in Maine and in Friedland). In 1762, the Provincial Synod in Bethlehem assigned Francis Boehler to visit the manor about once a month, a task he performed for the next four years. As the Moravians' popularity grew, Bethlehem agreed to grant a formal congregation to the manor in 1766 and to send Joseph Powell and his wife to minister full time to its members.[13]

For a worldwide organization engaged in missionary work to Christians and non-Christians alike, Carrollton Manor represented but one more opportunity to spread the word of Jesus' saving grace. The prospect of ministering to an English-speaking population was not at all troublesome to the German-based brethren. Instead, it was appealing, because they viewed the manor as a religiously apathetic place that needed some stirring up. By establishing a congregation at Carrollton, the Moravians believed they would be shining "a Light in a dark place, that thousands by Her light may See and joy in Her, and with Her find Shelter, Covert [Comfort], and Refuge in Jesus's Wounds."[14] The Reverend Powell viewed his mission in similar terms. In 1770, after four years of careful work on the manor, he described his congregation as a "Candle on a Hill" that was drawing the unconverted to the Savior by setting an example for others to emulate and by providing a place where the unconverted could learn how to be saved.[15]

The arrival of these German-speaking evangelists on the English manor aroused intense curiosity and, in time, some hostility. Nathan Peddycoard's oldest son, William Barton Peddycoard, was the first in his family to go hear the brethren preach. Curiosity, he recounted years later to a church chronicler, drew him to a sermon given by a missionary from the Moravian *Gemeine* at Lititz, Pennsylvania. William had never heard of the brethren up until then. The missionary, a Brother Sydrich, preached from John 1:9–12 on the true light. With little exposure to organized religion, William found the missionary's message intriguing, although it stirred up a host of conflicting emotions in him, ranging from excitement over the prospect of achieving eternal salvation to fear that he would be unable to actually achieve a new birth: "The discourse made a great impression on my heart, yet I did not understand all the phrases." The concept of a "true light" especially puzzled him. But William's curiosity was so aroused that he returned to hear more about his lost state and how he could escape it by turning to Jesus. The Moravians had entered William's life at a critical juncture. His father had died in 1759, and he had recently completed military service in the backcountry during the French and Indian War. As the oldest son, William was now considered the head of the family and had to help his mother raise his two siblings. Possibly because of these stresses, William "frequented their meetings incessantly" and found much comfort there: the Moravian message, he said, "became a balsam and nourishment for my heart . . . in good and bad days."[16]

On a small manor with a weak church structure, the Moravians rapidly became a force with their radical message that all true followers of the Savior could achieve salvation. During these first few weeks on the manor, Powell held the meetings at the house of a tenant named Zimmerman, where he and his wife were staying. Interested hearers crammed the front room, and Powell marveled at the diversity of attendees—Baptists, Anglicans, Catholics, and Reformed Germans. "This was a very extraordinary meeting, far exceeding last week—the power of God truly attending the Gospel word," Powell recorded in his diary of one such gathering.[17] Powell traveled throughout the valley, both inside and outside of the manor, and he held meetings wherever inhabitants expressed an interest in hearing him preach. One such meeting occurred in late August 1766. A large crowd was in town for court, and someone sent word that these visitors would like to hear Powell preach. He obliged. The Moravian pastor arrived promptly at the house of Noodley Masters along the Potomac, about twelve miles from his residence on the manor. The crowd was so large that Powell had to move the meeting outdoors. His host set up a "table under a large Tree in the field under which they sat close together on the grass entirely filling the shade." From a rustic pulpit by the tree, Powell preached from 2 Kings 5–13 on God's judgment of Ahaziah.[18] By September, Powell believed that he was making good progress: "One perceives a moving and awakening by Some, by others love and good will desiring to be better acquainted with us."[19] Within a few years, the Moravians had become the most successful church on the manor, persuading about one-fifth of all tenants to become converts.[20]

To aid the building of the congregation, Powell tried to make the Moravian presence felt in tangible ways by getting involved in tenants' daily lives. He helped neighbors raise barns, build houses, and husk corn.[21] He regularly crisscrossed the manor, visiting members and nonmembers alike, offering advice or lending a sympathetic ear to the troubled. For Powell, an important goal took shape: building a meetinghouse that would enable the congregation to function properly while allowing his wife and him to live in some basic comfort. His original accommodations, at the Zimmermans, were distressingly cramped:

eighteen persons occupied the house. Taking pity on the Powells' domestic situation, congregation member Matthew Markland offered the pastor and his wife the use of their new house, an offer that the Powells readily accepted despite its poor location. Congregation members donated furniture for the couple, and in August 1766, the Powells moved in with help from Markland. In their new accommodations, they had more room but still faced a major drawback. Markland's house was relatively isolated, or as Powell noted: "Our aboade [sic] now not lying so convenient for the people as hithertofore." Ironically, the Powells now lived among the tiny German-speaking population on the manor. Powell promptly introduced himself to his new neighbors, but in a further irony, none expressed an interest in participating in the German-based Moravian movement, "all as yet seeming satisfied with thare [sic] Religion."[22]

Powell viewed this latest living arrangement as temporary. A meetinghouse, he reasoned, was badly needed. It would become a concrete symbol of the Moravians' commitment to the manor. But just as important, a commodious and centrally located meetinghouse would presumably allow the pastor to build a more durable congregation, because it would have sufficient space to preach the word and to conduct school and meetings. In 1768, Powell and Joseph Johnson turned to Charles Carroll for help. Johnson and fellow member John Padget hand-delivered a letter to the squire in Annapolis that laid out the needs for a meetinghouse. They asked Carroll to donate a tract of manor land. Carroll rejected this initial plea, dismissing the two messengers with the declaration that "there was Religion enough already in the world." Powell was undaunted, however, and he authorized construction on the desired tract without Carroll's permission—and without the approval of the Provincial Synod. On September 27, twelve men gathered to begin building a meetinghouse that was to be thirty-two feet long by twenty feet wide. The men felled and squared fifty-eight logs, and Powell noted that they "all labored with such love and willingness as one likes to see." In early October, Powell suspended construction while Johnson again pleaded with Carroll to donate the tract for Moravian use. This time, Johnson found Carroll in a friendlier mood, although the esquire peppered his steward with questions about this German evangelical sect that was proselytizing on his manor. Finally, Carroll agreed to a deal: the brethren could use the ten-acre tract "for the consideration of a rose per year" for twenty-one years. The promissory note was dated October 3, 1768. Not wasting any time, the men resumed work on October 4 with renewed vigor. A week later, they laid the bottom logs for the building. Sixteen men, with supportive female congregants in attendance, then "raised the Chapel in readyness for the frame of

Rafters." The roof came on November 13, and the two chimneys and fireplaces were finished then as well. On December 3, the Powells moved into their new home, using Matthew Markland's wagon to haul their furniture.[23] Powell, of course, was quite pleased. In a letter to Bethlehem, he described the meetinghouse as a large house "finely Sittuated [sic] on a Town Road, with each necessary convenience." Powell had gone out on a limb to build this meetinghouse, beginning construction before he had the permission of both Carroll and the Synod. A bit sheepishly, Powell defended his actions in the same letter as necessary and proper.[24] In a later visit, Carroll himself approved of Powell's handiwork: "Through your Industry, it by far is the neatest, prityest on my Manner [sic]."[25]

All this success bred resentment from some tenants who did not share their neighbors' zeal for evangelical religion. Some tried to talk people out of attending Moravian services, but Powell maintained that this tactic backfired: "Instead of hurt, it occasions strangers to visit our each and every meeting." The most potentially violent incident occurred on November 29, 1768, while the brethren were building the meetinghouse. Enemies of the Unity tried to evict Powell's wife from her house while she was home alone, but she foiled the attempt by bolting the front door and leaning against it with all her might. Matthew Markland and his son came to her rescue "and gave them a smart Repulse," and the attackers were forced to "retreat with shame." Powell believed that the completion of the meetinghouse further discouraged these foes: "Some of our Disaffected Neighbors having had hopes we'd leave this part for want of a place of Dwelling are now quite still and seem better satisfied."[26]

The building of the meetinghouse and the hostility that it engendered among some tenants brought the congregation closer together. As Powell's diary indicates, congregation members took great pride in the building of the meetinghouse. Its construction was a communal task that the congregation undertook with enthusiasm. And as Powell intended, its completion benefited the entire congregation. The meetinghouse not only provided an all-important gathering place for the congregation to meet, talk, and pray but also served as the physical symbol of the changes that were occurring in the brethrens' lives. Within its log walls, members could renew their vows of commitment to their Savior. That some neighbors objected to their affiliation with an evangelical sect did not seem to bother them. Indeed, the evidence is in the other direction: members drew closer in these years.

For many, congregational life was a family affair. When one family member joined the Moravians, others in that family followed. The Peddycoards were typical. William Barton, as the oldest son, took the lead in bringing religion to his kin. He became active in the congregation and encouraged his mother and siblings to join him. They agreed to, and so did other members of the growing Peddycoard clan. Sophia Elisabeth Peddycoard, the wife of William's brother Basil, was raised as a Quaker. She learned of the brethren through the activities of her husband and brother-in-law. As her memoir later explained, "The gospel of the atoning sufferings and death of the Savior for us soon made such an impression upon her that the Holy Ghost was able to convict her of un-righteousness." In 1767, she was quite worried about her unsaved state and approached Powell "in tears, desiring we'd visit her." Her "earnest desire" was to be baptized for the first time. Such feelings, her chronicler explained, "began at her first awakening about four weeks prior."[27]

This commitment extended in other ways. Some county residents found congregational life so appealing that they moved to the manor solely to be closer to the brethren. Two prominent examples were Daniel Smith and Elizabeth Goslin, both of whom played a pivotal role in the founding of Hope. Smith, a fisherman and tobacco farmer, lived along the Potomac about eleven miles from the manor. He became acquainted with the brethren well before Powell's arrival in 1766, likely having heard a missionary preach in the area. The pastor described Smith as a "loving friend" who persuaded Powell to come and preach in Smith's neighborhood after his arrival. Smith, Powell noted with satisfaction, "intends to move from thence and settle near us." In January 1767, Smith kept his promise, and Powell repaid this act of commitment by helping Daniel and his family raise their new house.[28] Goslin, a widow since 1763, expressed equal determination to join the brethren on the manor. Like the Smiths, Goslin attended Moravian preaching in her neighborhood and underwent a new birth that saw her develop "trust in her heart." She told Powell that she wanted to "leave the Dark neighborhood wherein she lives and move here amongst us." In November 1770, she relocated to the manor with her family, "purely to be nearer the sound of the Gospel," Powell recorded in his diary.[29]

Maine and the Moravian Diaspora

Broadbay, Maine, was a world removed from Carrollton Manor. In this northern outpost of Moravianism, no tobacco plantations were to be found. Maine was then part of the northern Massachusetts frontier, a cold and forbidding place where farmers struggled with the harsh weather, short growing season, and rocky soil.[30] They grew corn, potatoes, and some wheat. Broadbay itself was not a Catholic-owned manor populated by English speakers. It was mostly German, with a few Scots-Irish.

The settlers lived in the Waldo Patent, near the Medomak River, which widened at one stretch into a so-called Broad Bay. In 1732, Samuel Waldo, the Boston agent for a Hamburg merchant house, sent his son to Germany to seek migrants to settle on his patent. The Waldos promised one hundred acres to every man who made the treacherous transatlantic journey; by 1760, a thousand settlers had taken up their offer. In 1742, the first Moravian in the area—George Hahn, a single brother from Herrnhut—arrived at Broadbay, where he found a predominately German-speaking population of Lutheran and Reformed settlers from the Palatinate. Hahn was not a missionary, but he became one anyway because of the barren religious scene he encountered. "At the place where we lived there was neither school nor church, so a group gathered around me of those who were concerned for their own and their children's salvation," he recalled in his *Lebenslauf* (life story).[31] He held prayer meetings and lovefeasts and preached in the parlor of his home. Thanks to Hahn's careful work, "the desire of the people to come under the care of the Moravian Church grew daily stronger," according to the Unity's account of the Broadbay congregation.[32] The response to Hahn's impromptu evangelizing was so strong that the Unity dispatched missionary George Soelle to begin ministering to the settlers; in 1762, he became their regular pastor when the settlers formed a congregation and built a meetinghouse.

In 1765 in the Unity's northern province, Broadbay and Carrollton represented the farthest outposts, both geographically and ethnically, of the Moravian missionary empire among Christians: a southern, English-speaking congregation that was light years away from a northern, German-speaking one. Yet their experiences were remarkably similar. "Unsaved" settlers learned of the brethren, asked to have a full-time missionary sent, and later formed a Moravian congregation that remained small and vibrant despite internal troubles. The mere existence of these two far-flung congregations demonstrated the ability of an evangelical religion to bridge ethnic, cultural, and geographic lines. Carrollton and Broadbay represented the flowering of Count Nicholas von Zinzendorf's ecumenical vision. His Diaspora produced members from widely different backgrounds and origins who shared common religious and familial values centered on the new birth and a commitment to Moravianism.

Zinzendorf began his Diaspora in Europe in the late 1720s to awaken the supposedly spiritually dead laity to Jesus Christ's saving grace while preserving the individuality of specific churches. He instructed his itinerants "to seek opinions and sectarianism. . . . Seek everywhere only those in churches who after Luke 6 have dug deeply and found Jesus to be the only one."[33] The Diaspora was meant to nurture deep spiritual communion with Christ by encouraging fellowship and biblical study. "The people" of the Diaspora, Zinzendorf counseled, "should only sing, pray and talk with one another. What goes beyond the discussion of Christian experience is offensive."[34] In other words, the count wanted Moravian missionaries in Europe, and later in Pennsylvania and elsewhere, to encourage Christians to organize societies for fellowship and spiritual growth, while giving these Christians the option of joining the Moravian congregations or remaining members of their home churches.[35]

The Diaspora sprang from a very pietistic impulse: the desire to reform the territorial church. Pietist reformers in Germany and elsewhere in the late seventeenth and early eighteenth centuries were critical of the territorial church, whose inclusiveness they believed resulted in congregations with large memberships and few true believers. Church life, they concluded, had become sterile and empty in the early modern period. It allowed people to lead seemingly religious lives without actually experiencing true faith and the saving grace of Jesus Christ; worshippers could go to confession, take communion, and return to their supposedly flawed lives. To revive the church, Pietists formed conventicles that were to meet in small groups for Bible study and Christian fellowship. Their goal was to plant seeds for Christian renewal that would blossom into genuine reform as the number of awakened believers grew.[36]

The Moravians launched their Diaspora activity in Pennsylvania in 1742 following the conclusion of Zinzendorf's failed ecumenical synods, where he had tried to unite that colony's feuding German sects under one Christian banner. The founding of Bethlehem and the arrival of the first "Sea Congregation" of Moravian pilgrims in 1741 supplied Diaspora leaders with the resources they would need to conduct broad evangelizing activity.[37] On July 15, 1742, Bethlehem sent out its first wave of missionaries—ten itinerants in all—with the goal of bringing "unchurched men and women to a saving knowledge of Jesus Christ."[38] The Moravians' timing was fairly good. Throughout the 1740s and beyond, the Great Awakening led by Presbyterian and Anglican dissenters was creating numerous opportunities for ecumenical-minded evangelists of all ethnicities to find eager audiences in Pennsylvania and elsewhere. The greatest awakener of them all—George Whitefield—was himself taking his message of spiritual renewal to anyone who would listen. Before huge and ethnically mixed crowds, Whitefield downplayed denominational distinctions and preached the commonality shared by Christians. "Don't tell me you are a Baptist, an Independent, a Presbyterian, a Dissenter—tell me you are a Christian, that is all I want," he asserted on one occasion. Whitefield's latitudinarian message was heard by crowds of German and English speakers who belonged to the Presbyterians, Baptists, Lutherans, Quakers, and others. In stirring up thousands of people across the middle colonies, the Great Awakening created an evangelical ferment that helped prepare the way for Moravian itinerants and others by breaking down the walls of separation between people of different ethnicities. As one historian concluded about the period, "Conversion was beginning to draw people into a worldwide community of imagined strangers bound together by a power transcending local church covenants: a common experience of new birth."[39]

Traveling on horseback amid the tumult and excitement of the Great Awakening, Diaspora workers visited remote and scattered German- and English-speaking settlements. There, they performed baptisms, held worship services, and preached to people hungry to hear God's word. Moravian itinerants during this first decade concentrated on Lutheran, Reformed, and other church settlers, avoiding German sectarians at first because of the bitterness that the failed synods of 1742 had produced.[40] Under the supervision of Bishop Spangenberg, the Diaspora produced swift results. By 1748, the Moravians had established a strong presence in at least thirty-one communities throughout Pennsylvania and Maryland, and the total number of affiliated members in the Unity's northern province stood at 1,969 by 1759.[41]

The center of the Moravians' Diaspora activity was Pennsylvania. It was this colony with its strong religious freedoms and its bewildering array of churches and sects—Mennonites, Amish, Old Dunkers, New Dunkers, Arminians, Seventh-Day Baptists, Socians, and others—that Zinzendorf decided was the perfect place to pursue his ecumenical vision. Approving the count's plan, the General Synod authorized the founding of Bethlehem on the Lehigh River in 1741 as the base for an ambitious missionary program that would include schools for boys, evangelical activity among the Christian populace, and missions to the Indians.

Complex local conditions dictated whether Moravian congregations took root among the churched of Pennsylvania. Other sects and churches, including the Lutheran leadership under Henry Muhlenberg, viewed the Moravians with deep suspicion, seeing the Diaspora as a thinly veiled attempt to build up Unity membership at their expense. In Lancaster, for instance, Zinzendorf's efforts to spark a revival set off a complex chain of events that culminated in the founding of a Moravian congregation. The count visited Lancaster on December 3, 1742, and delivered a well-received sermon at the courthouse. "His sermon," a Moravian historian noted, "made a deep impression . . . but it also aroused much suspicion and fear on the part of the strict sectarians." Worried about Zinzendorf's intentions, the Lutheran Church in 1743 sent pastor Lawrence Nyberg to shore up the support of the Lutheran laity and to counter Zinzendorf's influence. But Nyberg, the defender of the Lutheran faith, turned out to be sympathetic to the Moravians and their mission of winning converts to Christ. And so did many of his flock. He sought to lead a revival of piety and unify German-speaking settlers by building a union church in Warwick in 1744 for Lutheran and Reformed members. At the same time, however, Nyberg attended several synods in Bethlehem over Muhlenberg's objections. Muhlenberg and his supporters saw Nyberg's presence in Bethlehem as treason, insisting that "since Nyberg is in agreement with the Moravians, he cannot be a genuine Lutheran." Relations became so tense between the two camps that Nyberg and his allies withdrew from the union church and erected a meetinghouse in Lancaster in 1746. Muhlenberg responded by expelling Nyberg from his Lutheran pastorate, an action that pushed Nyberg even closer to the Moravians. In 1748, he moved to Bethlehem, and his Lancaster congregation asked to affiliate formally with the Moravians. Bethlehem's response was positive.[42]

Muhlenberg had good reason to worry about the brethrens' activities. Moravian missionaries found the centers of Pennsylvania Lutheranism to be a fertile recruiting ground for Christ. Despite the hostility of Lutheran leaders toward Moravianism, the two faiths shared much common ground. The most important one was the Unity's acceptance of the Augsburg Confession, the statement of faith that united the Lutheran Church. Moravian liturgy was similar to the Lutheran as well, providing an important comfort level for those Lutherans attending Moravian services. Ironically, given the great hostility he aroused, Count Zinzendorf himself served as a link between the two faiths. The count was raised as a Lutheran and was ordained as a Lutheran minister. Indeed, he at first wanted the Moravian movement to remain within that church. Up to the mid-1740s, Zinzendorf saw the Moravians as a branch of Lutheranism. Zinzendorf even accepted the Lutheran pastorate in Philadelphia in 1741. The Moravians in Pennsylvania saw Lutherans as kindred spirits and ripe targets for their brand of evangelizing. In 1746, for instance, Leonard Schnell visited sixteen Lutheran settlements alone, while Nyberg served Lutherans at Lancaster and the lower Susquehanna Valley.[43]

The experience in Heidelberg in Berks County was typical. Zinzendorf traveled extensively through Berks in 1741 and 1742 in an attempt to awaken the laity. In 1742, Lutheran settlers at Heidelberg responded positively to Zinzendorf's message of salvation by asking the Unity to supply them with a preacher. A member of the count's traveling party, Gottlob Butner, agreed to remain and work with the Lutherans and others, including members of the Reformed Church. In March of that year, Butner delivered his first sermon to a large gathering in the neighborhood, an event that the congregation marked as its beginning. In 1743, the Lutheran settlers formally requested that a brother and sister "be sent to live with us here, to administer to our needs, and the school." Bethlehem complied with their request by dispatching Anton Wagner and his wife in January 1744. The Wagners opened a school and began holding religious services. The response was so strong that these Diaspora members began clearing a site for a meetinghouse in August; in November, they asked the synod for permission to organize a Moravian congregation, stressing to the elders that "while they were Lutheran and Reformed, they had a desire to be a congregation of Jesus without name." By 1745, the fledgling congregation enjoyed a membership of seventy-six, including fifty-three children.[44]

All areas where Moravian congregations formed in Pennsylvania, Maine, and Maryland shared common traits: a weak presence by the formal churches; "unsaved" settlers, usually of Lutheran and Reformed heritage, who were hungry to make changes in their lives; and intense evangelical activity following the Great Awakening and Zinzendorf's failed synods. These factors resulted in the establishment of Moravian congregations, most notably in Heidelberg and York County, which supplied most of the settlers to Friedberg. But the success or failure of the Diaspora went deeper than this. Its success came down to the individual hearer and his or her receptivity to missionaries' messages.

Moravian itinerants delivered a simple message that sought to appeal to the maximum number of people, regardless of ethnicity or sectarian affiliations: by embracing Jesus Christ, one can be "reborn." At Carrollton Manor, the Unity informed English-speaking tenants in 1766 that it was sending an evangelist "to visit You and in their daily conversation to invite you to the Love of Jesus, who first loved us, to direct you to Him."[45] Moravian missionaries, the forerunners of the famed Methodist circuit riders, delivered this theme with relentless consistency at meetinghouses, in private homes, and in open fields. In all places, among all hearers, their message reflected Zinzendorf's emphasis on "heart religion." The locus of a person's faith, the count believed, should be the heart and not the head; one was to feel God. Religious faith, in other words, was to be gained through an understanding of Christ that was to be based on not only the testimony of Scripture but also personal religious experience.[46] He disdained faith through works and moralism, instead preaching the centrality of Jesus Christ. Zinzendorf himself had arrived in Philadelphia in December 1741 with his daughter Benigna and six other church members. He gave a series of sermons in that city that outlined his views on salvation and the need to unify all the German churches and sects into a larger community of faith he called the Congregation of God in the Spirit.

The count divided Christendom into three types: "dead people"; "awakened people"; and "people who have gone their own way." As he explained to an audience gathered at a Lutheran church on March 11, 1742, the awakened were those "people in whom the Holy Spirit has made an impression of the truth from the hour when Jesus' voice sounded among them."[47] His missionaries sought to spark a broad revival that would target not just the "dead" but the awakened and the wanderers. To accomplish this ambitious task, the brethren described Christ's crucifixion and death in graphic terms and contrasted it with the unworthiness of man. Their purpose was not merely to shock the unconverted; it was to guide them to the first step in the conversion process— vocation, the feeling that one was utterly lost and worthless. Before someone could accept Jesus into his heart, he had to understand that he was a sinner with an utterly corrupt nature.

This message had a powerful impact on the unconverted, regardless of ethnicity. When the Reverend Powell informed John Padget of Carrollton that he was a sinner, Padget recalled how he retreated to a "barn, fell on my knees, and wept for grace."[48] Daniel Smith and his wife, Catherine, wrote a plaintive letter to Bethlehem officials in 1770: "This comes to let you know that I love our Savior, exceedingly," Daniel began in the letter, which was also signed by his wife, "because [he] died for me pore Siner [sic]. When I think how he Bleed to Death for me then am shame of myself and think that I Can never Love him anuff [sic]."[49] In 1745, congregation member Tobias Bockel of Heidelberg, a German speaker, thanked "my dear Savior that he has received me as a member of his Church. The Grace he bestows on me poor miserable Worm makes me ashamed before him."[50]

The missionaries' harsh message was meant to lead to the second stage in the conversion process—justification, where a sinner would open his or her heart to the healing power of Jesus Christ and become truly reborn. Unlike Calvinists, who believed that God preordained who would be saved, the Moravians and some Pietists softened the harsh message of human error with the reassuring thought that all individuals, through Jesus, possessed the power to achieve a spiritual rebirth. Peter Pfaff Sr., who later moved to Friedberg, was working in Yorktown as a smith in 1749 when "I soon had the opportunity to hear the Brethren preach their comforting witness that nothing counts in God's sight except grace in the blood of Jesus." For Pfaff, this "was a joyous message to me."[51]

Traveling across the countryside on horseback, the Moravians pioneered an evangelical weapon used to great effect in later years by the Methodists and Baptists. Their pietistic message of hope drew crowds of all persuasions to Moravian gatherings throughout the North. In Pennsylvania, Moravian services often drew Quakers, Presbyterians, and other English speakers. Diaspora workers visited as many settlements as they could. Pastors' diaries matter-of-factly recounted their many travels, ranging from Mennonite gatherings to neighboring townships.[52] Many of the awakened flocked to join Moravian societies, which formed small but thriving congregations in a process that mirrored the building of the congregation at Carrollton. Diaspora members learned of Christ—and the Unity—and came to identify closely with the Moravian cause. Peter Frey was typical. Born in Wingen, Alsace, in 1689, this German-speaking Lutheran moved his wife and seven children to Pennsylvania in 1734, presumably to escape the hard times in his native land. The Freys eventually settled in Berks County and, like countless settlers before them, built a cabin. In this outpost of Western civilization along Muddy Creek in southeastern Pennsylvania, the family encountered an evangelical movement that shook up their lives in ways they probably could not have anticipated when they left Alsace a decade earlier. Peter and his family heard a Moravian bishop preach on the saving grace of Jesus Christ, or the "free grace in the blood" of Jesus (*freie Gnade im Blute*). Deeply moved by the hopeful message of the new birth, the Freys abandoned the cabin they had so recently built and moved to Heidelberg to be closer to a growing Moravian congregation that had gathered in this farm hamlet. Living among other pilgrims, they reasoned, they could learn more about the evangelical message that all who embrace Jesus Christ could be spiritually reborn. In Heidelberg, the Freys became active members and participated fully in congregational life. Within a relatively short time, these expatriates from Alsace became thoroughly Moravian.[53]

The Migration to North Carolina

On many fronts, Moravianism and the Diaspora seemed by 1765 to be thriving. Membership remained healthy in the northern province as Moravian itinerants continued fanning out across Maryland and the northern colonies. The congregation at Carrollton appeared to be thriving as well. Attendance at weekly preaching remained strong, and the Reverend Powell had succeeded in building his meetinghouse, which he believed would ensure the congregation's survival. Yet by 1774, the Freys, Peddycoards, and several hundred other society members from across the North and Maryland had departed for North Carolina, and the congregations at Carrollton and Broadbay were soon defunct. Unlike in the *Ortsgemeinen,* the Unity did not tell them to move. No church official selected migrants to the North Carolina *Landgemeinen* and told them when to leave and where to go, as they did in the populating of Bethabara in the 1750s, Bethania in 1759, and Salem in 1772. The migration to North Carolina's three *Landgemeinen* was fairly spontaneous and consisted of three separate streams of settlers from Maryland, Maine, and Pennsylvania. Individual members and their families decided for complex personal reasons when they would leave and where they would go.

But, of course, the general migration to the *Landgemeinen* did not just happen. A confluence of events in the northern province and in North Carolina produced it, and despite their haphazard and chaotic appearances, the three separate migrations shared many traits and were a natural outgrowth of the Diaspora and its ability to mold a Moravian identity. These diverse groups of migrants shared a common outlook after having undergone a new birth and having participated in congregational life for several years. The emigrés to Wachovia were motivated by the desire to find both religious security and land. The "saved" moved in search of a stable religious home that would allow them to raise their children in God's ways. In the cases of Friedland and Hope, serious problems with the founders' home congregations "pushed" the migrants to consider relocating elsewhere in hopes of finding stability and spiritual fulfillment. In the case of Friedberg, more-individualistic reasons predominated. But in all three instances, the search for a nurturing religious environment was a crucial "pull" factor that drew them to Wachovia. But as strong as this pull factor was, it did not work alone. The desire for a religious home operated simultaneously with another key factor: economics. Land—that is, parents' wishes to provide farms for themselves and for their offspring—helped push migrants from their old homes to a new one. This interlocking desire for land and God was the common link between pilgrims from widely different geographic, ethnic, and congregational backgrounds.[54]

The 261 settlers who traveled to the North Carolina *Landgemeinen* in the 1760s and 1770s moved as extended families, linked by kinship and religious

Table 1.1. Migration to the North Carolina *Landgemeinen*

Departure	Year	No. of Migrants
To Friedberg		
Heidelberg, Pa.	1755	5
Heidelberg	1765	21
Heidelberg	1767	31
York, Pa.	1771	12
York	1772	2
York	1774	40
Total		111
To Friedland		
Broadbay, Maine	1769	28
Broadbay	1770	50
Total		78
To Hope		
Carrollton Manor, Md.	1772	19
Carrollton Manor	1774	18
Carrollton Manor	1775	35
Total		72

Sources: Diaries, memorabilia, and historical accounts for individual congregations, Moravian Archives, Northern Province, and Moravian Archives, Southern Province.

ties. They hailed from three main locations: Carrollton Manor (whose English-speaking settlers founded Hope); Broadbay (whose German-speaking settlers founded Friedland); and southeastern Pennsylvania (whose German-speaking settlers founded Friedberg) (table 1.1). The founding of Hope provides the clearest example of how land and God motivated pilgrims to relocate to North Carolina. As in Friedland, but unlike in Friedberg, internal congregational problems in the home colony of Maryland served as a significant push factor.

By 1772, congregational life at Carrollton Manor had atrophied. Joseph Powell and his wife were old and tired after a lifetime of missionary work. In his congregational diary, the pastor appeared upbeat. Attendance remained strong, and he was even finally gaining a following among the manor's small but growing German-speaking population. In June 1770, these German tenants asked for preaching in their native language, and the bilingual Powell complied the next month.[55] But in his letters to Bethlehem, Powell told a different story. The pastor was anxious to retire and return to Bethlehem because his wife was dying and she wanted to see her home again. In May 1772, Powell, who himself was in bad health, asked Nathaniel Seidel in Bethlehem to let them return to Pennsylvania for their sake and the congregation's. After six years at the manor, he explained in the letter to Seidel, "we not only are become quite Old, and near the close of our Days, but seem also to have become something Old to our hearers." Powell hoped that a change in leadership "might Occasion a fresh stir, or an awakening in the Neighborhood." "Our auditors," he noted sadly, had fallen off, "becoming fewer."[56] The dampening of congregational enthusiasm, combined with the Powells' impending departure, influenced both the vanguard's decision to emigrate and its timing. A move to Carolina represented a chance to recapture the spark that had brought the founding families to Moravianism in the first place. Led by Daniel Smith and the Goslin family, a vanguard of four families began making preparations in early 1772 to leave by spring. In February, Smith and his wife discussed their plans to begin an English-speaking settlement in Wachovia with Powell, and they asked him to recommend them to Unity leaders in North Carolina. The pastor promised to, "knowing them as very industrious people whose principal views are to get nearer and amongst the Lord's peoples. On our willingness to let them go, they rejoyced [sic] above measure."[57]

But land proved to be an equally important lure for the settlers from Carrollton Manor. In Wachovia, these Maryland tenants would have a chance to own their own farms and to acquire enough land to bequeath holdings to their heirs. In late 1772, Wachovia's administrator, Frederick Marshall, helped Daniel Smith select tracts and arrange financing that allowed his family and the other Marylanders to purchase farms. Smith, who lacked the cash to buy land, took out an indenture with Marshall on December 21, 1772, for 221 acres. Marshall offered Smith the standard terms for leasing land in Wachovia with an option to buy. Smith was to pay an annual rent of six pounds, two shillings, and nine pence sterling—lower than what he paid at Carrollton. The purchase price for the land was to be 110 pounds. The leases for Smith and the others allowed the Marylanders to apply one shilling per twenty shillings toward the purchase price, plus 5 percent interest. Marshall, however, gave these Marylanders ten years to come up with the purchase price instead of the usual three or seven years. As a further incentive, the Marylanders could clear as much land as they wanted for building and fencing, "together with full Liberty of hunting and ranging upon the Premises."[58] In contrast, leases at Carrollton contained no options to buy. Tenants after 1750 leased their tracts "at will," meaning that they relied on oral, probably annual, agreements that were renewable at the will of the landlord. Rents themselves, while still reasonable, had risen steadily in the eighteenth century, increasing from eight shillings, four pence sterling for every one hundred acres to about five pounds by midcentury. And they rose again in the 1760s to more than six pounds for a one-hundred-acre tract, and tenants faced a new charge of two capons per one hundred acres on top of a quitrent of four shillings sterling.[59]

Not surprisingly, Wachovia's lease-purchases proved to be enticing for these Moravian tenants, including the Peddycoards. William Barton Peddycoard took out a lease-purchase on a 150-acre tract in 1775. His rent of four pounds, three shillings was lower than what tenants paid for a one-hundred-acre tract at Carrollton, and he had seven years to pay off the purchase price of seventy-five pounds.[60] His brother John Jacob Peddycoard, who bought two tracts totaling 305 acres, made out equally well: church chroniclers noted that he moved his family to North Carolina not only for religious reasons but also that he "might . . . get Land on better terms."[61]

The decision by the Smiths and Goslins to leave set off a chain reaction that led to others in the congregation emigrating. With each departure, the struggling Carrollton Manor congregation became progressively weaker. And as membership tailed off and interest dwindled, Bethlehem decided not to send a missionary to replace the Powells, to the great disappointment of those who had stayed behind. Bethlehem's decision to leave the pastorship vacant sealed the fate of the congregation. The demise of the congregation in 1773, in turn, forced others to leave, including the Peddycoards.

In 1772 and 1773, the remaining congregants were unhappy about the turn of events. In early August 1772, Powell had announced his intention to retire in the fall and to return to Pennsylvania with his wife, who was near death. The Carrollton brethren, Powell recorded in his diary, assumed that he would be easily replaceable, that "the Congregation had such plenty of preachers that they [Bethlehem] sent them immediately on a slender Invitation." He was forced to disabuse them of that notion, reminding the congregation that the Unity was a small church with global missionary responsibilities: the *Brudergemeine* (Moravian Church), he told the assembled congregation, faced "the vast Expence and Consumption of Laborers in the torred [sic], temperate and frozen Climes of the four Quarters of the Earth."[62] In late August 1772, the Peddycoards and several other members of the congregation wrote a plaintive letter to Bethlehem's elders, imploring them to send replacements for the Powells: "We trust and hope, Dear Brethren, that your compassion and tender love will still reach us, furder [sic] favoring us with a Brother and Sister, who shall continue the ministration of the blessed, saving Gospel." The Peddycoards and others characterized the departure of the members to North Carolina as a blow. But the bigger setback, they pointed out, was "to have the saving power of the blessed Gospel withdrawn from us."[63]

These members did not want to move. They wanted the congregation to survive and Maryland to remain their home. But when Bethlehem refused to send a replacement for Powell, they believed they had no choice but to leave. John Padget, for one, moved to Wachovia reluctantly and only because all of his neighbors had left. Padget had been a leader in the congregation since its founding in 1766, and he had put down deep roots in Maryland. With sadness and growing consternation, he watched his fellow congregation members move to North Carolina beginning in 1772. Padget believed he had only two options: to stay in a "godless" place that was his home, or to move to a strange place where he and his family could "hear the Gospel." Cast in those terms, Padget concluded he had no choice but to move. Family considerations were critical in his calculations. With the brethren gone, Padget said he "feared for my children . . . that they might be led astray." By moving to Wachovia, Padget believed he would be "bringing [his] children into safety." Family and religious considerations, in other words, reinforced each other. He wanted his children to remain under the brethren's care.[64] Because the nucleus of the congregation had, in effect, picked up and moved to North Carolina, the Padgets and others believed they had to move also. The news that an English-speaking congregation founded by former friends was forming in Wachovia overcame their initial reluctance to head south. The raw numbers hint at the snowballing effect of these interlocking developments: the first four families who arrived in late 1772 were augmented by three families in 1774 and seven in 1775.[65] By 1780, when Bishop Johann Friedrich Reichel stopped at the old meetinghouse at Carrollton Manor, he found a desolate scene. The building was in "ruin," and Mr. Johnson and the Schau family "are the only Brethren still living at Carroll's Manor, the rest have moved away."[66]

In Broadbay, the migrants also faced severe problems within their congregation. For them, a move to Wachovia represented a chance for their children to grow up in a safe haven, where they could prosper spiritually and materially. The Reverend George Soelle's tenure on the Maine frontier had turned out to be a difficult one. Some society members of the Reformed persuasion had hired a pastor from New York to minister to them. When the pastor arrived, he objected to Soelle's presence. The presence of two pastors divided the settlers, and the dispute became so fierce that the followers of the Reformed pastor had Soelle and George Hahn arrested in May 1762.[67]

Poverty also bedeviled the struggling and divided congregation. The people, Soelle wrote, "are as poor as church-mice, and the land is not rich. . . . They all have large families: They cannot plow, and if they wish to sow rye, they must use the hoe to stir up the soil."[68] To add to the settlers' misery, they learned in the 1760s that their land titles from Waldo were worthless and that their leases were nonbinding. Such was the scene in the mid-1760s: a Moravian congregation internally split, facing an uncertain future on the Maine frontier. Congregation members concluded that their prospects were poor on all fronts. Farming was a struggle, and their neighbors appeared hostile to their religious beliefs.

In 1767, a discouraged Soelle and other Unity leaders debated abandoning Broadbay and urging the congregation members to relocate elsewhere in New England. They considered establishing a congregation on the Kennebec River, but the plan held little appeal to Broadbay's membership because they feared they could not acquire secure land titles there, either.[69] Bishop Ettwein of Wachovia visited Broadbay in May 1767 and told congregation members of North Carolina's virtues, including "its genial climate and fertile soil." Soelle returned from a trip to Bethlehem to "find a large number of them bent on removing" to Carolina because of its powerful religious and economic attractions. Soelle advised congregation members to move cautiously because of the need to plan carefully and thoroughly for a difficult move south. Ettwein could offer encouragement, but no practical assistance, to these Moravians in Maine. The settlers, convinced that moving to North Carolina was in their best economic and spiritual interests, pressed ahead with their plans in 1768. In a letter to Ettwein after the bishop's visit in 1767, Hahn succinctly summed up the interlocking motivations: "Our children are going to ruin; we want to live near a congregation of Brethren."[70] Other members cited the same reasons. The parents of Catharine Rominger moved the family to Wachovia because they were "desirous of seeking the salvation of their souls and mindful of the everlasting happiness of their children."[71] The name these settlers chose for their new community in Wachovia also said a great deal about their motivations—Friedland, the land of peace. They wanted to be free of the hostility of their neighbors. Soelle cited this very weariness. The migrants, he explained to Wachovia's administrators, "honestly wish to be farther from the tumult and temptations of the world, that in quiet they may learn more of Him."[72] Of the three North

Carolina *Landgemeinen,* Broadbay's desire to live in a religious haven apart from the world was by far the strongest.

Friedberg's case differed from Hope's and Friedland's in one crucial regard: it lacked the clear internal congregational problems that plagued Carrollton Manor and Broadbay. Yet it was not so different in another regard: religion and family stirred these settlers from Pennsylvania in nearly identical ways. Three areas in Pennsylvania supplied the majority of migrants to Friedberg: Heidelberg, Conewago, and Yorktown.[73] Friedberg's settlers began moving to North Carolina as early as 1755, but most migrants left those three communities in 1765, 1767, and the early 1770s in separate waves in search of more and better land in a religiously stable environment. Individual family needs, including finances and personal circumstances, dictated the timing of their departures from Pennsylvania. The Freys were, again, typical. Despite having moved twice already, and despite Peter's advanced age, the Frey clan decided in 1765 to move for a third time. But they did not pull out of Heidelberg until Peter's son Valentine was finally able to sell his remaining two tracts on April 29, 1765, only a few weeks before their departure on May 10. Valentine's tenth child, Tobias, was born on January 10, 1764, and this birth surely factored into the family's decision as to when they could make the difficult trek south. A journey through the wilderness would be too dangerous for a pregnant woman or a newborn.[74]

In some ways, the migration to Friedberg resembled the massive exodus to the backcountry that was occurring on the eve of the Revolution. North Carolina had become one of the most popular destinations in this secondary migration; the colony's population more than doubled, from 65,000 in 1750 to about 175,000 in 1770.[75] Only Georgia had a greater rate of population growth during this period. On the most elemental level, population growth in the northern colonies underlay the massive movement of people south. The years from 1760 to 1775 saw, in one historian's phrase, an "extraordinary" migration of people from Europe to British North America, a migration that sent population soaring in the North.[76] This immigration, combined with natural population increases, placed great pressure on land. In Maryland and especially in Pennsylvania, the growing population resulted in land shortages and rising land prices. In Lancaster County, Pennsylvania, for instance, arrivals had snapped up the best lands as early as 1730. The scarcity and expense of farmland caused many farmers to look to the frontier, an exodus that reached new heights in the 1760s and 1770s following the French and Indian War.[77] But the border controversy between Pennsylvania and Maryland threw many land titles into doubt and forced thousands of settlers to look farther south, to such places as the Cumberland Valley, the Shenandoah, and ultimately the Carolinas, where land was even cheaper and more plentiful. By the 1730s, land prices had risen in Pennsylvania from two pounds per hundred acres to more than fifteen pounds. In the Granville District in North Carolina, where Wachovia was located, land could be had in the 1750s for only five shillings per hundred acres. The French and Indian War did not interrupt this exodus—ironically, it encouraged it, as people fearful of Indian depredations in Pennsylvania sought safer havens far removed from the fighting.[78]

For Friedberg's migrants, Wachovia's cheap and plentiful land proved to be irresistible as well. But unlike in secular migrations, these settlers treated religion, family, and land holistically. The wanderings of Matthias Wesner, a Lutheran, show how these three motives intertwined. He was born in Stuttgart, Germany, in 1730, came to Pennsylvania in 1758 for reasons that are unclear, and later joined the Moravian congregation at Emmaus after hearing the brethren preach. Wesner built a life for himself in Emmaus, where he worked as a tailor, started a family, and built a house. But Wesner's family struggled financially. He decided to move his wife and five children to North Carolina in 1771, a church chronicler of his life explained, "in order to improve his outward circumstances." But family and religious factors were also decisive: he turned down an offer of land from his brother because it was sixty miles from Wachovia—too far for his family to worship with the brethren. Wesner settled, instead, in Friedberg, where he and his family could worship at the meetinghouse. In that Moravian settlement, he planned to work as a farmer and tailor "until he could turn the farming over to his son Jacob." The move to Wachovia, in other words, represented a chance to worship with like-minded evangelicals; equally important, it meant that Wesner could provide enough land for his heirs in an environment where they could grow up in God's ways.[79]

An energetic Diaspora movement thus underlay the formation of the North Carolina *Landgemeinen*. It "awakened" members of other faiths, drew them to Moravianism, and helped to produce migrants to Wachovia with a common outlook and common goals. Without this missionary work, the congregations of Friedberg, Friedland, and Hope would not have been founded. Nor would the migration have been as large as it was. The Diaspora produced committed pilgrims who were desirous of finding land and spiritual fulfillment in the southern backcountry.

Wachovia offered them the chance to pursue both. Founded in 1753 as a haven for the Unity's European refugees, Wachovia by the 1760s was aggressively seeking to develop the nearly one-hundred-thousand acre tract. Unity leaders had abandoned plans to restrict development to a central city and thirty-five European-style "villages of the Lord" populated by full church members. Only *Gemeine* members were to live in these European-style villages, and they were to farm small, scattered tracts totaling about twenty-two acres. But the concept proved to be both unworkable and unpopular, and the Unity decided to allow both full and society members to purchase land on individual farms. Wachovia's administrators began offering generous land deals in the 1760s to spur this development. They placed advertisements in Pennsylvania in the mid-1760s, for instance, letting would-be migrants know that they could get farms on easy terms in a religious community endowed with abundant land, water, meadows, and woodland.[80] Although the Unity did not directly help migrants move, it welcomed their arrival as a boon to Wachovia's economic and spiritual development, and it encouraged settlers to relocate to North Carolina.

Clearly, these land deals helped spur the migration and account for its timing. Settlers in Heidelberg, after all, could have remained with that congregation or have chosen to move to a neighboring Moravian village in Pennsylvania—as so many did in the 1740s and 1750s. Broadbay's settlers could have started a new congregation elsewhere in New England or have relocated to Pennsylvania. The members of Carrollton Manor could have gone to nearby York, as a handful did. These settlers, in other words, had plenty of local choices available to them. Yet the movement to Wachovia began in earnest in the 1760s, precisely when Wachovia's administrators made the land deals available to newcomers and precisely when land prices were rising in Pennsylvania and Maryland.

The land deals proved to be so effective because of the common aspirations that the *Landgemeinen* settlers brought with them to Wachovia. Moravian parents in Wachovia's agricultural settlements wanted the opportunity to strengthen their families' religious commitment through well-conceived land use and inheritance practices. Their goal was a simple one: to anchor their children securely in the religious haven of an evangelical sect. To achieve this goal, families in the three *Landgemeinen* settlements built up ample landholdings in the late eighteenth and early nineteenth centuries. Landholdings, as a result, averaged two hundred acres and up. In Friedberg and Friedland, the holdings of the largest landholders averaged just over one thousand acres, and the overall average was 265 acres in the former and 224 acres in the latter. In Hope, the largest holdings averaged 705 acres, and the overall average was 181 acres.[81]

The migrations to the *Landgemeinen* and the motivations involved contrasted sharply with the elaborate church-led populating of the *Ortsgemeinen*.

The Unity's ambitious global missionary goals, small size, and relatively meager financial resources placed a premium on planning. Church officials were organized and thorough in their preparations for the dispatching of settlers to the *Ortsgemeinen* in Europe and America. Church members migrated from Europe in congregation groups, "usually on ships owned by the church and operated by church members or others connected to the church," as historian Aaron Spencer Fogleman has noted. The Unity transported 566 of the 830 immigrants it sent to the mainland colonies on fourteen voyages aboard Moravian ships, manned by Moravian crews.[82]

The migration of *Ortsgemeinen* settlers contrasted with that of the *Landgemeinen* in a more fundamental way. To a large extent, Unity leaders in Herrnhut, Bethlehem, and Salem controlled whether these religious refugees could emigrate. They balanced religious and economic considerations in deciding who was to depart and when, with the scales often tipping toward the practical needs of the community. It was a given that any candidate for emigration had to be a full congregation member in good standing with the Unity. This meant that the emigré had been fully inculcated in Moravian teachings; had partaken of communion; and was willing to move on short notice for service to the Lord while still being able to contribute to a new community as a craftsman or worker.

Exactly who went and where came down to the needs of the individual *Ortsgemeine*. Congregation towns across the globe especially wanted craftsmen—carpenters, weavers, potters, and the like—to keep their economies functioning smoothly and efficiently. Moravian planners also considered demographic factors. They sought to achieve a proper sex balance among the population that would allow the smooth functioning of the choir houses and the congregation, as well as individual families. In all situations, the Unity considered the needs of the community paramount over those of the individual. Although no one was forced to move against his or her will, an *Ortsgemeine* resident was expected to display the pilgrim spirit and to relocate when the Lord asked him or her to. As devout followers of Jesus, Moravians were to put the Savior first. Church members, the Unity instructed, should "always keep the pilgrim spirit and whenever they could be used at any place to be ready and prepared immediately."[83] As the research of historian Daniel B. Thorp has shown, Unity leaders selected settlers for Wachovia's *Ortsgemeinen* based on these criteria. Their first concern was that the colony survive, and they sought pilgrims who would help Wachovia establish itself in the North Carolina wilderness. In 1753, Rowan County's population totaled only thirty-six hundred, and most of the early settlers lived across the Yadkin River, relatively far from Wachovia. The colony's isolation meant that it would have to be almost entirely self-sufficient its first few years. Because of the perceived dangers of clearing a wilderness, planners in Bethlehem did not want women involved in the early phase. They also wanted men who were acclimated to the harsh New World climate, that is, those men who had been in America for at least several years and had gained experience in wilderness living. These requirements meant that Wachovia's population was entirely male from 1753 to 1755.[84]

By fall 1755, Moravian planners believed that Wachovia's survival was assured, and they began focusing on developing the colony's economic and social structure. They now wanted craftsmen, including millers and potters, for the economy so that Wachovia could begin producing the goods it would need to develop trade. Most of all, they wanted women and children to begin living in the new settlement. No Moravian congregation would be complete without the participation of sisters, and no family life would be possible without their presence. This shift in goals meant that Bethabara, Bethania, and Salem moved rapidly toward normal demographic patterns in the pre-Revolutionary period. In 1754, the adult sex ratio in the congregation towns was all male; by 1759, it was 146:100 male:female; and by 1771, it was 114:100. The percentage of children in the three congregation towns rose from zero in 1754 to 21.8 percent by 1771.[85] The populating of the *Ortsgemeinen,* in short, was a model of expert planning, as recent historians have noted and admired.[86] Moravian leaders carefully planned migrations to the congregation towns in order to fulfill the practical and religious needs of those communities.

In the *Landgemeinen,* of course, migration worked far differently. Individual settlers and not the Unity decided when and how to come to Wachovia. Yet this is not to say that the church played no role in these migrations; it is to say that the role was far different than in the *Ortsgemeinen.* In the migrations to all three farm *Gemeinen,* the settlers employed a collective strategy that drew on informal church networks. Even in Friedberg, where the congregational role in the migration was weakest, settlers took advantage of the elaborate Moravian network that had been developed in 1753, when the Unity founded Wachovia, to transport migrants from Pennsylvania to North Carolina safely, a journey of several hundred miles over bad or nonexistent roads and thickly forested wilderness.

The key to this internal migration was the assistance that Moravian congregations provided to their fellow brethren heading south. These congregations served as stopping points in Pennsylvania and Maryland. In Virginia, where the

Moravians had failed to establish a presence, travelers relied on friends of the Unity for food, lodging, and other assistance. The Freys' route to North Carolina was typical. From Heidelberg, they headed to the Moravian congregation in York and then on to Monocacy, Maryland, the German-speaking congregation that was north of Carrollton Manor. From there, the Frey party crossed the Potomac River and headed south through Virginia. Unlike many other backcountry migrants, Moravians did not travel the Great Wagon Road that ran just west of the Blue Ridge Mountains to Salisbury, North Carolina, the county seat of frontier Rowan. Moravian travelers followed an easterly route that took them through Leesburg and across the Potomac, Rappahannock, James, and other rivers farther south.[87] The trip took the Freys four weeks, with the family and their baggage pulling out of Heidelberg on May 10 and arriving at the South Fork in Friedberg on June 10. The journey was marred by only one tragedy: a single man accompanying them drowned in the Potomac.[88]

This collective strategy, however, worked far differently than for *Ortsgemeinen* settlers: the Freys traveled as a family unit on their own, and they financed their own move by selling their farms in Pennsylvania. Their plans to leave elicited no offers of help from authorities in Bethlehem or from their congregation pastor. Indeed, Unity leaders in Pennsylvania barely took notice of the Freys' departure. Congregational diary entries recording the Freys' departure were, without exception, brief and to the point: "The old Peter Frey and his son Valentine Frey, with their wives and eleven children, along with their son-in-law and daughter, left for North Carolina," read one entry.[89] Heidelberg's memorabilia recounting events for the year 1765 was even more succinct: "Peter and Valentine Frey, with their families, moved from here to North Carolina—a total of twenty-one persons."[90]

The congregation's role was less obvious in this migration to Friedberg, but its members' movements resembled Hope's in one crucial way. Emigrés left in waves, first from the congregation at Heidelberg in 1765 and 1767 and then from the congregation at York in 1771, 1772, and 1774. A snowball effect was at work, with more families leaving in the last year than in the first year. One departure in a congregation would lead to another and to another. These Pennsylvania Moravians moved as multigenerational family units, often with elderly parents in tow, and they moved in waves from specific congregations for individualistic reasons.

Because they moved almost exclusively as individual families over a period of nearly three decades, Friedberg's settlers relied much more on internal networking between German speakers in Carolina and Pennsylvania than did mi-

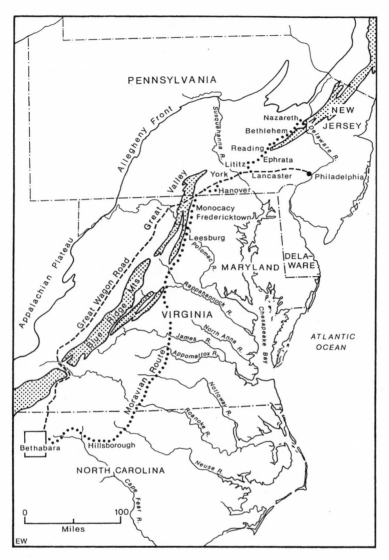

The primary Moravian migration route from Pennsylvania to North Carolina ran east of the Great Wagon Road. *Map by Eugene Wilson, courtesy of Aaron Spencer Fogleman.*

grants in Friedland, Hope, and the *Ortsgemeinen*. Close contacts with former family and friends both fed the exodus to this *Landgemeine* and sustained it. Friedberg residents regularly sent wagons to Heidelberg and other Pennsylvania communities, usually in late fall after the harvest had been brought in. These wagons carried agricultural goods, letters, and encouragement. Returning travelers brought Friedberg residents "many cordial greetings from Pennsylvania, not only from brethren and sisters but also from their friends, and told them many stories." One wagon from Yorktown groaned under the load of nine packages of letters and German newspapers.[91] Equally significant, some of the migrants had served as missionary helpers in Pennsylvania. They accompanied the pastor during his rounds, talked with people in the field, and regularly conversed with congregation members. Much information about conditions in Carolina was likely exchanged during these visits. Future migrants also observed firsthand the passing of *Ortsgemeinen* travelers. For instance, brother Bernhard Adam Grube and a small party of brethren left Bethlehem on October 8, 1753. Their first stop on their way to Wachovia was Heidelberg, where the congregation provided them with food, clean beds, and companionship. Grube noted that the sojourners' arrival was a festive time for local Moravians. "There were other Brethren there working on a new hall who rejoiced to greet us once more," he recalled.[92] For members of the northern *Landgemeinen,* these encounters increased the awareness of events beyond their borders and very likely helped pique their interest in emigrating.

In Broadbay, the story differed in several particulars. Living the farthest north, Maine's migrants obviously did not want to take the overland route through Pennsylvania, Maryland, and Virginia that other Moravians followed. The vanguard instead bought passage on a ship headed to Wilmington, North Carolina, and hurriedly left Broadbay with no firm plan about what they would do once in Wachovia. The settlers apparently had done no advance planning despite their small numbers and extended discussions in Maine about where they would go. And despite Bishop Ettwein's earlier entreaties, Wachovia's administrators were unaware of their departure and were not expecting them—a stark contrast to migrations to the *Ortsgemeinen*. Hahn led a vanguard of six families from Broadbay that arrived in Bethabara in late 1769 after a harrowing journey. Their schooner sank off the Virginia coast during a November storm. The cold, weary survivors promptly became ill after reaching the port of Wilmington, North Carolina. Several died on the long trip to North Carolina. The larger group of settlers—fifty in all—led by Soelle followed in 1770.[93] Because of the compactness of their move, networking did not play any role in the formation of Friedland, unlike in Friedberg. The first arrivals from Maine were unsure of how to proceed; with nowhere to go, a few families stayed temporarily in the Salem tavern and others at cabins at the Salem mill. The emigrés simply waited for the second, and larger, group to arrive in Wachovia before making any decisions on whether to start a settlement and where. The Broadbay settlers then decided as a group to keep together, although several families opted to relocate to other settlements within Wachovia. The settlers chose a site several miles north of Friedberg and southeast of Salem.[94]

The Marylanders from Carrollton moved south as a congregational unit *and* as extended families: kinship linked three of the four original families. "Widow Goslin," as church documents identified her, was Daniel Smith's mother-in-law, and Smith's sister had married into the third family that traveled to Wachovia. Blood ties then prevailed on less-enthusiastic family members to make the trek south; they would rather stay with their families than be left behind in Maryland.

As the experience in Hope shows, German speakers were hardly unique in their use of the collective strategy. "Cultural brokers" also were at work at Carrollton and Hope, serving as leaders for this ethnic group. They told members of conditions in Carolina and encouraged them to move south with the rest of the congregation. Yet such a collective strategy served different ends. It was not used to enable an ethnic group to maintain its ethnic cohesiveness; it was used to forge a Moravian one.[95] The congregation and its collective strategy helped give coherence to scattered members, instituted a sense of community, and facilitated the worship of Jesus Christ. The Carrollton congregation played a far stronger role in Hope's formation than it did any home congregation in Friedberg. As in Friedland, the Carrollton congregation moved relatively intact, although the move was not as compact. The formal church, though, played even less of a role in this migration than it did in Friedland. No missionary accompanied the migrants from Carrollton, and no Unity leader ever considered relocating the congregation to another northern location. Congregants' pleas for a new pastor for Carrollton Manor went unheeded. The congregation helped give structure to the migration, but congregation members acted independently of the church and their Maryland pastor. The migration to English-speaking Hope, in short, was a cross between Friedberg's and Friedland's.

✝

Arriving in Wachovia, the emigrés had undergone two difficult journeys—first to Moravianism, then to North Carolina. Within a relatively short time, they had become evangelicals and committed members of the Moravian movement. The desire to draw even closer to the brethren brought most of them to Wachovia. Once there, they wanted to provide for their families and to construct *Gemeinen* that would endure for years to come. Family and kinship, as chapter 3 will show, were important in the acculturation process. But so was religion. And it all began with that mysterious, difficult journey known as the "new birth."

2

A Community of Believers

After a lifetime of searching, George Soelle believed he understood the answer to a mystery that Christians had been pondering for centuries: how to achieve eternal salvation. Open your heart to Jesus, Soelle told anyone who would listen, and he will come into your life. Soelle was hardly bashful about delivering this message of eternal life. An energetic missionary who came to Wachovia in 1770 in the twilight of his career, Soelle traveled extensively throughout the North Carolina backcountry, spreading the word.[1]

Soelle's eagerness to deliver the joyful message of the new birth was hardly unusual among evangelicals. His spiritual journey was remarkably similar to other pilgrims searching to find communion with Jesus Christ, and of those missionaries seeking to help them find it. In an evangelical world, the striking fact was not the differences expressed by leading theologians of the day, but the commonality of the conversion experience among the faithful. In the South, evangelicals shared a loose kinship based on experiential conversion. This conversion experience transcended race, nationality, and ethnicity, and it helped to create a community of believers that transcended differences along denominational and cultural lines.[2]

In Wachovia, the new birth provided the sturdy base that allowed the brethren to construct a durable religious community that survived into the twentieth century. The conversion experience underpinned congregational life, helped unify a disparate group of pilgrims, and reinforced Wachovia's other religious institutions. It enabled German-speaking Moravians from many confessional backgrounds to find common ground with English-speaking brethren from different countries. An evangelical culture, in short, helped facilitate the process of community formation in the southern backcountry. This culture had one overriding objective: to cement an individual's relationship with the Savior. The process began with the conversion experience but did not end there. The Moravians developed an elaborate and multilayered religious community that sought to reinforce the tenets of their heart religion. Like other evangelicals, the brethren treated religion holistically, with the church permeating all aspects of an individual's life. The congregation formed choirs to facilitate unity and the worship of Christ; held festivals to celebrate Unity milestones; and enacted solemn Brotherly Agreements to regulate behavior. But for the brethren, living as a saint was no easy thing—and neither was the Unity's task of building a religious community built on such high standards of conduct. The tensions created by the rigors of a new birth and the difficulty of maintaining a proper state of grace came to define community in Wachovia as much as the lofty goals of brotherhood and piety. Religion, paradoxically, proved to be both a unifier and a divider.

The New-Birth Experience

Like other evangelicals, Soelle brought to his missionary work the fervent determination of someone who had undergone that life-transforming experience known as the new birth. The new birth was both intensely personal and ritualized, with seekers undergoing a basic three-step process that varied among hearers in length and difficulty: *vocation,* where one was in a lost spiritual condition seeking but unable to find salvation; *justification,* where one experienced the liberating power of Jesus Christ; and finally *sanctification,* where this new relationship with Jesus was cemented. Soelle's conversion was typical in its intensity and difficulty. He was born on the island of Erroe, Denmark, in 1709 and was raised as a Lutheran in the world of God. But, as Soelle later recalled, he did not truly know him. At age twelve, "I was overcome with such an alarm and fear of God that I went into the church, threw myself on the floor, and besought the dear God with many tears to forgive my sins. My fear passed, and I felt safe, but for twelve more years, I went my own way." As was the case with countless others of the "unsaved," Soelle's spiritual rebirth did not come easily or quickly. The tearful young Dane recognized he was unsaved, but he did not know what to do about it. Such helplessness led to even deeper feelings of chagrin and self-loathing. While in school, "I felt how terrible sin was. . . . For several years, I was greatly oppressed and miserable." Soelle, in short, was rudely experiencing that first terrifying step in the conversion process that all pilgrims had to undertake—vocation, the feeling that one was utterly worthless.[3]

Getting to the second stage of the conversion process—justification, where Jesus offered assurance for the pardon of sins—proved to be as daunting for

Soelle as it was for others. He credited two sources for putting him on the path to salvation, one mystical and the other earthly. In a series of dreams, Soelle learned of the Savior and, more mysteriously, of the Unity of Brethren, whom he had never heard of up until that point. Soelle could make no sense of these nightly visions; "it seemed that I was one of the men who were carrying the body of the Savior, and as it disappeared from our hands, I heard a voice say three times: 'The Brethren have overcome.'" These dreams led to a great deal of soul searching.[4] While true conversion remained beyond his grasp at this point, Soelle decided in 1741 at age thirty-two to become a Lutheran minister. The earthly help came a year later, in 1742, in the form of a Moravian missionary. Brother Grassman was the first Moravian Soelle had ever met, and his appearance apparently fulfilled the vision that Soelle had had years earlier. Through this chance meeting with Grassman, Soelle said he "first learned of the sins of all sins, the lack of faith in the atonement of the Savior, which I had not hitherto felt in my heart. Now at last my lost condition was evident to me, and it was hard for me to speak and to preach of the Savior, for I did not yet know Him." Grassman's plain but persuasive words had struck Soelle with great force. Grassman's evangelizing set the stage for Soelle's spiritual rebirth. For Soelle, Grassman's words reinforced his earlier feelings that he was lost and corrupt. What he finally came to comprehend was that he had to open his heart to Jesus. Only then did "the crucified Savior appear to me, as He died on the cross for my sins." By placing his total trust in Jesus Christ, Soelle had at last crossed the bridge of understanding to justification. His rebirth, after long years of effort, brought about a miraculous change in its wake. In Soelle's words, "I felt the peace of God in my heart."[5]

Soelle's difficult journey to salvation was a lonely one, but he was not alone in taking it. Other Moravians and southern evangelicals underwent similar, and equally difficult, journeys. John Littlejohn, a Methodist, could not have been more different from George Soelle: the two were from different countries, followed different occupations, spoke different languages, and joined different churches. Yet their conversion experiences were virtually identical. Littlejohn was a raucous, English-born artisan who came to America in about 1767. After moving to Norfolk, Virginia, he first heard revivalists preach in 1769 and was intrigued enough to continue attending preaching on a regular basis. Like Soelle, Littlejohn regretted that "the word did not reach my heart, although it did for many others." Five years later, Littlejohn remained unconverted until he heard the words of a Methodist exhorter from Philadelphia, who played the same role for Littlejohn that Brother Grassman did for Soelle. The exhorter "related to us what God had done for his soul. His words got to my heart as never any did before, tears gushed from my eyes. . . . I acknowledged my sin & cryed [sic] unto the Lord to spare an pluck me as a brand from ye burning." Littlejohn had at last made the step from vocation to justification. As Methodist historian Dee E. Andrews concluded, "The pattern of Littlejohn's religious experience was replicated among a remarkable variety of Methodists, male and female, across social, racial, and ethnic lines."[6] The conversion experiences of German and English speakers were virtually identical. As another historian of southern evangelicalism has noted, "If the paramount issue was conversion, then all those who shared this experience in some way were members of a vast spiritual community."[7] Indeed, some of the earliest converts to Wesleyan Methodism in America were German Palatines.[8] These German immigrants found a congenial home in a religious reform movement transplanted to a British colony from England. Ethnicity mattered little; achieving a spiritual rebirth was what counted.

Soelle himself intuitively understood that his experience as a sinner was typical and that he had much to offer to those trying to find spiritual peace through Jesus. Having successfully been reborn, this Lutheran minister asked to join the Unity in 1747 and to become a missionary in the Diaspora. The brethren in Copenhagen advised him to stay where he was and to serve the Lord in his old post in the Lutheran Church. But Soelle rejected this advice; "I had no rest in my heart until I preached my farewell sermon [at my church] and set out for the Unity." Soelle reached Herrnhaag in October of that year and then moved to Marienborn, where he was received into the Moravian congregation there on December 1. When Soelle received his call to go to America in 1753, he eagerly accepted.[9]

Soelle's transatlantic move launched a missionary career that took him to numerous Moravian outposts in Maryland, Pennsylvania, and New England: Oley, Lynn, Yorktown, Philadelphia, Newport, and finally to Broadbay for eight years. In the final three years of his remarkable career, he settled in Wachovia in 1770 and traveled tirelessly throughout Wachovia and the North Carolina backcountry, spreading the word of Jesus' saving grace. Soelle died on May 4, 1773, at the age of sixty-three.[10]

Soelle brought to his task an empathy for those struggling to achieve a new birth and a certain toughness that the unsaved needed to confront his or her sinful ways. In 1771, for instance, Soelle was both patient and stern with George Lang of Friedland who was trying to find the "light." Patiently, Soelle explained over and over again to Lang during pastoral visits to Lang's house over many months that no one could be saved until he took that first step to justification and admitted his worthlessness. Soelle even stayed overnight at Lang's house so they could better talk about what this society member needed to do to achieve a relationship with the Savior. On July 24, Soelle noted that he was making progress with Lang: "Grace is becoming more and more active in him and makes him more conscious of his misery and ruin."[11]

Although Soelle displayed patience with those unsaved souls who were struggling to achieve a rebirth, he had no patience for those unsaved who proclaimed to be good Christians and to know all the answers. In February 1773, Soelle encountered a Presbyterian, a member of a church that Soelle felt lacked "spark and light." This Presbyterian considered himself to be "wise," an assertion that only earned Soelle's ire. "I asked him whether he had in all his life been in spiritual distress and experienced the power of Christ's death for forgiveness," Soelle recounted in his diary. "He replied, 'No.' I told him he should go and first learn to become a penitent sinner and a fool, and then experience in his own soul what it means to be a Redeemer."[12] Soelle's harsh words were quite clear: unless the unsaved let Jesus into his heart, he was not a true Christian.

Those "unsaved" whom Moravian missionaries succeeded in reaching understood this well. Adam Hartman of Friedberg was so moved by a sermon that L. C. Bachhof gave on the need to repent that he approached the pastor "and said that in the sermon yesterday, I had spoken of his situation exactly." Hartman's admission gave Bachhof the chance to repeat his earlier point: "I said to him, 'You are under the influence of the Holy Spirit. Hear Him and follow not just your head, but rather give yourself to the Savior with body and soul.'"[13] In 1771, Martin Walk approached Bachhof about joining the Unity as a member of the Friedberg congregation. This pledge of commitment did not impress the pastor; he made it clear to Walk that "the way to conversion did not begin with their being accepted [into the congregation], but rather in their saying, 'Oh, how can I bring Jesus into my life!'"[14]

Moravian views of salvation reflected Count Zinzendorf's Christ-centered philosophy. For the count, a love of Jesus was at the core of an experiential "heart religion." The locus of one's faith was to be the heart and not the head. The essence of true belief, he preached, was an individual's loving relationship with God and Jesus Christ. Central to this conception was the count's views of Christ, whom he saw as *Spezial-Gott:* "The Savior is our God. Through him we know the Father and the Holy Spirit."[15] Bachhof had put it well. To undergo a new birth, Hartman and others could not merely think about Christ; they had to *feel* his presence. What the pastor meant was that conversion was to be a matter of feeling and not of reasoning. Pilgrims could not use their minds to achieve a rebirth; they had to use their hearts. They had, according to Zinzendorf, to directly experience God through identification with Jesus Christ.

The count was not a Calvinist who believed that God preordained who would be saved and who would be damned. Like other evangelicals, he saw vocation as an absolutely critical first step to conversion. The seekers, Zinzendorf preached on numerous occasions, could not achieve a new birth through good works or careful study of the Bible. A seeker must "entrust everything to Him," and a person could do that only if he or she had the strength of faith to rely completely on the Savior. On one level, Zinzendorf's message was aimed at those Christians who believed they could "work" their way to a new birth, either through virtuous acts of charity or through diligent study of the Bible that would allow them to "amass holiness." The count disdained those scholastics who believed that piety could be achieved through the study and understanding of theological propositions. Zinzendorf firmly rejected the views of those later Pietists at Halle who espoused "legalistic" conversions and who promoted intellectualism and moralism over regeneration and repentance.[16]

Zinzendorf viewed attempts to earn salvation as manifestations of pride—the "devil's greatest vice"—because it was the opposite of humility. "Pride," he concluded, "is the most loathsome vice, the most repugnant to God, and humility is the virtue closest to God." In one sermon, he recalled the parable of the wedding feast, where a well-dressed guest was cast out for rejecting the humble wedding robe that was offered to him. The count's point was that a prideful person was a "haughty" and "sanctimonious" person who believed he was holy and thus deserving of salvation. Yet the well-dressed, vain person, Zinzendorf warned, was exactly the one who would *not* receive salvation.[17]

Yet Zinzendorf did not believe that the new birth was entirely up to the individual. He saw salvation as a gift of the Savior. By totally trusting in Lord Jesus, the individual was placing his fate in the Savior's hands. Justification could not occur unless the seeker took a crucial step during vocation. The unsaved, Zinzendorf explained in a sermon in 1742, have to "come to Jesus as poor sinners, who bring no righteousness, no words, no holiness, nothing but nakedness and poverty." The count stressed that the unsaved needed to be totally humble and helpless before their Savior. If a person believed he deserved salvation, he would be rejected by Jesus as vain and unrighteous. Zinzendorf put it baldly to an audience in Germantown, Pennsylvania, in 1742: "The judgement of rejection is when a person who desires to be saved, who seeks to be saved, cannot be saved. As it [the Bible] says among other things, 'Many will strive to get in and will not be able to do so.' Now this is a divine truth." The vain and the righteous, the count said, will forever remain outsiders. Zinzendorf, in short, believed that Jesus would grant salvation only to those who came to him with open and humble hearts.[18]

Zinzendorf was walking a fine line in these sermons. He argued that the sinner could not achieve salvation on his own, that only Jesus in his wisdom and goodness could grant it. To seek salvation consciously would lead to rejection. Yet Zinzendorf also argued that the sinner had the ability to receive Jesus's good graces through the exercise of proper faith: admit your worthlessness before the Lord, and you too can be saved; come to Jesus as a poor sinner, and you will receive the "garment of honor." This was a complex message that could confuse listeners at first, as the memoirs of William Barton Peddycoard and others demonstrate. Who did the saving—Jesus or the individual? Moravian missionaries emphatically answered it was the former, but they emphasized the important role that the latter played in his or her own salvation. It was the individual who had to take that first crucial step of admitting his or her worthlessness. The pastors stressed repeatedly that a person thus had the ability to bring about a new birth by turning to Jesus. In delivering this mixed message, the pastors were not rejecting their Zinzendorfian heritage. Indeed, the General Synod of 1775 had codified it by declaring "since the Fall we have no power to save ourselves."[19] Missionaries instead emphasized the more mainstream elements that one could be saved through the good graces of Jesus Christ. As Bachhof had told one seeker, you must bring Jesus into your life.

Wachovia's pastors, who preached repeatedly on the glories of Christ's martyrdom and the healing power of his resurrection, used their sermons to point the unsaved toward the correct path. Their goal was to elicit both guilt and joy in audience members—guilt for their sinful natures and joy that they could be saved by opening their hearts to Jesus. Unlike Baptist and Methodist evangelicals of the late eighteenth and early nineteenth centuries, Moravian pastors did not want their hearers to fall into ecstasy, do the jerks, or exhibit other forms of behavior associated with camp meetings that the brethren considered excessive and offensive. Instead, Moravian preachers sought to deliver addresses that would cause people to contemplate maturely and seriously their lost conditions without the Savior. This was not to say that the pastors did not want to tug on listeners' emotions. They did. Preaching to Friedland's congregation on March 4, 1772, Soelle drew a "picture afresh of the agony of our God [that is, Jesus Christ], and the drops from His wounds and His side, opened after His death." Through the use of such graphic language, Soelle had two goals in mind. One was to bring audience members literally to tears. He wanted them to feel real anxiety over the state of their souls. Approvingly, he noted that his sermon worked on this occasion because it "forced out many tears" in the audience. If such tears were not shed, Soelle believed he was not doing his job. A sermon that Soelle delivered in May 1772, for instance, got off to an indifferent start among not only the audience but also the pastor himself. "At first my heart was pretty much unmoved; however, I then experienced a release, so that I was able to speak with unction and grace, which stirred my [hearers] and called forth their tears."[20]

The second goal of such graphic language was to educate people about Jesus' sacrifice on the cross and the need for sinners to let the Savior into their lives. Soelle's use of blood and wounds imagery drew directly on the heritage bequeathed by Zinzendorf. In his own sermons, the count did not preach of eternal damnation for those who failed to embrace the Savior. Instead, he delivered another message that was meant to shock his audience into comprehending—and feeling—the tremendous sacrifice made by Jesus for mankind: that, in the words of one Moravian historian, "Christ was the slaughtered Lamb who purchased salvation with his blood."[21] Zinzendorf's "Litany of Wounds" employed extremely graphic language about Christ's crucifixion on the cross. For the count, the piercing of Jesus on the cross and the terrible wounds he endured were more important than the crucifixion itself. That was because the side wound became an opening into Jesus—the blood that poured from this wound represented the very source of life. The wound's opening, in other words, was the passage "through which souls pass on their way to a new life in Christ." For those who believed in the Savior, the wound's opening invited the believer in.[22]

Soelle and other pastors used this blood-and-wounds language in their sermons to shock their audiences out of any complacency they may have been feeling. But they also wanted to guide the unconverted toward the first step in the conversion process. In deploying such language, the brethren were separating themselves from other evangelicals. Many Lutheran Pietists and others were appalled by both the sensuousness of the language and its bloody imagery.[23] More-mainstream evangelicals preached that an individual possessed the ability to achieve salvation on his or her own.

Critics of the *Brudergemeine* also accused the brethren of espousing quick and superficial conversions that did not stand the test of time—a charge that other evangelicals faced as well, especially during the height of the camp-meeting movement in the early nineteenth century.[24] In Wachovia, few would have called their conversions superficial. All understood too well the difficulty of achieving a true rebirth. All understood that vocation was a difficult, drawn-out process. And nearly all understood—and feared—the dangers of "back-sliding," as the unsaved embraced Christ and renounced their worldly ways, only to relapse and to return to old bad habits until they turned to Christ yet again.

Such a cycle was well known in Wachovia. Indeed, when congregation members died, pastors routinely read their *Lebenslaufs* to the assembled congregation as a lesson in human weakness and Jesus Christ's ultimate triumph. This lesson was familiar to pilgrims but was likely awe-inspiring nevertheless: Moravian evangelicals struggled to achieve a conversion and to maintain it. For the faithful, Jesus won out in the end. The struggles of Cornelius Schneider were typical. He was born in Broadbay in 1751 to parents who later joined the Moravian Society. His family came to Wachovia in 1770 for a familiar reason, according to Cornelius's *Lebenslauf:* that the parents and "their children might come into closer fellowship with the *Brudergemeine*." Schneider, his life's chronicler said, "was not accustomed [to talking] at length about the state of his heart, but he did express himself to the end that it was his earnest wish to follow our Lord faithfully as his possession." In 1779, he was received into Friedberg's congregation, and in 1780, he took communion for the first time. But despite having undergone a new birth, "for several years, something seemed to be troubling him in the serene walk of a pardoned sinner." Schneider became so troubled with the state of his soul that he declined to take communion and eventually severed his ties with the congregation. After returning from Gnadenhutten, Ohio, Schneider tried to recapture the spark he had earlier experienced, but he struggled to achieve it. As his chronicler put it: "He declared various times that he would turn soon to the congregation in Friedland in a new commitment." His efforts at reconciliation drew the support of the church community. "The circumstances of this dear man," noted his memoir, "and the darkness into which he had come were of great concern to the Wachovia workers, and they wished to be able to help him soon to come back into the light again."[25]

Valentine Frey was another member who struggled to avoid backsliding. When his family moved to Pennsylvania from Europe and joined the brethren there, he joined as well. He became a founding member of the Friedberg congregation and a respected community figure. Despite his conversion, a deep dedication to Moravianism, and his close ties to the Friedberg congregation (and later to Hope's), Valentine was unable to avoid straying in the 1790s, and he left the congregation for a time. As his memoir explained: he "turned to various by-paths, which interrupted his fellowship with us." Like so many others who wandered, Valentine eventually came back to the church, bringing a great deal of guilt and remorse with him. When Valentine "spoke of this time," his memoir recalled, "he wept bitter tears."[26] Jacob Roth of Friedland found so much temptation around him that Soelle reported "he is fighting against sin with all his might." Soelle told this struggling brother he knew of but one solution: "to surrender himself to the Savior and accept mercy from Him as an ungodly person."[27]

The difficulty of achieving and maintaining a new birth meant that membership in the *Landgemeinen* was extremely fluid, consisting of those seeking salvation and those struggling to maintain it. Communicant, or full, members made up about 40 percent of the adult membership, or some 17 percent of the total congregation. Children constituted the bulk of the *Landgemeinen* membership—about 53 percent of the total—and they were not considered full members.[28] The one constant was that all struggled to remain faithful to Jesus and the *Gemeine*. *Landgemeinen* members may have lived on scattered family farms, hailed from different countries, grown up in different faiths, and descended from different ethnicities, but they were all evangelical cousins who struggled together to achieve a new birth and to maintain it. For those who succeeded, the conversion experience forged a bond that was deep and lasting. The converted became brothers and sisters in Christ, and conversion drew them together in ways that transcended kinship and ethnicity. Someone who had experienced the helplessness and terrors of vocation—along with the joys of justification—readily identified with someone who was going through a similar experience. The same held true for those who were "backsliding." Here, a congregation pulled together to help when the righteous strayed, as Schneider and countless others learned.

The *Gemeine* itself stood for something far more significant than a congregation. It represented a community of believers who shared the new birth and an all-encompassing commitment to Jesus Christ. To impress upon the brethren the seriousness of this commitment, the Unity required *Gemeine* members to draw up, sign, and adhere to Brotherly Agreements that outlined a code of conduct for the brethren to follow. In late 1780, for instance, the board of pastors overseeing the *Landgemeinen* decided that it was time for Friedberg to have a Brotherly Agreement. "This would serve as a foundation for the better administration of discipline," board members declared. "To this end, some articles can be derived from the basic Principia and discussed several times with the *Haus Vaters* in the *Gemein Rath* [Congregation Council]. The extract out of the Synodal *Verlaß* [synodal report] can also be taken as an aid."[29]

The Brotherly Agreements, drawn up with the aid of Wachovia's leaders, became one of the basic organizing principles in the *Landgemeinen,* and all who wanted to join the *Gemeine* had to agree to abide by its rules. Hope's agreement of 1785 was typical. *Gemeine* members there pledged to be a "living congregation of Jesus." In practical terms, that pledge meant that full members had to have undergone a conversion experience: "We will therefore receive none into our congregation, but such whose hearts desire is to surrender themselves to our dear Savior with Soul and body, and to live for Him only." This obligation was stressed repeatedly in the Brotherly Agreement. "The only ground of our salvation is Christ Jesus and his blood. Thro' free election of God the father, we are called by the Holy Ghost to believe in Jesus Christ our Lord, and to prove by word and deed that we are his property." Service to the Lord, in other words, entailed turning one's life over to Jesus Christ; the Savior had to come first.[30]

Such a requirement carried a second important component. It meant that the brethren had to avoid the "many worldly customs" enjoyed in rural America, specifically, drinking liquor, horse racing, and shooting matches, "as well as all sorts of frolicks, such as spinning and cotton picking and cornhuskings at night, intended for merriment." Not content to stop there, the Brotherly Agreement admonished members not to lie, slander, or engage in "foolish talking."[31]

Not surprisingly, members in the *Landgemeinen* struggled to live up to such high standards of piety. How they dealt with their inevitable human failings tells a great deal about the influence of evangelicalism on community. As in all things, the Brotherly Agreements advised the congregation and its pastor on how to deal with the quarrels and inevitable backsliding that arose in their settlements. When problems occurred, the brethren were to let the Savior be their guide and beacon, and patience was to be paramount. If a brother or sister strayed, the congregation should try to "restore such a one in the Spirit of meakness." Quarreling parties were not to air their problems in public or, worse, "make use of the Law for redress." Instead, the Brotherly Agreements advised the brethren to talk among themselves. If this did not work, they should turn to the "minister or other qualified members of the community for their mediation."[32]

The *Landgemeinen* did follow this advice as much as possible. One May morning in 1772, Friedland's congregation was wrapped not in love but in anger. Soelle took to the pulpit to remind the brethren that "hatred, envy, quarrelsomeness is the mark of the children of the world, for Satan is incapable of love." With that reminder, Soelle recounted in his diary, the congregation aired the problems surrounding a "quarrel caused by a family. . . . It was discussed [among themselves] fully and buried."[33] On another occasion, the men in the congregation gathered at sundown at a nearby farm after finishing their chores to deal with a fistfight involving the son of Valentine Frey and an unnamed person. The mediation process involved a good deal of talking and explicit reminders of their duty as Christians. Soelle, quite characteristically, joined the gathering and reminded "old and young about the friend of sinners."[34] He fully expected them to work out their differences as a Christian family, in the spirit of forgiveness personified by their Savior.

Despite admonitions not to quarrel, slander, and lie, the brethren of course did just that. These were small congregations bound tightly by religious and familial kinship. Personal quarrels were common and consumed a great deal of pastors' time. Peter Rothrock of Friedberg, for one, found himself on the wrong end of a slander; upset and worried about his standing in the congregation, he went to the pastor and "cleared himself of the lies that someone had been spreading about him."[35] Friedrich Bockel, also of Friedberg, became very angry at Christian Frey, "because in a survey, Frey cut off his land up the fence without his knowledge," Bachhof reported in his diary. "Friedrich and his brother John Nicholas brought Valentine Frey across Muddy Creek in a canoe and went to Christian Frey's to call him to account for the matter. Thus they were more eager to quarrel than to come to the sermon." Congregation pastors acted as mediators in these disputes and did all they could to reconcile the quarreling parties. Bachhof, for instance, crisscrossed Friedberg every Wednesday and Saturday, not just spreading Christ's word but acting as a mediator and a counselor. Bachhof repeatedly implored members not to meddle in others' affairs, "for it is most dangerous." When necessary, the pastor summoned the quarreling parties to the *gemeine Haus* for a conference and lecture on Christian love and forgiveness. When the Mullers and Hartmans were unable to resolve their differences, Bachhof "found it necessary to ask them to come to the schoolhouse tomorrow for a thorough discussion about the quarrel they are having over their children." Bachhof also mediated between Adam Hartman and Adam Spach over some unnamed problem. After a "cordial" discussion, the two men "embraced again in love and forgave each other."[36]

Settlers in the *Landgemeinen* expected neighbors and friends to deal with each other in a forthright and brotherly manner. Peter Volz of Friedberg learned the hard way that one violated this code at a cost. By all accounts, Volz was difficult to get along with. He constantly criticized his neighbors and the pastor. The congregation suspended him in 1771, but he continued "slandering" people into the following year. The usual punishment of barring him from communion and participation in *Gemeine* activities proved to have little effect. By late fall, congregation members were physically shunning Volz. The situation was so tense that Sarah Frey became alarmed when her husband agreed to dig a cellar for Volz. She asked Bachhof for advice. His reply was succinct: "Do not have dealings with Volz, who is a wicked man." Finally, in 1773, the pastor excluded Volz from the congregation. He had repeatedly violated the Brotherly Agreement and was to pay the price.[37]

Volz's case was an extreme one; the Moravians did not follow the Amish and Anabaptist practice of physically shunning those members who broke the rules. Their inclination, instead, was to help guide the sinner back to the correct path. Patience was crucial, and forgiveness was paramount. Volz, who was given countless chances to change his quarrelsome ways, could himself testify to that attitude. In November 1771, before his later expulsion, he had again found himself in trouble for things he had said about other congregation members, including the pastor. After the morning service, he called Bachhof "aside and confessed that he had said bad things about me to many people. He asked for forgiveness and requested that the church readmit him." Bachhof, who had been one of the targets of Volz's crankiness, was sympathetic. "I told him, 'As far as I'm concerned, I will forgive you, for you have caused me little injury, but you may have caused damage to the souls of those whom you spoke. Thus you must above all ask for forgiveness from the Savior.'" Wachovia's boards excluded someone as only a last resort; even then, the sinner could seek readmission if he amended his ways. The key, the central elders in Herrnhut agreed, was for the sinner to demonstrate that he "sincerely repents." If he did, then his readmission to communion or the *Gemeine* rested with the Lord: administrative boards, including the Land Arbeiter Conferenz (the ministers' conference for the farm congregations), put a readmission to the lot. If the answer came up "yes," the person was allowed to rejoin; if it was "no," the person remained excluded for the time being.[38]

The return of the excluded was meant to be a triumphant time that helped to reunify the congregation and to signal Jesus' superior wisdom. It almost always involved an elaborate mediation process among the wanderer, the pastor, and the congregation itself. Pastors in the late eighteenth century spent countless hours arguing, discussing, and pleading matters of profound personal faith with people whose behavior had slipped or who were thinking of leaving the congregation. The many quarrels and disputes added stress to communal life, but the process of resolving those arguments ultimately left the bonds of community stronger as the power of Christian forgiveness manifested itself.

Here, historian David Sabean's thesis of "mediated" relationships contains important insights into understanding how community functioned in Wachovia. As Sabean argued in *Power in the Blood,* a study of European village life in the early modern period, frustration and anger helped define community as much as harmony, because the negotiating process strengthened relationships among people. In the case of Sabean's European villages, the give-and-take process between lord and commoner, and between peasant and peasant, gave a degree of power to all sides and a stake in the dispute's outcome—and, ultimately, in community itself.[39] When congregation members in Wachovia quarreled, pastors would often call the offending parties to the *gemeine Haus,* where they would try to work out their differences with the pastor's help. Such a process could be seen at work in Friedberg in 1772, when several members were bickering among themselves. With pastor Bachhof looking on, "these men, who had fallen out with each other, once again had discussed the matter thoroughly with one another and had admitted, apologized for, and forgiven their mistakes and wrongdoings . . . and they again embraced in love and affection."[40] These brethren, in other words, managed to put aside their differences and restore some harmony to the congregation.

Tensions among the brethren, caused by their failures to live up to their Brotherly Agreements, sharpened the issues and made all parties reassess their commitment to the congregation, to each other, and to their Savior. This was especially true in the all-important issue of *Abendmahl,* or holy communion. In all Christian faiths, one of the most important rituals was communion—the partaking of bread and wine symbolized one's wholeness with Jesus Christ. Wachovia's *Gemeinen* held communion about once a month, usually on Saturday evening.[41] For a Christocentric faith that lived by heart religion, it was an especially meaningful event and one ripe with symbolism. Only *Gemeine* members—and the saved—could attend. Because it was such a momentous event, memoirs noted almost without fail when a person had first partaken of communion. The brethren marked this milestone with the same reverence that they marked the birth of a child or the death of a parent, because the taking of communion was such an important step in a Christian's life journey. It symbolized the brethrens' oneness with Christ.

The *Landgemeinen* did not believe they were complete and accepted members of the Wachovia church community until they could offer communion to their *Gemeine* membership.[42] Communion was so important that some settlers told the minister that they wanted to join the congregation specifically so they could participate in this Christian ritual. And at least one excluded member had second thoughts about his behavior because he was denied participation in communion: on a Sunday in 1772, Friedrich Bockel handed the pastor a "letter in which he expressed very contritely his hunger and thirst for communion." A year later, the wife of Martin Walk "was very perplexed over her not being permitted to communion. . . . At Peter Frey's, the longing for communion was likewise powerfully stirred up."[43]

In his study of German villages, Sabean found communion to be one of the most important rituals that rural communities engaged in. The church polity intended that the sacrament of the Lord's Supper be a meal of reconciliation, and village pastors took advantage of this importance to settle conflicts among villagers and to control behavior. In other words, if someone wanted to take communion, he would first need to make amends for any un-Christian behavior he had engaged in. Thus, for Sabean, "the central mediating institution was communion. It was the ritual that constituted the social order and defined its tensions."[44]

Communion served virtually the same function in Wachovia. Before communion was administered to full congregation members, church authorities held *Sprechens,* or speakings. At *Sprechens,* pastors carefully interviewed each congregation member "to learn from them their present heart's situation."[45] Only those of the proper mind could attend communion. As the Unity's central elders explained: "We are instructed it is true faithfully to examine ourselves before we draw nigh unto the Lord's table—that is to say, we are required to put all such questions to ourselves as may be conducive to point out to us the real situation of our hearts."[46]

The speakings became a powerful tool to control members' behavior; only those deemed worthy could partake of the Lord's Supper. Christian Zimmerman of Friedberg, for instance, opted not to partake of communion "because he considered himself too unworthy."[47] In the *Landgemeinen,* the Land Arbeiter Conferenz decided who could attend communion based on the speakings. Salem's elders fulfilled the same role for the congregation towns. Ultimately, the decision rested with the Lord through the lot. Pastors and elders did not hesitate to bar someone from communion if he or she had misbehaved in some way. In 1781, for example, "the Friedberg members who attended corn-huskings, and by their behavior gave offense and broke their Brotherly Agreement, were not allowed to attend the last Communion." The reaction of the cornhuskers to their exclusion was telling: "Some of them regret the offense given; others are not sorry, and accuse Br. and Sr. Beck [who had replaced Bachhof after his death in 1774] of harsh judgment."[48] Denying entry to communion often angered congregation members. Thus, as in Germany, communion served both as an important source of tension and as an integrating force. Those who wanted to partake of the Lord's Supper had to be on their best behavior and be members in good standing.

Tensions over communion took two forms. On one level, members resented being excluded from communion. Such a punishment embarrassed and wounded them, and they often protested to the pastor. During one communion service in 1773, Bachhof closed the front door to the *gemeine Haus,* barring entry to those forbidden to attend. The obvious symbolism of a closed door did not escape the attention of those congregation members prevented from attending. One excluded member angrily let Bachhof know what she thought; another "came to me with tears in her eyes and asked me to forgive her."[49]

Communion proved to be divisive on a second level as well: some congregants objected when the supposedly unpure were allowed to break bread with them. Here, there were echoes of Roger Williams and his allies in the seventeenth century who condemned fellow New England Puritans for not being pure enough.[50] In 1773, George Frey became angry when the Land Arbeiter Conferenz barred some of his friends from communion. For Frey, the whole thing was hypocritical. As he explained to Bachhof, "I have often desired to come to communion; but I heard that communicant members through no fault of their own must stay away from communion while the boot-lickers among the brethren come out on top. That is why I am quite distressed." In protest, he and his wife refused to participate in the Lord's Supper.[51]

These disputes could divide the congregation outside the meetinghouse. Friends and relatives would back the protester's side; others would side with the pastor. This was what happened in Frey's case. His brother Christel defended George and enlisted the support of another brother, Valentine. Christel "expressed his animosity toward the Congregation," Bachhof sadly noted in his diary, "and said flatly that the Congregation was not functioning according to the Savior's intentions and will."[52] Christel and Valentine announced they would not attend communion, either. Peter Frey went so far as to argue that the congregation should allow unconverted Christians to attend communion.[53]

As with the problem of straying members, disputes over communion forced the congregation to talk, to cajole, and to work out its problems. Certainly, Bachhof and other pastors were not willing to compromise on who could attend. Bachhof advised Christel and Valentine Frey to stay away, and he pointedly told Peter that the taking of communion would be an empty exercise if the unconverted participated—*Abendmahl* "exists only for the new person and not for the old one."[54] The communion service itself helped heal the very tensions it created. As the *Abendmahl* began, the pastor granted an absolution for the congregation, with members corporately giving their confessions to their choir leaders. Then, with members lying prostrate before the communion table, they prayed silently as the pastor offered a prayer of confession. This act of confession served an important function: it transferred the individual sins of the brethren to Jesus, who took responsibility on his broad shoulders for their misdeeds. With these sins thus forgiven, congregation members exchanged the kiss of peace to seal the act of reconciliation. The service thus became a time of joy for participants. As the pastor distributed the communion elements to the seated congregation, members sang a series of stanzas that reflected the theme of redemption.[55] Religious values, as a result, paradoxically introduced tension within individual congregations and helped to resolve them.

Governing the *Gemeinen*

For members of the *Landgemeinen,* the Moravian congregation gave structure to their lives, helped foster unity among members from different ethnicities and faiths, and made them part of a church family that spanned more than two continents. The Unity's central elders based in Germany set broad policy on doctrinal matters; Wachovia's administrators, with help from numerous church boards, oversaw life in Wachovia. But each congregation had responsibility for day-to-day affairs in their settlements. As a result, the Unity was a complex federation that deftly mixed local autonomy with central direction from Germany. On the one hand, the General Synod recognized that "every separate congregation . . . must have its own particular direction." But on the other hand, these congregations were part of a whole: "The Congregations of the Brethren, tho' differing amongst themselves in local regulations and scattered over the world, all together constitute one Union and an intimate connection in the Lord subsides between them."[56]

In practice, this meant that church elders in Salem and Germany provided central direction, maintaining a final say in all liturgical and doctrinal matters. A local congregation, for instance, could not choose its own pastor, as independent Baptist congregations could. In Wachovia, Salem's Aeltesten Conferenz (board of elders) oversaw the *Landgemeinen* until the formation of the Land Arbeiter Conferenz in September 1780. This new board, which was composed of Wachovia's pastors and their wives, had direct administrative responsibility for religious affairs in the three country congregations.

The pastor was the formal leader of the congregation, but all members had a great say in how their community was run. As in the *Ortsgemeinen,* a conferential system of governance predominated in the *Landgemeinen.* A Haus Vaters Conferenz consisting of the heads of households regularly met, as did a Haus Maters Conferenz for the married sisters. These committees discussed issues of importance to families and decided how to implement resolutions approved by the congregation's other governing boards, such as the organization of work teams to clean up God's Acre. The most important of these other boards was the settlement's general committee. This committee, consisting of the pastor and about five congregation members elected by their brethren, oversaw settlement life. It, among other things, determined the pastor's salary and how it should be paid; helped settle disputes among settlers; determined who could be buried in the congregation's God's Acre; decided when school would open and end; and oversaw the building and maintenance of the meetinghouses. Congregational councils dealt with a narrower purview: religious affairs, such as when to hold a lovefeast and how to pay for it. Stewards assisted the pastor, served as spokesmen for congregants, and acted as community representatives with church authorities.[57]

The *Gemeine* functioned as a surrogate government. It provided structure to the community, a vehicle for decision making, and a forum for airing the concerns and complaints of settlers. The governing structure in the *Ortsgemeinen* was similar but more elaborate. The *Ortsgemeinen* ideal meant that the church owned all property, including houses, and the church tightly controlled the economy, determining who could work at what crafts. This more demanding lifestyle, in turn, meant that the congregation boards had a more extensive role to play in settlement affairs. It was the Aufseher Collegium—akin to a board of supervisors—that regulated the guild system in Salem and decided who could build a house and where. It was the Aeltesten Conferenz that determined who could join the congregation and who would be punished if congregation rules were broken.[58]

The *Gemeine,* as a result, combined the secular and the sacred. The word itself meant more than "congregation"—a *Gemeine* represented a community of believers that made no distinction between the civil community and the congregation.[59] It was developed in Herrnhut in the late 1720s and had its origins in German Pietism and the European village. On the sacred level, Pietism encouraged members to be active in church life. Reformers believed the revival of staid churches was to begin from the ground up; through their piety and energy, individual members could spark a collective reformation. This would be best accomplished through conventicles, where Christians would meet in small groups for study and fellowship. Such small gatherings would promote piety and carefully fan the sparks of reform. Closely intertwined with these conventicles was the pietist impulse to provide charity and schooling for villagers—functions that brought religion even closer into the daily lives of people. Reform was not to be confined to the parish church but was to extend into the village itself. On the secular level, the Moravian *Gemeine* arose out of a German milieu that saw the village government heavily involved in its citizens' lives. In Herrnhut, the first *Gemeine* that became a model for the rest of the Unity, the elders acted as village overseers, passing regulations that emulated village ordinances. The difference was that in the *Gemeine,* these rules were intended to enforce not civil peace but devotion to the Savior.[60]

The differences between the *Landgemeinen* and *Ortsgemeinen* were both practical and philosophical. Wachovia's administrators recognized that it would be unrealistic to institute a regimented lifestyle in farm communities on the southern frontier. As administrator Frederick Marshall explained in a 1780 letter:

> It appears to me that the life on a farm lends itself to a patriarchical mode and to daily worship of God in the home better than to residence in a congregation town, with numerous and daily meetings, and with strict Choir organization. Even when persons trained in the Choir Houses marry and take charge of a farm, the care of cattle and other farm work does not always permit rigid adherence to rules.[61]

Country living required a different approach, Unity leaders reasoned. They accorded the farm settlements more leeway precisely because they were not towns. The *Landgemeinen,* the General Synod of 1764 explained, were subject only to the church's spiritual and moral regulations because these congregations conducted their civic life independently of the Unity.[62] Settlers, as a result, could decide where they wanted to live, how big of a house to build, and what kinds of crops they could grow.

These differences between a restricted congregational town and an open congregation of society and *Gemeine* members also reflected the differing roles the two settlement types were to play in this evangelical community. Unity leaders saw the *Ortsgemeine* as a city on the hill. The *Ortsgemeine,* with its superior piety and behavior, was to set an example for others to emulate. This vision had obvious parallels to seventeenth-century Puritanism in New En-

gland. By leading exemplary lives, members of congregation towns were to inspire others to follow their example and thereby help lead a reformation within
the Protestant world. Such a lofty goal meant that only the truly devout could
live in an *Ortsgemeine*. Inhabitants of Salem and other congregation towns not
only had to be absolutely committed to the Savior but also had to be willing
to subordinate all aspects of their lives to religion. Only the most committed
could live in an *Ortsgemeine;* hence, the church restricted residency and promoted stricter rules for inhabitants.

The *Landgemeinen,* by contrast, had a more basic pietistic goal: they were
to help introduce others to the Savior's ways. Because of this mission, the
Moravian farm settlements were inclusive. They sought to introduce as many
hearers as possible to the Moravian message of redemption. Those wishing to
affiliate with the Unity could do so as society members; those wanting a closer
affiliation could join the Unity as full members. Thus, the *Landgemeinen* were
open places that tolerated different levels of membership.

The Unity, however, did not lower the standards for those people in the
Landgemeinen wanting to be full members. It insisted that these settlers be committed evangelicals who had undergone the new birth. At its inaugural meeting in September 1780, the Land Arbeiter Conferenz tried to explain exactly
who a *Gemeine* member was in those "open" farm congregations outside of the
congregation towns. A full member, the board said, had to "live truly in the
Savior." Devotion to Christ, it continued, also meant a devotion to discipline.
The board expected a society member to be devoted to Christ, of course. But
it expected a higher degree of sacrifice from a *Gemeine* member; such a member was someone "who wholeheartedly choose[s] to endure insult, hardship,
and persecution with the *Gemeine* . . . or [who] wholeheartedly loathes sin. . . .
Those who do not fall into one of these two classes and who do the works of
the flesh, or who have no yearning for the Savior and for the forgiveness of their
sins are not true *Gemeine* members."[63] The pastors reasoned that they had to be
especially diligent in the *Landgemeinen* precisely because of the looser church
controls in those congregations. When the conference discussed the procedures
for admitting single society members into the *Gemeine,* it concluded that "a
profound examination of the spiritual and material progress of the persons to
be proposed is even more necessary," because choirs in the *Landgemeinen* provide less oversight than in the *Ortsgemeinen*.[64]

The power of the church was not as encompassing in the *Landgemeinen*. The
Unity, however, still considered these congregations *Gemeinen* (that is, a community of believers), and the farm settlements could not be awarded the status

of a *Gemeine* unless they met several exacting requirements that mirrored the process for individual applicants. Settlements hoping to become Moravian congregations had to show a sustained commitment to the Unity on both spiritual and financial levels, and they had to serve a probationary period as a society that lasted years before they could be awarded the status of a *Gemeine.* Only after an applicant was declared a *Gemeine* could its pastor offer communion and other benefits to full-time members. As with individuals seeking entry into the Unity, congregational applicants had to show that their members were devout followers of the Savior and committed to him in all ways. This commitment carried a monetary obligation as well; the Unity could offer advice and structure to those settlements forming congregations—but little or no money. Applicants had to possess the resources to build a meetinghouse and to feed, clothe, and house a pastor and his family. They also had to have the financial means to contribute to the Unity's missionary work and its other reform work.

Most applicants in the North Carolina backcountry floundered on one or all of these requirements. Fox Nap, a difficult sixty-mile ride from Wachovia in western North Carolina, was one such place. This isolated German-speaking settlement was "poor in religious and in material matters," the Salem Diary reported, and these settlers "rejoiced" at the visit of missionary George Soelle in 1772. The settlers promised to build a meetinghouse if Soelle would return periodically. He did, but the tiny settlement was never able to fulfill its promise, and nothing came of this initiative. The brethren had high hopes in the 1760s that Town Fork and other settlements near Hope would build meetinghouses and affiliate with the Unity. These hopes never materialized, because the settlements lacked the sustained interest, the financial means, or both, to join the Unity.[65]

Of the three North Carolina *Landgemeinen,* Friedberg was the one whose efforts to become a formal Moravian congregation proved to be the longest and most difficult. That was because of Friedberg's chaotic, unplanned beginnings and its lack of previous ties to the northern Diaspora in the 1750s and early 1760s. The settlement lacked both the existing population to justify designation as a congregation and—unlike in Hope and Friedland—the seeming likelihood that additional Diaspora members from elsewhere would soon be joining the settlement. For a twelve-year period beginning in 1755, Friedberg's formal ties to the Unity were relatively tenuous. The settlement possessed no *gemeine Haus* and no pastor. Literally and figuratively, Friedberg stood outside the Wachovia community during this period. The earliest settlers lived just beyond Wachovia's borders, and authorities in Bethabara did not yet recognize Friedberg as part of their religious community. Instead, they viewed the settlers at South Fork as an outreach of Zinzendorf's Diaspora—German speakers who were receptive to the Savior's message and who could possibly affiliate with the brethren if they met the criteria for joining. They treated South Fork, as the brethren then called Friedberg, no differently from Fox Nap, Town Fork, and other settlements in western Carolina that were considering joining the Unity.[66]

Indian attacks in 1759 that killed several settlers in the Yadkin area caused South Fork's settlers to retreat to the safety of Bethabara's palisades. There, they received the chance to witness the Moravian community anew and up close. As one missionary put it, South Fork's settlers were "struck and captivated in their hearts by the power of the Spirit and the grace of His blood."[67] In October of that year, the settlers at South Fork formally "asked that a Brother might hold services for them and instruct their children; they wished to build a school-house, and asked for a place on our land for that purpose."[68] Church authorities rejected this request as premature. They did agree to send Ludolph Bachhof for a visit in 1759, but missionaries returned only sporadically to South Fork in the early 1760s. The settlers, however, kept pressing to join Wachovia. The arrival of several families from Pennsylvania in 1765 and 1766, including the Freys and Bockels, was a turning point in Friedberg's efforts to affiliate with the Moravians. These families not only bolstered the settlement's population by at least fifty-two persons but also greatly added to the number of Moravian expatriates from Pennsylvania societies. These newcomers were society members in good standing, and they gave the settlement credibility in its efforts to persuade Bethabara that it had the proper evangelical fervor to contribute to Wachovia's religious life.[69]

By the mid-1760s, Friedberg finally possessed the population, the financial resources, and—most of all—the sustained commitment to the Unity that the church required for membership. In May 1766, the settlement went ahead and consecrated a God's Acre on Wachovia's southern line. The settlers were forced to open a cemetery for a distressingly simple reason—the settlement's first death (the elder Peter Frey) meant that they needed a burial ground. But the opening of a God's Acre increased pressure on Wachovia's leaders to provide South Fork with a pastor. They finally agreed in that year to send a minister on a semiregular basis, although another twelve months would pass until they were able to fulfill this promise. Having at last secured a commitment for a pastor, the settlers commenced plans to build their meetinghouse. Adam Spach, George Hartman, and four others donated eighty-one acres along the Wachovia line for a log house thirty-four feet by twenty-eight feet.[70] On February 23,

1767, during heavy rains, the settlers laid the sills for the *gemeine Haus*. But another two years would pass until the settlement officially became a Moravian Society. With this momentous step, Friedberg formally joined the Wachovia community and received its name. No longer did Wachovia's leaders refer to the community as the settlement at South Fork.[71]

The inclusion of Friedland and Hope into the church community, by contrast, proceeded relatively swiftly because of the compactness of the migrants' moves and because of the settlers' previous affiliation with the Diaspora movement in Maine and Maryland. In Friedland, George Soelle's role was especially critical. He guided the Broadbay's emigrés, encouraged them to form a congregation, and provided critical leadership both to the community as a whole and to individuals. Friedberg had no such ally. His leadership was decisive in Friedland's relatively fast inclusion into the Moravian community. Soelle was a powerful mentor who felt personally responsible for the Broadbay emigrants' security. But equally important, Friedland's members were all society members who were able to persuade provincial elders quickly that "love of the Savior and His people, not material advantage, led them to come here."[72] From the outset, Wachovia's leaders viewed the Maine emigrés as Moravians who deserved to be part of the church community. In 1769 and 1770, Friedland's settlers were unsure whether they should start their own congregation or join existing ones. Soelle and the provincial elders helped solve that question for them. Salem's elders concluded that the expatriates from Maine "do not fit at all into our congregation" and should form their own.[73] Wachovia's leaders then helped them select land for a settlement several miles northeast of Friedberg on the "Hartman tract."[74] On January 15, 1771, the first family moved into their completed house, and by July, the village consisted of at least four houses. The settlers and church authorities selected a twenty-five-acre site for the meetinghouse at the end of September, and they began construction after the holding of a ceremony.[75] Friedland gained society status in 1771 and became a full congregation in August 1780.[76]

Hope's settlers also gained swift entry into the Wachovia church community despite their uniqueness as English-speaking former Anglicans. Daniel Smith and the other early arrivals used their first year in Wachovia to build their settlement on 450 acres at a site they had selected along a branch of Muddy Creek. There, they erected their first homes, several hastily constructed cabins.[77] The emigrés worshipped at Friedberg and awaited the arrival of additional congregation members from Carrollton. In 1774, eighteen members came; in 1775, another thirty-five arrived, boosting the population of the still tiny settlement to seventy-two. That total was large enough in the minds of the emigrés to form a congregation. Hope's settlers asked church officials for permission to build a meetinghouse in 1774 and requested that a minister be sent to the settlement. Before receiving an answer, settlers were so confident of a positive response that they began building a bridge across Muddy Creek to the site of the proposed meetinghouse. Construction on the meetinghouse began a year later. The settlers' confidence was justified. In 1780, Moravian authorities granted Hope the status of a full congregation—the fastest of the three North Carolina *Landgemeinen*—and assigned Johann Fritz, a German pastor fluent in English who had considerable experience as a missionary, to pastor to the congregation.[78] The reasons for Hope's swift inclusion were simple: the Carrollton emigrés had established a successful congregation in Maryland and were able to meet the criteria for joining the Wachovia community. Their plans and firm resolve to start a congregation in North Carolina had impressed Unity leaders and ensured that their probationary period would be a short one.

Resolve alone, however, was not enough. Moravian congregations had to fulfill a substantial financial burden as well. Members kept the pastor and his family clothed, fed, and housed. For their minister, carpenters built corncribs, farmers helped till the family garden, and tailors stitched family clothing. The congregations in the *Landgemeinen* placed the arrangements with their pastors on a firm financial footing. Friedberg, for instance, signed an agreement on April 30, 1787, that spelled out in detail what members owed for Simon Peters's *Unterhalt,* or maintenance. The steward was to collect the amounts owed by members, including firewood for heating and cooking, produce for his family, and fodder for his horse. Friedberg members were also to pay Simon a small salary of $8 a year and were to ensure that the pastor's residence at the meetinghouse, along with his fields, gardens, and fences, were kept in good repair.[79]

Friedland and Hope, as their congregational records show, provided wheat, corn, flax, butter, milk, wool, and other products to their pastors. As in Friedberg, members there paid the pastor's annual salary: *Hausvaters* were required to pay $2 per person; *Ledige* (single men), $1; and *Witwers* (widowers), $2. In Hope, this contribution totaled $55 in 1808.[80] Much of this aid was to be given weekly—sometimes to the exasperation of individual members who complained that these obligations were onerous. Not surprisingly, the financial demands forced members to constantly reassess their commitment to the brethren and their church. Some members did decide that the financial demands were too much, and they withdrew from the congregation for a time. But those who stayed were making a commitment to their congregation, their neighbors, and their Savior.

Religious Life in the *Gemeine*

In the *Landgemeinen,* the meetinghouse became the physical and symbolic heart of these sprawling backcountry communities. Members constructed their church sanctuaries with great care and reverence, cutting down the trees, hauling the massive logs in their wagons, and erecting their buildings to the accompaniment of religious stanzas.[81] The meetinghouses' central location served symbolic and practical functions. If Jesus was to be at the center of their lives, so was this simple edifice they built to pay homage to him. The location also needed to be easily accessible to all members; a central site would obviously facilitate worship for the hundred or so members who attended weekly services.

The meetinghouses' architecture also reflected the Moravians' penchant for the spiritual and the practical. These buildings needed to be functional because of their multiple uses; they served not only as a residence for the pastor's family but also as a schoolhouse for the children, a church for the congregation, and a meeting hall for the settlers. They were built of logs because that was the cheapest and most accessible building material at hand. They were small—usually about thirty-two feet by twenty-eight feet—because the congregation lacked the resources in these early years to build anything larger. Yet they were two stories and big enough to fulfill their diverse tasks. And the congregations did try to give these *gemeine Hauses* some dignity by covering the logs with clapboards and by erecting small bell towers that summoned the faithful on Sundays. The meetinghouses were also simple by design. They were never intended to be grand churches that the Anglicans, Catholics, and other state churches built in homage to the power and glory of God. Instead, the brethren envisioned the *gemeine Haus* as a gathering place for those seeking Christ and those who had found him. Stained glass, ornate pulpits, and reserved pews for wealthy parishioners were not to be found; instead, the architecture was to reflect the humbleness of man before his Lord. Within its walls, all were equal. The Saals (main meeting rooms) were exceedingly simple affairs, with whitewashed walls, pine benches, and a small table and chair for the pastor. They contained no pulpit. In Friedberg, and possibly in others, the Saal was on the second floor, with the pastor and his family living on the first floor.[82] Hope's meetinghouse was sparsely furnished, containing a walnut table in the front hall

Hope's settlers built this meetinghouse in 1775 on a hill near Muddy Creek. It became the focal point of community and religious life. *Collection of the Wachovia Historical Society, Winston-Salem, North Carolina; courtesy of Old Salem Inc., Winston-Salem, North Carolina.*

and wooden candlesticks on the walls. It had a kitchen, dwelling room, cellar, and "appartment [sic] in the loft." Quite appropriately, the pastor owned in his meager library a copy of *Practische Bemerkungen die Fuhrung des evangelischen Predigt—amtes betrefftend,* or "Practical Notes Concerning the Guidance of the Evangelical Sermon."[83]

Surrounded by a garden, picket fence, and God's Acre, the *gemeine Haus* stood at the center of vibrant farm congregations. It was here that settlers sent their children to be educated, their parents to be buried, and their families to be inculcated in God's ways. At least twice a week, on Thursdays and Sundays, settlers gathered to worship, to meet, to talk—and at times to argue. Social and religious life, in sum, revolved around these log-constructed meetinghouses.

The *gemeine Hauses* hosted countless events throughout the year that brought family, friends, and neighbors together. Religious festivals ranged from anniversaries of a congregation's founding to choir festivals to Chief Elders Day. At sundown on December 31, settlement members assembled at the *gemeine Haus* for a general worship service, where prayers were said, songs were sung, and events in Wachovia for the past year were reviewed. Once a year, crowds gathered for the congregation festival, in summer for harvest lovefeasts, and in fall for Michaelmas Day. The celebration of Michaelmas on Sunday, September 29, 1771, in Friedberg was typical. Several leaders from Salem joined the congregation for a worship service and lovefeast—the sharing of a simple meal, usually coffee and cake. Pastor L. C. Bachhof approvingly noted in his diary, "In this way our dear hearts saw the whole local Society . . . with the exception of a few who were not present on account of sickness."[84]

Celebrated annually, these community rituals served at least two important functions. For starters, they helped provide social cohesion and stability within individual agricultural settlements. The rituals lessened the isolation that farmers living on the outskirts of the community, or on opposite sides of a river, must have felt. In 1775, Wachovia was a vast tract covering nearly one hundred thousand acres that was thinly peopled, and it remained that way well into the nineteenth century. Indeed, George Bahnson of Denmark, who had been assigned to pastor to Bethania's congregation in 1834, set out from his home to Salem one night in 1837 and took a "byroad" that he hoped would speed his journey. He reported riding "through a thick wood of at least four miles length, without meeting an inhabited cabin."[85] Congregational life was thus crucial to the social fabric of community: it brought people together to worship, to talk, to swap stories, to gossip. An evangelical religion helped to unify sprawling farm settlements in a frontier setting.

Equally important, religious rituals did much to connect individual congregations to the larger community that constituted Wachovia and the worldwide organization known as the *Brudergemeine.* In Pennsylvania, Europe, and elsewhere, Moravian congregations worldwide celebrated these same festivals. The festivals reminded members that they were part of a larger church that had a special mission. This educational function was especially important in the farm congregations with their mix of society and *Gemeine* members. Hope's congregation festival in 1782, for instance, instructed members about the settlement's founding and hailed the event as a milestone. Dignitaries from Salem attended to reinforce the day's importance. The congregation held a lovefeast, where "the story was told of the organization of the little congregation two years ago, and a suitable festal Ode was sung."[86] Those *Landgemeine* settlers who were society members in the northern province were well acquainted with these rituals. Celebrating them in North Carolina likely eased their transition to a new life in a strange place.

Wachovia's administrators worked tirelessly to instill a sense of community among the six settlements and a commitment to the larger mission that evangelism and Moravianism demanded. They regularly crisscrossed Wachovia on horseback and in carriages, bringing advice and encouragement—and often admonishment—to each congregational settlement. They distributed *Nachrichten,* or church reports, that kept each settlement informed of what the others were doing. Pastors routinely read accounts of Moravian missionary work in such exotic places as Greenland and the Caribbean; these reports piqued members' interests in a wider world and reminded them of their mission to reform Christianity.[87] The seemingly endless cycle of festivals and celebrations helped cement members' loyalties to the church community and made them feel, regardless of ethnicity, part of a larger whole.

So did the Moravian choir. These choirs broke the congregation down into pietistic conventicles of married men/women; single men/women; and boys/girls. The choir system dated to 1728. It was an outgrowth of "bands," where the Herrnhut community first divided its members by sex into small fellowship groups, and "classes," where the community subsequently divided members by age and sex. The choirs came to embody both. To further facilitate worship of the Savior and fellowship among the brethren, the single brothers at Herrnhut in 1739 built their own house. Here, they would live and work communally under one roof. A year later, the single sisters followed suit, acquiring their own house.[88] The brethren brought their choir system to the New World, building choir houses in all their *Ortsgemeinen,* including in Salem.

Choirs embodied a very pietist impulse: reformers, upset with the sterility of institutional church life, believed that small, intimate gatherings would better promote the true worship of Jesus Christ. People with common backgrounds and ages could gather to talk about their faith, to pray, and to read the Bible. Such closeness, reformers hoped, would facilitate discussion, build unity, and better enable members to achieve and maintain the piety that their activist faith demanded. Such small groups, in turn, would collectively help to reinvigorate church life. Reform of the church was to begin with the individual. In the Moravian *Ortsgemeinen,* choirs carried this goal to its logical conclusion. The conventicles would not be a weekly gathering but a daily one. Members' lives would revolve around their choir, as they slept, ate, and worked with their fellow brethren. Brothers and sisters would progress through the various choirs as they aged. The brethren would first join the children's choir until about age thirteen, then the young people's choir, the single brothers/sisters choir, the married choir, and finally the widower/widow choir. In all choirs, the goal was to be the same: to put the Savior first.

North Carolina's *Landgemeinen* did not have choir houses, but the choir's role was important nonetheless. The Unity believed choirs would ease the way for more intimate Christian fellowship and help build community cohesion. Choirs, which celebrated their own liturgies and held their own festival days, physically brought a geographically sprawling congregation together. The choirs helped on another important level as well: they unified congregations whose diverse membership hailed from different ethnicities, regions, and religious backgrounds. In the choirs, German mingled with English, Lutheran with Reformed, and Maine expatriates with Maryland expatriates. The choirs fostered intermixing on a religious level and ultimately a social one as brethren from different backgrounds got to know each other intimately. This integrating function was especially important in Wachovia's lone English-speaking congregation. From Hope's earliest days, choir life played a significant part in bringing German and English together. In May 1783, Brother Benzien of Salem visited Hope "and laid their Choir Principles before the unmarried men and boys. . . . This was the beginning of such instruction there."[89] Hope's choirs met once a month for fellowship and to discuss matters of mutual concern, including such issues as congregational discipline and the proper raising of children.[90] The choirs thus helped make Hope's English-speaking members feel a part of the larger community.

Religious life was rigorous in both settlement types. The Sunday morning worship services consisted of the litany, singing, a sermon based on a daily text provided by the Unity, and the reading of the *Nachrichten*. In the *Ortsgemeinen*, afternoon Bible readings and evening devotionals followed these morning services. The evening devotionals consisted of a *Gemeine Stunde* (hour) at eight o'clock that reviewed the texts for the day. A *Singstunde*, or singing hour, and prayer followed at nine o'clock. Bible readings, prayer meetings, and *Singstunden* dominated the rest of the week in the *Ortsgemeinen*.[91] The *Landgemeinen* held Sunday morning services that were virtually identical to those in the congregation towns. But because many members had to travel several miles over bad roads to reach their meetinghouse, the afternoons were normally reserved for congregational meetings and informal devotionals. Sundays were usually the only time the entire congregation was together, unlike in the *Ortsgemeinen*. Sundays became a time to mix on social and spiritual levels. The pastors took advantage of these gatherings to make their rounds, visiting individual families. On Thursdays at noon, the farm congregations often held a *Singstunde*. Pastors also held midday services when farm work permitted them.[92]

Pastors usually selected their sermon texts from the *Losungen*, or daily texts for the ensuing year, that Herrnhut began printing in 1731 and distributed to all congregations. The sermons were meant to inspire both the pastor and his audience. The texts used in Friedland in 1783 were typical. The pastor built his sermons around the New Testament passages from John and Luke. The month began with readings from John 15, on the true vine, with Jesus explaining in a homily, "I am the vine, you are the branches. He who abides in Me, and I in him, bears much fruit." Readings in the middle of the month dealt with that most evangelical of concerns, the new birth. John 3 tells the story of Jesus's encounter with a Pharisee named Nicodemus, who wants to know "how can a man be born when he is old?" Jesus's response lays out the basic tenets of the new birth—that "unless one is born again, he cannot see the kingdom of God" and that such a new birth can be achieved only through faith in Jesus Christ: "He who believes in Him is not condemned; but he who does not believe is condemned already."[93] The month concluded with a text from Luke that urged the faithful to leave all to follow Christ.

Sermons were one way to draw people closer to the Savior. Singing was another. Congregations in both settlement types routinely held *Singstunde,* where pastors wove a sermon or theme built around hymns. They designed these *Singstunden* to inspire their listeners and educate them on the Lord's ways. Music was a powerful part of the Moravian tradition. Zinzendorf saw singing as a critical component of the Unity's spiritual life and as the purest, most inspiring part of heart religion. The *Singstunden* date to 1728, when the congregation in Herrnhut began using them in its services.

The Saals in the meetinghouses of the *Ortsgemeinen,* and eventually the *Landgemeinen,* contained organs whose beauty and resonance drew neighbors from miles around. Trombones routinely announced the birth of a child or the "going home" of an elderly congregation member. Various congregations also used French horns, flutes, and violins at their services.[94] On the most elemental level, the *Singstunden* reflected the Moravian love of music. The Unity by the nineteenth century had a rich heritage in music composition. Steeped in the classical traditions of central Europe, Moravian composers produced some of the first classical music composed in America. Pastors in North Carolina were able to draw on more than twenty-three hundred hymns written or collected by Moravian musicians.[95] On another level, the *Singstunde* became another effective way for the congregation to celebrate their love of the Savior. Zinzendorf expected members to know the hymns by heart. As the pastor introduced a stanza, the congregation was to join in. By singing together, the congregation became one. On Christmas, for instance, members of the Friedland congregation gathered at Reverend Soelle's house for an evening devotional. "We had fellowship in love and blessing, and grace," Soelle recorded in his diary. "We were very happy together and closed with a most affectionate *Singstunde*."[96]

✝

Religious life proved to be an integrating force in Wachovia. Undergirded by the new birth and powerful church rituals, it fostered the intermixing of Moravians from various backgrounds. These Moravians got to know each other intimately not only inside the meetinghouse but outside it as well. The brethren came to share a kinship based on the conversion experience and a commitment to the Moravian version of evangelism. The intermixing among ethnic evangelicals had a profound impact on the direction that family life and cultural development took during the Revolutionary period and beyond.

3

An Anglo-German World

Adam Elrod's final resting place was a grassy patch on a knoll not far from Muddy Creek. The land sloped gently and offered an inviting view of the woods and farms that bordered the thirty-eight acres on which Hope's meeting-house and its God's Acre stood. In the world of the *Brudergemeine,* deaths typically elicited feelings of sorrow and joy—sorrow that a loved one had departed this earth but also joy that he was "going home" to his Savior. As Adam's family and the Wachovia community said their goodbyes to him that November day in 1812 at Hope's God's Acre, they surely felt such a swirl of conflicting emotions. Adam had been a good man. Indeed, his memoir praised him as a "faithful member" concerned not only with his own soul but also with the salvation of others in places "here and there."[1]

The funeral of this *Gemeine* member, however, had an air of routineness about it. It elicited no detailed accounts in church diaries or in *Nachricts.* Adam's memoir made no special mention of his seemingly unique status in the Hope congregation. Instead, Unity documents presented Adam Elrod as a fully accepted member whose life was judged on one criterion—his devotion to the Savior. The Wachovia community at large apparently saw nothing unusual in the fact that Elrod was a German-speaking Pennsylvanian who had married an English-speaking woman from Virginia; who had left the Lutheran Church to join the Moravian movement at a young age; who had become a member of an Anglo congregation founded by former Marylanders; and who was buried at Hope after an approximately thirty-one-year affiliation with that congregation. That the burial of a German-speaking former Lutheran in an English-speaking settlement in a predominately German enclave was so routine says a great deal about the state of community and ethnicity in Wachovia following nearly forty years of intermixing among Moravians of different backgrounds.

Extensive intermixing among the faithful facilitated the formation of community, hastened the adaptation of German speakers to a new land, and changed the very nature of family through the creation of creole unions. German and English first found common ground in the new birth and in Jesus Christ. Then they got to know each other outside of the *gemeine Haus.* As English- and German-speaking brethren met, mingled, and eventually married, the two sides began absorbing the ways of the other.

As these individuals changed, so did their families and their communities. The enclaves that settlers had initially formed following their arrival in North Carolina began to break down. Kinship networks grew and became denser and more ethnically complex. Hope, the Anglo-American congregation, took on a German accent, and Friedberg, a German congregation, took on an English one. With the formation of creole families, German and English ways began to meld, especially in the two sides' approaches to landholding and inheritance. Simultaneously, German-Americans in Wachovia became more open to outside ways and influences. Quite quickly, the concept of Wachovia as an enclave or a refuge from a corrupt world crumbled. Families built up their landholdings in an attempt to keep their children close to home and to church, but they did not hesitate to buy land outside of Wachovia's environs. The 1770 to 1800 period, in short, saw the creation of a new ethnicity based not on language and cultural heritage but on an evangelical religion.

Settling into Enclaves

Adam Elrod had been, if nothing else, peripatetic. He was born in 1744 near Conewago Creek, Pennsylvania, to German-speaking Lutheran immigrants, had moved to Frederick County in Maryland, and relocated to a farm along the Yadkin River near Wachovia. Along the way, as his memoir recounted, Elrod "learned to know the Savior" through the preachings of Richard Utley, a Moravian missionary; married Rachel Wainscot, an Anglican from Shenandoah County, Virginia; and started a large family that at his death totaled twelve children, fifty-one grandchildren, and five great-grandchildren. On June 10, 1781, he and his wife were formally received into the Hope congregation after having been society members in Friedberg for twelve years.[2]

The Elrods' decision to join Hope symbolized a significant change then occurring: the congregation's rapid transition from an English-speaking congregation to an Anglo-German one. As the Hope congregation welcomed this creole couple to its church family, Wachovia's social and religious landscape was being transformed under the impact of intermixing. Community formation had begun as a religious and family affair. New arrivals to the *Landgemeinen* settled near their meetinghouses and their former neighbors from the north. Then as a tight religious community bridged the ethnic divide, these enclaves began to crumble and a new social landscape began to take shape.

In Hope, English ways predominated in the early years. Daniel Smith and twenty-one others from Carrollton Manor had ridden into Wachovia on December 11, 1772, carrying letters of introduction and dreams of starting an English-speaking congregation that would affiliate with the Unity. With Salem still under construction, the *Brudergemeine* lodged these three families in the locksmith's shop in Bethabara in northwest Wachovia while the Marylanders scouted out locations for their settlement. The Carrollton emigrés wanted a site offering enough land for several families, good soil, plentiful water, and proximity to another Moravian congregation. These first arrivals quickly honed in on 450 acres in the southwest corner of Wachovia that met all four criteria. With Smith and his vanguard figuratively and literally clearing the way, congregation members from Carrollton Manor followed.[3] Later arrivals bought tracts in southwest Wachovia adjoining their families and friends. Most of the Carrollton emigrants settled just north of Friedberg on tracts ranging from 150 acres up to 221 acres. The Peddycoard and Faw families dominated the area south of Hope's meetinghouse, and the Douthits, Hamiltons, Padgets, and others dominated the region north of the meetinghouse.[4]

A similar process occurred in Friedberg in the 1760s and 1770s, with kinship ties, religious needs, and practical considerations dictating settlement patterns. Kinship and religion were especially important in determining where people lived. In Friedberg, new arrivals received significant help from their families and former northern neighbors who had already settled in Wachovia. Many sought temporary shelter with old neighbors while they hunted for a home site in Wachovia. And it was from these friends that they asked for assistance in finding land.[5] Old neighbors showed arrivals the area, advised them of a tract's availability, and explained the financing options available to them from the church. Networking in the *Landgemeinen* resembled the networking common among Lutherans and other German speakers in the New World: leading settlers in Friedberg acted as "cultural brokers" among their brethren by providing various kinds of advice and assistance to their German-speaking brethren.[6]

In choosing farm sites in Friedberg, Marylanders tended to settle near other Marylanders, and Pennsylvanians settled near Pennsylvanians. Former Yorktown residents lived on Friedberg's "upper farms," a group of at least five farms covering the settlement's northern reaches.[7] In the lower farms, the earliest arrivals to southern Wachovia—a group of former Lutherans from Monocacy and Heidelberg—dominated the area just outside of the Wachovia line. George Hartman, Adam Spach, John Muller, and Peter Frey owned tracts of at least two hundred acres south of the site where the Friedberg congregation constructed its meetinghouse in the late 1760s.[8] Moravian authorities observed the process with some wonderment. "The settlement of the Tract and its Lots is a difficult proposition," Wachovia administrator Frederick Marshall said in the mid-1760s, "but I must say this: The migration of men are like the movements of a flock of sheep, where one goes the flock follows, without knowing why."[9]

As important as kinship and religion were in choosing land, settlers in all three *Landgemeinen* did not—and could not—ignore the practical. Water was the lifeblood of farms; countless studies of "secular" migrations have shown that settlers were drawn to those sites that offered plenty of it. Moravian farmers in Wachovia were no different. Early maps of Wachovia showed the importance of water. Well into the nineteenth century, farms hugged the rivers and creeks that coursed through Wachovia. The main bodies of water were the three forks of Muddy Creek, and it was along these forks and their numerous tributaries that the *Landgemeinen* took shape. Friedland's long village, as Philip Reuter's 1773 map shows, formed along two forks of the Ens (or South Fork). Friedberg residents, who arrived years earlier than the emigrés from Maine, gravitated to the best sites along the Ens farther south from what later became Friedland. The English-speaking migrants from Carrollton huddled along the Dorothea (also known as Muddy Creek) that branched off from the Ens and ran north. Bethabara's diarist suspected that Smith and the other first arrivals wanted "to settle on Muddy Creek, as they are good fishermen."[10]

Water thus became a basic building block of community; farmers needed a ready supply of water for their families, livestock, and crops. The creeks also served as a source of food and a means of travel in a frontier lacking navigable roads. Yet another obvious practical consideration loomed large: Moravian farmers needed fertile soil that would allow them to grow the wheat, rye, and corn that became the mainstays in their fields. Settlers of all ethnicities gravitated to the best lands—near water, with good soils that were not too rocky or hilly. Such criteria eliminated nearly half of Wachovia's ninety-eight thousand acres in the early years. As Bishop Augustus Spangenberg conceded in 1755, "I knew from the beginning that Wachovia does not contain uniformly good land, but that at least half of it is poor."[11] For the first half of Wachovia's existence, settlement was concentrated where land was most fertile and well watered. Farmers developed the areas just north and east of Salem last, because of the poorer water supply and soil quality there.[12] Wachovia's English- and German-speaking farmers were not utopians in this regard; they resembled other colonists, who chose farmland based on the quality of soil, proximity to markets, time of arrival, and the material circumstances of the individual settler. As geographer James T. Lemon concluded in a study of early southeastern Pennsylvania, "Certainly in the manner in which they occupied, organized, and used the land, members of national groups did not behave very differently from one another."[13]

George Hahn's selection of a farm site shows how all these motivations merged. He arrived in Friedberg from Yorktown in September 1770 and first consulted Christian and Peter Frey, acquaintances from Pennsylvania, about the availability of land in that settlement. The Freys were unable to help Hahn, so he went on to Salem to meet with Marshall. Hahn explained his needs—accessibility to water, church, and friends—and Marshall promised the family that "a homesite with a spring would be picked out for them near the schoolhouse [meetinghouse]." On October 14, Friedberg's pastor showed the Hahns the various tracts that were available. "They chose the one closest to the schoolhouse, on Wachovia's land," the pastor reported. Religious, social, and economic considerations guided the Hahns in their selection of a site. The family wanted a well-watered tract, but one that was near former neighbors and the meetinghouse. The Hahns expressed pleasure with their selection and immediately went to work carving out a farm. Only one day after choosing a site, the Hahns began "blocking up" their log house; with help from neighbors, the family finished it by October 19, allowing them to move out of the "little private" room they had been staying in at the meetinghouse.[14]

With religious, familial, and practical needs driving the settlement process, the communities in Friedberg and Hope physically came to resemble their non-Moravian counterparts in the backcountry—a collection of individual family farms scattered in seemingly haphazard fashion. The nature of the migration partly accounted for this settlement pattern in Friedberg. Friedberg took shape over a fifteen-year period with no central planning or organization. Most settlers moved as family units and settled on family farms. Unlike in Friedberg, Hope's migration was more compact (but not as compact as in Friedland), and settlers could have designed a village if they had so desired. But for two reasons, they did not. One reason was that this migration lacked any central direction, with settlers arriving on an ad hoc basis. Emigrés followed their own personal preferences and family needs in choosing farm sites. The second, deeper reason reflected cultural preferences. The settlers turned to what was familiar. In Hope's case, that was the individual family farm. Scattered family farms were the norm at Carrollton Manor, where Hope's residents had recently come from, and in eastern Maryland, where most of Carrollton's tenants had emigrated from. Their cultural heritage was firmly planted in an American soil that lacked European-style agricultural villages.

Friedland's settlers, by contrast, brought a different orientation with them, one that extended to their former homeland in the Palatinate. These settlers formed one of the most cohesive groups of migrants, and they built the most distinctive of the three *Landgemeinen*—a "long" village, in the words of Frederick Marshall, of nine farms. At the village's founding, each family received two hundred acres in rectangular strips. This regularity was intended to facilitate the creation of community. Their goal, Marshall explained in 1771, was to "buy adjoining farms, laid out in the form of a village, so that none shall be more than a quarter of an hour from the center, where they want to have a schoolhouse or church."[15] Unlike in Friedberg, which took shape ad hoc over a far longer period, the migration of the Broadbay *Gemeine* in two main waves made the creation of a German-style farm hamlet possible. This long village apparently reflected the landscape these migrants had known in southwest Germany. Hamlets in such places as Hohenlohe and Wurttemberg consisted of about seven households grouped together, as in Friedland. These "villages" lacked the spatial sophistication of towns. They had no markets, no squares—they were just a group of farms huddled together in the shadow of a castle or a road. Sometimes they had a church, sometimes not. In Friedland, the result was a deceptively simple Germanic farming hamlet that stood out both in Wachovia and in the southern backcountry for its unique shape.

Kinship Networks in the Countryside

Underpinning community formation was the family. In the *Landgemeinen,* kinship and family were especially strong because of the looser church controls and the settlers' general orientation toward farming, which required a great deal of labor in an unmechanized age. Although Unity leaders in the *Ortsgemeinen* feared the influence of family and land on religious commitment, settlers saw no such conflict. Indeed, they viewed family and religious commitment as mutually reinforcing.

Unity elders did agree that the family had an important role to play in religious life, seeing the family as an extension of the *Gemeine.* As the elders put it, the family was "a little church of Jesus."[16] In the battle to remain true to their Savior, families were to serve as one of the first lines of defense against straying.

Spouses were to support each other and keep one another from backsliding. Most of all, parents were to help instill a love of the Savior in their children and to teach them to be good Christians. "The main Matter in the Children's Education is chiefly this," the Unity's elders agreed in 1775, "to let the Children from their Cradle know nothing else, but that they exist for Jesus."[17] Count Nicholas von Zinzendorf stressed that families existed for the sake of children. Although schools played an important role in the religious education of young Moravians, Unity leaders placed far greater responsibility on the shoulders of parents. Wachovia's pastors and church boards expected parents to serve as exemplary models for their children and to inculcate in them a love of Jesus. Wachovia's leaders understood how much they were asking of parents. In October 1780, the pastors on the Land Arbeiter Conferenz discussed how they should deal with parents. "The training of children always remains a difficult matter," the pastors conceded. "It will be very useful to try to render all admonitions to the parents in such a way that they are received as Gospel advice than as judgmental pronouncements concerning their failings."[18]

Because of evangelical values, this advice was generally simple: *Gemeine* members "must constantly rely on the dear Saviour" in all their doings.[19] This meant, for starters, that the home must function as a small church, where devotions and prayers were to be as important a part of the family's day as chores in the morning and meals together in the afternoon and evening. With its formation in September 1780, the Land Arbeiter Conferenz took on the encouragement of home worship as one of its first tasks. "Since there is a great lack of home devotions in the families in the country, it should be explained to them that they . . . are expected to hold the Morning and Evening Blessings in devotions with their families." The conference expected *Gemeine* families to show even more "faithfulness and diligence therein so that they set an example for the others."[20]

Most of all, the church expected households in the *Landgemeinen* to adhere faithfully to strict standards of conduct. Parents were not to allow the mixing of sexes among young people; they were not to permit such worldly activities as dancing and drinking in their homes; and they were to avoid quarrels, slander, and other signs of an "irregular life."[21] These concerns with behavior were so important to the pastors that it often colored their views toward parenting and the rights of children. In 1780, the Land Arbeiter Conferenz was disturbed to learn that "Peter Pfaff for various selfish reasons has not made up his mind to establish his son, who is already twenty-six years old," on a farm. On one level, the pastors were concerned about the rights of the son; young adult men should be in their own households. But their deeper concern was for the morals of the household's inhabitants. Pfaff's decision to keep his son at home could eventually lead to "misfortune," the conference warned, because "all sorts of people of either sex go in and out of this house."[22] The pastors believed that such mixing of the sexes was improper and dangerous and would lead to temptation that had best be avoided. The institution of the family, they reasoned, represented one of the best ways to counteract such temptation.

The battle against temptation was often lost, of course. But when a family member stumbled, pastors almost without exception held one party responsible: the parents. Although they did not view children as blameless, the pastors believed that youths were inherently good who merely needed the proper guidance to become devout Christians. Unlike the Puritans, Moravians did not see children as sinners who needed to be converted.[23] In 1771, the Reverend George Soelle visited the home of Valentine Frey of Friedberg, where he had a long talk with Frey's son, Heinrich. The boy confessed to Soelle that he could "make no progress" in his effort to follow the Savior despite his "conviction of there being a better [life]." Soelle admonished Heinrich to try harder, but he reserved his most pointed criticism for the parents. Soelle confided in his diary, "I believe that were the parents more on fire with love for Jesus the children would gain some profit thereby and be won" to the Lord.[24] In contrast to the supposed shortcomings of the Frey parents, Soelle later recounted with satisfaction the positive role the Fiedler family played in helping lead the twelve-year-old daughter of the Voglers to Jesus. The girl, who lived with the Fiedlers in Friedland as a servant, sang in her sleep one Christmas night, "Jesus, thy passion is for me." Soelle recalled with wonderment how she sang the entire song in her sleep before wailing "aloud in great fright." Her surrogate parents awakened her, and she recounted how she had dreamed about the Savior and how he would soon appear for judgment. The Fiedlers explained the meaning of the dream to the frightened girl and the explicit message it carried: she must repent and turn to her Savior.[25] In this case, a nurturing family environment provided important guidance in the religious education of the young.

Because of cultural and religious imperatives, the pressure to construct strong families was fairly intense in the *Landgemeinen*. Men were expected to marry and set up farms of their own, and women were expected to serve as their husbands' "helpmaids."[26] Both the Unity and individual brethren in the *Landgemeinen* viewed marriage as an important stage in the life cycle. When young men turned twenty-one, fathers owed them the chance to set up an independent household, and they faced criticism if they did not, as Peter Pfaff could attest to.

Kinship networks strengthened the institution of the family and improved its ability to provide oversight as a little church of Jesus. The selection of baptismal sponsors, or godparents, for children became an important way to strengthen kinship and thus the family and the congregation. The Moravians were not unique in this regard. In Western society, families traditionally viewed godparenthood as a way to broaden a family's support network. In many cases, this obligation carried an economic responsibility: the godfather or godmother might be expected to raise a child whose parents had died or to take charge of a child's religious education. In Wachovia, such an economic responsibility was less important, but the spiritual one was not. Parents in the *Landgemeinen* selected neighbors or friends as godparents to serve as spiritual complements. In other words, they viewed godparenthood as another layer of support to help them raise their children in the Lord's ways. Baptismal sponsors, as a result, complemented the choirs' social and educational functions and played an important role in congregational life.[27]

An analysis of Friedberg's baptismal sponsorships from 1774 to 1778 shows what was involved. One elementary goal of parents in selecting baptismal sponsors was simply to strengthen existing kinship ties. The relationship between adult siblings could be very close, and they turned to each other for help as their children entered the world. Peter Frey demonstrated how close this relationship could be. In 1774, he and his wife, Catharina, named their son George Jr. after Peter's brother George Sr. and chose him as a baptismal sponsor.[28] Philipp Rothrock also turned to his brother, Peter, and his wife in 1777 after their son, George, was born.[29] The decision to select relatives as godparents served to acknowledge the existing love between family members. The decision was also meant to tie relatives closer to the stem family by giving them a vested interest in that child's welfare.

The ties of neighborliness proved to be strong as well. The expatriates from Yorktown—the Pfaffs, Rothrocks, Hahns, Eberts, and others who settled on Friedberg's upper farms—turned to each other for support when their children were born.[30] They routinely selected their neighbors as godparents. Such a step further drew them together and was a fitting recognition of their already deep ties that stretched to Pennsylvania.

Most parents chose two to five sponsors, relying on a mix of kin, friends, and immediate neighbors. Such a broad selection of sponsors created a dense network of fictive kinship that radiated outward, across Wachovia. In numerous instances, Friedberg's families selected brethren from Salem, Bethania, and other congregations to serve as godparents. These selections helped tie disparate congregations together, further bridged the ethnic gulf between English and German, and made the church family even more inclusive. Within Friedberg, baptismal sponsorships tightened the bonds of community. The families from Heidelberg, Pennsylvania, including the Volzes, Graeters, Holders, and Staubers, mingled regularly with the Hartmans, Spachs, Mullers, and others living in southern Friedberg near the *gemeine Haus.* Close working relationships in the congregation, as well as intermarriage between families, made such alliances normal and natural. Such proximity combined with a shared evangelical zeal to create enduring friendships. Baptismal selections reflected these close friendships.

Living in a community of spiritual equals, parents seemed less inclined to select godparents in the interests of financial security. In Germany, poorer villagers sometimes chose nobles or persons of higher social status in an attempt to win material advantages.[31] That rarely happened in Wachovia. Martin Walk of Friedberg was one of the few with such a possible motivation. Born to Lutheran parents in Culpeper, Virginia, his family moved to the large and growing German settlement at Abbotts Creek, about sixteen miles east of Friedberg. At age twenty-two, Walk went to work for Peter Frey, as well as for other Moravians in Bethania and Bethabara, but it was to Frey to whom he apparently felt gratitude. Walk later married, settled in Friedberg near the *gemeine Haus,* and started a family that grew to twelve children. In 1775, he and his wife asked Peter Frey and his wife to be sponsors for their daughter Elisabeth.[32] Whether Walk saw Frey's selection as a bid for protection is unclear, but it was likely meant as a token of affection and gratitude for the help that Frey had given him earlier and for the friendship that had developed between them.

The brethren perceived the selection of a baptismal sponsor as an honor. Parents often turned to certain leading families within the congregation, apparently as a token of the esteem they held for longtime and influential members of the society movement. In Friedberg, several families stood out in the 1774 to 1778 period. Congregation members chose the Frey clan the most, with George Sr. and Christian being the most popular choices. The frequency of their selection partly reflected their leadership within the settlement. Peter Frey, who arrived from Heidelberg in 1755, was one of the first settlers in Friedberg. His father and brothers came with the Bockels in 1765. During these early years, the Freys assumed a degree of prominence, but this stature as first arrivals alone does not account for their popularity as baptismal sponsors. Adam Spach was also a first arrival who played a pivotal role in the founding of the Friedberg congregation. Yet he and his wife were chosen as sponsors only once between 1774 and 1778.[33] The Freys very likely were popular choices because of their close religious and social ties to other members.

Martin and Eva Barbara Ebert were esteemed patriarchs whom younger members of the Friedberg congregation looked up to as well. They served as sponsors to nine children from various families, the most of any couple during this period. Their service as godparents drew together families as diverse as the Hartmans and Mullers on the lower farms, to the family of Martin Ebert on the upper.[34]

Other factors contributed to the extensiveness of kinship and godparenthood in the *Landgemeinen*. One basic one was that Moravian families were large—they averaged seven children in the eighteenth century in the farm congregations—and each child had several godparents. Men and women married younger in the *Landgemeinen* than in the congregation towns. In the *Landgemeinen*, the average marrying age in the eighteenth century was 24.7 for men and 23.75 for women, increasing a woman's opportunities to have children.[35] Young people generally married before taking their places in the congregation as full members. This desire to get established combined with other familial and cultural pressures to produce younger marital ages, larger families, and more extensive kinship networks. Another basic demographic factor also contributed to the strength of kinship in the countryside: men and women, on balance, lived shorter lives outside of Salem than in the central *Ortsgemeine*—65.76 in Salem versus 57.31 in the other five settlements during the 1770 to 1794 period.[36] Both widows and widowers felt a social and religious obligation to remarry—they needed partners not only to raise their children and run the farm household but also to serve as helpmates in the "little church of Jesus." These imperatives meant that remarriage was common throughout Wachovia. In fact, it was not unusual for some brethren to marry three times or more. Often, these later unions would produce children, leading to a tangle of half-brothers and half-sisters within Moravian households. A population that routinely lived into its sixties, in turn, meant that parents and step-parents lived long enough to see grandchildren and great-grandchildren enter the world. Extended families thus became even more extended, with plenty of relatives living nearby in physically small and religiously tight communities. Families as a result were large, and kinship networks were extensive.

Intermixing in the *Landgemeinen*

Intermixing fostered by religious contacts shaped the direction that family, kinship, and community took in the late eighteenth century. Intermixing's impact was felt first in the congregation: contacts between English and German drew German into the English orbit and English into the German. Then as the composition of congregational membership began to change and the initial enclaves began to break down, kinship ties started to change as well, with brethren selecting members from different ethnicities to serve as godparents for their children. Intermixing affected the family last but most likely the deepest.

First came change to the congregation. The most basic gauge of this change was the number of German speakers who decided to affiliate with the congregation at Hope: by 1810, the number of identifiable German speakers in Hope constituted 32 percent of the population. This was especially significant considering that the settlers who arrived in 1772 were all Anglo-Americans who had come with the express purpose of starting an English-speaking settlement. Moreover, this intermixing came relatively rapidly. By 1780, less than eight years after the first English Marylanders arrived, the settlement was 12 percent German. Such a swift rise in the German population indicates that intermixing was not merely a generational phenomenon, where second- and third-generation Moravians were less concerned with ethnic divisions. Intermixing began with the first generation (table 3.1).[37]

The proximity of Friedberg to Hope helped ensure that its German and English members enjoyed especially close ties. This was particularly true during the 1772 to 1780 period, when Hope's members attended services at Friedberg because their settlement did not have a full-time pastor.

Hope bordered Friedberg to the north, but there were no firm geographic boundaries between the settlements. Friedberg's members lived mainly along the South Fork, but its upper farms spilled over into territory occupied by residents of Hope near the Middle Fork, also known as Salem Creek. More than half of Hope's society members lived outside of Wachovia. But those residents who chose to reside within this evangelical community lived along Muddy Creek and the Middle Fork. Only one German-speaking family lived along the north bank of the Middle Fork—this was strictly English country. But the south bank contained a pronounced ethnic mixing. An English Marylander, Horatio Hamilton, and his family occupied two tracts. German farms sur-

Table 3.1 Hope's Congregation by Ethnicity

Year	Number	Ethnicity	Percentage
1780	30	English	88
	4	German	12
1810	60	English	68
	28	German	32

Note: Numbers include those known to belong to the settlement as congregation members. All major families have been identified, but the numbers are understated because of the difficulty of identifying whether children or spouses joined the congregation. Hope's population, according to church records, was about 70 in 1780 and 150 in 1810. Ethnicity was determined by examining family history, place of birth, and surnames. Sources include memoirs, Church Book for Hope, settlement committee minutes, and other primary sources in Moravian Archives, Southern Province.

rounded the family. Settlement patterns on Muddy Creek, near Hope's meetinghouse, also revealed a mix of the two groups. Germans lived to the south, near Friedberg, and English speakers grouped near Hope's meetinghouse. But the tracts north of the meetinghouse showed a variety of German and English. One can discern an English enclave only on the north bank of the Middle Fork, and even there they had German neighbors directly across the river. In all other parts of Hope, Germans and English lived side by side. Given this proximity, several members of the Friedberg congregation drifted into Hope's orbit.[38]

The presence of so many Germans living in Hope, combined with the extensive religious and social contacts between settlements, ensured that Anglo-American Moravians got to know their fellow brethren intimately. German and English, as a result, forged strong friendships that were reflected in their choice of baptismal sponsors. Parents who had their children baptized chose their most trusted and respected friends to be their children's godparents or baptismal sponsors. In Hope, the number of English and German choosing sponsors outside of their ethnic groups was high in the early years—30 percent in 1774—and soared to 59 percent by 1812.

The use of German and English godparents served to link families of different ethnicities and to extend kinship ties even deeper into the fabric of community life (table 3.2). As families drew closer and more interethnic friendships were formed, the opportunity for children to find marital partners from a different ethnicity increased.[39] In Hope, 30 percent of first-generation settlers married outside their ethnic group—English took German spouses and vice versa. That figure rose in the second generation to 38 percent (table 3.3).

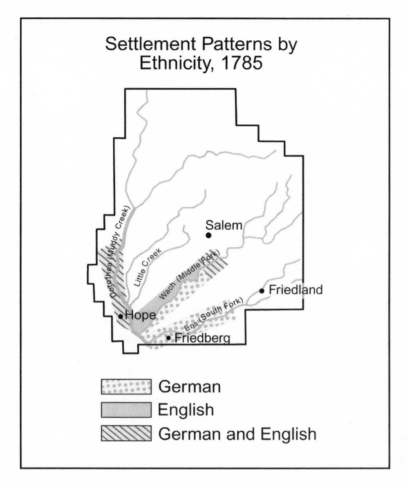

Map by Jodie Morris.

It would be tempting to conclude that geographic proximity alone was enough to reduce the gap between ethnic groups. Yet studies of other communities in early America have not found that to be the case. Historian Laura Becker examined eighteenth-century Reading, Pennsylvania, a heterogeneous, urban town founded in 1751 about fifty-six miles northwest of Philadelphia. Like Wachovia, Reading was predominately German: 83 percent German and 12 percent English. Despite the shared landscape, Becker finds that only 0.6 percent of English and German taxpayers intermarried. She concludes that ethnic divisions were pronounced in Reading as Germans and English married within their own groups.[40] In Germantown, Pennsylvania, 18 percent intermarried—a figure

Table 3.2 Baptismal Sponsors in Hope Outside of Ethnic Group

Year	N	Percentage
1774	4	30
1780–89	21	31
1810–12	26	59

Source: Hope Church Book Register A, Moravian Archives, Southern Province.

Table 3.3 Intermarriage in Hope

Generation	N	%	% of German Husbands/ English Wives	% of English Husbands/ German Wives
First	11	30	33	66
Second	8	38	60	40

Sources: Memoirs, Hope Church Book, and other church records in Moravian Archives, Southern Province, and cover the years 1772–1820.
Note: N equals number of intermarriages. *First generation* is defined as those who were of marrying age when Hope was founded in 1772 or were first generation in the sense that they were the first in their family to join the Moravian Church. *Second generation* is defined as those who were born into Moravianism. Numbers are for those with identifiable spouses of known ethnicity whose membership in Hope congregation could be confirmed. The criteria understate the number of second generation who intermarried. When all known second-generation members are included, regardless of church status, the percentage of those intermarrying rises to 44 percent (48 out of 110).

historian Stephanie Grauman Wolf considers high.[41] Farther south, Warren R. Hofstra argues that Scots-Irish settlers did not intermix with their German neighbors in the Opequon settlement in the Virginia backcountry, despite their proximity. Instead, the Scots-Irish "chose marriage partners within their own ethnic group . . . they seldom conveyed land outside nuclear families . . . and they worshipped together in a single Presbyterian congregation."[42]

What distinguished Wachovia from Opequon and Reading was religion. The Moravian version of evangelism and the strong sense of community broke down the walls of ethnicity in Wachovia. Both Reading and Opequon lacked such a cohesive religious force. Wachovia's sense of brotherhood and commitment to Christ ensured that its members regularly met and mixed, although the mixing was greatest between Friedberg and Hope because they were the closest neighbors. Their members shared the bond of the new-birth experience and more. This religious commitment overcame language and cultural barriers to an impressive degree. It allowed Wachovia to form a tight community despite the stresses of an evangelical life, where members struggled to live up to high standards of conduct, and the great diversity of backgrounds that Zinzendorf's Diaspora produced.

A closer look at the phenomenon of intermarriage shows how religion succeeded in blurring ethnic lines. Among the first generation in Hope, 66 percent of those intermarrying involved English grooms taking German-speaking wives. In the second generation, as more creole families were created and ethnicity became even less important, more German-speaking men married English speakers—60 percent versus 33 percent in the first generation.[43] Unity doctrines did not discuss ethnicity. They, instead, advised the brethren to marry not only out of love for their spouses but also out of concern for the Savior, the community, and the welfare of their souls.[44] The Unity saw all four as inseparable.

Pastors in the North Carolina *Landgemeinen* stressed to parents that they should encourage their children to follow religious considerations and not economic ones in choosing a spouse. Love for their mate and their Savior should guide members' selections, not the desire for a bigger and better farm. Parents, the pastors advised, were to avoid *Kuppeleien,* or matchmakings, that try to set up "their son or daughter . . . in the material sense." To give some weight to these wishes, the pastors agreed to exclude from communion those brethren who engaged in *Kuppeleien.*[45]

Other evidence indicates how important religion was to society members in selecting a mate. For Adam Spach Jr. of neighboring Friedberg, marriage represented a chance to remain true to his evangelical principles. Like other evangelicals, this German speaker struggled mightily to achieve a new birth and to sustain it. Adam's background was typical of second-generation *Landgemeine* settlers. He was born in Maryland in 1753, the year his family moved to Wachovia, and he grew up in Friedberg, where his father was a founding member of the congregation. Young Adam felt the first religious stirrings when the brethren came to preach at his house in the early 1760s, before Friedberg's meetinghouse had been built. These sessions planted the seeds of his faith.[46]

But young Adam did not know what to make of these stirrings, or how to proceed. He wandered in a spiritual wilderness for more than four years, until the death of his sister in 1777 forced him to confront his beliefs. Adam, at last, was experiencing vocation. "Oh, how wholly reprehensible I felt myself to be! I had become an enemy even toward my dear Savior. . . . I now acknowledged that I was completely dead and cold toward him." After taking this momentous step—acknowledging his sinfulness—justification followed.[47]

Adam was only twenty-four when he experienced this new birth, but it represented a lifetime of searching. He well understood that his next challenge was equally daunting—to avoid backsliding, or "how I might remain in His possession," as he put it. His solution was an interesting one—he would find someone to marry. Adam reasoned that his chances of staying true to his religious principles would improve if he married a devout woman. That way, they could battle the forces of sin together. To find such a woman, this German-speaking brother cast his eyes across the meetinghouse benches—and upward. "I prayed without ceasing," he recalled. "I asked: 'Dear Savior, bring me a person with whom I can live in love and joy, someone with whom I can follow you in my progress through life.'" His prayers were answered in the earthly form of Catharina Tesch, a member of the Friedberg Society, whose views on marriage were identical to Adam's. She was also searching for a deeper communion with the Savior, and she also wanted a partner who could reinforce her religious commitment. On November 23, 1779, the two young seekers married.[48]

Such a shared belief in Christ made it easy to bridge the ethnic divide that separated German from English in Wachovia. Ethnicity was not important to these pilgrims; religious commitment was. In Hope, those English men taking German-speaking wives were, with two exceptions, society members who lived outside of Wachovia. As society members, they had the freedom to marry whomever they wanted. And because they lived outside of Wachovia, they had a wide choice of potential partners. Yet they chose to marry German-speaking Moravians. Obviously, the attraction of this religious world proved to be powerful; they opted for marriages built on the foundations of evangelical experience. For these "outsiders," marriage to a Moravian evidently represented something more: it was a way for them to achieve closer ties with this evangelical sect on both an individual and a community level. Economic motivations appear absent from their considerations. John Riddle, for instance, was a middling landowner who owned a couple of hundred acres near Wachovia. He dabbled only occasionally in the land market, buying a hundred acres on Mill and Raccoon creeks in 1795 and selling two hundred acres seven years later.[49] His marriage to Mary Elrod, a German speaker, evidently brought no land, and no later land transactions with his wife's family were recorded. But by marrying an Elrod, this society member gained something else: a spiritual union with a fellow pilgrim and a tangible alliance with a respected family within the Hope congregation.

Unlike Riddle, Isaac Douthit lived within the Hope settlement. Isaac, who was born in 1756, grew up in a Presbyterian household along Wachovia's border, in Rowan County. Like other members of the Hope congregation, the Douthits journeyed to this religious colony following a detour in Frederick County, Maryland, after their arrival from Europe (in this case, Coltrain, Northern Ireland). But unlike Hope's founders, the Douthits were not members of the Carrollton Manor congregation. They, instead, came to North Carolina in 1750 and settled in the southwest corner of what was to become Wachovia in 1753. Isaac's father, John, found the brethren to be congenial neighbors who practiced an exciting brand of religion. According to his memoir, John shared food with the first Moravian arrivals; "when he saw that he was dealing with upright people he not only became a good neighbor, but came to have a real love for them and trust in them." He liked the brethren so much that he invited them to preach in his home. When John converted to Moravianism, his wife and eleven children did so as well. Later, the family worshipped at Bethabara, and then at Friedberg, when migrants from Pennsylvania founded that congregation. With Hope's founding, the Douthits became active society members there, and they helped build the meetinghouse. As a result, Isaac, who was the seventh child, was exposed to the Moravian faith at an early age. When it came time to settle down and select a marital partner, he looked to a neighboring congregation. On April 6, 1782, Isaac married a German-speaking sister from Friedberg named Sarah Frey. This English-speaking society member did not lack for marital choices. The large Douthit clan owned plantations both inside and outside of Wachovia. His siblings had no problem finding English-speaking spouses; only he and his sister Sarah married German speakers.[50]

For German-speaking Moravians entering into Anglo unions, religious motivations also predominated. As the Elders Conference explained in 1781, when a couple is contemplating marriage, "the chief thing is to consider whether the person whose marriage is suggested has yielded his or her life entirely to the Lord."[51] Evangelism was so strong a force that the possible loss of ethnic identity seemed to matter little to these German-speaking Moravians. From Unity boards on down, Wachovia's inhabitants appeared to be little concerned with preserving their Germanic heritage. Salem's elders, for instance, did not require that schools be conducted in German, nor did they insist that church services be in German, although they did prefer the use of their native language. Language, to them, was a practical instrument of the Lord—it was a tool that enabled them to take the gospel to more hearers. The attitude of Herrnhut's Board of Unity in 1766 was typical; it told a mixed company of English- and

German-speaking brethren leaving for Wachovia that "our German Brethren should learn English, & our English Brethren German" so that they could more readily converse with each other and with outsiders.[52] Such an attitude meant that all of Wachovia's settlements were conducting services in English at least once a month by 1803, including in Salem. Elders began allowing English for the simple reason that large numbers of English-speaking visitors were attending services throughout Wachovia. They also allowed English services because more second- and third-generation brethren were conversing in English. As the 1803 Wachovia Memorabilia explained, "That our English neighbors might be better served with the Gospel than heretofore, and also for the benefit of our young people, we began this year to have preaching in English monthly in Friedland and Bethania. . . . In Salem the monthly English preaching and the *Singstunden* have been attended by many visitors and travelers; and on one Sunday a month there has been an English service for the children."[53]

From its earliest years, Wachovia was operating in a bilingual environment. German and English settlements surrounded this Moravian enclave, especially to the west of Hope near the Yadkin River and to the east of Friedland. Moravian missionaries routinely visited these settlements, and inhabitants of these places frequently attended Moravian services. In 1771, missionary George Soelle traveled to a neighborhood near Blanket Creek, where he preached at the house of Christopher Ellroth. Soelle reported that he "waited for two hours for the Germans" to arrive until "finally a few came. It was chiefly the English who attended the service, most of whom understood some German."[54] This was no isolated incident. A couple of months later, Soelle returned to Ellroth's house. This time, more German speakers attended the service. Out of that group, "only four are unable to understand any English; the rest understand English just as well as German."[55] A year later, he visited a settlement at Deep Creek; "all Germans in this area understand English."[56] The Friedland congregation regularly entertained English-speaking visitors at its meetinghouse, with Soelle switching back and forth from German to English to German as the occasion demanded.[57] For the baptism of an Anglo-American daughter, for example, he would speak in English; for the funeral of a German speaker, he would give his discourse in German. The brethren did not hesitate to converse in English; their goal was to reach the maximum number of people in an attempt to increase their chances of converting the unfaithful to God's ways. Such a mandate cut two ways: in the late eighteenth century, Hope began offering German services in addition to English ones as the German-speaking population grew in that former English enclave.[58] Services were held in German intermittently through 1830.[59]

Judging by the debate over schools, many German-speaking parents shared the Moravian leadership's indifference to ethnicity. The striking fact was the lack of discussion over language and culture. Instead, the main concern of parents was improving the quality of schools and ensuring that their children received a quality education.[60] In 1804, some parents in Friedberg did ask that the school be taught in German, but they apparently were a minority. The settlement's Haus Vaters Conferenz delayed the opening of school because of a "difference of opinion, for some wanted it conducted entirely in English, others wanted it all German, and still others desired both languages used." The conference reached a decision, presumably reflecting the will of the majority: in January, the evening school for boys began—in English.[61]

This indifference to the German language and ethnicity shows how ingrained evangelical values were throughout Wachovia. The twin drive to reform Christianity through the new birth and to lead upright lives as followers of the Savior meant that evangelical religion dominated the brethrens' worldview, not a sense of Germanness. German Lutheran leaders, by contrast, saw their native language as an important marker of their faith and identity. In 1813, a German magazine cautioned North Carolina's Lutherans that "teaching Children only English is a sign of religious indifference. Children are thus deprived of German religious literature, which, because of the poverty of the English language, cannot be translated."[62] For many German-speaking Anabaptist groups, including the Amish, Hutterites, and Amanites of Iowa, language helped set them apart from the Anglo world and enabled them to maintain a degree of distinctiveness. As historian Harry S. Stout has noted, ethnicity and religion reinforced each other, enabling minority groups to maintain a group identity in a strange new land. Church services, Stout concludes, "become a symbolic rite of affirmation to one's ethnic association and a vehicle for preserving the ethnic language."[63]

The maintenance of language and culture, in turn, resided on the twin pillars of church and school. These interlocking institutions inculcated the young in the ways of religion and Germanic culture, allowing German sects to maintain their religious and ethnic identity.[64] Even for Lutheran and Reformed settlers, maintaining their membership in the church of their homeland was an act of allegiance to their heritage. As the research of historian Steven M. Nolt has shown, Lutheran and Reformed settlers in greater Pennsylvania avoided evangelicals in the early Republic because they perceived the movement as "American" whose social, religious, and political reforms threatened their distinctive German-American identity. These Lutheran and Reformed members, instead, used their churches to maintain a sense of German ethnicity at a time when a new Anglo-based nation was forming around them. A German religion, Nolt explains, "provided the intellectual resources, community setting, and public arena for sorting out the claims of culture and ideology that emerged in the often disorienting days of the early nineteenth century."[65] Historian Stephanie Grauman Wolf would agree. "To belong to a church," she maintains, "was to accept its cultural orientation along with its doctrine."[66]

Evangelism worked far differently. Moravian heart religion produced a diversity of people based not on ethnicity but on a shared religion centered on the new birth. Religion, in effect, became the most important glue in both creating a community and holding it together. Evangelism's broad emphasis on the new birth dampened ethnic identity among Moravian leaders and followers alike. It helped overcome the kind of hostility that German and English speakers could sometimes express toward each other in colonial Philadelphia and backcountry settlements. Some first-generation German speakers in Wachovia did express a stereotyped view of their English counterparts. In 1766, Lorenz Bagge took stock of the laborers at work in the construction of Salem. He noted that "James Horst, an old English Brother, here for the first time, has the Englishman's peculiarity." But Horst, Bagge quickly added, "is faithful to the Savior."[67] Horst's devotion to Christ, in other words, made him acceptable regardless of his ethnicity and "Englishman's peculiarity." A shared religion thus allowed people such as Horst and Bagge to find common ground despite their widely different backgrounds. These evangelicals in effect were creating a different kind of ethnicity—a self-identity centered on religion, not language and a common cultural heritage.

The Cultural Impact of Intermixing

Extensive intermixing with outsiders and with Moravians of different ethnicities meant that German speakers were increasingly exposed to "American" values, and English-speaking Moravians were exposed to German ones. Both sides changed as a result. This amalgamation of values can be seen most clearly in the German and English approach to family and testate practices. As A. G. Roeber, Kathleen Neils Conzen, and other historians have shown, German colonists from southwest Germany and Prussia showed an attachment to land and family that rivaled their English counterparts. In rural Pennsylvania and elsewhere, German speakers devised testate practices whose purpose was to protect the family and keep the family farm running smoothly and efficiently.[68] Anglo-Americans' attachment to family was equally strong, but they followed different strategies to achieve the goal of family protection. English-speaking colonists tended to devolve all of the family land to one or two sons in an attempt to protect the family line[69]; German colonists, by contrast, tended at first to follow southwestern German practices of partible inheritance, where heirs shared equally in family property.[70] In the late colonial period, as acculturation proceeded, the initial German pattern of devolving land equally gave way to the Anglo system of favoring sons.[71]

In managing their estates, Moravian parents of both ethnicities shared several overlapping goals. On the most elementary level, parents wanted to provide for their children while keeping the family farm running smoothly. Accumulation of land was central because both English- and German-speaking fathers viewed land as an inducement to keep their children in, or at least near, Wachovia. Unity leaders, ironically, disagreed with this strong desire to acquire land, warning that individual accumulation of land would entice people to worldliness and profit, as well as create jealously and envy among those whose holdings were smaller.[72]

Fathers in the *Landgemeinen* and in Bethania, however, rationalized that proper bequests of land could help keep their children close to home. Their reasoning was similar to Quaker parents in the Delaware Valley. There, fathers built up large holdings and liberally bestowed land grants on heirs in an effort to keep their children nearby.[73] In Wachovia, family and religious needs blended in fathers' decisions to buy land. Farmers of middling means built up their holdings to provide for heirs' material and spiritual comfort (table 3.4). Such a dual strategy was evident by looking at not only those brethren with children but also those without. Two members of the large Hauser family in Bethania, a settlement that by the late eighteenth century shared the country congregations' love of land, showed the differing motivations. Abraham, who was born in 1761 and died in 1819, worked as a farmer, mason, and tavern hostler. He married in 1786 and saw his first child born by March 1787 and his fourth son by 1799, giving him and his wife a total of five children. In August 1800, less than a year after Martin was born, Abraham bought one hundred and twenty-six acres on Peter's Creek in Wachovia for this last-born son.[74] In 1813, he bought a one-hundred-and-ninety-eight-acre plantation on Brushy Fork that he held for three years. In 1816, Abraham divided the tract into halves and sold them to sons Jacob and Timothy for $600 apiece.[75] With the exception of a tract of two hundred and twelve acres that he bought in 1805 and sold in 1809 for a loss of $100, all his purchases were for family purposes.[76] The timing of the purchases was also telling. He bought the one hundred and ninety-eight acres in 1813, just a few years before the two middle sons reached their majority. He sold them the land when Timothy reached the age of twenty-one; Jacob was only twenty-three. Frederick Hauser, by contrast, had no children. Although the rest of the Hauser clan was active on the land market, he made no purchases. His will of 1807 was brief and to the point: he left his wife, Elizabeth, his estate.[77] Although other factors may have been at work, the absence of children appeared crucial. Those brethren of middling means who did not have children lacked the incentive to participate actively on the land market.[78]

Both English- and German-speaking brethren shared this zeal for buying land as an enticement for their children to remain active in the church. The religious motivations, however, did not mean that families focused exclusively on Wachovia. By 1800, the brethren were actively participating in the surrounding land market, with many families settling just beyond Wachovia's borders. Several forces drove this shift outward—the attachment to family and a concomitant desire to build up holdings was one; the others were the creation of creole unions, which made German speakers more amenable to Anglo-American ways, and extensive intermixing with different ethnic groups, which made outsiders seem less different. More than half of Hope's society members, as a result, came to live outside of Wachovia. Most of this group lived several miles from the meetinghouse along the Yadkin River to the west of Wachovia. In the other settlements, land east of Wachovia in Stokes County, at places that became Germanton and Clemmons, was especially popular. In the *Landgemeinen,* Friedberg had the largest number of wealthy landholders, defined as those owners with holdings of seven hundred acres and up, and the settlement's "middling" class was extensive, with 75 percent of its settlers falling into this category (table 3.4). The vast majority of the settlers in Hope and Friedland also fell into the middling group, but these settlements had only three families in the wealthy category. Still, holdings in the three country congregations were remarkably similar, and so were the overall trends: more families were looking outward at the same time they were using land as a component of heart religion.

The critical difference between the two ethnic groups was in how English and German speakers passed on their land to heirs. The two groups' management of their estates was a complex question that reflected their cultural and religious heritages. In Germany, the types of tenure in this formerly feudal so-

Table 3.4 Landholdings by Class and Settlement

Category	N	Total Acreage	Average Acreage
Betharbara			
Wealthy	1	734	734
Middling	15	4,181.15	278.75
Small	4	61.25	15.31
Bethania			
Wealthy	19	27,642.14	1,454.85
Middling	71	16,603	233.84
Small	20	1,501.50	75.07
Salem			
Wealthy	12	29,088.75	2,424.06
Middling	29	9,004.5	310.50
Small	13	711.25	54.71
Friedberg			
Wealthy	7	7,158.2	1,022.6
Middling	61	13,769.75	225.73
Small	14	775	55.36
Friedland			
Wealthy	1	1,081.92	1,081.92
Middling	51	11,450	224.50
Small	8	509.25	633.66
Hope			
Wealthy	2	1,411	705.50
Middling	52	10,918.75	209.97
Small	24	1,826.25	76.10

Source: Stokes County Deed Books.
Note: Wealthy is defined as those landholders with 700 acres and up; middling is 101 acres to 699 acres; and small is 100 acres and under.

ciety went a long way in determining whether farmers followed partible or impartible inheritance. In the southwest principality of Calenberg, for instance, most peasants held their land under *Meierrecht,* or hereditary tenure, where the lord owned the land and imposed manorial restrictions. It was in the lord's and government's best interests for tax purposes that landholdings stay intact. These policies helped encourage impartible inheritance.

But this province was an exception in southwest Germany. Most fathers tended to divide land equally among heirs. The majority of peasants who followed partible inheritance held their land under *Eigenland,* which meant that the land was free of manorial control. Landholdings could be divided, unlike property held in *Meierrecht.*[79] Despite the differences between partible and impartible, both systems rested on similar conceptions of the "perennial family" that sought to tie the generations to land and family. German parents wanted to provide sufficient incentive for their children to stay on family land. Under the impartible system, this meant devolving the home place on one heir while providing bequests in the form of cash or "movable" property to the other children. Under partible, it meant dividing the land and movable property equally, although in America one heir would often get the home place. Both systems sought to keep the family farm running efficiently while allowing the parents to retire comfortably.[80] In southwest Germany, Pietism did not make significant inroads into these traditional practices. One of the family's essential functions in an agrarian society remained the transfer of assets between generations. Pietist villagers generally followed partible inheritance. They tended to pass the home place on to a single heir and gave spouses some control over the distribution of the estate. But overall, pietist testate practices differed little from other Protestant groups.[81]

As in southwest Germany, German speakers in Wachovia sought to keep their children close by. But there was one significant difference: the abundance of land in America meant that parents could maintain the principle of partible inheritance while abandoning its most pernicious effects that saw the family farm divided repeatedly until it was no longer economically viable. In other words, wills in Wachovia transmitted the home place to one child while helping other children get large farms of their own. Extant wills show how strong the attachment to home place was. Only 19 percent of the estates in Wachovia sold the main farm at the death of the father.[82] Not surprisingly, Bethabara's residents possessed the strongest attachment to the home place—only 16 percent sold it. Also not surprisingly, Hope showed the least attachment—28 percent—because of its strong mix of Anglo and German ways (table 3.5).[83]

Most German-speaking fathers accumulated land for later division among their children, including, in many cases, daughters. During his lifetime, Jacob Miller of Friedland gave his eldest son, John, 250 acres, and his other three sons received tracts of about 218 acres. Jacob gave one daughter 203 acres as a dowry. His will of 1796 awarded these tracts to these five children and decreed that the rest of his property be sold with the proceeds being divided among the three remaining daughters. The children with land were to pay the other three money

Table 3.5 Moravians and the Home Place

Settlement*	Total Testators	Wills Selling (%)
Bethabara	19	16
Bethania	45	18
Friedberg	30	20
Friedland	28	25
Hope	28	28
Wachovia (TOTAL)	150	19

Source: Rowan, Surry, and Stokes County Will Books.
Note: Salem is not included because residents rented their land and often their houses.
*Home place at parent's death.

if the sale failed to raise enough money.[84] Miller's will demonstrated how the principle of partible inheritance survived in complex form among German-speaking brethren. The goal of equality endured—all children received equal portions—but the sons were favored with land. Although Miller gave land to a daughter, she received her tract because of her marriage. In most instances, daughters received money or livestock as a dowry or inheritance. The exceptions merely proved the rule. Lazarus Hege of Friedberg had seven daughters and only two sons. Lazarus's will of 1816 awarded the home place, with its house, gardens, and 341 acres, to Christian. As the oldest son, he was also to receive three tracts of about 120 acres. The other son, George, received four adjoining tracts totaling almost three hundred acres. Four daughters received land ranging from one hundred acres up to two hundred, but not nearly as much as their brothers. The remaining daughters received money.[85] The six daughters of Peter Frey divided a total of 400 acres, whereas one son received the main plantation of 334 acres and the other son 212 acres. Frey, like most others, divided up his holdings among all his heirs but in favor of his sons.[86]

The English-speaking settlers in Hope, by contrast, descended from a different tradition. In England, primogeniture was the dominant practice during the early modern period because of the scarcity of land in that country. To keep the family estate viable, fathers passed on their land intact to the eldest son. Maryland and Virginia codified this practice in 1670 by passing a "Statute of Distributions" that mandated primogeniture be followed when a property owner died intestate. Despite this statute, primogeniture, of course, did not survive intact in the New World, but the idea that one or two sons should be favored did. English fathers generally believed that devolving most of the family land to one member would best protect the family estate. Daughters rarely got land; instead, fathers left them livestock, household goods, slaves, and other personal property.[87]

English-speaking residents of Hope—products of a Maryland society that mimicked English traditions in so many ways—showed a similar inclination in its inheritance practices. In the eighteenth century, fathers there generally rewarded favored sons with the main farm and home place. Matthew Markland Sr. was typical. He was a farmer at Carrollton Manor who had joined the Moravian movement and assumed a leadership role within the congregation. It was Markland who let the Reverend Joseph Powell and his wife live in his house, and it was Markland who came to the rescue of Powell's wife when she was attacked by enemies of the brethren. With his wife, Ancibel, Markland raised five sons and one daughter. The Marklands' holdings in Wachovia were modest. When Matthew arrived in 1774 from Maryland, he took out a lease-purchase for 168 acres in the northern reaches of Hope. His only additional purchase was a 101-acre tract he bought in 1794 for fifty-five pounds, North Carolina money, that adjoined his and Matthew Jr.'s land. When Matthew made out his will in 1796 shortly before his death, he left his eldest son, Joseph, only seventeen acres; his youngest son, Nathan, received all the other tracts. The remaining sons received no land. Instead, his daughter and the sons divided his personal property equally.[88]

By the early nineteenth century, intermixing had made subtle but significant changes in these cultural approaches to land and inheritance, with not only English ways making inroads among German speakers but also German values penetrating English ways. In the 1760 to 1800 period, 42 percent of German speakers in Hope and Friedberg divided their property equally, but only 33 percent did in the 1800 to 1830 period. While these German speakers in southern Wachovia were absorbing Anglo-American values, English-speaking Moravians were absorbing German ones: 43 percent of the Anglos in Hope made an unequal distribution of property in the eighteenth century; only 22 percent did in the later period.[89]

Such a two-way acculturation was also evident in the treatment of sons. German speakers' practice of granting land to sons before their passing to ensure a more rational and equitable distribution of family property began to give way to the Anglo-American practice. Before 1800, no English-speaking member of Hope passed on land to their sons before their deaths. But after 1800, 46 percent of first- and second-generation English fathers followed the German practice of bequeathing land while they were alive. At the same time, 53 percent of Germans in Hope and Friedberg in the 1800 to 1830 period followed Anglo practices of waiting to pass on land.[90] Historians of the German immigrant experience typically cite economic factors in explaining such changes in testate practices, especially for the greater use of impartible inheritance: a growing shortage of land, combined with rising familiarity with the Anglo-American commercial system, caused German colonists to adopt Anglo-American ways. But the experience in Hope shows the importance of cultural contact: intermarriage and close friendships changed both sides on the most basic social levels.

Intermixing's Impact on Community

Land and family, religion and intermixing—all this came together to produce explosive change on the community level. The impact of evangelism and intermixing can be seen most clearly in a place that Moravian leaders invested so much of their hopes and dreams: the congregation town of Bethania in northwest Wachovia. Founded by the Unity in 1759, Bethania by 1800 had evolved into a fiercely independent place that constantly aggravated Wachovia's leaders with its freewheeling ways and its strong attachment to family and land. As Marshall noted dryly in 1771 when discussing the differences between Bethabara and Bethania, "Although Bethabara and Bethania lie close together, there is as great a difference in their methods as if they were far apart. Bethania does things as they come, Bethabara plans."[91] The 1775 Wachovia Memorabilia had little good to say about the place: "During the past year the Savior has dealt earnestly with this congregation, and has shown His displeasure with its misdeeds and lukewarmness by thrice forbidding the holding of Holy Communion, which caused many a hour of sorrowful heart-searchings."[92]

It was not supposed to be that way. At Bethania's launching, Wachovia's leaders instructed founding members that this village was to be a place where the Savior would come first and land and family second. Planners wanted the physical design of Bethania to reinforce the town's religious mission and to keep inhabitants' familial impulses in check. Bethania, as a result, began as a German-style village with the agricultural fields and orchards placed behind a row of houses that lined a central street. Moravian leaders' detailed plans called for every house to have an acre and a half of land behind it, with room for an orchard and a garden.

The inspiration for this village design came from Germany. The roots of the Moravian Church extended not only into the southeastern corner of Saxony, where Herrnhut was located, but also into Moravia and Bohemia to the south and southeast. Many of the villages in these regions consisted of houses grouped along a single street. They had equal lots with the common fields behind the houses. The common fields were usually divided into ordered strips, with open areas serving as pasture or woodland.[93]

Such a landscape was clearly in the minds of Moravian planners as they drew up their designs for Bethania in 1759. The village's fields, Spangenberg wrote in a report, would be behind the orchards and "perhaps will be set out in the manner which is usual for villages in Germany."[94] Order and regularity greatly appealed to them for social and religious reasons. In this village of the Lord, all were to be equal before God. No one should have more land than he can properly use: if landholdings become too unequal, "in the long run the way will be paved for hard feelings."[95]

But such regularity also fit in nicely with the Unity's social vision for what a congregation town should be. In 1752, as he scouted for a tract in North Carolina for the Unity to buy, Spangenberg could scarcely contain his dismay with the southern backcountry and its inhabitants. "Trade and business are poor," he wrote in his diary in September. North Carolina's "towns are few and small" because of the lack of navigable rivers. He was equally displeased with the colony's farmers because the "work is poorly done."[96] Farms were scattered; livestock was set loose in the woods to forage as it pleased; and fields were used up with no regard to fertilizer or soil and then abandoned.

Bethania was to avoid these pitfalls. Surveyor Gottlieb Reuter, who helped implement the Moravian leadership's vision for this agricultural village, wrote at length on what the brethren had in mind. Landholdings were to be small and intensively cultivated. Their tillers were to follow the three-field rotation, as in Germany. One reason for such small holdings, Reuter explained, was that land should not be wasted; all residents must use what they possess. This meant that an inhabitant could not acquire fresh holdings "until he has carried out the designated clearing. Otherwise, uncultivated areas might result." But there was a deeper social reason as well. The sites, Reuter noted, "are to be carried forward in a way that is equal in proportion, without regard to residents, until each site contains six acres of land." Such rough equality meant that the church did not want "to give someone less than he can use . . . nor to limit a person in any way. They are intended not to harm an individual or the whole group by giving someone what he cannot use. For when it is given to one person, it is consequently given to no one else. Then the land is . . . rendered useless."[97]

Such a philosophy neatly blended spiritual and worldly goals and sought to make them virtually inseparable. All of God's people were to be equal in the spiritual realm, and all were to enjoy his fruits on the earth. The fear of Reuter and Marshall was that excessively unequal holdings would breed discord and jealousy among the brethren. They also worried that a person accumulating more land than he could use would be striving after worldly gain in an attempt to get ahead. It was imperative that a farmer possess only what he needed. The real fear was of individualism and all that that meant—people putting their own needs ahead of the Savior and the congregation. Marshall and Spangenberg hoped that houses clustered in a village setting, with small fields close by, would enhance the sense of community and devotion. As Spangenberg explained in 1759, the Unity wanted the houses to be far enough apart so that each inhabitant would have "room for barns, stables, or other out-buildings." But "neither are they too far from one another, so that the inhabitants can better reach out a helping hand to one another."[98]

Wachovia's and Bethania's governing boards worked hard to try to keep holdings both small and relatively equal. In the early years, they were quite successful. Inhabitants' holdings averaged twenty-two acres in 1769, and no one held more than thirty-three acres.[99] Such small farms were a far cry from the *Landgemeinen* of the 1770s and the rest of the North Carolina frontier, where holdings averaged 250 acres.[100] Bethanians' holdings were also scattered European-style, with farms being divided into about six tracts, often far from each other.[101]

Because Bethania was an *Ortsgemeine,* villagers did not own their tracts but leased them from the church. From the church's standpoint, maintaining ownership of land outside of Salem held great advantages. It allowed Wachovia's boards to keep tight control over its occupiers. No one could move into Bethania without the church's permission, and all residents had to agree to abide by the Brotherly Agreement. The Brotherly Agreement spelled out just who could live in Bethania. For starters, of course, the applicant had to be fully committed to the Lord and willing to live with a "People of God." But church elders considered a host of practical concerns as well: "whether the Person be of Age; whether bound to any body; whether promised in Marriage; whether in Debt; and if the Person be married, who and what sort of People belong to their Family; with what Business they intend to get their Livelihood; that neither the Congregation nor the Persons themselves may thereby suffer unexpected Losses."[102] Such strict criteria were intended to keep the unconverted away from the pious. Church control also meant that leases could not be transferred to another resident without the church's permission. This rule, among other things, was intended to prevent a congregant who had strayed from God's ways from acquiring more land.

The brethrens' attachment to family and land, along with extensive contact with Anglo-Americans and the *Landgemeinen,* changed all this. The residents of the upper part of the village—a group of eight families that in July 1759 asked to affiliate with the Moravians as society members—were the unhappiest with the strict rules and led the challenge against them.[103] At Bethania's committee meetings, they pushed for larger farm sizes. One such session in 1768 was typical: "Brother Sponhauer . . . said that he and the residents of the upper village wished they [their fields] could be enlarged through the vacant farm Lotts [sic] that lie nearby."[104] Several of these members simply ignored the rules. George Hauser Jr. was the first to transfer his lease without Marshall's permission; Jacob Lash was the second. Lash built a house without the consent of the village committee, refused to sign the Brotherly Agreement, sold wood without permission, constantly "quibbled" with the committee, and yet claimed "all the Benefits of an Inhabitant."[105]

The inclusion of society members in an *Ortsgemeine* was having disastrous results in Bethania.[106] None of these brethren were English, but they were German speakers from diverse cultural and religious backgrounds who, unlike the founders of the *Landgemeinen,* had little or no previous experience with Moravianism. In one sense, it was merely dumb luck—and a war—that had brought them to Wachovia in the late 1750s. The circuitous journey of Heinrich Schor to Bethania was typical of these society members. He was born in 1735 in Muttenz, Switzerland, and was raised in the Reformed Church. His parents migrated to the New World in 1749. The Schor family passed through the port of Philadelphia and settled in Pennsylvania. Schor's childhood was not an easy one; his mother died during the sea voyage to Philadelphia, forcing the family to split up after they left the port city. Heinrich stayed with a family near Lancaster, where, according to his chronicler, "he became quite concerned and troubled about the state of his soul." Heinrich, of course, was experiencing vocation, but during his youth he never found a way to achieve justification, the second step in the conversion process. He went to live with a Mennonite family for six months, then served as a carpenter's apprentice for another eight months.[107]

Heinrich's travels were just beginning. In 1753, he moved to New River, North Carolina, with his father to help run a plantation the father had purchased, but the son returned to Pennsylvania in 1754 so he could resume his carpentry work and find a bride. Heinrich decided to return to New River in 1755 with his new wife, Barbara Mueller, but they encountered a terrible blow as they approached North Carolina: war, a fellow Swiss expatriate boarder warned them near the Virginia border, had come to the backcountry, and Indians had killed or captured the entire settlement at New River. Heinrich and his wife turned around and retreated to the safety of Maryland, where they anxiously awaited news of the father's fate. With relief, they learned that the senior Schor was alive and living in Town Fork, and they promptly headed back to North Carolina so they could join him. Then, their plans took another unexpected turn. On the last night of their journey, Heinrich and Barbara spent the night within the palisades of Bethabara. Sleep did not come easily. Tossing and turning, they heard something that both startled and deeply moved them: a night watchman singing. "It made such a deep impression upon their hearts," recalled Schor's chronicler, "that they came to the decision to either stay with these people, or if they could get permission, to settle in their neighborhood." Thus in 1758, Schor bought land in Wachovia two miles from the future site of Bethania so he and Barbara could learn more about the brethren. The settlers' Indian troubles, however, were not over. New attacks sent area inhabitants scurrying to the safety of Bethabara, where several families, including the Schors, stayed at the village's mill. During their confinement, they learned more about this evangelical religion through the preachings of various brethren, including Bishop Spangenberg. These families were captivated by what they heard and asked to affiliate formally with the brethren. Wachovia's leaders agreed to settle them in the upper part of the *Ortsgemeine* known as Bethania. On August 9, 1759, Schor and the other families moved into their new homes in Bethania.[108]

These mill families, as they were known in Wachovia, became good Moravians and devout followers of the Lord. Their interest in joining the brethren was sincere, and their motives for affiliating with the Unity differed little from the hundreds of other members who came to know the Moravians through the Diaspora. Quite simply, they wanted to get closer to Jesus. Yet their position in the 1760s and 1770s was extremely complex, even by the confusing standards of the Diaspora, which tolerated different levels of membership. For one, the mill families had not undergone the long years of apprenticeship in the northern colonies, as had the founders of the *Landgemeinen*. They did not travel to North Carolina specifically to start new Moravian congregations, as had many emigrés from Maine, Pennsylvania, and Maryland. In 1758, the mill families found themselves facing Indian attacks; in 1759, they found themselves living not in a settlement of society members but in a newly founded *Ortsgemeine* with the then-strictest list of rules in Wachovia. With so little acclimation into the ways of the brethren, it was no surprise that the mill families were so quick to question congregational rules and so quick to chaff at the restrictions placed on them. Their unhappiness only grew in the late eighteenth century and spread to the rest of the village as they learned more about the *Landgemeinen.*

Intermixing among Moravians, then, was proving to be extremely volatile. "Outsiders"—that is, German speakers from Lutheran and Reformed backgrounds who had little exposure to Moravianism—were living in an *Ortsgemeine.* And these outsiders lived only a few miles from an Anglo-American congregation and two *Landgemeinen* of mixed ethnicity, where members were allowed to live on bigger farms with fewer church rules. By the mid-1760s—only a few years after Bethania's founding—these brethren were looking with envy at the *Landgemeinen* who possessed the freedom and the flexibility to accumulate holdings far larger than twenty-two acres.

In 1768, Bethanians politely pointed out that "we must have a little more room than what a mere craftsman needs."[109] When their pleas went largely unheeded, congregation members came up with a creative but obvious way to avoid church rules: they moved. The number of *Austwartige* members—those members who chose to live in Bethania's environs but still affiliate with the congregation—grew so quickly that by 1792, half of the congregation was living on unregulated plantations outside of the village.[110] By living beyond Bethania's borders, members were able to evade the strict rules that limited landholdings inside the village. They then plunged into the land market until, by 1800, Bethanians had become the second largest landholders in Wachovia. They trailed only Salem, whose numbers were inflated by the huge holdings of Traugott Bagge and other wealthy merchants who accumulated tracts as large as ten thousand acres. Bethania had the largest number of wealthy landowners in Wachovia and the broadest middling class with the largest holdings. Within less than twenty years, Bethanians had surpassed the holdings of their brethren in the country congregations.

Contact with Anglo-Americans helped fuel the drive for land and freedom. Bethanians readily mixed with their English-speaking neighbors and were comfortable in the presence of the "English." As in the *Landgemeinen,* the congregation's pastor frequently conducted services in both German and English. A congregation diary entry of 1809 was typical: "The German sermon was preached in the morning at ten o'clock by Brother Reichel; and Brother Benzien preached in English at one o'clock in the afternoon."[111] And as in the *Landgemeinen,* conducting the school in German was not an issue for Bethanians. In fact, in 1805 parents requested that the congregation committee start an "English school," Bethania's diarist reported, "and it looks as though this might be possible."[112]

As landholdings increased and contact with "English" ways grew, cultural change inevitably followed. Slowly, Bethania took on an English accent in a process that mirrored the social changes in the *Landgemeinen*. In 1790, Wachovia's leadership bowed to the village's headstrong ways and agreed to drop the use of the lot for *Gemeine* members wishing to marry.[113] This sea change in policy meant that congregation members were free to marry whomever they pleased, subject to the usual restrictions in the *Landgemeinen*. That is, the parents and pastor of a prospective bride and groom had to approve of the match. Intermarriage in Bethania was lower than in the country congregations but far higher than in other German-speaking communities elsewhere in America: 15 percent of Bethanians intermarried in the 1790 to 1820 period. Bethanians mingled with Anglo-Americans, sometimes married them, lived on American-style farms, and pushed for American freedoms.

Bethania, too, had created an Anglo-German world.

✝

Religion and intermixing among Moravians produced waves of change between 1770 and 1800. Creole families were created, kinship networks were reconfigured, and settlement patterns were altered. But such developments, sweeping as they were, were only half of the acculturation story. The evangelical impulse to reform a "worldly" culture and revive Christian life meant that the *Brudergemeine* was actively engaging the outside world on numerous fronts. This engagement with the outside had far-reaching implications—none more so than the Revolution that shook the brethrens' world beginning in 1776.

PART TWO
Growing Together
The World from Without

The brethrens' Anglo-German world, a complex melding of distinct cultures, never existed in isolation. Religion and the nature of Moravianism itself propelled the brethren to look outward at the very time they were looking inward, at the state of their hearts. They built an economically thriving community and plunged into the workings of the market. They remained aloof at first from the political controversies of the day, but the demands of the American Revolution soon made such a stance impossible. The brethrens' engagement with the political and economic spheres changed the way they saw the world around them. Yet religious values influenced this engagement in a very profound way. And extensive contact with the outside was occurring at the same time that the brethren were creating their new ethnicity. In the end, the complex interplay between the two stages of acculturation produced a third stage that led to an even more distinct, and ultimately "American," identity.

4

Becoming "American"
The Revolutionary Years

On May 12, 1780, Charleston, South Carolina, fell to British forces, and the reverberations were soon felt all the way to Friedberg, North Carolina. The enemy's capture of this pivotal southern port sent American soldiers and civilians alike fleeing northward. News of the disaster, which included the surrender of fifty-five hundred American soldiers—the third-largest capitulation in U.S. military history—reached Friedberg on June 1. "The beginning of this month was much disturbed, for we heard on the 1st that Charlestown had surrendered to the English," Friedberg's pastor reported. "Those [congregation members] who live on the road had much to bear, partly from those passing in flight, partly from the soldiers released on parole in South Carolina. They took a horse out of old Greter's stable, and he was thankful to get it back, though he had to pay $200 to ransom it."[1]

Geography goes a long way in explaining this seeming peculiarity—how the surrender of American forces some three hundred miles to the south could result in the theft of a Moravian's horse a few weeks later. Unity leaders envisioned Wachovia as a refuge from the world, but a 1770s map shows just how exposed Friedberg was during wartime. A series of roads ran right through this farm hamlet, connecting the settlement to Salem, the central *Ortsgemeine,* to the north and to the non-Moravian towns of Salisbury and Lexington to the south. The South Fork and its two tributaries, meanwhile, snaked their way through the heart of Friedberg, serving as a different kind of highway for those who preferred the ease of water travel over that of rough roads. The settlement, as a result, was a jumble of roads and rivers, and it served as a key entryway into Wachovia for visitors and thieving soldiers alike, as Brother Greter learned to his dismay on that June day in 1780. Friedberg's open terrain meant that the settlement's residents could not retreat from the world for very long—although they tried to do just that during those times when the American Revolution was most threatening. Companies of "Liberty men," as the brethren called the rebellious American colonists, repeatedly passed through Wachovia in search of guns, supplies, and recruits.

The impact of the American Revolution on Friedberg and the other five settlements was multifold. The war increased Wachovia's contacts with the outside American world while temporarily cutting off contact with Germany. It ended British rule and left Wachovia's inhabitants as citizens in a new American nation. And it hastened the process by which Moravians of all ethnicities began to see themselves as "American." Being "American," of course, meant different things to different people. Historians have traditionally defined the term as a sense of peoplehood centered on core American values—democracy and equality, for instance.[2] For German-Americans living in pre–Civil War America, being American meant, in the words of one historian, "learning how to succeed in the very pluralistic, diverse America they [German immigrants] had helped to create."[3] For Moravians living in North Carolina in the early national period, Americanization meant something different. It was not about developing a strategy for surviving as ethnic Germans in a new land. The Moravians' primary concern remained how to develop, and maintain, a religious identity as evangelicals. The war, however, intruded on this critical process, with the Revolution coming along at the precise time that the intermixing described in chapter 3 was producing such momentous changes in Moravian community life. The two developments overlapped, with war influencing acculturation and acculturation influencing Moravian participation in the war. This dual process meant that, as Moravians in North Carolina were developing their Anglo-German communities, they were absorbing American ways and developing a dual identity as evangelicals and as Americans.

War Comes to Wachovia

In the middle of July 1776, ten days after the Continental Congress had approved the Declaration of Independence, Friedberg's congregation met to discuss the latest demand for men to serve in the militia. They were of one mind. "The brethren consulted together," pastor L. G. Bachhof recorded in his diary, "and agreed that none of them would go out to fight, but would endure whatever this course might bring upon them." This resolve was tested quickly. As the meeting broke up, "a Lieutenant came to the [meetinghouse] door and ordered the first and second Classes of our Rowan . . . Brethren and their sons to appear before Capt. Ekel next Tuesday, ready to march against the Indians," Bachhof recalled. "He at once received the answer: 'We are not going to fight.'"

To emphasize their resolve, the young men most in danger of being hauled off "retired into the woods," where they hid from the lieutenant and his soldiers.[4]

For the brethren in Friedberg, this was no spur-of-the-moment decision. Months earlier, on February 18, 1776, the married members of the Friedberg congregation and society had met to discuss "their position in these disturbed times." Again, there was little debate about what this position should be. The congregation would follow the lead of their brethren in the three congregation towns. This meant that Friedberg's members would honor the new government and pay their taxes, but they would not take up arms for either side. And as in July, their resolve was tested quickly. Fearing they would be forced to enlist in the Rowan County militia, the men "retired" to the forest. As Bachhof put it, "On account of danger from the soldiers who were marching through, practically all the young men and boys, and some of the men, were hiding in the woods." There they stayed, hidden, until the danger had passed.[5]

The physical act of hiding highlighted in dramatic fashion the great issues confronting this religious community. From a moral standpoint, Moravian leaders and laymen alike found war repugnant. An evangelical culture discouraged the taking up of arms, as well as the swearing of a formal oath of allegiance to one side or the other. But the brethrens' views on these related issues were complex. Moravians were not formal pacifists, and they owned guns and could use them to defend themselves against attack from robbers, Indians, or wild beasts. Yet they rejected participation in offensive operations against a rival army—a distinction that was often lost on recruiting officers who recalled the role played by the brethren during the French and Indian War. The brethren denied any such inconsistency. The Savior, Bishop John Ettwein explained, allowed a pilgrim to protect himself against attack. Because of the threat posed by Indians in the 1750s, the brethren believed they were completely justified in fortifying Bethabara and its mill and in allowing neighbors to seek protection behind their walls.[6]

In the early stages of the American Revolution, an evangelical culture helped to foster an aloofness and passivity among Moravian leaders and followers alike. With war at their doorstep, the brethren placed their fate in the hands of their God and Savior. They trusted that Jesus would protect them. Salem's Memorabilia of 1776 captured this attitude well. It praised "the many instances of His wonderful help, counsel, and direction [in the past year]. Had He not been this to us, had the Guardian of Israel not watched over us and turned aside the evil which the enemy planned against us, we would have perished."[7] As the crisis with Great Britain deepened in 1775 and 1776, the brethren turned to prayer with greater fervency, strongly believing that Jesus Christ was watching over them. "This year more difficult and unpleasant things have happened than in any preceding year," stated the 1776 Salem Memorabilia. "But we must say with truth and humility that our dear Lord has not only lightened the heavy load, but when misfortune and harm was [sic] threatening, He either turned it aside or made it work to our advantage."[8]

Evangelical values did more than encourage passivity—they helped shape the Moravians' reaction to the competing British and American governments. The Bible was quite clear on what the brethren should do: the followers of Jesus must obey their earthly ruler. The Moravians would accede to whoever seized the mantle as the rightful government. Yet, when King George's rebellious subjects formally declared their independence, the decision was not so black and white. One complication was whether to take the oath of allegiance demanded by the newly independent North Carolina government. The Moravian position on oaths differed little from that of other Anabaptists and Pietists. The brethren based their opposition to oath taking on James 5:12: "But above all, my brethren, do not swear, either by heaven or by earth or with any other oath. But let your 'Yes' be 'Yes,' and your 'No,' 'No,' lest you fall into judgment." This refusal to swear oaths landed the brethren in trouble with American authorities, who questioned the Moravians' loyalty to the rebels' cause. For many revolutionaries, oath taking signified something more than a perfunctory declaration of support to the government; it represented an important symbolic act to the new republic taking shape. In the early years of the war, declaring allegiance meant an individual was declaring his fealty to the cause of liberty and republicanism. As historian Gordon S. Wood describes it, "This oath-taking was so solemn and ceremonious because the revolutionaries . . . were creating new social bonds by making individuals swear a new 'attachment to the body of the people.'"[9]

Another serious complication was that the Unity had no real grievances with the British Empire. In fact, the Unity's relationship with British authorities was quite good. The king had allowed the Moravians to worship in peace within his vast dominion. In 1749, Parliament formally recognized the Unity as an ancient Protestant Episcopal Church, and the brethren had thriving branches on both sides of the Atlantic. If Moravians in British North America sided with the rebellious colonists, they risked the safety and well being of Moravians in England, the Caribbean, and elsewhere in the empire. Moravians in North Carolina and the northern colonies, however, faced retaliation from their American neighbors if they sided with the king.

Unity leaders in Wachovia, as a result, watched the growing revolutionary crisis in the 1770s with trepidation. When the 1775 Halifax Convention directed North Carolina's congressional delegation in Philadelphia to vote for independence, Wachovia decided to stay neutral. As Wachovia's leaders succinctly explained, "[We] wished to remain true to the King." Caught in the middle of two warring sides, the brethren hastily reassured their American neighbors that "they desired all good for the Province of North Carolina . . . that they would never do aught which might work harm to the Province; and that they would pray to God to end the present distress and grant an honorable peace."[10] The brethren tried to straddle the fence well into 1776 when both Patriots and Tories approached them for their support, declaring, "It does not accord with our character as Brethren to mix in such political affairs, [as] we are children of peace."[11] The Americans' decision to declare independence formally in July forced the issue; North Carolina's Moravians now had to choose a side or risk being treated as traitors by both the British and their rebellious subjects. With little hesitation, Wachovia's leadership backed the Patriots, and the king's name was dropped from the litany for support of the rulers of the country.[12] This decision, however, was no Jeffersonian declaration for the rights of man. It was a carefully calculated decision designed to protect the Moravians' interests. Their neighbors had formed their own nation, and Wachovia's leaders believed they had to go along with independence or risk physical retaliation from American forces. Friedberg's pastor captured well the ambivalence that the brethren felt during this early phase of the Revolution. "The brethren had a short conference concerning the conditions of the country," he recorded in his diary on August 11, 1776, "and decided that as long as Congress is dominant it will be well to obey its orders, when they do not conflict with our conscience; and to conduct ourselves toward every man as true and peaceable citizens."[13]

Evangelical values were never far from the brethrens' thinking as they grappled with the complex political problems posed by the Revolution. The Moravians took seriously the admonitions of Jesus to obey thy earthly ruler. For philosophical and practical reasons, Wachovia was reluctant to challenge state authority, which in 1776 became the Continental Congress and the state of North Carolina. Much of the Moravians' safety rested in the hands of these rulers. Having faced nearly four centuries of persecution in Europe, Moravians did not want to risk antagonizing the new government and its citizens. In 1777, the leadership reminded Salem's congregation that "the welfare of a congregation rests upon its childlike simplicity and its loyal obedience to those in authority over it."[14] And Bishop John Michael Graff explicitly instructed

Wachovia's brethren to appear as loyal citizens: "It is our duty, in speaking to outsiders about our position in these political circumstances, that we allow no one to doubt that we are faithful subjects of the state. . . . Even without an Affirmation our conscience would have required that we be loyal to the State, according to Romans XIII, 1 . . . for in all the world it is required that fidelity be pledged to the party of government that is in power, and that due submission shall be made to it." Otherwise, Graff said, uninformed outsiders could brand the brethren as Tories—a term of opprobrium that would be not only "painful for us," he warned, but "in the end dangerous."[15]

Events would prove Graff's warning to be prophetic. The Moravians may have declared their allegiance to the new nation, but their neighbors still viewed them with suspicion, and with good reason. In 1776, support for the Patriot cause was lukewarm in parts of Wachovia. Some brethren did not identify deeply with the colonists' grievances and had no reason to be suspicious of a king and his ministers who had treated the Unity with respect. Support for the British, as a result, could be found in nearly every settlement, even after Wachovia had formally thrown its backing to the rebels. Wachovia's leadership, with some success, did all it could to keep the brethren in line. In 1777, for instance, it gave an "earnest warning" to members of Salem's congregation about making "ill-considered and quite unauthorized remarks and opinions concerning the present war between America and England."[16] The brethren, instead, were continually reminded to keep their focus on the one thing that really mattered—their Savior. "It was impressed upon the Brethren and Sisters that they were not called of the Lord to be judges of the actions of the world, but to be a quiet and patient flock, walking worthy of the Gospel, giving no offense to our neighbors, but watching and praying for our needy Brothers and Sisters." With rebel forces camped on Salem's outskirts in August 1776, the issue became a very real one for that congregation. After Bible reading, the adult members met in the Saal to discuss the war. "They were reminded that in these critical times, they should be very careful of word and deed, and especially that they should not express an opinion before strangers, still less declare themselves for either side, and that if asked any questions on political matters they should excuse themselves from answering on the ground of ignorance."[17]

This seeming indifference to affairs of the world made the brethren highly suspect to those Americans who believed that they were engaged in a truly glorious cause. They questioned whether the brethren really did support the colonists in their fight against King George. Admonitions to feign ignorance about the political issues did not help matters. It only made the brethren appear uncaring or insincere, because some brethren did inevitably talk, and this talk could land them in trouble, as a 1778 incident in Friedberg showed. "Br. Beck reported from Friedberg that last night Capt. Ekel and some of his men took young Tesch out of his bed, and would have done the same with young Spach had not his father promised to bring him before Justice Moore today," Salem's diary reported. "The accusation is trifling, but the gossiping of the Brethren there gives opportunity for such things."[18]

Also making the brethren suspect was the fact that German speakers predominated in the religious community. Despite the presence of Hope and a growing creole population, Wachovia remained home to a seemingly foreign sect whose main church was based in a country that was supplying troops to suppress the American rebellion. To uninformed outsiders, Wachovia looked suspiciously foreign. The Moravians' Germanness made many Americans wonder whose side the brethren were on. This was hardly an unusual reaction. Revolutionaries viewed another evangelical group—the Methodists—with equal suspicion because that movement was based in England and because its founder was rabidly pro-British during the imperial crisis between the colonies and the Crown. As historian Dee Andrews notes, "Formerly a movement of small account espousing the apolitical teachings of an English religious reformer, the Methodists were now widely perceived as presumptuous outsiders bent on betraying American independence."[19]

The refusal to bear arms and to swear an oath of allegiance only increased suspicions of the Moravians and other evangelicals. Bishop Ettwein reiterated in a letter of November 16, 1778, that the brethren opposed taking an "abjuration oath against the King because of our Missions and our connection with European congregations." But with the war going badly for the Americans, such a stance raised suspicions that the brethren were hedging their bets in case the British prevailed in the conflict. A newly elected member of the North Carolina Assembly put it bluntly to Ettwein: "He said we evidently wanted to make our estates safe if the other side won."[20] These suspicions also involved sheer resentment of the Moravians and their success in building a thriving community in the southern backcountry. The same assemblyman pointed out that "the Brethren were hated by their neighbors because they were *too* religious and *too* industrious for them."[21]

The most troublesome problems between the two sides involved oath taking and military service. At the end of 1777, North Carolina's assembly passed a series of laws outlining punishments for those individuals who did not support the war effort and the new government. Anyone who refused to take the oath of allegiance was to lose his right to citizenship. The assembly also passed a confiscation act that permitted authorities to seize the land of nonresident British landlords who did not return to the state by October 1778. The first act worried the Moravians for obvious reasons, but so did the second one, because the title to Wachovia remained in London in the hands of James Hutton, the trustee of the Moravian Church. If the authorities followed the confiscation act to the letter, enemies of the brethren could lay claim to Wachovia and evict its inhabitants.[22] This was no fanciful fear; Salem merchant Traugott Bagge wryly noted how "many persons around us . . . planned to take advantage of the opportunity and fish in troubled waters, and to possess themselves of land belonging to the Brethren in Wachovia and elsewhere." Salem, Bagge huffed, was claimed by a "lame drummer," Bethabara by a "no-account fellow," and the remaining settlements by "one and another." These usurpers believed they could succeed because of the assembly's act and because "the Moravians had not sworn allegiance to the land, so no one would listen to them if they complained."[23]

In August 1778, Wachovia dispatched Bagge and Jacob Blum to lobby the assembly in Hillsboro for an exemption from the provisions of these laws. The two Moravian emissaries offered a deal to benefit both sides: the brethren would pledge their loyalty to North Carolina, but the state would not force them to repudiate all allegiance to King George. Bagge and Blum stressed to the assembly that the Unity was a worldwide church and that its members would face charges of treason if the Unity transferred them to parts of the British Empire still under the rule of His Majesty. The assembly was not persuaded, but it did agree to postpone until January, when the assembly was to next meet, the requirement that the Moravians had to take oaths. When January came, Wachovia promptly dispatched two different emissaries to Hillsboro to plead anew the Moravian cause. This time, they succeeded: the assembly agreed to let the Moravians take an affirmation instead of a formal swearing to the new government that did not contain an explicit renunciation of the king. Equally important, the act exempted the brethren from military service and, in the words of the Salem Memorabilia, promised that "we should be left in the peaceful possession of our lands." Individual brethren called to serve, however, would have to pay triple taxes in lieu of military service.[24]

The compromise reached in Hillsboro gave the brethren some temporary respite from the incessant demands made earlier in the war. Recruiting parties had repeatedly entered Wachovia, especially in the *Landgemeinen,* whose society members were viewed as not being "real" Moravians. The complexities of

Count Nicholas von Zinzendorf's Diaspora with its varying degrees of membership were lost upon militia officers, who questioned why certain brethren deserved an exemption from service on religious grounds. The problem became even more complex when residency was taken into account; half of Hope's membership lived in Rowan County outside of Wachovia, and a significant number of members from Friedberg did so as well. Early in the war, for instance, a recruiting party expected those members of the Friedberg congregation who lived outside of Wachovia to serve in Surry County's militia, and they sent a scouting party to look for them. These misconceptions about the society movement forced members to prove that they were truly brethren. When Surry's recruiters rode into Friedberg, "Br. Pfaff and Martin Ebert came to me in great distress," Bachhof recalled in one typical incident, "and asked for a signed statement from me concerning their sons." Bachhof obliged the two worried fathers, drawing up a certificate that declared, "I, the undersigned, testify herewith that N—N—from childhood on has belonged to the Unity of Brethren, and is now a member of the Brethren's Society in Friedberg."[25]

American authorities questioned not only the validity of these brethrens' membership but also the motives of people who joined Moravian Societies during the war. Their suspicion was that such people were affiliating with the Unity not out of commitment to the Lord but to avoid military service. This suspicion only grew as the war dragged on and as it became harder to find able-bodied men willing to serve in the militia and army. As late as 1781, the Land Arbeiter Conferenz recognized that "to give our Certificates, and to receive many persons into our Societies, would look as though we were depriving the land of able soldiers." So the pastors from the country congregations agreed that "for the present there should be no receptions into the Societies . . . and no Certificates shall be given except in cases where the man behaves in all respects as a Brother and has paid the three-fold tax."[26] For a heart religion whose very raison d'etre was to bring converts to Christ, the temporary closing of societies to new members was an extraordinary act that revealed the tremendous pressures the Moravians were facing during the war. Residents of the *Landgemeinen* apparently understood the need for such a step. Friedberg's society had voluntarily undertaken equally drastic action a few months earlier, when the Haus Vaters Conferenz "agreed that no one should employ a doubtful, unknown, or drafted man, as it would injure the credit of our Society."[27]

At times, the North Carolina militia could be quite harsh in its demands for recruits. In July 1776, Colonel Martin Armstrong of Surry County "notified" the brethren that the commanding officer in Salisbury had ordered both the

Moravians and the Quakers to "send their proportionate number of men to take part in the expedition against the Indians, who had murdered white persons on Broad River, or provide substitutes, or pay a fine of 10 pounds for each." Armstrong "excused himself for bringing such a hard proposition" and urged the brethren to appeal directly to his commanding officer in Salisbury.[28]

These demands placed the brethren in a terrible bind—serve in the militia or face a heavy fine (they did not see sending a substitute as an option). Two days after Armstrong's appearance, members of Friedberg rode to Salem asking for advice. "They were told," the Salem diarist recounted, "that if they wished to claim the exemption from military service as Brethren they must be prepared cheerfully to put their faith in the Savior, and to bear whatever they might have to suffer."[29] Most members decided to follow this advice, but several from Friedberg and Friedland opted to attend muster. A few days later, militia officers ordered "all the young men at Friedland" to march. Recruiting parties also went to Bethania and Friedberg, taking those young men who seemed to be willing to serve—three from Bethania and the sons of three families from Friedberg. Salem's diarist dismissed the three from Bethania as "entirely worldly-minded" who were lukewarm followers of Jesus.[30]

Ethnicity was not an accurate barometer of Moravian support for the war; nor was religious commitment. One would have expected Anglo-American brethren in Hope to be more willing to support the American cause than, say, German-speaking Moravians in Bethabara. That was not the case. In Hope, Anglo-Americans wanted little to do with the war. Their Brotherly Agreement, adopted in 1780, even codified this pacifism: "Whereby Grace we are Children of peace, we will follow peace with all men. We will in no way entangle ourselves into political affairs or disputes, but if God should suffer any to happen, we will conduct ourselves as orderly, still, and quiet Citizens ought."[31] Hope's settlers had developed a strong Moravian identity following their years in Maryland, where they built a successful Moravian congregation. As in the other two *Landgemeinen*, Hope throughout the 1770s was absorbed in the task of building a new congregation in North Carolina. Along with Friedland, Hope was awarded congregation status during the middle of the war—a joyous and triumphant time for both young settlements.

Possibly because of their Anglo-American backgrounds, these Moravians, including Daniel Smith, the leader of the Maryland expatriates, faced sharp questions from American forces about their reasons for not enlisting and more actively supporting the Revolution. Smith had an answer for them in the winter months of 1776, when a party of militia entered Hope and confiscated members' guns and powder, according to the account of the Salem diarist: "He would do nothing against the liberty of the Land . . . [but also] declared himself a Brother."[32] When proving their pacifist leanings involved surrendering valuable weapons needed for hunting, Hope's members apparently did not hesitate, as another incident in February 1776 showed. "Our English members, living on Middle Fork and on Muddy Creek, were called to meet at the home of Valentine Frey, where Capt. Folbs and his Company were gathered, there to sign the test [oath] and give up their arms," pastor Bachhof recorded. "They obeyed the order." Folbs and his men moved on to Friedberg, where they helped themselves to more muskets. Unlike in Hope, these German-speaking Moravians were not very happy about the confiscations. Bachhof visited Christian and George Frey four days later and found them "still grieving over the loss of their guns."[33]

Hope's inhabitants remained so aloof from the war that their settlement earned a reputation as a bastion of loyalism. In one incident, members of the "English settlement" found themselves before two justices defending their loyalty to the new nation "because of things said against the cause of Liberty."[34] In another incident, in 1780, a company of light horse seized cattle "from persons [in Hope] whom they suspected of being Tories." The cattle were returned—but not because their owners' loyalty to the American cause was proved, but because the troops had acted on their own initiative, "without order."[35] Whatever the political leanings of its members, this Anglo-American settlement clearly did its best to keep its distance from the war. Settlers there were among the most pacifist in Wachovia, wanting to be left alone so they could practice their religion in peace. Indeed, William Barton Peddycoard went so far as to move back to Maryland in late 1780, "as he is disturbed over the question of military service." He did not return to North Carolina until he felt safe.[36] By contrast, some German speakers in the *Landgemeinen* could be quite enthusiastic in their support of the American cause. For instance, George Frey, a German-speaking member of Friedberg, returned home from Salisbury after meeting with Colonel Armstrong, grabbed his gun, and told his wife, "I must go; I am a *Liberty Man.*"[37]

German-speaking Bethania, to the discomfort of Wachovia's leadership, had the reputation of being the most ardent supporter of the Revolution. Bishop Johann Friedrich Reichel, for one, complained in 1781 that Bethanians had "really declared themselves for Americans too loudly."[38] Unlike in the *Landgemeinen,* many in Bethania were willing to attend muster, although their reasons for doing so were more complex than the leadership realized. As

Traugott Bagge observed, "Many residents, including older Brethren, went to Muster and to Drill, though for no better reason than to avoid trouble." Considering Bethanians' rebellious ways, enthusiasm for liberty may not be so surprising. But Bethabara's support was. This village was the former capital of Wachovia and was among the most devout and insular of settlements. Yet, in 1777, Bagge lumped this *Ortgemeine* with its more unruly neighbor to the immediate south: "Many in Bethabara and most of those in Bethania embraced the cause of Liberty," he noted.[39]

Ironically, the never-ending demands to serve in the militia and to supply food, shoes, clothing, and guns helped to heighten Moravian identification with the American cause. Revolutionary forces repeatedly entered Wachovia throughout the war seeking supplies for their troops because of the community's reputation as prosperous. In the agricultural settlements of Friedland, Friedberg, and Hope, farmers regularly supplied the militia and army with cattle, grain, and other supplies, albeit not always willingly.[40] The heaviest demands for help came in 1780 and 1781, when fighting between the main armies moved dangerously close to Wachovia. In early February 1781, British General Charles Cornwallis and his troops spent two days in the Moravian community. His lordship was not in a good mood during his brief visit. Things had been going badly for his forces following their destruction of an American army commanded by General Horatio Gates at Camden, South Carolina, in mid-August 1780. In that stirring victory for British arms, Cornwallis's army had captured a thousand Americans and killed and wounded another eight hundred. Buoyed by this success, Cornwallis decided to move into North Carolina in September, where he would march to Hillsboro and issue a proclamation calling on all loyal citizens to rally to the king's cause. But he got only as far as Charlotte because of illness among his troops and raids by rebel partisans that disrupted his supply lines and made life miserable for his soldiers. In an attempt to quiet the backcountry and relieve pressure on the main army, Cornwallis ordered Patrick Ferguson and his Tory militia to peel off and pacify western North Carolina. A confident (and overly brash) Ferguson warned patriot forces to cease their raiding or face destruction of their country by "fire and sword." His proclamation only succeeded in stirring up even more hostility toward the British. A thousand frontiersmen gathered at Sycamore Shoals in late September and set off to meet Ferguson and his Tories. On October 7, the two forces met at King's Mountain; in just over an hour, Ferguson had lost the battle and his life.[41]

For the Moravians, the repercussions following the battle of King's Mountain were nearly immediate. American troops seeking badly needed supplies were the first to arrive in Wachovia, and their presence forced the brethren to feed six hundred hungry soldiers and nearly three hundred prisoners of war.[42] Cavalry camped at the tavern meadow and split up into small parties to "scour the surrounding country for grain and cattle for General Sumner; he and his men are in Mecklenburg County, and are in great need of food." A few days later, a company of soldiers marched through Friedland, where they ordered a supply of grain. To their disappointment, though, the officers "found that not as much can be secured in this district as Captain Paschke had led them to expect. Apparently, Captain Paschke had intended to bring General Gates' army here, but Colonel Armstrong will try to prevent this." Bethabara was forced to host a large contingent of troops and bore the brunt of the soldiers' misbehavior. As the Salem diarist reported, "There is much distress in Bethabara, for 300 soldiers from Virginia are there, who have camped in the orchard, where they do as they please."[43]

Cornwallis, meanwhile, had decided after Ferguson's defeat to return to the supposed safety of South Carolina, and his troops began their retreat from North Carolina on October 14. The general, however, found things no pleasanter in South Carolina, a state he had supposedly subdued with the capture of Charleston and the rout of General Gates at Camden. Francis Marion, Thomas Sumter, and other partisans were successfully harassing the British and disrupting their vulnerable supply lines. While Cornwallis was trying to figure out what to do next, Nathanael Greene, Gates's replacement as commanding general in the southern theater, made a decision that would eventually lead to more trouble for the Moravians in North Carolina: he divided his small army and sent Daniel Morgan and his cavalry westward to South Carolina. When British forces under Lt. Col. Banastre Tarleton gave chase and were badly mauled at Cowpens, South Carolina, on January 17, 1781, an angry Cornwallis bent on revenge followed Morgan into North Carolina in hopes of defeating the American commander and freeing the 525 British prisoners he had taken.

Thus, Bethanians found themselves face-to-face with a polite but unhappy Lord Cornwallis on a rainy February day in 1781. The general was in the midst of chasing Morgan and was having no luck capturing the elusive American officer. Equally frustrating was the fact that Cornwallis had burned most of his supply wagons in an attempt to turn his plodding army into something more mobile.[44] Tired, cold, and hungry British soldiers camped at Bethania the night of February 9 and at Friedland on the 10th. Cornwallis's officers, meanwhile, warmed themselves in village houses. Fearing the approach of Cornwallis's

British forces under the command of General Cornwallis camped in Friedland on February 10, 1781. In desperate need of food and other supplies, both sides targeted the farms of the *Landgemeinen* throughout the war. *Courtesy of Old Salem Inc., Winston-Salem, North Carolina.*

army, the brethren had sent two emissaries to General Greene asking for protection. But the American commander was in no position to help. Greene was struggling with immense problems of his own and was helpless to halt Cornwallis's advance into North Carolina. Greene, as a result, could not even offer the brethren encouragement, telling the two emissaries that "he could not protect us, as the English must already be in our towns."[45]

During their mercifully short two-day stay in Wachovia, the British soldiers took what they wanted. Their most pressing need was for food, and they seized meal, cattle, sheep, geese, and chickens. Bethania's losses—in cattle, grain, hay, brandy, and destroyed property, including fencing—totaled as much as fifteen hundred pounds. Cornwallis's men treated the brethren quite imperiously. They singled out several brethren from Friedberg and arrested them on "the charge that they were enemies of the country." In Bethania, the congregation received a "sharp order": the village had to supply twenty good horses by 6:00 p.m. or face an unspecified penalty. "Everything was in the greatest confusion and no one knew what to do," Bethania's pastor recalled. "Between eight and nine o'clock we made an attempt to explain to General Cornwallis that it was impossible to furnish twenty horses; he was not at all moved. . . . I had hardly reached the house when an officer arrived to seize me as hostage until the horses were furnished, but the officers lodging with me interfered, and he went away without me."[46]

Camp followers caused as much trouble as the British troops themselves. "The people who followed the baggage stole various things at the store and in the houses," Salem's diary reported, "for example, the Single Brethren lost all their wash, Br. Meyer lost nine head of cattle, Br. Bonn lost 40 pounds." With relief on the brethrens' part, Cornwallis marched away on the eleventh. But no sooner had he left than an American lieutenant informed the Moravians that "tomorrow an [American] army of fifteen to eighteen hundred would come from the Shallowford, which led to planning for their needs."[47] The Americans were as good as their word. On February 16, troops began arriving in Wachovia, and the whole cycle repeated itself. The officers, described by their hosts as "very polite," did all they could to keep things under control. A Presbyterian minister accompanying the officers also vowed to help: "If any one made a disturbance during the night he and the officers would stand by us." Despite these pledges, unruly soldiers proceeded to wreak havoc over the next few days, looting Salem's store, starting fights in Salem's tavern, and threatening to burn the town. The mayhem peaked on February 17—a "hard day" where "the powers of darkness made themselves felt." Roving soldiers accosted brethren in the streets and took what they pleased. "Hardly one house remained unrobbed," Salem's diarist complained. The disruption was so great that the congregation could not hold Sunday services on February 18.[48]

The Rise of Nationalism during the Revolution

The constant harassment and demands for help involved the brethren in the war in a very real way. Church members nursed the wounded and buried the dead; congregation members drove off thieves who broke into their houses; and farmers turned over the fruits of their labors to hungry soldiers.[49] These trials destroyed the passivity that Moravians had felt in 1775 and 1776. With soldiers constantly entering Wachovia, remaining aloof was impossible. The brethren became participants in the Revolution whether they liked it or not. Because of these hardships, the Moravians came to understand that they were part of a larger cause and that they were helping fellow Americans involved in a bloody but important business.

Bonds of affection did develop between the two sides despite the militia's unruly behavior. In 1776, for instance, Adam Spach and Peter Pfaff carried Friedberg's declaration of support to a Captain Macay "who took it very well." He accepted the petition and told the two brethren that he was "glad to find your kind and friendly Disposition, and your kind Wishes for the Welfare of the Country. You may rest assured, that I mean not to disturb you, nor Other Persons, that behave peaceable."[50] Sympathetic officers and soldiers alike repeatedly pledged to protect Wachovia from looters and mischievous soldiers. Although far from successful, they did help to minimize the damage inflicted on Wachovia. Seeing this religious community up close, many visitors came to admire the Moravian movement and all it had built since 1753. That admiration included an appreciation for evangelical religion. Soldiers frequently asked to attend worship services, out of both curiosity and a need to visit a house of God amid the carnage of war. In spring 1779, cavalry from Pulaski's Legion spent four days in Wachovia, typically needing lodging and food from the brethren. But "the good feature of this," Salem's Memorabilia noted, "was that they behaved well, most of them came every day to preaching, and in the end they paid for all the supplies furnished. When they left they could not say enough concerning their appreciation of the care which had been given them." A year later, Bethabara's congregation diary recounted the visit of a company of soldiers. These men "remained over night. In the evening we sang: 'Oh Head so full of bruises:' and the soldiers were attentive and quiet."[51] The affection ran both ways. The brethren modified their litanies to include expressions of well-being for the "welfare of the land where Thou has placed us." On a Sunday in 1777, Salem's congregation concluded its service with "a prayer . . . for this land, for its rulers and its people, and they were commended to the mercy of God."[52] Out of such acts was a sense of nationalism born.

The war boosted a sense of Americanness in other ways. It not only increased contact with Americans of all stripes—from assemblymen on down to common soldiers—but also disrupted communications with the main seat of the Moravian Church in Herrnhut. For several years in the mid- and late 1770s, North Carolina's Moravians were pretty much on their own, unable to send mail to brethren in Germany or receive packets from them. For the brethren in North Carolina, this isolation only increased the feeling that their fate rested with their countrymen in the newly declared United States.[53] Another basic— but extremely important—consequence of the Revolution was that the war ended British rule and left Wachovia's inhabitants as American citizens. No longer were they subjects in His Majesty's realm. North Carolina's Moravians were now republicans in a democratic regime. The transition from "subject" to "citizen" was not at all passive. The creation of a republic led to the brethren becoming far more involved in the political process, and this involvement only increased their sense of identity as "Americans."

Before the Revolution, Wachovia's leadership espoused an Old World view of politics. Politics was to be avoided as much as possible because it risked entangling Wachovia in the corrupt affairs of the world. When involvement was unavoidable, it was best to limit that contact as much as possible by designating a few brethren to deal with the political system. This meant in practice that the leadership wanted to keep individual brethren as far as possible from the corrupting influence of elections and electioneering. The reason was simple: elections were a dirty business that the Lord's people had best avoid. Wachovia administrator Frederick Marshall put it well. "The natural consequence of republican elections is that people interested in office must stand for it long in advance. That creates parties and counter-cabals which in consideration for expected support from one another become blind to all others and seek only to accomplish their [own] affairs."[54] Politics bred factionalism, and factionalism bred individualism. Moreover, Moravian leaders viewed with horror the raucous behavior that surrounded the election itself. Drinking, fighting, merrymaking—such mayhem was all part of election day in both the colonial and early national periods. To avoid these horrors, the leadership before the Revolution selected brethren to go to the polls with proxy votes for the rest of Wachovia. Proxy voting was very un-American, of course. Democratic elections rested on the premise that voters were acting independently of the church, the gentry, or whoever was the controlling influence in the community. Indeed, such a premise was behind the requirement that only freeholders were eligible to vote. To be a truly fair and free election, a voter had to be beholden to no one. The German-based Moravian movement operated from a very different premise. The individual's will was not important; the Savior's was, as expressed through the community. Proxy voting thus had two related goals—to keep individual brethren far from the sordid world of politics and to ensure that the community spoke with one voice that would best defend Moravian interests.

To further these goals, Wachovia's leaders in the 1750s sought parish status for their community. Under a 1741 law, Anglican parishes in North Carolina enjoyed the right to appoint ministers, pay their salaries, construct chapels, levy poll taxes, and collect the money. Parish status would give Wachovia greater flexibility in organizing its affairs while minimizing the control that outside political authorities could exercise in Wachovia. Poor relief, for instance, would now be a Moravian responsibility, and Moravians would fill parish offices. Equally important, the church—and not outsiders—would control the elections for these parish offices. All of these goals were fulfilled in October 1755, when North Carolina established Dobbs Parish and made its boundaries roughly equal to Wachovia's. North Carolina authorities, of course, expected the parish to be nominally Anglican and overseen by an Anglican minister, although they well understood that the Moravians would be establishing a parallel system within its borders. The brethren, however, had other ideas. As historian Daniel B. Thorp concludes about the affair, "Dobbs Parish was a fraud designed to serve the needs of the Unity. Its vestry contained no Anglicans; its minister was a Moravian; and decisions affecting it were actually made by leaders of the Moravian Church."[55]

Dobbs Parish was also something else. It represented an anachronistic system of governing that would not survive the American Revolution. For the Unity, the parish concept was predicated on the idea that the church would enjoy significant control over members' political lives. The parish, in other words, would enable the Unity to limit the brethrens' contact with the outside political system. In 1778, however, North Carolina's assembly abolished all parishes and reorganized the state's counties. Under this reorganization, it placed Wachovia in Surry County, whose seat was a town called Richmond. Because of changing times, Wachovia's leadership well understood what was happening and was powerless to stop it; as a church document drawn up during the war succinctly put it, "During this year all Parishes were abolished, for no denomination was to rank above another, and so our Dobbs Parish came to an end."[56]

Gradually, so did the idea of proxy voting. In Wachovia, the act of casting a ballot was becoming an individual's decision. The demise of Dobbs Parish gave a push to this very American idea, and so did the rhetoric of the Revolutionary War. The effort to establish America's independence raised all kinds of momentous issues that required the input of voters at the ballot box, from electing delegates to the Continental Congress to deciding who should serve as captain in the local militia. With elections continually being held, and with democracy gaining in practice and in spirit, brethren throughout Wachovia began going to the polls to see how it all worked. In 1776, for instance, a Heinrich Schmidt was elected captain in the Surry militia. "Many of the young people" in Wachovia, Traugott Bagge reported, "attended the Election out of curiosity, and gave in their votes."[57] County officials did all they could to encourage Moravian participation, placing ads throughout Wachovia announcing the holding of elections and asking the brethren to attend. "The sheriff posted an

Advertisement on our taverns here and in Bethabara," the Salem Diary noted on one such occasion, "announcing that on the 10th of this month an Election will be held at Richmond for a Senator and two Representatives to the Assembly. All Freeholders, and all who have made Improvements on vacant land, are called to attend."[58] These notices helped increase awareness of events outside Wachovia's borders and helped to pique the brethrens' interest in elections. So did the steady stream of voters passing through Wachovia on the way to the courthouse to vote. One election in mid-October 1776 was typical: "Yesterday and today many were here, on their way to the Election at Richmond town," Bethania's diarist recorded. "Some of our people rode with them."[59] Less-stringent voting requirements also encouraged more brethren to participate. Pre-1775 laws restricted voting to freeholders, which effectively disbarred many brethren living in the congregation towns because they did not own any property. After 1775, North Carolina allowed householders to vote, thus widening suffrage and enabling more brethren to vote.

In the charged times of the American Revolution, voting itself became an act of political significance: to vote in a local election was seen as an act of allegiance to the new nation. Revolutionaries expected the Moravians to cast ballots as a show of support for the governments then forming, and the 1777 law passed by the assembly specifically linked citizenship and the oath of allegiance. Moreover, to vote in a militia election had some direct consequences—the voter became eligible for muster. Indeed, authorities saw voting and mustering as closely related. Voting in elections, serving in the militia, and observing days of prayer for the troops in the field were all part of being a good republican citizen. An incident in March 1777 showed just how direct the connection could be: the sheriff informed Wachovia's inhabitants that Surry County would be observing a day of humiliation and prayer while holding an election and a militia muster. "Many of our neighborhood rode through on their way to Richmond, partly to the Election and partly to Muster," Salem's diary said. "The sheriff issued a Proclamation, ordering all who were in hiding, and all who have shown themselves to be active Tories, to come forthwith and take the Oath of Allegiance to the Commonwealth."[60] This linking of voting and mustering, of course, did much to temper Moravian enthusiasm for participating in elections. If voting meant mustering, many brethren sat out the election. Despite all that, proxy voting did wither throughout most of Wachovia. The demise of Dobbs Parish and the great issues raised by the Revolution served to heighten political awareness among the brethren. They watched the electioneering around them closely and were often swept up in the excitement. Repeatedly, members watched voters pass through their settlements on the way to an election and decided to ride along.[61]

There was one significant holdout to this more open political system: the Salem leadership. It remained reluctant to get involved in political affairs, and it still preferred that the Salem congregation follow proxy voting. The Salem Diary noted that in 1776, the congregation stayed out of Richmond during the election of delegates to Congress because it had "decided not to meddle with any political matters."[62] When the time came to vote for a new assembly in 1780, the Aufseher Collegium met to discuss the election. "Certain brethren were selected," the Salem Diary recalled, "who will cast their votes for those candidates who are opposed to the division of our County."[63] Thus, the collegium expected a few brethren to act on behalf of the congregation, and it instructed them to cast votes for those candidates who would best represent Moravian interests. Understandably, Wachovia's leaders sought to elect candidates who had defended the brethren during these dark times. Colonel Martin Armstrong was one such candidate who drew the thanks—and support—of the Moravian leadership. Salem's Congregation Council agreed that, with the election coming next week, "it will be well for the Brethren to arrange that some of them go to Richmond on Monday and some on Tuesday to cast their votes. Colonel Armstrong is our choice as Senator, and Br. Bagge and Colonel Martin as Burgesses."[64]

Still, proxy voting was becoming anachronistic, and Salem's leadership slowly recognized that. Not only outside trends undermined it, however; inside ones did, too. The leadership tried to influence voters in the *Landgemeinen,* but it could not dictate who could vote or how. The contrast with Salem was startling. While the Congregation Council was arranging to send selected brethren to Richmond to vote for Armstrong and other favored candidates in the election of fall 1783, the Land Arbeiter Conferenz could merely "urge" its "brethren in the country congregations . . . to go to the election and cast their votes for members of the Assembly who will be of real service to the public."[65] As in so many other things, members of the *Landgemeinen* were accorded far greater freedom in voting than their counterparts in the congregation towns. And as in so many other things, this freedom set a precedent that eventually spread to the *Ortsgemeinen.* The existence of American "freedoms" in the *Landgemeinen* meant that proxy voting would not last much longer in the three congregation towns. By the end of the war, the Salem Diary could report, "Many of our Brethren went from our three towns to cast their vote" in the assembly election. The diarist still found the whole thing distasteful—the act of voting "was made dangerous by the terrible commotion caused by the rough element, inflamed by strong drink"—but the importance of voting overcame this fear of democracy's ugly side.[66]

The demise of proxy voting was a less-than-subtle blow to the older notion of communal brotherhood. No longer would brethren vote as a bloc but as individuals. It also weakened the church's hold over members' political lives by giving individual members a greater say in their own daily affairs. Finally, individual voting meant that the brethren were becoming more involved in local politics. They attended elections, observed the fierce campaigning that could precede them, and directly participated through the act of voting. All of this increased their contact, and identification, with the young American nation.

The Cultural Impact of War

It was no surprise that war's rough ways pulled North Carolina's Moravians into a sense of oneness with other Americans. The never-ending demands of war meant that the brethren were forced to participate in American affairs, both as suppliers of the army and as voters at the polls. Nationalism, as a result, grew alongside the demands of war. But cultural changes occurring at the community level aided this process in important ways. Religion did, too. The creation of creole families, along with the spread of evangelical values, influenced greatly the views of English and German speakers during the Revolutionary period. Cultural intermixing and latent tendencies within evangelical religion made the brethren far more receptive to American values and the political changes that the Revolution was unleashing throughout North Carolina and the other former colonies.

This receptivity to American values can be seen most clearly in Wachovia's embracing of American "freedoms." As the research of historian Elisabeth Sommer has shown, Moravians in Saxony had a very different view of order and freedom than did their counterparts in America. Saxony Moravians were products of a society that emphasized order, with "freedom" representing obedience to paternalistic authority. These Moravians also exhibited evidence of a second Germanic tradition, usually found within southwest Germany, in which inhabitants associated freedom with the absence of constraint and in which they were far more suspicious of authority. German Moravians absorbed both these traditions, Sommer has found: they accepted the traditional German view of feudal society that offered protection to its members, and they held a paternalistic view of authority. Their ultimate ruler, though, was not a prince but Jesus

Christ. The Saxony-based Unity, as a result, expected members "to submit freely to the government of the Savior and to subordinate their self-will to the good of the whole," in Sommer's words. German Moravians thus came to hold an essentially paternalistic view of authority. Christ would oversee their spiritual lives and communities, and a benevolent secular authority would guard their secular affairs.[67]

The implications of this paternalistic view of authority were readily apparent in Germany. Herrnhut, the spiritual center of Moravianism, reflected the severe gradations in German society that saw a nobility at the top of the social pyramid and a large mass of commoners at the bottom. Nobles constituted an important part of the Moravian membership in Germany, beginning with Count Zinzendorf himself, and these nobles continued to enjoy the trappings of their power despite having joined a movement that stressed the spiritual equality of the saved. Herrnhut, as a result, came to convey a sense of order and hierarchy, with members subscribing to a list of ordinances that was twice as long as Salem's. Although German Moravians did periodically challenge authority in the tradition of southwest Germany, Sommer concludes that they did not do it in the direct manner that American brethren did. That is, German brethren challenged authority by pleading ignorance, shirking their duties, or resorting to anonymous satire.[68]

North Carolina's Moravians, by contrast, lived in a British-dominated society with a long tradition of defying authority. As Gordon Wood has noted, "Liberty, insubordination, and unwillingness to truckle to any authority were what distinguished Englishmen from Frenchmen and all the other enslaved and deprived peoples of the world."[69] Such distant events as the Glorious Revolution remained part of the cultural memory, but so did more recent uprisings, such as the Regulator Movement in the Carolinas. The open challenge of Parliament over taxes and political sovereignty in the mid- and late eighteenth century only intensified this ingrained English willingness to challenge one's superiors. The Revolutionary period gave a significant boost to democratic forces throughout American society, from the ruling assemblies that seized power from the executive branch and declared themselves the voice of the people, on down to the yeoman farmer who now believed he was the political equal of any member of the gentry.[70]

Individual brethren in North Carolina were attuned to this rising democratization for two reasons. One was their extensive contact with Americans and American authorities during the Revolution. The war brought a never-ending parade of visitors and soldiers to Wachovia. The brethren met and mingled with these visitors in church, at taverns, in houses and farm fields, and at musters. Because outsiders were so uncertain of Wachovia's loyalties, these encounters involved a good deal of political discussion and give-and-take by both sides. Such contact, moreover, was not fleeting. The war lasted seven long, wearying years, and Wachovia was rarely free of the demands of outsiders. Even after Cornwallis's surrender at Yorktown in late 1781, Wachovia could be found debating, and struggling with, war-related issues. This prolonged contact with Americans and their Revolution helped spur Americanization by increasing the brethrens' knowledge of American ways, beliefs, and values.

The second reason was the acculturation process within Wachovia. It facilitated the spread of American values because it created families that melded American and German ways. Culturally, as chapter 3 showed, such a melding meant that there was a meeting in the middle in families' approaches to inheritance, treatment of sons, and landholding. For German-speaking Moravians, intermarriage with Anglo-Americans exposed them to American ways. And this exposure gave them a unique perspective as the Revolution unfolded around them. The creolization of German and Anglo-American made German speakers more likely to embrace American ways. In short, the blending of families allowed American values—that is, an appreciation for American-style freedoms—to gain ground. Historians have long identified the generational aspect as a key to the assimilation of German-speaking brethren in America: Moravian youths born in America were more receptive to American freedoms and ways than their elders.[71] This generational model, however, misses the complexity of what was really happening. Intermixing, and specifically the creation of Anglo-German families, enabled the values of a newly born republic to take root in this religious colony. As early as 1780, Moravian families were showing blends of American and German culture. English married German with increasing frequency after 1770. Even when German married German, such families were in close contact with their English-speaking brethren in Wachovia. The offspring of these all-German unions were born into a multilingual and a multiethnic society that found common ground not on a sense of ethnic peoplehood, but on the new birth and heart religion. Even in the congregation towns, Moravian youths often spoke English, sometimes had English mothers, and came of age during the excitement of the Revolutionary period when a new nation was forming. It was a short and easy step for them to absorb the values of their American brethren and neighbors.

The process of Americanization proceeded the fastest in the *Landgemeinen,* where intermixing was the most extensive and was taking place the earliest.

Settlers there had spent long years in Maryland and the northern colonies, and the acculturation process that saw them become Moravian and American had begun during that period. These Moravians then came south, to North Carolina, where the acculturation process accelerated. Their absorption of American ways was so deep and rapid that it worried the governing board that oversaw the *Landgemeinen*. As the Land Arbeiter Conferenz put it in November 1780 at one of its first meetings, "Members are beginning to feel the spirit of freedom in the land, and to think that as soon as the children attain their majority they are at liberty to do as they please." From the board's perspective, this love of freedom meant that young people in the *Landgemeinen* were doing as they pleased and were too readily engaging in the "worldly excesses" and unruly behavior of their American neighbors.[72]

The board's pastors had identified something very important—the Revolution and its spirit of freedom had rather easily pervaded the three country congregations. The board intuitively understood that the family was playing a critical role in the spread of American values. Creating creole families meant creating families that were becoming more "American," and more "American" during the Revolutionary period meant that families were placing more emphasis on the rights of the young. Youths sought, and parents granted, greater control of their lives, and at an earlier age, as the father's hold over the family loosened.[73] Patriarchy within the family, in other words, was weakening. In this Revolutionary age, youths in the *Landgemeinen* wanted the same freedoms as other Americans because they increasingly saw themselves as Americans, not as Germans. To counter this development, the pastors during the Revolution and beyond preached to parents that they must raise sons and daughters committed to heart religion. The advice of Wachovia administrator C. L. Benzien to Friedberg's parents in 1805 was typical. Benzien was alarmed that many in Friedberg were participating in "worldly merrymakings," and he "urged all true-hearted fathers and mothers to hold fast to the desire to live to the Savior and not to the world, and by the grace of Jesus to rule their families in godliness, and not allow anything to creep in among us which would bring discredit to the name of Jesus." An incident a few weeks later was typical of the type of behavior that so worried the leadership—a congregation member had "allowed a traveling showman to use his house on assurances that the show contained nothing objectionable." The hapless brother "went to bed and learned that they were preparing to dance"—immoral behavior that the brother sternly stopped. Here, two decades after the Revolution, was the classic statement of Moravian views toward the family—the parents were to oversee the little church of Jesus, rejecting all worldly enticements and freedoms within their households. Fathers and mothers were the rulers in their families, and they alone had the authority to keep their offspring in line. When members of the household slipped and engaged in "merrymaking," the Moravian leadership held parents responsible.[74] In 1780, the Land Arbeiter Conferenz put it bluntly: "A house-father is responsible for all that goes on in his house, and nothing should be done without his approval."[75]

The pastors, though, saw the family as only one defense in the battle against American freedoms. They also emphasized proper brotherly conduct and the role of schools in educating the young. The three country congregations received their Brotherly Agreements in 1780 as the Revolution wound down, and members were required to sign these strict codes of conduct after the rules were carefully explained to them. These agreements specifically targeted offensive "American" behavior, from rowdy cornhuskings to dancing and merrymaking. The documents tried to instill in members the need to put Jesus and the church first and individualism and freedom second. There were many reasons for implementing these Brotherly Agreements, but pastors likely saw them as vital to their efforts to restrain encroaching American freedoms. In Friedberg's case, for instance, the Land Arbeiter Conferenz wanted an agreement reached there as soon as possible because "this would serve as a foundation for the better administration of discipline."[76]

Schools in the *Landgemeinen* were to supplement the efforts of parents and the Brotherly Agreements. Within the classroom, children were to learn the tenets of heart religion and the all-important role of Jesus Christ. As Christmas approached one year, for instance, Friedberg's pastor used the occasion to explain to "the schoolchildren . . . what the Savior did for us, and what moved Him to become a man, that he might lead us out of the misery into which sin had brought us. . . . They listened attentively, and one said of his own free will: 'I will love the dear Savior,' to which most of the others agreed."[77] Such instruction, the pastors hoped, would instill in youths the desire to become good Christians who would have the fortitude to avoid the worldly ways of their American neighbors.

The "spirit of freedom in the land" could be found in the *Ortsgemeinen,* too. There, youths were showing a streak of rebelliousness and individuality that in some ways surpassed that of their brethren in the *Landgemeinen.* After all, in the more closely regulated *Ortsgemeine,* young Moravians had far more to rebel against than did those brethren living in the more relaxed *Landgemeine.* Sommer documents two distinct phases of this rebelliousness in Salem—the first occurred in the late 1770s and early 1780s, and a second took place in the late 1780s and mid-1790s. In both periods, discipline problems worsened and the leadership fretted that devotion to the Savior was waning. Sommer attributes the problems in the first period to the Revolution itself: the presence of soldiers fascinated Salem's youths and led them to engage in less-than-brotherly behavior.[78]

Because of extensive intermixing, American ways penetrated deeply in the *Ortsgemeinen* and involved far more than misbehavior by the young. The attitudes of the *Landgemeinen* and the outside were seeping into every corner of the *Ortsgemeinen,* from views toward individualism to attitudes toward work. The career of master craftsman Johann Gottlob Krause demonstrates the unusual ways that American values infected the communal society of Salem. Raised in the nurturing atmosphere of a congregation town, Krause was the product of a complex ethnic environment within Wachovia: he was born in Bethabara in 1760 to two native German Moravians, Matthias and Christina Krause, who were originally from the Moravian settlement of Herrnhaag. Gottlob never got to know his mother—she died in 1761, when he was only a year old. His father died a year later, in 1762. Thus, the church literally became his family, with the Bethabara congregation raising him during his first decade of life. At age eleven, Krause went to live with Gottfried Aust, Salem's master potter. At this point, Krause's life appeared fairly typical, despite the loss of his parents. He was raised in the church and was learning a trade in a congregation town. Soon, he would take his place in the church as an adult member and in the shop as a craftsman. Countless other Moravian youths had followed the same path.[79]

Krause's skills were anything but ordinary, however. The Revolutionary period exposed him to all things American and gave him the opportunity to express his individuality in imaginative ways. In 1777, a glimpse of his playful rebelliousness could be found: it was a period when Wachovia's leadership was advising the brethren to stay quiet on all things political. Relations between Tories and Liberty Men were also "very hot," with Tory sympathizers taunting an American recruiting officer at Salem's tavern with shouts of "King George, hurrah!" During this tense time, Krause and another boy were found shouting "very loudly, the one: 'Hurrah, King George!' and the other: 'Washington'!" The Aufseher Collegium was not amused by the prank; it rebuked Krause and the other boy.[80]

It was through his work that Krause most absorbed outside "American" ways and came to show his fiercest independence. At Aust's shop, Krause observed the delicate and difficult task of making Queensware, an elegant china developed in England and named in honor of Queen Charlotte. Cream colored and rococo in design, Queensware required a great deal of skill to make. Aust learned this skill through a Charleston potter who came to Salem in 1771. Two years later, another outside potter came to town to help Aust build an experimental kiln and to teach them the complexities of making Queensware. During his apprenticeship, Krause learned all aspects of the pottery trade, from the tedious task of digging up clay to the intricacies of burning and molding the clay into cups, bowls, and plates. Unhappy with Aust's stern ways and difficult personality, Krause asked to learn another trade—masonry. His request was granted.[81]

Krause's brickwork became his symbolic declaration of independence. In the Revolutionary period, he built some of Salem's finest buildings that remain admired and studied today. Krause was the first craftsman in Salem to act as a contractor overseeing all aspects of a building project. He used this power to pursue highly flamboyant—and Americanized—brickwork. Moravian values discouraged ostentation in architecture. Houses and churches were to be handsome but functional. Moravian leaders dismissed elaborate brickwork and other decorative architectural elements as excessive and worldly. They wanted architecture to enhance the worship of their Savior, not to detract from it. Krause, the rebellious youth who had shouted his support for the American Revolution, had his own ideas. Drawing on techniques used extensively by outsiders, he introduced Flemish bond brickwork to Salem and went a step further, using glazed headers to form herringbone and diamond-shaped patterns on the gable ends of the buildings he constructed in the postwar period. His most impressive creation was the house he built for Christoph Vogler on Salem's Main Street in 1797. The house retained some elements of early German architecture—an unbalanced front façade and steep pitched roof, for example. But Krause put his own stamp on what would have been an ordinary house built for a Moravian gunmaker. With great skill, Krause, the master mason, used darkened headers to form elaborate herringbone patterns that dominated both the north and south gables. He also placed rubbed brick arches over the windows and doors. Krause apparently was so pleased with the quality of his work and these decorative effects that he inscribed his initials in yard-high letters on the south gable using darkened headers in the shape of "JGK." Through these glazed headers, Krause was practically shouting his disdain of the more staid ways of the brethren.[82]

His artistic brickwork, imaginative and richly executed, was a radical depar-

Johann Gottlob Krause built this house on Salem's Main Street in 1797 for Christoph Vogler. The house blended German and American elements. *Courtesy of Old Salem Inc., Winston-Salem, North Carolina.*

ture from Moravian norms, which emphasized simplicity and functionality. In building houses for Christoph Vogler, Samuel Vogler, and others, Krause was expressing his individuality and appreciation of American ways. Equally significant, the church chronicler of Krause's life never mentioned his great skill as a master craftsman nor his importance to Salem's architectural history. His flamboyance possibly remained too controversial in 1802, when Krause died. He or she did allude to Krause's independent ways, saying that throughout his life, "his walk was changeable." Krause *was* a devout brother; that same chronicler noted that "it was very meaningful and important to him to belong to God's people." His "changeable" ways, however, meant that he liked to follow his own inclinations in most things.[83] This feistiness included the freedom to pursue the craft of his choosing. In the mid-1780s, Krause sought to quit his masonry business in Salem and return to Bethabara as a potter. The leadership objected to Krause's plans on practical grounds—Krause's skills as a mason and builder were badly needed in the growing capital of Salem. The congregation's elders "admonished" him that, "since he has invested so much in his brick manufactory," Krause was better off staying put instead of "setting up a pottery in Bethabara." But the elders also objected because of Krause's explicit challenge to their authority, which they saw as an embracing of American liberty. In discussing Krause's and another brother's case, the Elders Conference noted that such requests exhibited "a spirit that would establish the American freedom . . . and [we] held it to be good to have a discussion and prudent inquiry in the *Gemeine* Council in order to arrive at the reason for this and to abolish such a dangerous thing from among us."[84] Thus, this son of two native Germans was acting quite American, seeking the freedom to work at the craft of his choosing and to pursue this craft in the manner that he saw fit.

Krause was not alone. His behavior was indicative of the way American values were gaining throughout Wachovia, especially in the more "closed" *Ortsgemeinen*. Intermixing was greatly enhancing this growing Americanization, although in Krause's case, intermixing involved not intermarriage with an Anglo-American but contacts with outside craftsmen and ways. The forming of friendships and, in many cases, intermarriage with Anglo-Americans brought German speakers far closer to American ways and made them more open to American values. A second cause, ironically, was evangelism itself. The Revolution could not have promoted individualism and other American values so effectively without the interceding influence of evangelism. That was because the individualistic tendencies inherent in evangelism made Moravians and other evangelicals more receptive to the cultural changes transforming American society in the late eighteenth century.

As historians of this religious movement have noted, evangelism, because of its emphasis on the new birth, promoted a theology of individualism. Despite the theological differences among Baptists, Presbyterians, Methodists, and Moravians, evangelicals shared a belief that the new birth was critical to conversion and that the individual played an essential role in his own salvation. Evangelicals rejected the Catholic notion that the church was a universal institution encompassing all members of society. Instead, they saw the true church as a voluntary society of converted believers. The "emphasis on the individual in the conversion-centered theology . . . accented the personal role in religion," historian John B. Boles notes. "The individual Christian was the measure of evangelism. If the individual convert composed the true church and participated in the beginning of his own religious life, then quite obviously evangelical religion was almost wholly an individual matter." This emphasis on the individual did not end with a successful conversion. For all evangelicals, sanctification was pivotal, too. The reborn sinner was to lead a virtuous life, striving constantly to be a better person and Christian. "Christians," Boles points out, "were called upon to make themselves more like Jesus Christ. They were expected to reform themselves, not society in general, though of course it was assumed that one led to the other."[85]

Such an emphasis on virtue blended almost seamlessly with republicans' notion of a civic society. Political thinkers in the late colonial period believed that a successful republic rested on the virtue of its citizenry. For a republic to survive, people had to sacrifice for the common good. Moral decay from within, caused by a selfish and profligate citizenry, had destroyed many a republic in ancient times. Factions—and all the selfishness that such groupings implied—contributed to the threat. Some revolutionaries saw the war for independence as a chance to reform American society and to rid it of its British-inspired corruptions. In this new society led by a disinterested meritocracy, frugality, honesty, and industry would guide a virtuous citizenry.[86] Evangelicals expressed a basic comfort with the main tenets of republicanism, especially the emphasis on virtue and the moral reform of society. Virtue, after all, was vital to sanctification. After undergoing the new birth, the reborn was supposed to lead a virtuous life. Layman and leader alike thus identified with republican efforts to reform society and to create a republic built on a moral foundation.[87]

Of course, things did not go as planned during the Revolution. Reformers pinned their hopes on the "people," and the people disappointed. "The American people," Gordon Wood writes, "seemed incapable of the degree of virtue needed for republicanism. Too many were unwilling to respect the authority of their new elected leaders and were too deeply involved in trade and moneymaking to think beyond their narrow interests or their neighborhoods and to concern themselves with the welfare of their states or their country."[88] The radicalism of the Revolution itself helped lead to the new American society that did emerge after the war—"the most egalitarian, most materialistic, most individualistic—and most evangelical Christian—society in Western history." Classical republicanism was replaced by a liberal democracy, where, in the words of one contemporary, "the public good is best promoted by the exertion of each individual seeking his own good in his own way."[89] In this liberal world, individualism and the pursuit of private interests became two hallmarks of American society—the opposite of what republicans had envisioned in 1775 as they launched the war for independence and moral reformation.

Evangelism did not isolate its followers from the swirling changes that were buffeting republicanism and American society during the Revolutionary period. Quite the opposite: impulses deep within the movement made evangelicals open to the cultural and political developments in American society, despite their earlier support of republicanism. As Nathan O. Hatch has so vigorously argued, evangelism itself became democratized following the Revolution. During the Revolutionary period, according to Hatch, "America's nonrestrictive environment permitted an unexpected and often explosive conjunction of evangelical fervor and popular sovereignty." The war itself, he continues, "dramatically expanded the circle of people who considered themselves capable of thinking for themselves about issues of freedom, equality, sovereignty, and representation. . . . Ordinary people moved toward these new horizons aided by a powerful new vocabulary."[90]

Moravianism shared the evangelical belief in the new birth and all that that entailed. Heart religion placed a tremendous emphasis on the individual's relationship with his or her Savior. Religious fervor began with the individual; each person needed to own up to his failings, make a new start as a reborn Christian, and then fight sin to remain a disciple of Jesus Christ. Over the long run, this emphasis on the new birth, when placed in the ferment of Revolutionary America and coinciding with the creolization of Wachovia, served to exalt the individual. It meant that North Carolina's brethren intuitively understood, and often sympathized with, the new libertarian society that was taking shape during the early republic. That evangelism helped to promote individualism among Moravians was deeply ironic. Rising individualism was a development that Moravian leaders vigorously denounced and had long resisted. When Bethania was founded in 1759, for instance, Bishop Augustus Spangenberg stressed that "although the Brothers and Sisters dwell by themselves and are to care for their own families, they should not think on that account that they live for themselves as do other people in the world."[91] Brotherhood, the leadership preached repeatedly, must take precedence over individualism. In the Moravian worldview, the Savior was to come first in all respects.

The leadership was fighting a losing battle. Evangelism's inherent stress on individualism came galloping to the fore during the heady days of the Revolution and all of its heated rhetoric on the rights of the people. A post-1776 world saw the creation of a democratic society that glorified the individual. It made explicit what had been implicit in the evangelical world. Because of the war and the never-ending parade of visitors to Wachovia, Gottlob Krause and other brethren witnessed firsthand the changes that were overtaking American society. Some brethren in the *Ortsgemeinen* did lament the passing of an older communal society and decried an increasing emphasis on private interests. Most brethren, however, welcomed the new freedoms that the Revolution brought in its wake, and they fought to increase the rights of the individual in economic, religious, and social spheres.[92]

In a further irony, the Moravian system of governance enhanced the role of the individual during the Revolutionary period and beyond. The Unity, after all, was a deftly designed federation that placed a great deal of authority with individual congregations while keeping the major decisions in the hands of central elders in Herrnhut. The *Brudergemeine* loved conference boards, and these boards could be found at every level of this worldwide church. A conferential system meant that individual brethren, including the sisters, enjoyed much say in the running of their church, especially on the congregational level. Each congregation had its own housefathers' and housemothers' conferences that dealt with a wide range of issues affecting their daily lives. And every congregation had its own boards that decided everything from what to serve at a Sunday lovefeast to which member should till the pastor's garden. During the Revolutionary period, this conferential system took on added meaning by helping to empower the individual and by easing the transition to citizenship. The brethren were used to voting and to expressing their opinions from their church activities.[93]

None of this is to say that North Carolina's Moravians became radicals or threw themselves wholeheartedly into the politics of the day; they did not. Heart religion demanded that its adherents put their energies into conversion, not politics, and this mandate put a brake on Moravian involvement in the world of politics. Evangelical religion always remained paramount during the Revolutionary period. Indeed, the stresses of war made many brethren even more devout. They knew of but one way to deal with the pressures they faced and the deep fears they felt. In 1780, Johannes Hohns of Friedberg recounted to his pastor the tenseness he experienced when taking meal to American soldiers. The experience, the pastor said, has "turned him to the Savior, and he cannot be thankful enough that He graciously helped him through, and brought him home safely."[94] Few brethren ever actually ran for office; Frederick Muller of Friedland served briefly in the assembly in the late 1770s, as did Traugott Bagge of Salem. The Moravians were hardly alone in this reluctance. Other evangelicals kept their distance from politics because of their conversion-centered outlook on life. Like the Moravians, they believed that the running of government should be left to the politicians and that evangelizing should be left to the faithful.[95]

✝

War and its offspring—individualism and a rising participation in politics—meant that North Carolina's Moravians were being increasingly drawn into the affairs of a young nation. With increased participation came increased accommodation with American ways. Brethren of all ethnicities, including German speakers, now saw themselves as "American" following the Revolution. The political realm had mixed decisively with religious and cultural trends to produce this result. Accommodation, meanwhile, was also occurring in the economic realm. As the nineteenth century dawned, North Carolina's Moravians were showing an affinity for southern ways, including for that most peculiar of southern institutions, slavery.

Becoming "Southern"
The Slaveholding Years

The town of Salem stood on a hill in the center of Wachovia, its main buildings huddled around a central square. Built with energy and purpose from 1766 to 1772, the village had grown steadily in its early years until by 1822 it had finally overtaken Friedberg as the most populous settlement in Wachovia. Salem was thriving. Throngs of customers from Wachovia's environs walked or rode into the village, past the single brothers' house and the handsome brick church to T. Bagge's former store and the other shops that lined the main streets, where one could buy pottery, or shoes, or fine china imported from England. Amid this bustle of economic activity, the brothers and sisters scurried to their daily devotionals and prayer meetings, where they contemplated the saving grace of their Savior. The seemingly odd juxtaposition of work and worship was not really so odd. The Unity purposely placed Salem, the commercial and religious capital of Wachovia, on a hill in the center of the ninety-eight-thousand-acre Wachovia tract, where it would serve as the symbolic heart of the Moravian mission in the American South. And, indeed, Salem did fulfill its function as a powerful symbol. Here was where the chosen people were to live, their piety plainly visible for all to see.[1]

On a neighboring hill, just across the creek from the town's southern end, stood another community that represented something quite different—something so different that a visitor to Salem who came upon it might think he had stumbled on another part of the South. Plainly visible from Salem was a large, stately house that stood at the center of a small but diverse plantation. Bustling about the grounds and on the dusty road that led from the creek to the "big house" were the black slaves who helped till the fields, run their master's household, and cut the firewood that warmed Salem's rooms.[2]

Ironically, the symbolism of this plantation was as apt as Salem's. A working southern plantation, complete with a slave workforce and big house, stood almost mockingly in the very shadow of Wachovia's religious capital. It was run not by a West Indies expatriate or a member of the local gentry, but by a rebellious, German-born Moravian who had come to the United States only a few years earlier, in 1801. Friedrich Schumann's plantation was representative of a larger story unfolding in the evangelical world in the early nineteenth century. The saintly had begun embracing a not-so-saintly institution. Slavery was becoming entrenched in the post-Revolutionary South, and most evangelicals were no longer resisting the trend. The reasons were not hard to find. Contact with a wider world was blunting the egalitarian thrust of a movement that stressed the spiritual equality of the saved. In Wachovia, the same phenomenon was occurring but with a twist: acculturation was producing accommodation with the brethrens' southern neighbors. This accommodation was nowhere more evident than in the institution of slavery. As Schumann's story reveals, many Moravians, regardless of ethnicity, were turning to slavery with relative ease and with only a few pangs of conscience. The shift to a bound labor force came fairly easily because slavery, in a terrible irony for its victims, meshed comfortably with the family and religious values of those brethren living in the countryside. In another irony, however, these same values also served as a brake on the spread of slavery. The emerging Anglo-German society, with its mix of Anglo-American, German Moravian, and creole German-American ways, meant that the adoption of slavery would be uneven and its impact on acculturation complex.

A German Slave Plantation in the American South

The slave plantation run by a German Moravian who came to thoroughly exasperate the Salem leadership was never meant to be. Friedrich Schumann did not begin the plantation—the church itself did in June 1768, but merely as a tenant-run farm that would supply milk, vegetables, eggs, and cheese to the commercial town then undergoing construction. In 1769, the brethren built a log house and stable for the first tenant, George Holder and his wife. The farm, however, proved to be a major disappointment, thanks to a long line of indifferent or incompetent tenants who followed Holder. Peter Rose, who succeeded Holder in 1774, may have been one of the most inept. Only two years after he took over management of the farm, Salem's Aufseher Collegium complained that under Rose's stewardship, "the fields and the acres and the meadows, yes, the whole household is in an impossible status." Twenty years later, the collegium was no happier despite a succession of tenants who had tried their hand at running the place: "J. G. Ebert is neglecting the plantation now completely. His cattle are running around on the meadows, through which the hay crop is spoilt, so that his successor cannot exist."[3]

By 1814, when Schumann wanted to move in, the old farm was in a ruinous state. Its size had shrunk from three hundred acres to a hundred, and the farmhouse was virtually uninhabitable. The Aufseher Collegium saw Schumann's offer to take over the farm as something of a godsend that seemingly would solve two problems at once: Salem would gain the services of a talented physician, and the commercial town might finally see the farm produce something other than headaches. The Salem congregation was so pleased with the impending arrival of Schumann that it readily agreed to allocate $1,500 for a new house, at a time when craftsmen's houses in town were being built for about $700 apiece.[4] The arrival of a slave plantation at Salem's doorstep was thus something of an accident. If earlier tenants had managed the farm properly, Schumann and his slaves never would have moved in. Yet more than bad luck, of course, was involved. The founding of a slave plantation on the outskirts of Salem was intimately tied to events in Salem itself and the ongoing debate there over whether slavery should be allowed in the capital of Wachovia.[5]

The man who helped renew the debate in Salem over slavery was not your stereotypical slaveholder. Schumann was born in Gnaden, Germany, in 1777 and raised as a Moravian. He arrived in Pennsylvania at age twenty-four, settling in the Moravian village of Hope, New Jersey. In 1807, he asked to migrate to Wachovia. Salem's elders were happy to oblige Schumann, because his skills as a doctor were in short supply in backcountry Carolina. They assigned him to the Bethania congregation, which was badly in need of a doctor. In these early years in Wachovia, Schumann lived the life of a good brother. His medical practice was highly valued and appreciated by patient and church alike. He even contributed to Wachovia's religious mission, traveling to the Moravians' outpost at Flint River in late 1809 for work among the Creek Nation. C. L. Benzien, who succeeded Frederick Marshall as administrator of Wachovia, had nothing but praise for Schumann's effort there, noting that the doctor not only took care of the sick but helped the mission "in every way . . . even assisting them with the cooking, slaughtering, making of sausages, cutting of wood," Benzien recounted in a letter of February 12, 1810. "Blessed be our good Br. Schumann."[6]

The good doctor's acclimation to a new life in a new country proceeded swiftly. He was fluent in English and came to identify with, and apparently support, the young nation he was now residing in. On July 4, 1812, as war came with Great Britain, Schumann could be found in Bethania's meetinghouse participating in Independence Day celebrations. "In the afternoon," the Bethania Diary reported, "our doctor, Br. Schumann, made an address in English, which was much appreciated by those who heard it. At the close of the meeting, several American songs were sung by a chorus."[7]

Schumann found another part of his new country very much to his liking—the right to own slaves. In Bethania, he relied on the services of a slave woman named Coelia and her four children, who worked in his home as servants and as nurses to his ailing wife and two children. The doctor became so reliant on his servants that he did not want to give them up when he requested permission to move to Salem. He told the Aufseher Collegium that his slaves had to remain with him because his wife was sick; two of his black servants, he explained, were needed in the short term to care for her. This request landed Schumann in the middle of the debate over slavery in the central *Ortsgemeine*.[8]

Wachovia's elders had agonized for years over the impact slavery would have on Salem's religious mission. Although the church itself had owned or rented slaves since the 1760s, the elders feared that the use of captive labor by individual brethren would undermine church members' work ethic. The brethren could become lazy and unmotivated. Such a declension in ideals would threaten Wachovia's spiritual and economic health and risk bringing down the censure of God on the community. Slavery, in short, could defile the central *Ortsgemeine* and snuff out its role as a "city on the hill" and the exemplary example it was supposed to set.[9]

Because of these fears, Wachovia's boards did all they could to keep slavery out of Salem. They did not want bound labor undermining the apprentice system and ruining the purity of the chosen people. In the eighteenth century, the Salem congregation barred the use of all slaves in town. Congregation members could neither own slaves nor rent them. With a few exceptions—the Congregation Council, for example, allowed Adam Elrod of Hope to bring his slave into town when he took over management of Salem's tavern in 1803—this ban held firm. Pressure against the rule had been building, however, and Schumann's request to move to Salem and bring his slaves with him helped to bring the issue to the fore once again in the summer of 1814.

Schumann, because of still formidable opposition to slavery in Salem, couched his request in the most humanitarian way possible—he needed servants to care for his ailing wife. He promised he would remove the slaves from town once his wife had recovered. The collegium found this reasoning unpersuasive, concluding "he would not be likely . . . to give [them] up later." Schumann's request and the unseemly round of negotiations that followed showed the great ambivalence that the church leadership still felt toward slavery. The collegium opposed Schumann's request not out of concern for Coelia and her family. Instead, board members feared that she would have more children; if this were to occur, the board warned, "the number of Negro slaves in Salem would be increased, and with it the growing unpleasantness and danger to the inward welfare of the congregation."[10] For the collegium, then, the real issue was the supposed threat the presence of blacks posed to the purity of Salem's mission and not the morality of slavery itself. In the midst of Schumann's negotiations with the Aufseher Collegium, Salem's householders held a meeting on August 22, 1814, to discuss whether slavery should be allowed in their village. A majority remained opposed to allowing slaves in Salem, but householders also recognized that times were changing and that slaves were becoming more important to the economy in North Carolina and Wachovia. So the town meeting agreed to soften the ban somewhat; the congregation would still bar slavery from Salem, but a member could petition two of the congregation's governing boards—the Aufseher Collegium and the Elders Conference—for permission to use a slave in exceptional cases. On a case-by-case basis, the boards would review whether it was truly justified for a member to use a slave in Salem.[11]

On August 16, Schumann made a counteroffer to the collegium: he would sell two of Coelia's middle children if the other children were allowed to come to Salem with him. The board again said no. Instead, it told Schumann that he could bring the woman but not the children, and if this was not feasible, the board said, the doctor should sell the entire family. Schumann rejected this deal out of hand.[12]

The final compromise did keep the family intact—but not for humanitarian reasons. Schumann, the board decided, could not move to Salem. He could, however, lease the neighboring farm, which not coincidentally was floundering. The board believed it had come up with a satisfying solution to several interlocking problems. It had stood its ground and kept the corrupting influence of a slave family out of Salem. Yet this brother would not have to sell his slaves; indeed, he could now have as many as he wanted. The farm would finally get a new tenant and a new chance at fulfilling the modest (and still largely unfulfilled) goal of supplying milk, cheese, and eggs to a growing commercial town.[13]

To the board's initial delight, Schumann began expanding the farm's operations. Within a few years, he had increased the farm's size to 157 acres. Schumann, however, showed a disdain for congregational rules and the tiresome boards that propagated them. Soon, the Aufseher Collegium was complaining of Schumann's "despotic" ways. The board was especially angry at the way this tenant went about expanding the plantation's operations—without permission and with no regard for the property rights of the Salem congregation. He dumped stumps and hedges into Salem creek and began clearing land inside village limits—practices that the collegium sternly ordered him to end.[14]

The collegium, however, had no objection to Schumann's decision to expand the labor force. He invested thousands of dollars in slaves, who worked in both the main house and the fields. No longer would the farm be dependent on family members and white day laborers to do the tilling, planting, and harvesting. By 1820, Schumann had deployed four slaves in the fields and slowly doubled their number until he had eight working as laborers in 1832. As early as 1817, the plantation had at least ten slaves—one of the largest holdings in Wachovia.[15]

Throughout the South, the landscape of large plantations became an important statement of the gentry's power. The grand houses and their formal, ordered dependencies were meant to impress and intimidate. Often, designers placed the main house on a knoll or hill so that it would literally stand above others. They placed the house at the center of the plantation and set it off from the countryside by fences or terraces. Planters wanted these architectural elements to reinforce their power and status as leading members of society. They also wanted their plantations to take on all the trappings of a village, providing for its inhabitants' economic, social, and religious needs.[16] Friedrich Schumann did not go so far, but he clearly wanted to make a statement through his plantation's landscape, albeit a different one from that of a nabob in Chesapeake Virginia, or Charleston, South Carolina.

In its early days, the farm south of Salem had a small log house and a stable. George Holder, the first tenant, added other structures common to any family farm, including a smokehouse, chicken house, corncrib, and bake oven.[17] Before agreeing to take over management of the farm in 1815, Schumann asked that the Salem congregation give him the money to construct a grander house. It agreed, and his new residence ended up costing the congregation $2,000 (Schumann exceeded his original budget by $500, saying he needed the extra money for plastering and painting the interior).[18] It was a handsome house that became the subject of a portrait by Salem painter Daniel Welfare titled *Salem from the Southeast*. Welfare's painting reveals a two-story house that deftly blended the Moravian and the Georgian, with its clapboard siding, clean lines, and cedar-shake roof. But Schumann also abandoned the medieval irregularity of the German farmhouse that had been popular in Wachovia for so many years. The house's centered doorway and symmetrical fenestration gave it a stately appearance. More important, Schumann placed his house at the center of the farm on the tract's highest hill, where he could look down literally and figuratively on Salem. Certainly, Schumann had a practical reason for constructing such a large house. He very likely used part of the first floor to treat patients from his busy medical practice. He, however, did not build a larger house because of family needs; he and his first wife, Johanna Salome Leinbach, had only two children, and one of them, Timeleon, died in December 1810 at the age of three. The house, instead, represented something more than the practical. This brother very likely was making a statement through the size of the house and its symbolic location. The house stood on a hill overlooking Salem, with its front staring right at the *Ortsgemeine* and the boards that Schumann spent so much time feuding with. He placed a "free place," or open lawn, in front of the house, surrounded by dependencies that formed a compact, roughly symmetrical village. This former church farm now had the air of a plantation, overseen by a master with a large slave force.[19]

Wachovia's Growing Economy: The Underpinnings of Slavery

Friedrich Schumann's story was unique in some ways because of his tense relations with the church over congregational rules. Unlike other brethren, he used the plantation itself as a weapon in his battle with the church, both by defying the collegium in his clearing of land and by placing the house on a hill so easily visible from Salem. But in many other ways, his story was not at all unique. This German Moravian had come to the United States in only 1801 and to Wachovia in only 1807. Yet within a few years, Schumann had become an eager participant in slaveholding. The ease with which he wore the mantle of master was replicated elsewhere in Wachovia. His practical reasons for turning to slavery were also quite typical. On the simplest level, this busy doctor with an ailing wife needed help running his household. When he moved to the farm south of Salem, it was a logical and natural step for him to acquire more slaves, because Schumann did not have a brood of sons to work the fields. Earlier tenants had relied on their own brawn and their family members to run the farm. Clearly, Schumann believed that was not enough.

Moravians across Wachovia were reaching similar conclusions. The religious

From his house (visible on the near right), Friedrich Schumann could literally look down on the neighboring village of Salem, whose boards he constantly feuded with. The house was the center of a farm that took on the trappings of a southern plantation. *Collection of the Wachovia Historical Society, Winston-Salem, North Carolina; courtesy of Old Salem Inc., Winston-Salem, North Carolina.*

colony's steady economic growth in the late eighteenth and early nineteenth centuries fueled the demand for all kinds of laborers—field hands, carpenters, day laborers, and domestics, all of whom were in short supply in a region rapidly leaving its frontier days behind. Further spurring the need for laborers was the growth in the number of Wachovia's settlements from two in the 1750s to six in the 1770s, thanks to the founding of Salem and the *Landgemeinen*. On the most elemental level, more settlements meant more houses to build, more farm fields to clear, and more roads to build. All of that work required more labor than Wachovia could supply.[20] Slave labor helped fill the void.

Wachovia's economy was not only growing after the Revolution but also becoming more sophisticated. The religious community boasted a diverse economy of crafts, shops, farms, and industries. Salem and Bethania were the two most prosperous villages, with large merchant classes that invested their wealth in mills, stores, land, and slaves. As the Unity intended, Salem became home to an array of crafts upon its completion in 1772: a pottery, two tanneries, a gristmill, a tavern, a community store, and numerous crafts. The single brothers ran, among other things, a brewery, a distillery, and a slaughterhouse. Salem's regulated system, which restricted competition in an effort to help everyone in the community, ironically helped to enrich a few. Traugott Bagge was the most noteworthy example. He used his position as operator of Salem's main store to amass a landholding empire of 9,578 acres. These holdings made him the largest landowner in Wachovia. He acquired several thousand of those acres from customers unable to pay their debts at the store. Jacob Blum, a tavern keeper and farmer who first lived in Bethabara, was Salem's second largest landholder with 4,886 acres, and several other craftsmen had holdings of between 1,000 and 3,000 acres.[21]

Bethania's inhabitants were not far behind Salem's merchants. The town's merchants, who lived in the upper village, led a dynamic economy that mixed holdings in land, mills, stores, and taverns after the Revolution. The village had, among other things, a general store; a distillery; a tannery; and apple, oil, grist, and saw mills. The Conrad, Lash, and Hauser families displayed an especially strong entrepreneurial spirit. In 1771, Bishop John Michael Graff told Bethania congregation members that the brethren could not open a private mill.[22] But Bethania's leading families persisted, and in 1782, Salem's Elders Conference dropped its opposition. The Conrads and several other brethren began building a grain mill near Bethania on church land, for which they would pay a ten-pound "gratuity" as rent.[23] In 1784, they finished construction and began operating. The number of businesses grew in Bethania in the 1780s and so did the village's economic sophistication. Among others, Michael Hauser built a "still-house" in 1782; George Hauser Jr. constructed a smith shop in late 1784; in the mid-1780s, Peter Hauser operated a "guest-house" or tavern, and Jacob Conrad ran an oil mill; and in late 1789, George Hauser opened a store.[24]

The Conrads became one of the wealthiest families in Wachovia despite humble beginnings. Christian, the family patriarch who was born in Quittopehill, Pennsylvania, in 1744, moved to a farm four miles from Bethania in 1769 with his wife and children. He was a farmer and teamster with a love of hard work. That combination enabled him to acquire holdings of 705 acres and to build a strong foundation for his four sons and daughters. As his *Lebenslauf* put it, Christian "experienced in material [things] the blessing of God on the work of his hands."[25] The most successful Conrad was Jacob, the merchant, who was born in Heidelberg, Pennsylvania, in 1782. This branch of the Conrad family came to Wachovia in 1785, where Jacob's father, John, ran a successful store in Bethania. He groomed Jacob to take over the store at his death. In 1802, Jacob assumed the responsibilities of his father's business. Despite poor health, Jacob became a successful merchant and built up the largest landholdings in Bethania.[26]

Wachovia's administrative boards, which wanted Salem to remain the economic capital of Wachovia, tolerated Bethanians' burst of private enterprise but kept a close eye on the village's morals. In 1785, the Aeltesten Conferenz told George Hauser and Johann Conrad that their store in Bethania could "not handle wine, rum, or other strong drink." It also told Peter Hauser that the "guest-house" at his farm "must provide additional facilities so that his family and his children are separated from outsiders, and the visitors can thereby be better served."[27] In 1803, Salem's elders decided to become more involved in Bethania. The Aeltesten Conferenz opened a church-run store in the village for the benefit of a diaconie, or congregation account, to be established for Bethania's congregation. The board agreed to let merchant Christian Lash run it. The elders wanted to generate income for the church while nudging the economy in directions they approved. On May 1, 1804, the congregational diaconie became a reality with the transfer of Lash's distillery and tanyard to the congregation. Lash's holdings included a dwelling house, a still house, a bark mill, a lumber house, and vats worth $1,465.50.[28] Of the six settlements, Bethania had by far the largest number of landowners with holdings of more than seven hundred acres and a broad class of middling landholders.

The *Landgemeinen* were primarily agricultural settlements consisting of family run farms. The landholdings in these three settlements were considerably smaller than in Salem's and Bethania's, with Friedberg's average holdings the largest at 265 acres and Hope's the smallest at 181. The difference can be attributed to the more family based values in the *Landgemeinen*. As seen in chapter 3, farmers of both ethnicities built up holdings judiciously to keep heirs anchored at home and in the church. But such "conservatism" did not mean that the *Landgemeinen* were static places. These farmers participated in the market and were active in the land market. In the early national period, the largest growth rates in land values occurred in Hope and Friedberg, followed closely by Bethania and Salem. In Hope, the value of the settlement's landholdings increased 55 percent between 1799 and 1820; Friedberg's rose 49 percent; Salem's increased 47 percent; and Bethania's rose 44 percent.[29] In the *Landgemeinen*, Friedberg had the most diverse economy, including the most teamsters and craftsmen and the largest number of wealthy landholders. It also had the largest number of middling owners with holdings of between two hundred and seven hundred acres.[30] Not surprisingly, its growth was steady and strong in the late eighteenth and early nineteenth centuries.

At the other extreme from Salem and Bethania were Bethabara and Friedland, the most insular settlements in Wachovia. Although the values of their landholdings did enjoy healthy growth—36 percent for Friedland and 28 percent for Bethabara—settlers did not engage in the land and slave markets to the extent that their neighboring brethren did. In each of these two settlements, only one member had landholdings of more than seven hundred acres. Friedland was an especially sleepy place economically, with few crafts and no stores or taverns. At the settlement's founding, its inhabitants were the poorest in Wachovia. The missionary who worked with them in Maine and led them to North Carolina in the early 1770s worried greatly about their "hard material circumstances" during this first decade of colonization, as well as their "serious lack of physical necessities."[31] This lack of resources hampered Friedland's development. Up to 1830 and beyond, it remained a small agricultural settlement.

Bethabara had a more diverse economy than Friedland because of its founding as a commercial village in 1753, but it became an economic backwater with Salem's completion in 1772. No houses were constructed in the village from 1772 until 1810. Its tavern—formerly the second most lucrative enterprise after the village's store—consistently lost money and was closed in the early 1790s.[32] When Wachovia's leaders decided to end the communal farm because of losses and sell it to private owners in the 1790s, no one wanted to buy it. The community's gristmills and sawmills did well after 1772, generating profits every year but two, but the store was no longer a big moneymaker.[33] The village's loss in standing was both real and symbolic. As late as 1777, the value of Bethabara's estates stood among the highest in Wachovia. By 1820, it was the second lowest.

Moravian farmers grew an impressive range of crops, from tobacco to rye, but one crop stood out in the post-Revolutionary period: wheat. In the colonial period, Moravian growers found wheat to be an unprofitable export because of the primitive road network and unprofitable distance from the coast.[34] That began to change, however, in the 1770s for several reasons. For one, the road network improved. Salem's boards appointed road masters for each settlement in Wachovia whose job was to oversee the roads in their neighborhood. These road masters worked not only on maintaining the existing road structure but on adding to it. The goal, as Salem's Congregation Council put it in 1785, was to ensure that new roads would be of "service to our trade." One new road that year, for instance, went to the key trading town of Cross Creek, and another went to a ford that cut traveling time to the Shallowford River.[35] Settlements throughout the backcountry were also improving their roadways as their economies grew.[36] By 1800, decent roads radiated outward from Wachovia to its major trading partners in the South: Petersburg, Virginia; Cross Creek and Wilmington, North Carolina; and Charleston, South Carolina. Wachovia depended on roads for trade because of the poor river system in North Carolina. Unlike the James in Virginia, no major river flowed west to east, making water transportation from the backcountry to the coast unpractical.[37]

The population growth of the *Landgemeinen* in the late eighteenth century gave a significant boost to wheat production in Wachovia. It brought to the religious colony many farmers from the middle colonies who had grown that crop up north and who preferred to keep growing it in the South. In all three country congregations, farmers grew wheat as their primary cash crop. Although records do not exist to determine output for each settlement, increased wheat production can be seen in the amount of wheat ground at Wachovia's mills. An analysis of grains brought to Salem's gristmills from 1774 to 1805 shows that wheat dominated, constituting 55 percent of the grain milled. Corn was an important but distant second at 34 percent (table 5.1).[38] Wachovia's farmers preferred wheat for several reasons. For one, it was well suited to Wachovia's hilly terrain, unlike corn. Second, wheat fit in nicely with the needs of a family based farm. It was less labor intensive than tobacco. Tobacco's planting cycle was year-round and required as many as thirty-nine separate days of labor. But wheat needed intensive attention only during planting and harvesting, requiring about twenty-six days of man labor.[39] Farmers in Wachovia did grow tobacco in the early national period, but only in small amounts. It was not until after the 1840s that tobacco's importance grew in Wachovia's environs, with production rising from 596,103 pounds in 1840 to 2,064,482 pounds in 1860. Despite the growing use of slavery, cotton cultivation remained small throughout the later antebellum period, with 56,481 pounds grown in 1840, none in 1850, and 121,600 pounds in 1860.[40]

These farmers also preferred wheat because of market trends. By the mid-1760s, population growth in the Atlantic world was spurring the need for food; European farmers were unable to meet this growing demand. Prices rose, and corn and wheat exports from British North America soared as a result.[41] In the 1750s, wheat brought a price of about two shillings, six pence a bushel.[42] By 1800, it stood at about seven shillings a bushel. Prices varied locally, however, depending on supply and the quality of the grain. At Salem's gristmill in 1796 and 1797, for instance, the price varied from a low of six shillings to a high

Table 5.1 Crop Production in Wachovia, 1774–1805

Crop	1774		1786–87		1799–1800		1804–5	
	Bushels	%	Bushels	%	Bushels	%	Bushels	%
Wheat	287	53	666.5	44	706	58	777.5	62
Corn	170.5	32	487.25	35	373.75	31	393	31
Rye	53	10	138.5	10	127.75	11	74	5
Malt	24.25	5						
Barley			81	5			15.75	1

Source: Inventories of the Salem gristmill, Moravian Archives, Southern Province.

of eight shillings.[43] By contrast, farmers received lower prices for corn than wheat. Wachovia's farmers could get up to eight shillings for a bushel of wheat in 1797, but they could get only five shillings for corn. Some bushels brought only two shillings. Teamsters from Bethania and the *Landgemeinen,* especially from Friedberg, ranged up and down the East Coast. They brought back not only goods but also valuable information about developments in the Atlantic economy. Their contacts with the coastal merchant houses enabled Wachovia's farmers to move fast to meet market needs, as an incident in 1790 showed. Gottlob Rancke and Peter Schor of Bethania hurried to Petersburg with at least two wagonloads of flour because they had learned that "a French ship lying there has offered a good price."[44]

All this activity translated into economic strength, as the tax records reveal. In 1768, when Wachovia was part of Rowan County, the taxables for the entire county totaled 419 polls. That figure included not only Wachovia but also Salisbury, the Yadkin River, and other settlements in this sprawling backcountry region.[45] In 1790, Wachovia's taxables alone totaled 357, and the number steadily rose, from 401 in 1800 to 510 in 1820.[46] Moreover, Wachovia's economic growth kept pace with Stokes County, which saw its population nearly double from 7,745 in 1790 to 14,033 in 1820.[47] In 1790, Wachovia's polls represented 26 percent of the county's polls; in 1820, it remained at 24 percent.[48] From 1790 to 1820, Wachovia had the most polls of any district in Stokes, another sign of its economic strength, because its population increase did not keep pace with Stokes'. In 1790, Wachovia constituted about 14 percent of the county's population; in 1820, it constituted only 10 percent. Thus, the percentage increase in polls can largely be attributed to economic development. See table 5.2.

Another indicator of this economic strength was Wachovia's active land mar-

Table 5.2 Wachovia's Tax Base, 1790–1820

Year	Districts	Polls	Total	% of County Polls
1790	Capt. Shouse	357	357	26
1800	Markland's	189		
	Bennett's	212	401	21
1810	Bethabara	93		
	Bethania	178	462	22
	Salem	191		
1820	Bethabara	120		
	Bethania	126	510	24
	Salem	264		

Source: Stokes County tax records. Not until 1810 did tax assessors divide Wachovia into three districts, which also included the *Landgemeinen.* The boundaries between Wachovia's districts were imprecise and changing, as the 1810 and 1820 figures show for Bethania. Salem gained polls at Bethania's expense. The 1830 returns did not give totals by district.

Table 5.3 Land Unsold in Wachovia, 1795–1830

Year	Acres Unsold	%	Year	Acres Unsold	%
1795	56,783	57	1815	46,073.25	47
1801	53,037.5	54	1820	37,679	38
1805	51,482	52	1825	35,807.5	36
1810	49,259.25	50	1830	34,700	35

Source: "Land lying in Stokes County, given for the tax . . ." for the above years, Moravian Archives, Southern Province.

ket. As Wachovia's population and economic activity grew, so did the amount of land sold by the church. In 1795, the amount of land left unsold in the 98,765-acre tract stood at 56,783. This figure steadily dropped to 51,482 in 1805, 46,073 in 1815, and 34,700 in 1830. In other words, the church sold 22,083 acres in thirty-five years. This figure represented 22 percent of the Wachovia tract. See table 5.3.

Wachovia's economic growth was also reflected in the tax assessments on

Table 5.4a Value of Estates, 1777

Settlement	N	Total Value (pounds)	Average Value (pounds)
Friedberg	16*	4,129	258**
Bethabara	15	2,984	199
Salem	36	6,807	189
Bethania	44	7,389	168
Friedland	24	1,982	83
Hope	13***	1,059	81

Source: Surry County tax returns.
*This number is vastly understated because many of Friedberg's residents were included in Rowan County's tax returns, but those returns give only polls.
**Two large estates—the Martin and Ebert estates—inflate the average value. When these values are not figured in, Friedberg's average value is 140 pounds.
***This number is significantly understated for Hope because of omissions by the tax assessor.

Table 5.4b Value of Landholdings, 1799

Settlement	N	Acreage	Value ($)	Average Value ($)
Salem*	22	12,726.75	10,611.25	482.33
Bethania	48	18,512.75	20,082.50	418.39
Bethabara	19	6,638	6,135.50	322.92
Friedberg	28	6,014	8,328.25	297.44
Hope	25	4,308	7,050	282
Friedland	16	2,470	3,791	236.94

Source: Stokes County tax records.
*This represents the landholdings of Salem residents outside of Salem. In Salem itself, residents rented the land on which their houses stood, so those holdings are not included.

land and estates. By matching residency with these tax records over twenty-year intervals, it is possible to not only give the parameters on growth but also correlate the relative wealth of each settlement within Wachovia: in the nineteenth century, Salem and Bethania were the wealthiest, and Friedland was the poorest. See table 5.4.

A strong economy was a critical prerequisite to the establishment of slavery. Frontier economies generally could not afford large-scale purchases of bound

Table 5.4c Value of Landholdings, 1820

Settlement	N	Acreage	Value ($)	Average Value ($)
Salem*	44	24,908	40,063	910.52
Bethania	95	25,286.25	70,936.25	746.70
Hope	25	5,711.5	15,800	632
Friedberg	43	8,048.25	25,298	588.33
Bethabara	29	4,806	13,122	452.48
Friedland	47	4,960.75	17,554	373.49

Source: Stokes County tax records.
*This represents the landholdings of Salem residents outside of Salem.

labor; developed ones could.[49] A growing economy gave Wachovia's farmers of all ethnicities the income to purchase slaves and the impetus to do so. As the research of historian Jon F. Sensbach has shown, the Unity in North Carolina first used slaves—it rented in these early years but did not buy—in the late 1760s when labor was in short supply and demand was rising because of Salem's construction and the founding of the *Landgemeinen*.[50] The shortage of slave labor in the North Carolina Piedmont likely kept the brethren from using slaves earlier. It was not until 1769 that the Moravian Church bought its first slave, when the owner of Sam, a slave rented to the church for work in Bethabara, offered to sell him to the Unity because of Sam's Christian leanings. In the early 1780s, the black community remained tiny; there were no more than twenty-five blacks who either were slaves owned by Moravians or were hired hands.[51] The 1790 census showed a smattering of slaveholders in Wachovia and the *Landgemeinen*. The largest slaveholder was a resident of Friedland—Frederick Miller, a saddler, mill owner, and farmer, who owned eleven slaves. The second largest slaveholder was George Hauser, a merchant and farmer in Bethania, who owned eight slaves.[52]

The numbers grew steadily in the nineteenth century, along with Wachovia's economy. By 1802, brethren in Bethania held thirty-six slaves, or 49 percent of the total for Wachovia. The settlement with the second highest number of slaves was Hope with twenty slaves, or 27 percent of the total.[53] By 1830, the number of slaves had grown in Wachovia to about four hundred, more than five times the number thirty years earlier. Median holdings remained small—the average slaveholder held fewer than five slaves—but there were more large slaveholders.[54] The largest slaveholdings were in Bethania and Salem, the two most commercially oriented settlements. Conversely, the fewest slave holdings were in Friedland, the settlement with the lowest land values. In Bethania, Christian Lash, who ran the village's distillery, store, and farm, owned the most slaves in Wachovia, with holdings of thirty. Jacob Conrad was next, with twenty-six slaves, and Abraham Conrad owned fifteen.[55]

The Cultural Imperatives of Slavery

The economy alone, however, was not responsible for the spread of slavery within Wachovia. Acculturation also encouraged the turn to slavery at the same time that slavery was furthering the acculturation of the brethren. Contact with outsiders helped lead to the use of slavery in two ways. The first was through the influence of those "outsiders" who lived in Wachovia—that is, those members of the *Landgemeinen* itself, populated by an ethnically complex group of settlers who joined the Moravian movement at the behest of Moravian missionaries and who did not live in the "closed" *Ortsgemeinen*. The first private owners of slaves in Wachovia could be found in Anglo-American Hope, and these new arrivals helped introduce individual brethren to the peculiar institution on a very personal level. Daniel Smith, the leader of the emigrés to Hope, grew tobacco in Frederick County and owned several slaves. He and the Goslins and Peddycoards brought their slaves with them—about six in all—when they came to Wachovia in 1772. In the climate of the 1770s, this instantly made them among the largest slaveholders in Wachovia. The cultural imperatives involved in slavery's use were strong enough that Hope had the second highest number of slaves by 1810 despite being the second smallest settlement with the smallest landholdings.[56]

For the emigrés from Carrollton Manor, owning slaves was nothing unusual. It was common and accepted in Maryland society. Indeed, evidence indicates that Hope's founders saw nothing wrong with bringing their slaves to Wachovia and that they never considered giving them up despite their relocation to a religious colony built on strict evangelical principles. The use of slavery in Hope, in fact, only spread. By 1790, the ranks of slaveholders in Hope had grown to include Anglo-American and German-American alike, from English-speaking James Douthit of Irish ancestry, who owned six slaves, on down to German-speaking Adam Elrod, who had at least one. These Anglo-American members helped make slavery seem less different, less foreign to German-speaking Moravians throughout Wachovia. In the 1770s, the presence of slave-holding brethren in Wachovia's farm congregations must have been jarring.

One can only imagine the wonderment and curiosity aroused among the brethren when Smith and his fellow expatriates from Carrollton Manor rode into Wachovia with their black slaves in tow. By 1800, the atmosphere was quite different. A generation of intermixing had thoroughly introduced German-speaking Moravians to Anglo-American ways. The sight of Adam Elrod bringing his slave to Salem's tavern in 1803 was likely not an unusual one.

Contact with the outside world, a contact leaven with a growing spirit of acquisitiveness, fueled the desire for slaves on a second and deeper level. The Moravian trading network—spearheaded, ironically, by Salem, the religious center of Wachovia—was extensive, and it ensnared Wachovia in the inner workings of the Atlantic world. The brethren, quite simply, saw what the world market had to offer and wanted to partake of its bounty.

Salem's role was critical in the process. In the late colonial and early national periods, the commercial town served as an entrepot. It gathered goods from neighboring areas for shipment to the coast. Teamsters, primarily from Bethania and Friedberg, ranged across Wachovia and settlements outside Wachovia's borders. From Briant's Settlement, Town Fork, and Belews Creek, wagons returned with wheat; from the Atkin, they came back with corn; from the Quaker settlement at New Garden, they brought cultivated hops; and from Dan River, they returned with lime.[57] Wachovia also transported tobacco from Southside Virginia to Charleston. Congregation diaries for both the *Ortsgemeinen* and *Landgemeinen* were peppered with the activities of these wagons. "Our wagons brought corn from the Town Fork," reported Bethabara's Diary in 1784.[58] Bethania's Diary noted in 1787, "At noon five wagons loaded with tobacco set out for Petersburg, following four that left last week; all were sent by George Hauser."[59] And Friedberg's Diary recorded in 1784 that Martin Walk, Peter Frey, and Adam Spach "took several wagons of white cabbage to Salem to sell."[60]

Salem's diaconie also accumulated an abundance of goods through barter because stores and craft shops accepted agricultural goods as payment. Gottfried Aust, for instance, accepted cotton, flax, guns, and other products worth forty-seven pounds in return for his pottery.[61] Finally, Salem generated considerable surpluses of grain and produce through its milling operations. In 1789, for example, the Aufseher Collegium advised the miller, Abraham Steiner, "to make all haste" and grind the surplus wheat for shipment to Cross Creek; otherwise, the grain risked spoilage.[62] This gathering of grain and other goods enabled the Moravians to trade with cities ranging from Philadelphia in the north to Charleston in the south.

After the Revolution, Philadelphia became the Moravians' most important trading partner. The supplanting of Charleston was for partly economic reasons. As the leading port in the fledgling United States—albeit one about to be eclipsed by New York City—Philadelphia had extensive contacts in the Atlantic world and Germany and could offer the widest range of goods.[63] But the southern Moravians' close social ties with Pennsylvania were important, too. Philadelphia was the center of German-American commercial life.[64] Its merchant houses could offer a comfort zone that other cities found difficult to match. The two merchant houses Wachovia dealt with—Boller and Jordan, and George Haga—corresponded in German and employed religious language on occasion. Of extant trade records, they were the only houses that did this. Both houses had extensive contacts with Moravian towns in Philadelphia's hinterland, as well as Germany's major port in Hamburg. Networking among Bethlehem, Lititz, and Wachovia was extensive, and it was natural that Moravians in North Carolina had close contacts with Philadelphia and its environs. When Bethania's congregation made plans to open its store in 1804, it dispatched Christian Lash to Philadelphia to stock its shelves. To the accompaniment of prayer hymns, residents sent Lash, the store manager, on his way on May 7. He returned in the summer, and the store opened on August 15, when the goods from Philadelphia arrived.[65] *Landgemeinen* settlers, especially in Friedberg, stayed in close touch with Yorktown, Heidelberg, and other interior centers of Pennsylvania Moravian life, trading gossip and economic goods. Wagons from the *Landgemeinen* carried letters and produce to Pennsylvania. They returned with an array of products to sell to neighbors. In May 1774, for instance, Jacob Rothrock, whose family had migrated from Yorktown only three years earlier, brought a wagonload of goods to sell. His sale on a Sunday drew such a crowd that the pastor stared out at a half-empty meetinghouse at that morning's service.[66]

From Philadelphia, the Moravians obtained the latest goods and fashions from Europe for their stores. The diversity was impressive. They bought everything from coffee, wine, and such spices as nutmeg and cinnamon to copper wash kettles, Rittenhouse stoves, and pencils. Regardless of strictures against "worldly" goods, the Moravians seemed attuned to consumers' changing tastes in the late eighteenth century. Through the large mercantile houses in Philadelphia, they obtained knives, forks, fine wines, and other products of the so-called consumer revolution. They bought tin from England, rum from Jamaica, wine from Lisbon, and books from Hamburg, Germany. The Moravians paid for these purchases with a combination of cash, flour, tobacco, and tallow. In

1808, for instance, church accounts sent \$1,784 in cash to Boller and Jordan to cover debits on their account.[67] The merchant houses then sent the goods by schooner to Petersburg, Virginia, where a consignment house unloaded and stored the goods. Wagons delivered them to Wachovia and its clientele.[68]

Petersburg was an important way station for Wachovia. This Virginia town, along with Alexandria and Richmond, was part of a group of small cities that emerged in the mid-eighteenth century at the fall lines of settlement. These three towns all served the same economic function. They integrated the staples of the backcountry and the coast and forwarded them to Atlantic markets.[69] Petersburg and Wachovia developed close ties for practical reasons. Because of the lack of rivers and ports in North Carolina, Petersburg was a convenient stopping place to unload containers sent by ship for the overland journey to the backcountry. Wachovia's teamsters frequented Petersburg from the 1770s on. The trip to Virginia was relatively short and easy, and Petersburg was well connected to Philadelphia and the Atlantic world. Trade letters from Petersburg's merchants touted these advantages and others. In 1828, the firm of Henderson and Simmons promised that wagons would be "promptly dispatched" to Wachovia. Moreover, "we receive, store, and forward Goods or Produce, committed to our care, and we occupy a Store conveniently situated for the purpose, near the River, with a wharf in front. The Store is large, fire-proof, newly erected."[70]

Charleston remained important to Moravian trade in the late eighteenth and early nineteenth centuries, but not as important as in the colonial period. Deerskins, which played so prominent a role in trade before the Revolution, declined in significance after 1780 because of the Moravians' greater trading options.[71] Although Moravian tanners still gathered deerskins and sent them to Charleston, Philadelphia loomed larger because of its connections to Germany. Peter Yarrell, a leather-dresser, was in charge of Salem's tanning business from the mid-1770s until his death in October 1799. He prepared the casks of skins for shipment abroad. The amounts shipped varied, but inventories show that Yarrell sent an average of at least eight hundred dressed skins to Jacob Tentsch in Gnaden by way of Petersburg and Philadelphia in the 1790s. In January 1793, for instance, Yarrell shipped two casks containing 865 dressed skins worth 461 pounds; in 1794, he sent 757 skins worth 423 pounds. He sent the latter shipment aboard the ship *Star* bound for Hamburg. From there, the consignment merchant was to send the casks on to Tentsch in Gnaden.[72]

With the relative decline of the deerskin trade in Charleston, the Moravians traded small amounts of butter, whiskey, tobacco, and tallow in this southern port. In return, they bought products from the West Indies, including molasses, rum, and sugar.[73] Charleston was a logical choice to obtain such items; the port served as an important distribution point for the Caribbean trade. It supplied the West Indies with foodstuffs and lumber in return for the rum, sugar, and other items the Carolina backcountry coveted.[74] Moravian trading partners in Germany also used the port to send books that brethren in Wachovia had ordered.

In Wachovia's early years, the church preferred dealing with Charleston. It was a thriving city in 1753 with well-established links with the Caribbean, Europe, and Africa. As the Reverend John Ettwein explained to North Carolina's governor in 1766, Charleston had many advantages over Wilmington, its rival on the North Carolina coast: "We needed many things which could not be had in Willmington [sic], that goods were at least ten percent higher there than in Charleston, and that the deer-skins with which we paid in Charleston were worth more than in Wilmington."[75] That changed, though, as Cross Creek and Wilmington grew in sophistication during the Revolutionary years. Founded in the 1750s, Cross Creek parlayed a strategic location on the Cape Fear River, about halfway between Rowan County and Wilmington, into an important trading center with the backcountry. Scottish merchants played a significant role in the development of both of these trading centers, as Cross Creek became the dominant entrepot for North Carolina's western backcountry.[76] Population growth, which saw the number of people increase in North Carolina from about 30,000 in 1730 to about 175,000 in 1770, helped fuel a growing, more diversified economy that allowed the colony to compete better with Charleston.[77] Cross Creek served as a middleman in this bustling economy, gathering the products of the interior for shipment to Wilmington.

Wachovia sent most of its flour to Cross Creek and Wilmington. It also sent hogsheads of tobacco, which were then sent to Philadelphia for shipment abroad. In return, Cross Creek fulfilled at least two functions for the Moravians. One role was as an entrepot that gathered up the brethrens' goods for shipment to Wilmington. In this role, its merchants served as the eyes and ears for Wachovia's merchants, letting them know what price their flour and other goods would fetch on the coast and whether the market was glutted. They freely offered advice, too. In 1782, Robert Cochran thanked Samuel Stotz for offering to forward whiskey from Wachovia as payment on their account, but advised against it: "The Conditions of Sending it by your own wagon would make it rather high, as there is nothing to be had here, for backloading except a few Bushels of Country made Salt."[78] From Wilmington, consignment merchants sent these goods to Philadelphia. Second, Cross Creek allowed Moravian merchants to shop closer to home. When salt shortages developed, for example, Moravian businessmen dispatched wagons to Cross Creek. The Moravians also bought considerable amounts of leather in Cross Creek for its tanners along with iron and "West Indies Articles."[79]

Wachovia's farms, including in the *Landgemeinen,* were never self-sufficient. Retail stores in Friedberg, Bethabara, Bethania, and Salem supplied the brethren with such basic farming equipment as sickles, weeding hoes, saws, shovels, and whetstones, all items that farmers could not easily produce on the average family farm.[80] Wachovia's farmers also turned to these stores for a host of the mundane, from nails to thread to razors, all items that could be produced on the farm if they had wanted. Customers at Wachovia's stores had a taste for the refined. From the late eighteenth century and on, Wachovia's stores carried products of the "consumer revolution," including white Delph plates, spoons and forks, silk, fur hats, ivory, and other luxury items.[81]

But the availability of these goods reflected not just Moravian farmers' willingness to engage, and participate in, the marketplace. It also reflected their growing spirit of consumerism in a developing American economy. This acquisitiveness was a natural byproduct of acculturation and adaptation to American ways. This adaptation began not with later generations but with the first generation, especially in the *Landgemeinen,* which intermixed so extensively with outsiders and where creole families were created from an early date. From the outset, materialism alarmed Wachovia's boards, and they tried to stop its spread. Their difficult challenge was familiar to other religious reformers. To borrow Max Weber's term, Moravians shared with other "ascetic Protestants" the challenge of how to construct a Christian society while living in a materialistic, secular world. The virtues of Protestant ethics, with its emphasis on sobriety, discipline, and hard work, complicated the task by fostering a capitalist spirit that undermined the very religious commitment that the reborn was trying to maintain. Most famously, Puritan clerics in the seventeenth century expected the saints to work diligently in their calling, because economic success would show that they were among the elect. But working hard in one's calling led to a dilemma: frugality and industriousness would lead eventually to wealth, temptation, and worldliness.[82] Anabaptists, too, struggled with a similar dilemma, although their greatest fear was that economic striving would ensnare them in a commercial, and unconverted, world. Their solution, at least for the Hutterites, Amish, and some Mennonites, was to withdraw from the world and construct *Gemeinen* limited to the converted.[83]

An ecumenical, evangelical group such as the Moravians shared this Protestant dilemma, but they had an added one as well. They were to venture into the world to convert the unconverted. They rejected the Catholic notion of monastic ascetism, where the pious were to retreat behind walls to pursue a life of godly contemplation. They also abhorred the Anabaptists' hostility to the unconverted. The unsaved were to be engaged, not shunned, and introduced to Christ's healing message. Such a challenge meant living among the ungodly while striving to be free of the world's temptations.

Evangelicals saw the new birth as their main weapon in the battle against temptation. Being reborn would give the saved the discipline and the strength to reject his or her worldly ways and make a new beginning as a Christian. As Count Zinzendorf put it, the conversion experience "changes us, gives us new birth, and makes us completely different people in heart, spirit, mind and all our powers."[84] Such strength would enable the Christian to leave behind his or her corrupt, secular ways and lead a new life as a disciplined servant of God and Christ. Work, paradoxically, played an important role in helping the sanctified lead a disciplined life; indeed, evangelicals saw labor as religiously sanctioned, because God blessed his chosen ones through the success of their labors.

For Zinzendorf, weak discipline indicated the lack of true conversion. The reborn Christian, living for Christ, must follow his commandments in all aspects of his or her life. Work, in the count's view, was an important facet of a person's spiritual growth. Zinzendorf valued work because of its religious meanings and its implications for a person's salvation. For the same reasons, he abhorred idleness. A lazy person did a disservice to himself and Jesus. "In a Church we must work," he liked to say. "We should not work to live, but live to work."[85] In an ideal twenty-four-hour day, Zinzendorf believed, a person should devote three hours a day to the care of his soul and five hours to sleep. That left nearly sixteen hours for work.[86] Following Zinzendorf's lead, Wachovia's administrative boards strove to instill a proper work ethic in youths and adults. "It is important to impress upon our youth," members of the Aufseher Collegium noted in 1786, "the all-important things of human life—industry, faithfulness, obedience, economy, good manners, and to do unto others as they would be done by." Such a holistic approach meant that those who had undergone the new birth were to work hard and direct their energies into leading upright and exemplary lives. They were not to be concerned with getting ahead economically, but with working hard and living by biblical standards. Work and religion went hand in hand. The attitude of Salem's elders toward something as innocuous as hunting exemplified this spirit. The Congregation Council reminded Salem's master craftsmen in 1785 not to allow their workers to go off hunting. If a journeyman can get time off, board members reasoned, he will ignore his regular work and engage in frivolous leisure activities, thereby making it "difficult to bring him back to orderly ways."[87] Craftsmen and their apprentices, in short, were to put work ahead of leisure.[88]

Church elders in Salem repeatedly lectured residents about the dangers of trying to get ahead. Such grasping was unacceptable, they said; it was un-Christian. The Helfer Conferenz explained why. "A man is more blessed when he follows his calling faithfully and industriously. A man who tries to do too many things and mixes in matters which do not concern his business loses his sense of order and becomes restless."[89] Striving for worldly things, in their view, led only to unhappiness and spiritual emptiness, because it put the selfish needs of the individual ahead of God.

The evangelical (and Protestant) impulse to work hard meant that individuals could not act "worldly." Men and women were to work hard in their occupations while not striving for riches or material goods. Salem's elders urged Wachovia's residents to live plainly and simply. This stricture applied to clothing. The elders preferred that the brethren dress in plain shirts and clothes—black was preferred but not required—and simple leggings and breeches. The reason: "We should not follow the world," because those who follow the dictates of fashion would not be following the dictates of God.[90] Wearing pretty ribbons, flashy buckles, and large hats meant that an individual wanted to "become noticeable and attract attention." For the elders, such vanity was dangerous for another reason as well. It could mean that a brother or sister was striving to be something that he or she was not. The brethren, the elders noted in 1787, "should dress according to their station, and a poor person should not have the clothes which one more well-to-do might properly purchase."[91] Each congregation's Brotherly Agreement, drawn up with extensive guidance from Wachovia leaders, placed a great emphasis on proper economic conduct. Bethania's agreement, adopted in 1780, began by declaring that inhabitants should not seek "to grow rich or to acquire worldly Advantages." Instead, brethren should strive to save souls and lead "quiet and peaceful life [lives] in all godliness and honesty." No one was welcome in the village who sought "Riches, profitable Business and other worldly Views."[92]

These religious values were abundantly evident in the Moravian leadership's views toward money and credit. Wachovia's boards feared the improper use of credit because it led to temptation. In other words, credit made it easier for the brethren to acquire worldly goods. They especially worried about the ability of young adults to deal with the temptations of a secular society. As Salem's Congregation Council lamented in 1787, the young "are easily induced to buy things on credit which they do not really need and which good management requires that they do not buy."[93] Credit, the leadership complained, led to a keeping-up-with-your-neighbor syndrome: "No one must think, as it seems some do, that he must have everything that wealthier Brethren have."[94]

Wachovia's leaders, as a result, tried to limit the use of credit. Contracts with the settlement's mill owners, tavern operators, and store managers required that these businesses extend credit only as a last resort. An agreement signed in 1802 between Wachovia and Herman Buttner for the management of Bethabara's distillery was typical. The second clause in the contract stressed, "He should not contract any Debts for Account of the said Business, nor lend money out of the same to any."[95]

Such was the ideal. The Protestant dilemma, along with the contradictory policies of the church itself, hurtled the brethren toward a far different outcome. Cut off from the outside world, Wachovia's residents might have resisted the riches around them. But the brethren, thanks in large part to the church itself, were never isolated from the regional and national markets that grew in size and complexity during the early national period. The great irony was that Wachovia's boards admonished the brethren to avoid worldly goods at the same time church-run stores stocked Wachovia's stores with the latest products of the Atlantic economy.

Extensive trading throughout the Atlantic world accomplished two things. It enabled individual brethren to stay fully attuned to changing markets and tastes, and it put consumer goods within easy reach of them through their stores in Salem, Bethania, Bethabara, and Friedberg. Contact with the outside helped spur the brethrens' appetite for the luxury goods that were becoming available in the marketplace. Wealthier brethren, including merchants and large landowners, began purchasing the finer things in life. The holding of slaves became an important part of this consumer culture in Wachovia and throughout the South. Slaves, land, material goods—these aspirations all came together for many southerners, especially those of "middling" means. That is, many people worked hard to get ahead so they could acquire land and slaves. As one historian of slavery notes, "Slaveholding was the symbol of success in the market culture of the Old South. It was an ambition, an achievement, a reward for diligence, hard work, and tenacity."[96] The appeal of slave owning ran even deeper than economics. It brought a certain prestige for those masters who had the money to invest in a slave. Entry into the slaveholding class thus often became an end in itself. It was a sign of an individual's success in society.

In the South, slavery underwent a massive expansion following the introduction of the cotton gin in the 1790s and the subsequent spread of cotton cultivation. Within two decades, the South's slave population had soared to 1,191,354 in 1810, up 70 percent from 697,897 in 1790.[97] Slavery's importance grew in the North Carolina backcountry as well. As early as 1790, blacks constituted nearly 20 percent of the population in the central Piedmont.[98] While the South was increasing its reliance on slavery, the North was moving in the opposite direction, with state after state passing laws after the American Revolution that barred slavery by gradually emancipating its slave force. The net effect of these developments was not only to sectionalize slavery but to increase slavery's importance in the South. The more "peculiar" slavery became, the more southerners defended it and fought to expand it.

As acculturation proceeded on economic and cultural levels, North Carolina's Moravians were fully attuned to these changes around them. They participated in the market as consumers and traders and observed close-up the concomitant rise of slavery and a consumer culture. The lure of the latter two was so strong that it transcended ethnicity. The desire of Friedrich Schumann, a German Moravian who had come to the United States in 1801, to own slaves was as strong as a native-born English-speaking Marylander who had come to Wachovia thirty years earlier. Admonitions against worldly goods to the contrary, brethren in both the village and the countryside found the purchase of a slave to be surprisingly easy to rationalize. On one level, most Moravians saw no contradiction in owning slaves. Zinzendorf himself, after all, had believed that the subordination of human beings was perfectly natural and proper in the divine order. As the Bible showed, some were meant to lead and some to follow. The ancient Hebrews, defenders of slavery noted, owned slaves, and Jesus had not censured the practice. Thus many evangelicals concluded that God did not condemn slaveholding and actually welcomed it, because the institution of slavery provided a chance for good Christians to expose "heathens" to the gospel.[99] Some of Salem's residents did not ignore the practical in seeking the right to own slaves. Artisans argued that employing bound labor would allow them to compete better in the marketplace, because they could lower production costs and the prices they charged. Many shop managers were tired of going to the expense and trouble of training apprentices, only to have these workers abandon them when their training period ended.

Apparently, Moravian farmers did not see slavery as morally repugnant either; most shared the common view that God had ordained leaders and followers. Certainly, Anglo-American brethren in Hope had no qualms about the owning of slaves. As Maryland expatriates, they accepted slavery as part of their worldview and perfectly natural in the order of things. But *Landgemeinen* settlers of Lutheran and Reformed background apparently had few qualms, either. Both the Lutheran and Reformed traditions from which these settlers were raised embraced a view of the social order with its God-ordained gradations.[100]

Culturally, the strong sense of family helped shape the views of Moravians of both ethnicities toward slavery. To borrow historian Daniel Vickers's phrase, the brethren desired a "competency," but not quite in the way that he and other scholars use the term. Because of their strong religious values and sense of community, Moravian farmers did not want a yeoman's independence. Evangelism was an outwardly looking reform movement. The idea of standing alone, of striving to be free of dependence from others, clashed with their sense of values. The ideal of a subsistence farm producing all it needed held no attraction to them. They saw themselves as part of a unique religious community that carried reciprocal obligations. Markets and profits were means to them so they could achieve their ends of providing for their families spiritually and economically. In this sense, Moravians wanted a "competency," a balancing of religious, household, and market needs. For farmers outside of Salem, land and slaves represented an important way to achieve security for their families.[101]

Slavery did not represent a radical break from these family based values. Instead, it was a new means to achieve old goals, in much the same way that some Pennsylvanians embraced commercial farming in the early 1800s to preserve the family better.[102] As the research of A. G. Roeber has shown, German speakers' obsession with household, family, and property survived the transfer to the New World, albeit in a hybrid form. In southwest Germany, family values played a significant role in the shaping of village life. German speakers, Roeber notes, aspired to material security and noninterference in religious and familial affairs. Pietism in southwest Germany worked within this tradition, tried to channel it in religiously acceptable directions, but did not radically change it. Pietist leaders understood the importance of property as a linchpin of familial life, although they believed that individuals needed to deal with property cautiously because of its corrupting influence. In colonial South Carolina, pietistic Lutheran settlers embraced slavery as a new form of wealth and defended it as a form of property that they had every right to hold. It was an easy step for them to expand the pietist definition of liberty to include freedom of choice to hold slaves. Slavery, in other words, was another way for them to achieve material comfort.[103] For Moravian farmers in Wachovia, slavery meant nearly the same thing. They did not see the holding of slaves as compromising their pietist principles but as a means to provide for their families. Indeed, owning human property was something of a reward for their religiously sanctioned hard work.

Farmers' emphasis on family values was quite "traditional" in many ways. The first generation, after all, had migrated to the *Landgemeinen* in the 1760s and 1770s out of a desire to provide for their families spiritually and economically. Parents sought to achieve this dual goal by purchasing farms in a religious enclave. They would provide for their children while raising them in an evangelical culture. In 1800, land and family remained important to the later generation, but the growth of markets and intermixing with the outside meant that the values of "modernity" and consumerism were infusing, but not replacing, the brethrens' traditional worldview. In an important sense, slavery and consumerism were natural outgrowths of their evangelical values. The church implored the brethren to work hard, and they did. By working hard and achieving material success, the reborn could show he had achieved sanctification. And, concurrently, the brethren worked hard so they could purchase land and slaves that would enable them to secure their families' financial and spiritual futures. Simultaneously pursuing property and piety, of course, posed a fundamental contradiction. The good Moravian was supposed to reject materialism and all that entailed. The threat to religious purity posed by the use of slaves—and the materialism and laziness that would follow—was one reason some brethren in Salem sought to keep slavery out of their village well into the nineteenth century.

The broader evangelical world struggled with the same dilemma. Some Virginia Methodists, for instance, denounced not only slavery but an obsessive concern with the materialism that permeated it: "The world is in their thoughts day and night," complained one minister. "The price of merchandise and negroes are inexhaustible themes of conversation. But for them the name of Jesus has no charms."[104] The Unity asked when an individual's pursuit of property for religious reasons turned into the pursuit of riches for selfish reasons. And it wondered when a love of land and slaves hurt the brethrens' devotion to the Savior. Wachovia's administrative boards had no answers to these difficult questions but only contributed to the perplexities surrounding them. Despite strong fears of slavery's corrupting influence, they did not attempt to restrict the use of slaves in the countryside. At the same time that they wrung their hands over the brethrens' seeming devotion to land and slaves, they did all they could to encourage the development of Wachovia's land through generous lease-purchase agreements that allowed buyers to build up their holdings. Both decisions contributed to the growth of slavery outside of Salem.

Despite the fears of slavery and a consumer culture, materialism did not run amuck in Wachovia. Family values, which contributed to the turn to slavery, paradoxically helped keep its use down. The daily demands of family run, grain-based farms meant that most brethren did not need large slave forces in their fields.[105] Unlike tobacco, which needed constant, year-round care, grain required intensive labor only during planting and harvesting. Feeding, housing, and clothing a slave year-round proved to be a serious expense for farmers in the middling and small landholding classes. The price of slaves was so high that purchasing one represented a significant investment. In the North Carolina Piedmont in the early nineteenth century, prices for children ranged from $150 up to $500, depending on age and sex. Prime male field hands could cost as much as $650, and purchasing slave families of three to four members topped $800.[106] By comparison, $500 could get a land buyer up to nine hundred acres, depending on location and the number of improvements. In 1830, Jacob Fry of Friedberg procured most of the implements for a working farm with only $187, or what a girl under ten years old would have cost: a horse, seven head of cattle, two sheep, twenty-five hogs, ten stacks of small grain, and a wagon and gears, as well as household furniture, including a spinning wheel.[107] For most farmers in Wachovia, the decision to purchase slaves involved carefully weighing their options, deciding whether to put their capital into land, slaves, or both. The building of large slaveholdings was left to the wealthy who had the money to invest in human capital and the holdings to put them to work productively. Most families, as a result, had anywhere from one to five slaves; they then used these workers to help them in the fields and the home.[108] Family values and economics, more than admonitions against materialism and riches, helped tamp down enthusiasm for slavery.

Slaves complemented family labor but did not lead to the abandonment of grain-based farms for lucrative staples such as cotton or tobacco, as often occurred elsewhere in the South. In Warren County, Mississippi, for instance, the opening of markets and the rise of slavery enabled planters to shift from subsistence farming to staple production, most notably cotton.[109] In Wachovia, the family farm and its focus on grains held firm, although cotton and tobacco did finally grow in importance in the late antebellum period. The slaveholdings of Dr. Schumann were far larger than those of other slaveholders in Wachovia. But despite this large labor force, Schumann was quite typical in one regard:

he did not abandon grains and dairy products to become a staple producer; instead, Schumann merely expanded the production of existing crops and products. His slaves enabled Schumann to run a better farm, but they did not drastically change the farm's makeup.

The Impact of Slavery on Acculturation

The presence of black laborers, in effect, introduced a third ethnicity to Wachovia. Now, there was intermixing not only among German and Anglo-American but among white and black. The effects of this intermixing between white and black were substantially different than between German and English. White-black intermixing did produce friendships and a sense of brotherhood between the races, especially in the eighteenth century, but no interethnic marriages and lasting social unions. Intermixing between German and English over the long run brought the two ethnicities closer together. Among white and black, however, sustained intermixing had the opposite impact—the two ethnicities drew further apart. And as the wedge between white Moravian and black Moravian widened, the gap between white Moravian and white southerner narrowed, with the brethren becoming more like their neighbors.

The widening gulf between white and black can be seen most clearly in the rise of segregated worship. As historians of the evangelical movement have documented, the push for universal salvation had the effect of downplaying racial differences during the late eighteenth century. Those sinners who had "died" and been spiritually reborn were all equal before the Lord. The saved became members of a spiritual community who enjoyed a rough equality with others who had undergone the new birth. The implications of such an equality were obvious to white and black alike. In the late eighteenth century, during the heady days of the Revolutionary era, this promise reached its fullest fulfillment, only to be dashed in the nineteenth as slavery became more entrenched.[110]

Wachovia's leaders in the late eighteenth century encouraged blacks to convert as a way out of a "quandary," in the words of historian Jon Sensbach. Wachovia needed laborers to help run its shops, clean its houses, and till its fields. Yet the presence of black "heathens" threatened the purity of the Moravian mission in North Carolina, especially in Salem, the supposedly purest congregation of all. The leadership came up with a simple way out of this dilemma: encourage the slaves to join the church. That way, the slaves would not be outsiders—they would be fellow Moravians. And by converting former Africans, the brethren would also be fulfilling one of Count Zinzendorf's fondest dreams—taking the message of Christ's love to all.[111]

For blacks in Wachovia, this attempt at evangelizing carried promise and danger. No matter how benevolent the message of Jesus's redeeming grace, it remained the message of the master race, which was intent on using religion to justify blacks' enslavement. Many slaves apparently resisted on those very grounds. But for others, the promise of salvation was an attractive one. By converting, they would gain a potent psychological means of coping with the harsh realities of slavery. Jesus would be their protector, and conversion would be the path to a better life in the beyond. Just as important, conversion offered the hope of some benefits in the here and now: to be black and a non-Moravian in Wachovia was to be the ultimate outcast, the strangest of "strangers." But to be black and a brother would theoretically offer some protection, because these members could claim to be the spiritual equals of the white Moravians who worshipped with them at the *gemeine Hauses* scattered across Wachovia. "By laying claim to the masters' covenant, slaves would undercut the supposed differences between them, chipping away at the rock of racism on which slavery rested," Sensbach notes. "They could, in effect, challenge slavery at its brute core—the negation of their humanity."[112]

This hope of protection and spiritual equality was not an empty one. During the Revolutionary years, black Moravians did become a part of the church family in Wachovia, worshipping and working alongside their white brethren. Those who became communicant members were held to the same standards as whites. The Unity expected black applicants to be reborn and to be committed followers of the Savior. It expected them to abide by congregation rules and to participate faithfully in choir and congregational life. "Prayer, song, and work provided important arenas of interracial contact," Sensbach concludes, "and fostered a rough-and-tumble leveling in some aspects of daily life." He characterizes relations between the two races as "fraternalistic"—a corporate relationship governed by the brethrens' allegiance to a higher authority. The church, in other words, sought to promote a spiritual kinship among the two races. Bishop Augustus Spangenberg summed up fraternalism well: "Because of our love to them we do not free them, for they would be in a worse condition if they got free as if we kept them. Actually they are not slaves with us, and there is no difference between them and other Brothers and Sisters."[113]

As Sensbach's research elegantly shows, such spiritual equality was always a rough one in practice. But even this limited promise of a biracial accommodation began to disappear in the 1790s. The causes of such a shift were many and complex, and they mirrored the forces that propelled Moravians to embrace slavery in the first place. That is, change came from within and from without Wachovia. As the outcry against slavery rose during the Revolutionary years, and as northern states banned the institution, southern slaveholders launched a vigorous defense of their rights to own black labor. This defense rested on the premise that Africans were inherently different from whites and ultimately inferior to Westerners. Because of their inferiority, blacks supposedly could not handle the responsibilities of freedom and citizenship. Left on their own, they would lead lives of squalor and idleness. Southerners (and others) argued that slavery thus benefited the enslaved by keeping them fed and clothed; by teaching them useful trades; and by inculcating Christian values in them. For southerners facing criticism from hostile northerners, it was an alluring argument that even Spangenberg mimicked: "Because of our love to them we do not free them, for they would be in a worse condition if they got free."[114]

The ethnic makeup of Wachovia's population aided the Moravians in their embracing of southern views on segregation. The *Landgemeinen* with its complex mix of Anglo-American members and creole German-Americans played a significant role in the shifting of attitudes toward blacks and spiritual equality. It was in Friedberg where one of the first protests against the presence of blacks was recorded. In 1797, an African-American girl asked to be baptized upon completion of study of the scriptures under the pastor's guidance. Martin Schneider had agreed to help teach her the scriptures and to let her attend a meeting of the older girls' choir. But the choir members and their parents opposed this, and they "persuaded these people not to tolerate any Negroes in these meetings," Salem's elders recalled. "And so when [Schneider] wished to hold the last meeting, they all walked out." The walkout appalled the elders, who sternly told the mothers and girls that "not the slightest distinction between whites and blacks can be made in matters of the spirit."[115] And it was in Friedberg where the brethren concluded they did not want to share benches with blacks anymore—the congregation decided to seat black visitors in the rear.

As important as Friedberg's role was, Hope's was even larger. By 1800, the largest number of black church members resided in Hope, and Wachovia's other congregations watched events in this Anglo-German settlement closely. In late 1801, Hope's committee decided that the settlement's slaves should have their own separate religious meetings. The committee couched its decision in the language of southern paternalism: "It is now the time to offer separate meetings for the Negroes in this area, in which one could present the truths of our beliefs to them in a clear and more comprehensible manner."[116] The reality, though, was harsher. Sunday worship services at Hope's meetinghouse were now for whites. Black Moravians were to be kept apart. The two other major slaveholding settlements followed Hope's example. Friedberg began separate meetings in 1802, and Bethania soon followed suit.[117] In these three farm settlements, the first momentous steps on the path to segregated worship were taken.

A confluence of events had driven the three congregations to take such action. Behind southerners' defense of slavery and white supremacy lay the palpable threat of rebellion. Armed revolts, of course, had been masters' darkest fears since colonial days. In the summer of 1802 in North Carolina, these fears intensified. Slaves in eastern North Carolina planned to overthrow their masters on June 10. Like so many revolts, the plot was uncovered and squelched before it ever got off the ground—in this instance, a week before the planned uprising. Authorities hanged the ringleaders and deported others suspected of being involved. And as in so many other cases, the aborted uprising scared slaveholders everywhere, including in Wachovia. There, the brethren decided to head off any prospective rebellions by intensifying efforts to take the word to blacks in the countryside. Reborn slaves, they reasoned, would be content slaves. And content slaves would be docile slaves. So the Moravians redoubled their missionary efforts among the area's blacks. The vehicle for this missionary work was the Society for the Propagation of the Gospel Among the Heathen, which had been founded in 1788 to proselytize among the Cherokee and other southeastern Indians.[118]

The threat of physical violence helped accelerate the process by which white Moravians viewed their black counterparts as "different." Although no armed uprisings ever occurred in Wachovia, African-Americans from the Revolution on had stepped up their resistance to their masters through time-honored means—by running away, by engaging in petty thefts, and by conducting work slowdowns. Others slept during services or refused to come to church at all. Evangelism, despite its emphasis on spiritual equality and brotherhood, was not able to thwart the sense of estrangement that crept in between the two races. Instead, another side of evangelism contributed to the feelings of mistrust between the two sides: missionaries, if nothing else, believed in the righteousness of their cause. The Bible to them was quite clear that the new birth was the only path to salvation. This conviction gave the missionaries the confidence—or arrogance—that they had the answers and that others did not. It allowed a missionary such as George Soelle in the 1770s to fume that the Presbyterians lacked the "true light." And it allowed missionaries and other evangelicals to dismiss Africans as heathens, pagans, and inferiors. As a cultural backlash against "upstart revivalists" muted the egalitarian thrust of evangelism in the early nineteenth century, evangelism's original tendencies were easily turned to the defense of the southern way of life. In dealings with blacks, to be reborn no longer meant one was among social equals. Conversion no longer freed the slaves on any level. Instead, southern evangelicals, including the Moravians, argued that slavery was necessary if heathen blacks were to stand any chance of converting and becoming good Christians. By the 1820s, evangelism in most places had become a tool to defend slavery. Indeed, evangelism in the nineteenth century had a strong following among slaveholders, with many plantation owners embracing revivalism.[119]

In Wachovia, the paradoxes in these developments were readily apparent. Blacks increasingly became different, and foreign, and threatening. Yet this very foreignness meant that the brethren stepped up their efforts to convert them and to make them evangelicals. These new converts, however, could no longer sit with their evangelical brothers and sisters. Nor could they worship in the same churches. Blacks, this thinking went, needed their own meeting places for their own sake. The trend to segregated worship moved steadily, if not inexorably, forward during the early years of the nineteenth century: separate meetings and seating began between 1801 and 1803. Separate burial grounds came in 1816. And finally, a separate meetinghouse for African-Americans was built in 1823. The erection of a log church in south Salem, within an easy walk of Schumann's plantation, meant that blacks would no longer belong to Wachovia's white congregations. They had their own church—but one overseen by a white pastor and white governing boards.[120]

The embracing of slavery and segregated worship were powerful manifestations of just how "southern" North Carolina's Moravians had become. The Moravians in Pennsylvania, by contrast, moved in the opposite direction: they had freed their slaves by the late eighteenth century and permitted biracial worship throughout the antebellum period.[121] Intermixing and acculturation had thus produced opposite—but quite predictable—results in the Moravian Church's two American provinces. The northern branch embraced the antislavery views of its northern neighbors; the southern one adopted the proslavery views of its southern compatriots.

Driven by a complex ethnic mix within Wachovia and by extensive economic contacts with the outside, the brethren moved quickly to the views of their neighbors, thus lessening the distance between the two. The journey to "southern" ways was shortest for those German-American brethren who had formed creole families; it was longest for those recent German arrivals such as Friedrich Schumann. For all groups, though, it was a relatively easy sojourn. Intermixing among fellow Moravians and with outsiders helped speed the process by which the brethren became "southern." An evangelical religion, with its emphasis on hard work and discipline, did the rest.

Economic developments that helped propel the Moravians toward a more southern identity meant that the pace of acculturation was accelerating by the 1830s. As the Reverend George Bahnson, a native German-speaking Danish Moravian, arrived in Bethania from Pennsylvania to begin a new pastorship, he witnessed firsthand how much Wachovia had changed—and not changed.

6

The New World of the 1830s and Beyond

George Frederic Bahnson arrived in Bethania after a "tedious" ride from Salem that tired not only him but his horse. His first impression of his new home was not a good one. "It is a tolerably large town for North Carolina," Bahnson recorded in his diary, "but contains only one house that may be called handsome by a lenient critic."[1] The year was 1834, and Bahnson had finally arrived at the village after an even more tiring ride from Pennsylvania to start his new job—the pastorship of an *Ortsemeine* that, while prospering in affairs of the world, had seen better days religiously.

Bahnson's sense of disorientation in these new surroundings was palpable. The young minister was a twenty-eight-year-old German-speaking Dane who had migrated to Pennsylvania from Prussia in 1829. Now, he had undergone yet another journey to a strange place—Bethania, a small village in the American South. The Dane from Christiansfeld brought with him a thoroughly European outlook. He spent his formative years at a Moravian boarding school at Niesky in Prussia. He later taught at a Moravian school in the upper Lusatia before receiving his call to come to the United States, where he taught for five years in Nazareth at the Moravian theological seminary and grammar school there. Bahnson was introduced to American—and northern ways—in Nazareth.[2] Thus, when he arrived in Wachovia, he had a unique perspective, being intimately familiar with both German culture and northern mores.

Wachovia in 1834 was no German enclave. Approaching the end of the first century of its existence, Wachovia had evolved into something quite different from its sister settlements in Germany. These differences were immediately apparent to Bahnson. The pastor, for one, was struck by how southern Wachovia's inhabitants had become. "They do not waste much in fine clothes," Bahnson noted in one early entry. "Land and slaves are the principal things wherein they invest money."[3] And Bahnson quickly grasped how American these North Carolina Moravians were. "The Salemites are prejudiced against every one that is not raised among them—strange enough!—but above all, against all Germans, whom they consider incapable of entering into the American *Gemeinschaft*! . . . Separation from Germany, suspension of all officers except preacher and inspector connected in one person and court, are their favorite plans."[4]

Nearly a century of intermixing had brought Wachovia to this state of affairs. As the antebellum period drew to a close, Wachovia had fashioned a unique identity that melded different traditions. Its inhabitants were evangelical, American, and southern. They retained elements of their German background; indeed, Wachovia's boards kept their records in German through the 1840s, and many residents still spoke German. But the use of English was extensive and growing. More important, North Carolina's Moravians, in contrast to German-American Lutherans in Pennsylvania, aligned themselves ever closer with the evangelical movement and with the Protestant mainstream. The brethren embraced the Sunday school movement, formed temperance societies, and participated fully in Protestant life. Yet befitting their complex heritage that saw a melding of German and Anglo-American cultures, they at first frowned upon the camp-meeting movement that had become so popular among southern evangelicals, and they decried its supposed emotional excesses.

Wachovia in the Antebellum Period

Pastor Bahnson took up residence in Bethania's *gemeine Haus* and tried to make himself at home in this foreign land. The Unity had appointed him pastor of an *Ortsgemeine* that was thriving economically but languishing spiritually. Congregational membership in 1834 stood at 218 persons—lower than in 1785, when 245 men, women, and children were members. Nor had the congregation grown any in recent years. In 1834, membership was the same as in 1830.[5] The problems did not end there. The congregation was not only smaller than in 1785 but also more scattered. As early as 1790, the majority of members lived outside the village. By 1834, when this German-speaking Dane came on the scene, Bethania's members had dispersed evermore widely, living in places that they in some cases had helped to found—places with names such as Schortown, Pfafftown, and Brookstown.

Bahnson spent his first year becoming acquainted with his far-flung dominion. He found the various settlements to be small and inconsequential groupings of houses that did not merit the name of "town." He visited Schortown first—a collection of four or five mostly empty houses. Pitiful as it was, Bahnson felt compelled to visit because Schortown's only two occupied homes were inhabited by members of the Bethania congregation. One member was Joseph Stockburger. Bahnson did not much like him. The pastor found Stockburger to be a man of business who distilled whiskey "and sells it in large as well as smaller quantities, [so] that his house often resembles a tavern of rather low character." He liked Brother Isaac Werner and his wife far better. "I believe," the pastor wrote on July 12, 1834, "they think much more of the *Gemeine* than Stockburger, who only looks for money." Bahnson then pushed on to Pfafftown, another inconsequential collection of houses a little over a mile from Schortown. Here, Bahnson confronted the complexity of his—and Bethania's—predicament. The town's founder, Peter Pfaff, no longer belonged to the congregation. But Pfaff's five sons and four daughters were "all very warm members of our congregation." The founder, in other words, had strayed while the younger generation remained devout. Pfafftown thus turned the idea of a declension, with a second and third generation failing to live up to the supposedly high standards of the founding generation, on its head. Overall, Bahnson was unhappy both with the congregation's meager numbers and with its seemingly lukewarm state of piety. Barely two weeks into his stay, he felt discouraged. "Would to God our dear Bethany would again spring up by the blessing of our Lord and flourish, as it did in bygone days," the pastor confided in his diary. "But there is very little prospect" of that.[6]

As he got to know fellow congregation members, Bahnson identified several problems. One was simple geography. Scattered about the countryside, many members had drifted away from the congregation. Another, and closely related, problem was these members' growing worldliness. The large and wealthy Conrad clan was one example of these two related phenomena. Bahnson, on a visit to Jacob Conrad's plantation, was both fascinated and repelled by what he saw. This planter lived in a "very elegant dwelling house," Bahnson observed. "It is a delightful place." Less delightful was Conrad's deep involvement with the secular world. He owned, by Bahnson's reckoning, "forty grown negroes," numerous children, three stores, and three plantations. Bahnson disapprovingly noted that this wealthy member of the gentry was a lightning rod for criticism, with his "neighbors, out of envy perhaps, saying many a thing against him." Sadly, from Bahnson's perspective, Conrad was not especially unique in his flagging devotion to the Savior. He used to be a communicant member but had now settled for membership in the society. The causes of this waning religiosity, according to Bahnson, were multiple and complex. "With some it is indifference, with others religious scruples." Still, as in Pfafftown, Bahnson recognized that he was not dealing with a simple declension where later generations failed

Rev. Geo. F. Bahnson

George Frederic Bahnson, a German-speaking Dane, became pastor of Bethania in 1834 and was often puzzled by what he saw in the American South. *Collection of Old Salem, Winston-Salem, North Carolina; courtesy of Old Salem Inc., Winston-Salem, North Carolina.*

to live up to the supposedly higher standards of their parents. Although Jacob's attention in religious matters had been wandering, his wife's had not. Bahnson concluded that she "seems to be a very pious and religious lady. . . . If you should see her, you would never more believe that she is the partner of the richest man in our immediate neighborhood."[7]

Bethania's problems were not unique. Although congregational membership in Wachovia nearly doubled in the 1790 to 1856 period, from 1,157 to 1,935,

Table 6.1 Wachovia's Congregational Membership, 1765–1856

Settlement	1765	1772	1780	1785	1822	1836	1856
Bethabara	88	54	69	90	120	104	98
Bethania	78	105	123	245	274	226	314
Salem		120	147	205	437	479	718
Friedberg			108	262	411	391	427
Friedland			56	132	277	236	98
Hope			70	152	171	129	62
TOTAL	166	279	573*	1,086	1,690	1,565	1,935**

Source: Memorabilia for Wachovia.
*This total does not include children in the *Landgemeinen*.
**Total includes membership figures for three new congregations: New Philadelphia, Mount Bethel, and Macedonia.

these figures masked several problem areas. Bethabara continued to lag, seeing its total membership drop from 120 in 1822 to only 98 in 1856. Friedland and Hope also struggled. Following a migration to Hope, Indiana, in the 1830s, Friedland's membership dropped precipitously and did not recover in the antebellum period. In 1856, only ninety-eight people belonged to the congregation. Hope stagnated as well, with membership dropping from 171 in 1822 to 62 in 1856. Its largest loss of membership came over a twenty-year period, from 1836 to 1856. Bethania's membership recovered somewhat after Bahnson left the congregation in 1838, rising from 226 in 1836 to 314 in 1856.[8] The two strongest congregations in terms of membership were Salem and Friedberg. Salem's population nearly doubled from 437 in 1822 to 718 in 1856. Friedberg, meanwhile, continued to hold its own. The South Fork area was a hotbed of evangelical activity, with the Methodists and Baptists active and with the Moravians starting a new congregation four miles from Friedberg called Muddy Creek. The cumulative effect of this activity was to drain membership from Hope. Friedberg, however, kept the allegiance of its members, with membership holding steady throughout the antebellum period at about four hundred. This made it the second largest congregation in Wachovia.[9] See table 6.1.

Cultural Changes in Wachovia

For Bahnson, the cultural scene was even more complex and confusing than the religious one. Wachovia's Moravians lived in a dual world following more than a half-century of intermixing, and he struggled at times to understand it. This duality—and Bahnson's struggles—were nowhere more evident than in the use of language. Many Moravians still spoke German in the 1830s, a testament to the longevity of the brethrens' cultural heritage. Indeed, Bahnson could write on August 3, 1834, "The audience was tolerably good, although English preaching is not as much frequented as German discourses. *Der gate alto Stamm* [the good old clan] does not understand English well."[10] But this "good old clan" was clearly a minority. The European-bred Bahnson, who preferred conversing in German, struggled at times to meet the demands of his Anglo-American environment. In 1837, he complained about Bethania's sisters, "The confusion of languages in our congregation puts me to some inconvenience. With the exception of one or two, they cannot read German, and some do not understand the German well at all."[11] Bahnson had two general, and related, criticisms: that the state of education in the congregation was so poor and that teachers conducted classes in English. In 1834, he reported, "The younger generation, if able to read at all, can read only English." Three years later, the pastor put his criticism even more forcefully: "It is a great pity that the young people receiving in English what little 'learning' is given them cannot understand preaching in German as well as in English."[12]

More than a generational phenomenon was involved, however. These Moravian children were products of a cultural environment that often saw two languages used in the home—yet each parent was not necessarily bilingual. The Lash family was one example. Bahnson spent an evening talking with Will Lash, but not with his wife. The reason was simple: Will was a German-speaking member of the Bethania congregation; she was not. And the wife was not a congregation member, according to Bahnson, "because she does not understand any German at all."[13] Nor was German speakers' command of English necessarily strong. On one Sunday, Bahnson preached in German and then delivered a few closing remarks in English. As always, he struggled to talk extemporaneously in his second language. "It went so-so!" he recalled. "One is under the necessity of using both languages . . . and that is rather perplexing." But on this day, Bahnson did not feel too bad about his struggles with the native language: "Our good people," he declared, "speak such a miserable English that I feel quite encouraged." On another occasion, he heard a Salem resident deliver an address on the Sunday school movement, and Bahnson was struck by this brother's delivery: it was "in a kind of English which I have never heard spoken before publicly by a native of America."[14]

The interplay between evangelism and acculturation had helped result in such a duality. On the one hand, religion nearly always took precedence over

Germanness. That meant that German-speaking Moravian parents were more concerned with passing on their religious values to their children than their ethnic heritage. Johanna Gertrude Hauser, for instance, who was born in 1792, received only "the rudiments of a German education" while growing up in Bethania, according to her *Lebenslauf.* But while she was learning little about her German ethnic heritage, she was receiving "regular Religious instruction." Quite predictably given this upbringing, Johanna joined the *Gemeine* and married an Anglo-American.[15] On the other hand, religion did inadvertently contribute to the persistence of German. Although the Unity never emphasized its Germanic background or required that school subjects be taught in German, its very history reminded congregants of the church's roots in Germany. Festival days taught members about the Unity's beginnings in eastern Europe, and bulletins, *Nachrichts,* and other church reports continually reminded brethren that the Unity was still based in Saxony. Wachovia's church records were kept in German, and German remained the preferred language of choice among Wachovia's officials, including most congregational pastors. This German-grounded religious milieu helped German culture survive in Wachovia despite powerful crosscurrents. Bahnson, as a result, discovered a Wachovia in a state of transition in the mid-1830s. The "old clan" preferred German, but they were in a minority. The use of English was growing, but some brethren spoke a poor version of it. By the late 1840s, the German language was increasingly on the decline in Wachovia, and church boards finally bowed to the inevitable and began recording their minutes in English. Intermixing was thus propelling acculturation forward as the antebellum period drew to a close. The offspring of Anglo-American and German were growing up in an American environment and were increasingly exposed to all things American. As Bahnson observed repeatedly, young Moravians were less and less comfortable with the language of their German-speaking parent or parents.

Language was the most obvious indicator of a cultural duality—German survived into the 1830s but declined after that. Family was another important one. This important cultural institution retained "traditional" aspects from an eighteenth-century heritage well into the 1830s until change accelerated in the late antebellum period. A traditional outlook meant that families outside of Salem remained grounded in land and church. For family members, tilling their farms and cultivating their souls dominated their lives. Inheritance practices reflected the Anglo-German desire to keep offspring anchored in or near Wachovia. Settlement life still revolved around the church, and families still sought to function as little churches of Jesus. The reality, of course, was complex. Friedland saw a large migration of its members to Indiana in the 1830s, and smaller numbers from the *Landgemeinen* went to Kentucky and Tennessee as early as the 1780s. Families, meanwhile, frequently failed to act as little churches of Jesus, as Bahnson was quick to recognize. Sometimes, the parents themselves wandered from the church, while the children remained loyal. Other times, some family members became Methodist while others remained Moravian. Yet others wandered away completely from the church.[16] But overall, there was much continuity with the eighteenth century: church remained important to families, with most members remaining loyal to Moravianism. And in language and outlook, Moravian families retained a decidedly Anglo-German flavor throughout the antebellum period.

Yet amid this Anglo-German traditionalism, Moravian families were becoming more "modern" over time—that is, they were becoming smaller in the nineteenth century as marrying ages rose. And because of extensive intermixing with the outside world and the creation of creole families, these families were also becoming more "American"—that is, patriarchy was lessening as children were accorded more American freedoms.

As Nancy Cott and other social historians have pointed out, the post-Revolutionary period was a time of deep change in the family. Strong economic growth in the United States during the early national period led to the start of sustained urbanization. This growth was accompanied by the transition to modern fertility patterns, with smaller family sizes and greater social stratification.[17] Within Wachovia, several changes from the eighteenth century stand out. The most dramatic was demographic: men and women in the countryside married later and families became smaller. In half of the settlements—Friedberg, Hope, and Bethania—men married at an older age. Friedberg saw the biggest age difference, rising from 24.58 in the 1753 to 1800 period to 28.23 in the 1801 to 1850 period, but Hope was not far behind. Bethania also saw a significant increase, rising from 25.13 to 27.03. Women in four out of the six settlements—Friedberg, Friedland, Hope, and Bethania—married at an older age. In Bethabara, women married at nearly the same age as in the earlier period, about 25.23. Only in Salem did they marry at a younger age, with the average age dropping from 27.50 to 26.99. See table 6.2.

Family size dropped in five of the six settlements, most dramatically in the *Landgemeinen*. Friedland, which had had the largest family size in Wachovia with 7.81 children, fell to 5.29; the decline in Hope and Friedberg was nearly as dramatic, falling from 7.60 and 7.18 to 5.41 and 5.63 respectively. Even Salem's family size dropped slightly. Only Bethabara saw its family size increase, rising

Table 6.2 Age of Marriage in Wachovia, 1753–1850

1750–1799		1800–1850	
Settlement	Average Age	Settlement	Average Age
Men			
Hope	24.14	Friedland	25.24
Friedberg	24.58	Hope	26.30
Bethania	25.13	Bethabara	26.90
Friedland	25.55	Bethania	27.03
Salem	32.37	Friedberg	28.23
Bethabara	32.60	Salem	28.34
Women			
Friedland	21.12	Friedland	23
Hope	21.88	Friedberg	23.37
Bethania	22.28	Hope	23.87
Friedberg	23	Bethania	24.68
Bethabara	25.52	Bethabara	25.23
Salem	27.50	Salem	26.99

Source: Compiled from biographical cards, MESDA research library.

to 5.37 from 4.63. The changes in the *Ortsgemeinen* are fairly easy to explain.[18] After 1800, communal control of marriages in the congregation towns loosened. In 1818, the Unity's synod agreed to no longer put marriages to the lot because of members' demands for autonomy in selecting spouses. This helped give congregation members greater freedom to marry who and when they wanted.[19] With fewer church controls, individuals married at a younger age in both Salem and Bethabara. Family size grew accordingly in Bethabara, and Salem's held steady while everyone else's was falling.[20] Bethania was a special case. By 1800, it was still technically an *Ortsgemeine,* but in spirit it was far closer to the *Landgemeinen,* with its members rebelling against tight church control of their affairs and insisting that they had the right to live on individual farms. Bethania's *Auswartige* played a huge role in settlement life and led the charge against strict church controls. The result of this rebelliousness was that Bethania resembled the *Landgemeinen* in more than just form; its demographic picture was strikingly similar, too. See table 6.3.

In the *Landgemeinen,* the key factor in smaller family sizes was likely the growing scarcity of land. As land in Wachovia and its environs became harder and more costly to obtain in the nineteenth century, men and women married later than in the earlier period. In these agricultural settlements, marriage was

Table 6.3 Family Size in Wachovia, 1753–1850

1753–1799 Settlement	No. of Families	No. of Children	1800–1850 Settlement	No. of Families	No. of Children
Friedland	49	7.81	Friedberg	121	5.63
Hope	71	7.60	Hope	27	5.41
Friedberg	83	7.18	Bethabara	41	5.37
Bethania	114	6.66	Friedland	87	5.29
Salem	54	4.88	Bethania	132	4.59
Bethabara	54	4.63	Salem	172	4.50

Source: Figures compiled from biographical listings of Wachovia's residents at MESDA's research library.

not feasible until the groom had the means to provide for a wife and family. Land prices rose in the early nineteenth century, and the availability of acreage in Wachovia dropped steadily. Farm sizes also fell in the *Landgemeinen*.[21] This made it harder for fathers to provide for their sons and daughters. The delays in marrying kept family sizes down. The land factor was not unique to Wachovia; historian Alan Kulikoff, for one, has found a similar process at work in the Chesapeake, where men and women postponed marrying in the eighteenth century as land became scarcer.[22] So has Barry Levy in his studies of Quakers in the Delaware Valley.[23]

This shift to a more modern family structure was only part of the story. Moravian families were also becoming more like their American neighbors as the influence of fathers waned. With great disgust, Bahnson noted on one occasion, "Children whenever they have come of age appear to feel no longer under any obligation to their parents—what a doctrine!"[24] The weakening of patriarchy began during the Revolutionary period and continued unabated in the nineteenth century. With Americanization proceeding on numerous fronts, these creole families embraced American-style freedoms. The father's sway over the family weakened as the rights of children grew—a shift that served as another strong indicator of the Moravians' acculturation to American mores.

The position of Moravian women in the antebellum period was complicated. Historians of the women's experience in early America have debated whether women's status improved or worsened in the nineteenth century. Most argue that women's economic opportunities declined after the American Revolution because of the appearance of "domesticity." As the Industrial Revolution took hold in the United States, the work functions of the household were lost to the factory. This development, according to these historians, limited women's economic opportunities and isolated them in the home. But historians also recognize that the cult of domesticity held its advantages because it allowed women to carve out substantial autonomy for themselves within a woman's sphere. For some historians, such a development was a step forward because it gave women greater power and shattered patriarchy; for others, the rise of domesticity was a step backward because it isolated women. Worse, these historians argue, by destroying the economic functions of the pre-Revolutionary household, domesticity decreased women's economic roles and hence their power.[25]

The Moravian family felt these crosscurrents as Wachovia's economy developed and became more integrated with the national economy, but much remained the same in the nineteenth century. Despite nascent industrialization in the North Carolina Piedmont, including in Salem, in the 1830s, work was still organized on familial lines. Women ran the household, produced butter, spun yarn; husbands tilled the fields and managed the plantation; sons and daughters remained important sources of labor, despite slavery's growing use. And the family still fulfilled many of the social functions that it had in the eighteenth century. The family was largely responsible for educating its children, taking care of ill members or the poor, and providing for the elderly, although the church helped out in all areas. Moravian women in the antebellum period did not live any longer, despite the smaller family sizes and reduced risk from giving birth. The average life span for women outside of Salem was 64.58 in the 1830s, virtually the same as it was in the 1760s. By one yardstick, women's position deteriorated. After 1800, fewer women served as executors for the family estate. From 1753 to 1800, women represented 14 percent of the estate executors; from 1801 to 1850, they represented only 10 percent.[26]

Although it was rare in the eighteenth century for women to have sole control of an estate, a husband's decision to make his wife coexecutor gave her some say in how the estate's assets were distributed. Suzanne Lebsock has found that women in Petersburg, Virginia, gained greater autonomy in the antebellum period through a wife's control of the husband's estate.[27] This did not happen in Wachovia. Of extant wills, there were only two instances in the 1753 to 1800 period when wives were named as sole executors of the husband's estate and only five in the 1801 to 1850 period. Nor did Moravian women marry less frequently and gain more independence, as in Petersburg. Outside of Salem, marriage remained an integral part of the community's expectations. This lack of progress is not to say that Moravian women's position was a poor one but that their position did not improve substantially through the 1850s. In the nineteenth century, they exercised power because they had had power earlier.

Moravian women had a chance to carve out a significant role for themselves within the household. That was because the religious imperatives of the marital union—husbands and wives were to treat each other with love and respect—combined with the ideal of the companionate marriage to give women a degree of power. Although men and women viewed Moravian marriages as matches sanctioned directly by God, these matches were also based on affection. Even in the *Ortsgemeinen,* brothers and sisters had the right to reject matches proposed by the church. No one was forced to marry against his or her will. The language employed in wills indicates that many men and women did marry out of affection. This was especially true in the *Landgemeinen,* where young people went to such great lengths to marry the spouse of their choice. As historians of the family have shown, companionate marriages were based on a more "modern" notion of love and respect between spouses and not domination by one party over another. It gave women rights and the expectation of happiness. Historian Linda Kerber and others have noted how the revolutionary ideology of equality raised expectations and aided companionate marriages.[28] Evangelism played a similar role before the Revolution and beyond. The new-birth experience carried the implicit message that the converted shared a rough equality in the eyes of God. Such a potentially revolutionary message, combined with evangelism's exhortations for the saved to regard one another as equals bound by mutual love, gave women the means to achieve meaningful roles for themselves in the house and church.[29] As spiritual equals, women could claim the right to exercise certain rights inside and outside of the home. Indeed, the Unity formally recognized the importance of women in church life by allowing the wives of pastors to serve on all church boards and by allowing women to run their own choirs and form their own committees within settlements.

The economic component of marriage, which saw the merger of two families' assets, greatly contributed to women's status as well. Men brought to the union land, money, and the labor needed to build and maintain a farm; women, in the form of dowries, brought livestock, furniture, and sometimes land. Most of all, women brought organizational skills to the match that became indispensable to the brethren. It was the sisters who had the responsibility of running the household. Women handled the endless chores associated with the farm household—cooking, cleaning, mending, and caring for the young children. They made butter, spun yarn, pulled flax, tended a garden, and helped care for the livestock. They also helped at harvest time. The weakening of patriarchy was probably a mixed blessing for Moravian women. Greater rights for children hurt the authority of *both* parents; yet a more democratic (and American) family could only enhance the power of women. In the long run, as families became more "modern," women's lot gained as well.

Religion and Assimilation in the Antebellum Period

The Unity's German roots contributed to the persistence of Germanic culture in Wachovia, but evangelism itself was sending North Carolina's Moravians in another direction. Evangelism in the post-Revolutionary period was egalitarian and reformist (with the important exception of slavery), and the brethren embraced much of what this very American movement stood for. The Moravians' decision to align more closely with evangelicals had the effect of drawing the brethren ever closer into American life. Evangelism's ability to mold an American (and southern) identity becomes clear when the experiences of North Carolina's Moravians are compared with those of Pennsylvania's Lutheran and Reformed settlers.

Like the Moravians in the American South, Pennsylvania Germans in the antebellum period had a dual identity. The difference, though, was that these German-Americans resisted full-scale assimilation and sought to maintain a distinct identity as a German-American ethnic group in American society. Religion became an important means for them to accomplish this feat. As the recent research of Steven M. Nolt shows, most Pennsylvania Germans refused to participate in evangelism and its close cousin, revivalism, because the movement was so closely identified with America itself. In the nineteenth century, evangelism became far more aggressive in its efforts to reform the individual and American society. The reformers' goals were closely intertwined with the camp-meeting movement and the two groups that led it—the Methodists and Baptists. Reform, as always, was to begin with conversion, and revivals and their "anxious benches" became the primary tools to win over converts. This religious ferment began in the Revolutionary period, when Americans of all creeds were pressing for rights and liberties. As Nolt observes about the period, "In an atmosphere charged with the ideas of self-evident truth, inherent human equality, sovereignty of the people, . . . the old religious order gave way to an energetic evangelicalism that tended to disparage tradition and clerical authority, often claiming no creed but the Bible." Evangelicals initially concentrated their reform efforts on the individual and expanded it to broader society.

If the reborn sinner was to lead a life of discipline that eschewed drinking, gambling, and other vices, then so should society. "Soon, appropriating the message of evangelical Protestantism and its methods of revivalism," Nolt observes, "also meant subscribing to a host of related commitments and assumptions about American society and an identity tied to the redemption of the nation."[30] Lutherans and Reformed in Pennsylvania resisted. For these two groups, rejecting evangelism and maintaining their traditional faith allowed them to keep their distance from the American mainstream. By holding fast to their pietist and German roots, Lutheran and Reformed Germans could thus maintain a distinct identity as German-Americans in an Anglo world.

The contrast with the Moravians could not be more startling. North Carolina's Moravians expressed no worries about losing their German ethnicity because their German identity was never a concern. Indeed, Bahnson ran across repeated contempt for "Germanisms," especially in Salem. And North Carolina's Moravians, unlike Pennsylvania's Germans, embraced the evangelical movement. For the Moravians, evangelism and Americanness became inextricably linked. By embracing evangelism, the religious mainstream, and religious-driven causes, the brethren could demonstrate that they were good Americans who cared deeply about improving the morals of a young nation. Wachovia's inhabitants rallied behind a number of religious-inspired reforms that, at the same time, demonstrated a middle-class sensibility for improving society and propagating good citizenship. Salem, the central *Ortsgemeine* that was supposed to be the bastion of religious conservatism, led the way on this front: congregation members there formed a reading society in 1818, a debating society in 1825, a Sunday school union in 1826, and a temperance society in 1842. These societies mimicked those started elsewhere in America whose goals were to raise the educational standards of Americans while improving the behavior of those citizens engaged in immoral behavior denounced by all good evangelicals. Yet the Moravian embracing of reform had a distinctly southern bent to it. Conspicuously absent from their civic-mindedness was any society that allied itself with the northern abolition movement. Even George Bahnson, that transported Dane who found the ways of the South so strange, could be found fuming about "hotheaded & inconsiderate abolitionists who do no good to anybody. The poor blacks are much worse off than they were before."[31]

As they became more "American," the brethren sought to move closer to the Protestant mainstream. Inside their meetinghouses, they abandoned worship practices that initially linked them with original Christians but had tended instead to separate them from more conventional Protestant worship. In the early

1800s, North Carolina's Moravians ceased to prostrate themselves in prayer during communion and knelt instead. In 1818, they no longer exchanged the kiss of peace. For the Unity, the kiss was meant to represent a moment of union with Jesus Christ, a holy act that signaled a new member's admission into God's society.[32] Now, like other mainstream churches, the brethren extended the right hand of fellowship. At the same time, the Moravians were dropping *Pedilaviums,* or foot washings—another act meant to symbolize one's attachment to the Savior. Drawing on John 13, the brethren had reenacted the washing away of sin that Christ performed on the disciples. Church historians J. Taylor Hamilton and Kenneth G. Hamilton, commenting on the kiss of peace, have called the change part of "minor concessions . . . made to the spirit of the age."[33] All these changes in ritual, however, were something more—they meant that southern Moravians were moving away from earlier, radical practices that had emulated primitive Christianity but that had tended instead to make them "different."[34]

Equally important, North Carolina's Moravians in the early nineteenth century joined the Sunday school movement, a decision that brought them into closer cooperation with other Protestant groups. Northern reformers intended the movement as an ecumenical tool among American Protestants, and Pennsylvania's Lutheran and Reformed objected to it precisely on those grounds. They feared that Sunday schools would damage home churches by enticing away young members.[35] In stark contrast, however, movement advocates found a willing audience among a group of southern evangelicals—the Moravians—committed to interdenominationalism and the spread of heart religion. In 1816, Salem brethren expressed interest in starting Sunday schools as a means to complement their missionary work. The single sisters of Salem wanted to work with neighborhood "children who have no other opportunity for instruction."[36] In August, the sisters began teaching children at a church near Friedberg run, ironically, by a Lutheran. In April 1817, they opened a Sunday school in Salem "for the benefit of poor children from the surrounding country." The school met at one in the afternoon on Sundays, after the morning worship service, and taught reading, writing, and "reckoning," as well as religious instruction.[37] In these early years, the Sunday school became an effective way to reach people who were not attending traditional church services and schools.

Settlers in the *Landgemeinen* embraced the Sunday schools, but for different reasons. Several married brethren in Friedland took the initiative in 1819, believing that the congregation's children needed more educational opportunities. The response was strong; "parents and children were happy over the plan," the pastor reported.[38] Whereas the brethren in the *Ortsgemeinen* saw Sunday school as an evangelical tool to reach outsiders, members of the *Landgemeinen* viewed the schools an extension of their congregations that would directly benefit their children. Friedberg was the second settlement to start Sunday schools, and Hope was the third. As was true for efforts elsewhere in Stokes County, these early efforts met with mixed success. The schools lapsed, only to be started again.[39]

The brethren also welcomed the arrival of the American Sunday School Union to North Carolina in the mid-1820s. Reformers had formed the Sunday School Union in Philadelphia in 1824 to strengthen religious instruction throughout the nation and to promote the intellectual and moral culture of the nation. The union's foundation was evangelical, built on "the essential truths of Protestant Christianity held in common by all Evangelical denominations," including "union with Christ and union with each other."[40] These were goals most Moravians supported. The union became active in North Carolina and Wachovia from 1826 on. In April 1826, a Reverend Witherspoon preached in English at an evening service in Salem on behalf of the union. Through the 1820s and 1830s, the union sent teachers and supplies and worked closely with the Sunday schools in the area. Bethania and Bethabara started Sunday schools, and the *Landgemeinen* resurrected theirs. Individual brethren and others founded the Stokes County Sunday School Union that year. Salem's elders watched the burgeoning movement with some concern because of the old German fear of disorder. The Elders Conference warned, "Although we were convinced that the purpose [of the founding of the Stokes Union] was praiseworthy and that it would do some good, still we felt that all possible care must be taken to prevent possible abuses, and certain disturbances which might result."[41]

Although fearful of disorder, Moravian Church boards sided with their Christian duty to work with the unconverted. Only two years after the elders fretted over "possible abuses," the Aufseher Collegium, in effect, threw open Wachovia's doors to outsiders, allowing the union to use Salem Square for large gatherings.[42] On March 29, 1829, about five hundred students from the various Sunday schools of the union's Stokes district assembled in the lower part of the town. The Salem Diary reported the ensuing spectacle in some detail: "Led by the Union, they marched in procession, singing, to the church." About three hundred parents and friends watched. The president of the union, Gottlieb Schober, who was a Moravian and a Lutheran minister, then spoke about "the beginning of Sunday Schools in England, in Europe, and in other parts of the world, including this neighborhood." The service concluded with a lovefeast on the square. Unlike the elders, the Salem diarist saw no danger of disorder here, only opportunity. "It was a pleasant sight to see so many young people from our neighborhood, who have through the Sunday Schools not only have an opportunity to learn to read, but also to become acquainted with the word of God. May the good seed which has been planted in their hearts this day bear fruit for eternity!"[43]

The Sunday school movement was a key marker of the Moravians' willingness to participate in both evangelism and American society. By opening Sunday schools, the Moravians became less "different" and more like their neighbors. It made Wachovia less insular and less "foreign." Evangelical values, in the end, spurred the brethren to reach out and participate even further in American life.

Revivalism and the Camp-Meeting Movement

When it came to opening Sunday schools, the Moravians quite easily overcame their long-standing German fears of disorder. Revivalism and all its "excesses" posed a far sterner test for the brethren: just how completely would they embrace the evangelical movement, and how willing would they be to repudiate their German past by doing so? These became key questions after 1800, because the southern evangelical movement was exploding all around them. Pushing evangelism forward in the post-Revolutionary period was the so-called Second Great Awakening, which began in the late 1780s and erupted in August 1801 following huge revivals at Cane Ridge, Kentucky, and elsewhere. From these flash points, the revival movement quickly spread from Kentucky and Tennessee to North Carolina in 1801, 1802, and 1803. As historian John B. Boles has noted, "In almost every section of the state, there were meetings marked by extraordinarily large crowds, cooperating ministers of various denominations, hundreds falling, shouting, convulsing, finding security in apparent salvation."[44]

These revivals, where thousands camped out to hear several days of preaching, singing, and praying, became one of the main weapons in the evangelical arsenal to convert individuals. Preachers urged camp goers to heed God's call and give up their worldly ways. In fiery language, they warned of the dangers of eternal damnation and the fate that awaited sinners if they did not seek Christ's saving forgiveness. Fearful and afraid, crying out for forgiveness, thousands attending the great revivals responded to these evangelical warnings.

Many participants were so moved by the preachers' exhortations, and so remorseful of their sins, that they lost control of their emotions. Some fell to the ground, rolling around in convulsions; others barked, "jerked," danced, and sang.[45]

In both the *Ortsgemeinen* and *Landgemeinen,* the reaction to this explosion of evangelical intensity was fascinating. The Moravians' extensive contact with outsiders ensured that they learned of the Kentucky and Tennessee tremors in timely fashion. When a visitor arrived in Salem from Kentucky in late October 1802 and "told us something of the great revival there," this was already old news to Wachovia's inhabitants. The subsequent growth of the revivals in the early 1800s, including one of North Carolina's largest held at Hawfields in Orange County not far from Wachovia, produced excitement and concern among the brethren.[46]

Wachovia's boards had been cordial about allowing evangelical ministers of other faiths to visit and even to preach in Wachovia, but that commitment to openness was put to the test in fall 1802 and later. In September 1802, Salem's Aufseher Collegium "heard that some preachers are intending to preach their sermons here publicly in the streets and have asked the Community to congregate for that purpose." The collegium was wary of allowing these outsiders in this instance because "we are afraid that only disorder and bad discipline derive from such doings, mainly for our youngsters." The collegium decided to try to prevent such meetings in Salem, and it dispatched a board member to the Yadkin Forks to see whether it was true that evangelical preachers had published advertisements touting the coming gatherings to be held in Salem's streets.[47] In early February 1805, the arrival of Lorenzo Dow, the legendary Methodist circuit rider, in Salem and Bethania caused an even greater commotion. In each town, Dow spoke to about three thousand hearers in the "open air." Bethania canceled Sunday morning services because of Dow's plans to hold a meeting in the afternoon. The large crowd, mostly strangers, packed the village's streets to hear Dow preach on Genesis 24:58, "Wilt Thou Go with This Man?"[48]

Moravian pastors did not object to the goals of the revivals—to gain converts to Christ through a new birth. In neutral language, the Salem Diary in October 1802 described these early camp meetings as "great religious gatherings . . . in which many thousand persons of all religious persuasions gather in the woods . . . filling the time with preachings, warnings, singing, and praying." But they did object to some of the evangelicals' methods. Zinzendorf himself had decried the mass meetings of the first Great Awakening as mob scenes and grand spectacles.[49] Such a suspicion lingered into the nineteenth century. In 1802, the Salem diarist summed up anew this fear: the camp meetings, he complained, produced behavior that was "very offensive and running contrary to the teachings of the Gospel, for example, people fell down and lay for a long time in a kind of swoon, experiencing the pangs of the new birth."[50] Throughout the antebellum period, Moravian leaders consistently criticized what they considered the excessive emotionalism that accompanied conversions at revivals and camp meetings. They opposed the "jerks," swooning, shouting, and other behavior as offensive to God's people. Moravian pastors refused to organize camp meetings or hold revivals for their congregations until the late 1840s because of their strong distaste for such emotionalism.[51] This was a very German, and Lutheran, fear. For Moravians, being reborn meant living disciplined lives. Although they sought a deep-felt and warmly emotional relationship with Christ, the brethren feared that the conversions gained at revivals were shallow and short lived, based on the heat of the moment. They instead saw the new birth as something hard to gain and harder to maintain. Conversion meant not only submitting oneself to Lord Jesus but also making a commitment to a life of discipleship and obedience. In other words, Moravians saw commitment to obedience as part of the conversion experience.[52] They questioned the instantaneous conversions of the camp meeting as superficial.

This view was changing, though, for practical and cultural reasons. On a practical level, the camp meetings were proving to be enormously successful and popular, and North Carolina's Moravians risked falling into complete irrelevance if they continued to oppose them. Although becoming a large church was never a goal, the brethren could not afford to let the Methodists grow too big at their expense. And the Methodist Church *was* growing quite large. In 1786, it had 18,791 white members; in 1801, it had 139,336.[53] The Methodists' growth in North Carolina was equally impressive. In 1780, they had formed a new circuit just west of Hope and Friedberg, at the Yadkin River, and they quickly became a strong force in Wachovia's very backyard.[54] The Methodists' success forced the Moravian leadership to reevaluate its stance on camp meetings during a time when membership in most Moravian congregations was stagnating.

The impetus to change also came from below. While church boards were fretting over disorder, settlers in the *Landgemeinen* and Bethania were flocking to camp meetings. These brethren, who not coincidentally were intermixing extensively with outsiders, viewed revivals as something new and interesting to watch. Curiosity continued to draw them to these religious gatherings as late as 1830. As the Salem Diary explained that year, "Generally, our neighborhood congregations attend [the camp meetings] for a change sometimes or to see something new."[55] The brethren found the camp-meeting atmosphere entertaining and the emotionalism of the Methodists a satisfying change of pace from the more liturgical Moravian services, which placed such a heavy emphasis on order and strict behavior. The camp meetings brought together thousands of people in the heat of the summer to not only hear sermons but also enjoy Christian fellowship and entertainment. Congregants welcomed these gatherings as diversions from the humdrum routine of farm life. Such a motivation was hardly unusual. Historians of the camp-meeting phenomenon have long noted that many participants attended for the same reasons—to watch and enjoy the show.

As a newcomer to North Carolina, Bahnson himself was ambivalent about camp meetings; he expressed hostility toward them his first year in Wachovia but grudgingly began to appreciate them. In 1834, he could be found complaining that "one meeting was very disorderly . . . several horses were stolen, and some other persons were thrown into jail on account of misdemeanor. Oh, these camp meetings!" In October, he noted that several young people from the congregation attended a four-day meeting near Hope. "No wonder," he commented. "It is an excess they are fond of. I should like to go to one myself."[56] He, of course, eventually did. In 1837, for instance, Bahnson went to a camp meeting at Clemmonstown, about ten miles from Salem. The pastor found it "very picturesque," although he still did not completely approve of the proceedings. He liked the sermon, except for the "closing part, calculated to produce shouting and such nonsense."[57]

Assimilation proceeded the fastest in the *Landgemeinen* and in Bethania, and it was here where the revivals were most popular. These four settlements contained the most vigorous societies of partial members and were the most willing to embrace American ways. Society members were loyal to Moravianism, but they displayed a greater willingness to attend revivals. As in everything else, Bethania's *Auswartige* members showed a fierce independent spirit. The most popular camp-meeting ground for the Methodists was at Peter Doub's, only four miles from Bethania. Almost every July in the 1820s and early 1830s, large crowds of all faiths gathered for several days of preaching and praying. Lorenzo Dow himself praised Doub's meeting ground, noting the site "has the most convenient room, with a pulpit and seats, of any I have seen in the south."[58] The revivalists were also active at the Yadkin River settlements, near Hope and Friedberg. In Hope, the camp meetings were so popular that the pastor often stared out at a nearly empty meetinghouse on Sundays "because a three-day camp meeting was being held beyond the Yadkin."[59] Hope's close cousin, Fried-berg, shared this enthusiasm. Revivalism's appeal, in other words, transcended ethnicity.

Yet the differences between settlements, as well as the differences between society and congregational members, should not be overemphasized. In all settlements, Moravians appreciated the message of the evangelicals because of its many parallels with their religious heritage. Even in Salem, Moravians flocked to hear these evangelical ministers delivering their messages of spiritual rebirth. In August 1810, after the congregation's evening meetings concluded, a Presbyterian preacher from South Carolina "gave an evangelical testimony in the entry to the [Salem] tavern, many of our members going to hear him."[60] A Baptist minister delivered his message from an even more congenial location—the pulpit at Salem church. From the very center of southern Moravianism, "he preached an evangelical sermon on the new birth of the heart, to the edification of the numbers present." A Methodist minister followed this sermon with a "short address on the working of the Holy Ghost to arouse a new spirit in the heart."[61] Such messages had such resonance because Moravians—leaders and followers alike—believed in a heart religion built on a close, personal relation-ship with Christ. In none of the settlements did the pastors, congregational committees, or Haus Vaters Conferenzes debate theological differences between Moravians and Methodists. In fact, other than fears of disorder, the revivals produced little extended discussion in Wachovia.[62] Unconcerned with theologi-cal niceties, Wachovia's inhabitants found the evangelical message both con-genial and compatible with the main tenets of their faith.

The Moravian stress on ecumenicalism also aided the revivalists' cause within Wachovia. From the 1740s on, Zinzendorf preached the importance of finding common ground with other Christians. Methodists and Baptists fre-quently attended Moravian meetings and found them appealing because of the similarities in doctrines. In 1810, for instance, the Salem diarist noted that a Methodist preacher and his wife attended the preaching in Hope "with plea-sure, and afterwards he told Br. Kramsch how glad he was to be able to say that he and they had one ground of faith."[63] The links between Methodism and Moravianism were especially strong. John Wesley, the founder of the Methodist movement, studied Moravian practices in the 1730s and was fascinated by the Unity's doctrines, although he concluded that the Moravians placed too much emphasis on the inner life. Methodists shared with Moravians an emphasis on the new birth and an intensity of personal religious experience and personal piety. And like the Unity, Methodism began as a church within a church that sought to revitalize larger Christendom. The heart of Methodism were societies, bands, and traveling preachers. The bands, which Wesley modeled on Moravian choirs, were small cells of men and women who gathered for religious fellowship. Lovefeasts were another Moravian contribution to Methodism. From the Moravians, Wesley came to understand the role that religious structures could play in nurturing heart religion.[64] These similarities between doctrine and structure helped facilitate contact between the two faiths after 1800.[65]

Still, the rivalry between the two in Stokes County could be quite fierce, with the Moravians sometimes seeing the Methodists as upstarts who were stealing away their members—an ironic charge, because Lutherans and others leveled that same accusation against Zinzendorf's Diaspora in the eighteenth century. Bahnson, for one, did not trust the Methodists, even when ministers of the latter faith tried to be accommodating to the Moravians. In 1834, for instance, Michael Daub, a Methodist minister, invited Bahnson to preach at the "Methodist Academy" near Bethania. Bahnson thanked Daub but declined the offer, "for politeness would require me to offer him our church here, for which he and others of his persuasion have been waiting many years, by which means they would gain entrance into the very center of our congregation—to convert which by making them Methodist is their most ardent wish," he wrote in his diary. "No Methodist preacher in our section of the country may be safely trusted."[66] Bahnson's hostility did not end there. He blamed Daub and other Methodists for Bethania's languishing membership: "Had it not been for the Methodists and their often very unbecoming practices and stratagems, our Bethany congregation would probably be in a very flourishing state."[67] Bahnson's hostility to the camp-meeting movement lessened over time, and so did his distrust of the Methodists. By 1837, this stern Moravian minister could be found attending a lecture at the hated Methodist Academy. Bahnson generally approved of the Reverend Bethell's address, praising this Methodist as "a very fluent and agreeable speaker." But predictably, he could not resist adding that Bethell was also "a great patron of that senseless shouting which is so entirely contrary to a 'reasonable' worship of our God and Lord."[68] Despite his hostility to Methodist emotionalism, Bahnson well understood the appeal of his rivals and the role that emotionalism played among his evangelical followers. In 1835, Bahnson let several congregation members borrow his carriage so they could attend a quarterly Methodist meeting. "I consented to let them have their fun. The oftener they go to such meetings, the less they will probably join the Methodists."[69] The Methodists and their ways, in other words, served as an outlet for those brethren seeking more emotional worship services. A few months later, Bahnson actually found himself facing criticism in Salem for having let a "shaking Quaker" preach in Bethania's meetinghouse. "I think this is a very narrow-minded view," Bahnson huffed in his diary, "for if I have a chance of becoming acquainted with an evangelical minister, shall he on account of the name be prohibited from preaching in our church, whilst our people would anyhow go and hear him somewhere in our neighborhood and call me 'bigoted'!"[70]

Bahnson's change of heart was representative of what was happening in Wachovia in the 1830s and later. The brethrens' extensive contact with other evangelicals led to Wachovia's congregations eventually embracing a more emotional style of worship. In the 1840s, Moravian ministers began directly participating in camp meetings, and in the 1850s, Moravian congregations began holding their own revivals, or protracted meetings as they preferred to call them. As the name implies, these protracted meetings were daylong affairs that ran late into the night. They centered on prayer and sermonizing, with the goal of boosting congregational membership and gaining converts to Christ. The pastor for Friedberg and Hope recalled one such meeting in August 1858. "At night before service, gave an invitation to persons wishing to join the church to come forward." Three persons responded. The pastor then "preached and at the close, invited inquiries. Eleven came forward to be prayed with. The meeting continued till 11 o'clock. Two professed to have found peace."[71] Congregational pastors kept the meetings under fairly tight control: no dancing or fainting, although crying was common, and shouting did occur. Thus, the Moravians' protracted meetings represented a compromise between two worlds—the exuberance of the American camp meeting and the German order of a Moravian worship service.

The impact of the outside evangelical movement—Methodist, Baptist, and shaking Quaker—on Wachovia in the early nineteenth century was significant. It nudged the Moravians away from the Unity's Lutheran origins, shared by Zinzendorf, many *Landgemeine* settlers, and others, with its emphasis on formal liturgy. Yet the distance the Moravians had to travel in the 1840s was less than in 1800, because evangelical leaders were trying to curb the worst excesses of the revival movement. As Christine Leigh Heyrman and other historians have shown, the evangelical movement began making compromises during the antebellum period in a bid for respectability with the southern gentry. The jerks, shouting, and other wild behavior of the camp meetings made southern white men uncomfortable, Heyrman notes. They also objected to the rigors of the conversion process.[72] As a result, Methodist and Baptist preachers began making accommodations with the white male power structure in the antebellum South. The evangelicals, in short, sought to tone down the worst excesses of the movement, especially after 1830, and to make it more respectable and thus more acceptable to more people.[73] The net effect of these changes for both evangelism and Moravianism was to bring both movements closer to the mainstream of American Christianity. There was something of a meeting in the middle as Moravian services became more emotional and as evangelical ones became somewhat more sedate.

A Changing Religious Piety

Surveying his congregation in the 1830s, Bahnson wondered repeatedly whether piety among his congregants in Bethania had slipped. His charges, after all, were more modern and more American than were their predecessors in the eighteenth century. They had assimilated so thoroughly into the fabric of American life that Bahnson often wondered where religion stood in their lives. Historians of the Salem experience have asked the same thing. They have argued, with a great deal of merit, that religion by the mid-nineteenth century was no longer as central to Salem residents. This *Ortsgemeine,* it is said, became more commercially oriented, more individualistic. Although the *Landgemeinen* have been unstudied, historians have speculated that religion was even less central in the countryside than in the restricted town of Salem. These settlers, it is believed, were the least attached to Moravianism and the most attached to family.

The reality was not so neat. Several generations of intermixing, which was accompanied by the shift toward a more mainstream religion, affected the very heart of the evangelical experience itself—a seeker's relationship with his or her Savior. Religion was not less central to the brethren in 1850 or 1860; it remained extremely important to them on several levels. But the nature of the brethrens' relationship with Jesus did change. The implications of acculturation, in other words, were quite direct: the creation of an Anglo-German world that saw German-speaking brethren become more American and more southern meant that all brethren began to view their Savior through the lens of the American evangelical South. They developed a more conventional view of Jesus Christ that saw them downplay the radical side of their heritage, where they had emulated the early Christians.

This shifting view of Jesus Christ was apparent on many fronts. One key change could be found in Moravian religious rituals. The congregation's decision to lie prostrate during communion had symbolized a partaker's complete submission to the Savior. The decision in 1802 to begin kneeling greatly altered the symbolism of this most solemn of Christian ceremonies. So did the decision to end the kiss of peace in 1818. Both changes signaled that worshipers would have a less intimate relationship with Jesus. There was now more distance between the brethren and their Savior and also among themselves, because brotherly fellowship would consist of shaking hands and not exchanging kisses.[74]

The language used in the Brotherly Agreements was another sign of an evolving relationship. In 1836, the General Synod agreed on a standardized Brotherly Agreement for Wachovia's settlements outside of Salem. The revised Brotherly Agreement of 1836 had far less to say about conversion than did its eighteenth-century counterpart; it rather blandly stipulated that when a seeker wanted to join a congregation, "it is the duty of the Committee to acquaint themselves with all the circumstances of the applicant, and especially with the object and aim of such application." Bethania's Brotherly Agreement of 1780, by contrast, vowed that the congregation would not receive anyone "upon mere Hopes, unless there be convincing Proofs of the work of the Holy Ghost on his Heart, and his being called to us."[75] Although the 1836 agreement still emphasized that members must have a loving relationship with Jesus, the language used was far more businesslike than in the eighteenth century.

The language in the *Lebenslaufs* of members also hinted at a less intimate relationship with Jesus Christ. After 1820 or so, most *Lebenslaufs* became highly formulaic, listing just dates (ranging from when someone was born to when he or she first took communion) and a few platitudes. In earlier periods, church members often wrote long, emotional firsthand accounts of their journeys to heart religion, with these accounts stressing the importance of the new birth to the deceased's salvation. In the mid-nineteenth century, a certain sterility crept into the *Lebenslaufs*. The story of Jacob Frey was typical. He was born in 1796 near Hope and joined the congregation there at the relatively young age of twelve. Frey remained a "faithful" lifelong member, according to his memoir, serving as a committee member and lovefeast steward. He bore a number of trials, including the deaths of three wives. In true Moravian fashion, he endured his setbacks "with a Christian's resignation." What was striking about Frey's memoir was the language used by the chronicler. It still talked of the "Savior's love" during Frey's earthly tribulations. But as death neared in 1847, Jesus was curiously absent from the account: Frey "expressed resignation with the will of God and readiness to depart." In these later memoirs, Jesus was a more distant figure; he was not the central actor in a drama whose plot revolved around an evangelical's search for a spiritual rebirth and the everlasting joy that would follow when he did become reborn.[76]

These changes in tone reflected the many paradoxes of the later generation. Heart religion remained important to the brethren. Indeed, antebellum Moravians in increasing numbers enjoyed the camp meetings that centered on prodding people into undergoing a new birth. In fact, some brethren enjoyed the emotional conversions so much that they defected to the Methodists. The growing popularity of revivalism among the brethren was strong evidence that the evangelical experience retained its relevancy and that the new birth remained pivotal to heart religion. Yet at the same time as they were flocking to camp meetings, North Carolina's Moravians were also going "mainstream" in the Protestant world, and this move to the middle was reflected in the Brotherly Agreements and in the *Lebenslaufs*. Another sign of this shift was evident in the most curious place of all—pastors' diaries. Their diaries in the eighteenth century were concerned with the conversion experience and with helping the unsaved undergo a new birth; diaries of the nineteenth were not. Pastors in the *Landgemeinen* and Bethania doggedly recorded their activities and listed their services and other daily activities, but they had little to say about conversion. The diary of George Bahnson was exceptional in its detail and length, but even this prolific writer barely mentioned the new birth. He apparently did not prod the unsaved, as Ludolph Bachhof, for example, did in Friedberg in the eighteenth century. Nor did Bahnson's diary record many instances of members coming to him distressed about their lack of conversion.[77]

The numerous paradoxes of this later period were evident in the wills the brethren wrote. As with the *Lebenslaufs,* wills after 1800 became formulaic in their use of language. Yet the writer's decision whether to include evangelical language was a telling marker of his or her attitude toward heart religion. Most important, these wills allow comparisons between settlements and periods of time. Such a comparative approach can shed light on the evolution of religious values in the nineteenth century. Most of all, it can shed light on differences between settlements, allowing one to test the thesis that *Landgemeine* settlers supposedly became even less religious than their counterparts in the *Ortsgemeinen.*

In southwest Germany, according to the research of A. G. Roeber, the testate practices of pietistic villagers tended to differ slightly from their Lutheran and Reformed neighbors. Two key differences were Pietists' tendency to use a written format and to employ pietist redemptive language in the opening paragraphs. Such language invariably paid homage to Jesus Christ, expressing the Pietist's love of his or her Savior. "My Dear Redeemer Jesus Christ with fervent prayers to pardon my Sins for his high Merits Sake to grant me a happy departure from this World into his Kingdom," read one typical entry. Pietist wills expressed the writer's belief in the saving grace of Jesus: "For perfect Remission and Pardon of my Past Sins and follies and through the Merits and Mediation of my Blessed Savior and Redeemer Jesus Christ."[78]

Unfortunately, little work has been done on Pietism in the South that allows for detailed comparisons between the Moravians, German villagers, and southern evangelicals—the heirs of Pietism. One exception is the research of Bruce R. Penner, an archaeologist with the South Carolina Institute of Archaeology and Anthropology, who has studied the German-Swiss settlement at New Windsor Township in the South Carolina backcountry. Penner finds that these Swiss-German Pietists employed language in their wills similar to those pietist villagers in southwest Germany. In the introductions to their wills, these South Carolinians, too, expressed a heartfelt relationship with the Savior: "I Commend my Soul into the hands of Almighty God, who gave it to me, and my Body to the Earth from whence it Came in hopes of a Joyful Resurrection, through the Merits of my Savior Jesus Christ."[79] In both Germany and the New World, Pietists shared an almost joyful view of death that expressed death as a passage from a troubled earthly world to a far better one. Their wills typically employed several euphemisms for death: The deceased "has fallen asleep in the Savior Jesus Christ." Or, he or she has "changed this worldly existence for an other-worldly existence." Or more joyfully still, he or she "was called by the Creator of all out of this temporal world and to Himself in the happiness of a God-given eternity."[80]

The Moravian view of death was virtually identical. Funeral sermons and memoirs referred to death as a "going home" to the loving embrace of Jesus Christ. The expiration of life meant the joyous chance for the deceased to be united with his Savior. Such a view of death did not vary between the eighteenth and nineteenth centuries. But the intensity of these views did change somewhat, as reflected in the language used in Moravian wills. Before 1800, Moravians in all settlements expressed a warm, personal relationship with Jesus. Peter Binkley's will, written in March 1791, was typical. This resident of Bethania "humbly hoped for a blessed Immortality through the Merits and Mediation of my blessed Savior and Redeemer Jesus Christ."[81] These Moravian wills in the eighteenth century placed their hopes for salvation squarely with

Jesus. Samuel Miller of Friedberg recommended his soul into the hands of God and his "Body to the Earth from whom it came, in Hopes of a joyful Resurrection, through the merits of my Lord and Savior Jesus Christ."[82] In 1788, George Hartman put it even more explicitly: he instructed that his body be buried in a "Christian like manner, firmly believing that I shall rise hereafter at the Resurrection of the living, and that our Savior for his mercy's sake will let me be a partaker of eternal happiness."[83]

After 1800, will writers mentioned Christ less often. Like George Hartman thirty-nine years earlier, Michael Spainhouer of Bethania demonstrated confidence in the "General Resurrection," but he placed this faith not in Jesus but in "the mighty power of God."[84] Joseph Pfaff, also of Bethania, asked for a Christian burial "not doubting but to have a happy resurrection."[85] He did not mention Jesus. Those wills that did mention the Savior tended to avoid the warmer language of the earlier period. References to my "dear" Redeemer were largely gone. Catharina Frey of Friedberg placed the hope for the "remission of my sins, by the meditations of Jesus Christ."[86] For Frey and others, Christ became a more remote figure in the later period, indicating a shift in the nature of Zinzendorf's heart religion. Heart religion had been synonymous with the Savior. Its very essence was an intense personal relationship with Jesus. The pietist language used in wills before 1800 demonstrated that most ordinary settlers shared the intensity of this experience, later settlers less so.

Certainly all of this reinforces the traditional view that religion became less central during the antebellum period. But a closer examination of the use of pietist language shows that the shifting landscape was not so linear or simple as one would first believe. The use of pietist language in wills dropped in all settlements after 1800, but it remained strong in surprising places and weakest in the most surprising place of all—Salem.

The breakdown by settlement reveals several interesting trends (table 6.4). One, it shows the strength of evangelical values in the *Landgemeinen*. In both periods, the use of pietist language was far higher overall in the three farm settlements than in the *Ortsgemeinen*: 81 percent in the first period versus 57 percent, and 41 percent versus only 27 percent in the second. The totals for the *Landgemeinen* were also significantly higher than the overall average for Wachovia. The use of religious language dropped in all settlements after 1800, but the drop was less steep in the farm communities. That fact indicates that evangelical values remained strong in the countryside. The use of pietist language in wills did not mean, of course, that religion was stronger in the *Landgemeinen* than in the *Ortsgemeinen*. But the belief that religion was weak

Table 6.4 The Use of Pietist Language in Wills, 1753-1850

	Ortsgemeinen			Landgemeinen	
	1753–1800 (%)	1800–1850 (%)		1753–1800 (%)	1800–1850 (%)
Bethabara	70 (n=9)	51 (n=10)	Friedberg	80 (n=10)	40 (n=20)
Bethania	78 (n=10)	40 (n=35)	Friedland	83 (n=6)	50 (n=22)
Salem	43 (n=21)	4 (n=44)	Hope	80 (n=10)	29 (n=18)
TOTAL	57	27	TOTAL	81	41
Wachovia	62				

Source: Two hundred and fifteen wills from Rowan County and Stokes County Will Books and wills at Moravian Archives, Southern Province.

in the country congregations needs to be discarded. Evangelical values endured throughout Wachovia, albeit in a different form. The use of religious language remained high in Bethabara and Bethania and was comparable with the three *Landgemeinen.* Salem, as always, was a special case. As the commercial center of Wachovia, its extant wills demonstrate a businesslike approach to the division of estates. Its use of pietist language badly lagged the rest of the settlements in both periods.

The enduring importance of religion in Moravians' lives was apparent elsewhere. For one, the tremendous concern with behavior remained. The Unity still expected its evangelical followers to lead upright lives and to avoid the worldly corruptions around them. And it still required *Gemeine* members to sign and adhere to Brotherly Agreements, although the standard 1836 agreement was not as strict as in the eighteenth century. For all the changes in tone, love of Jesus remained at the center of congregational life: "The doctrine of Jesus Christ and his Apostles . . . shall be the ground of our faith," the agreement declared. And the Brotherly Agreement retained some of the "blood" language favored by Zinzendorf in the eighteenth century: "We ought never to forget that our children are the property of the Savior, redeemed and purchased with his holy and precious blood." But this declaration came far later in the agreement and was less explicit than its forebears. Parents were still expected to encourage home worship and to educate their children in God's ways while preserving the morals of their households. That mandate included barring late-night visits from strangers, preventing the improper mixing of sexes, and halting anything that was "at variance with the precepts of the Bible and the principles of strict morality." And all members, regardless of age, were to avoid the worldliness of their surroundings: "Agreeably to the form of sound doctrine, we will earnestly strive to cultivate property, temperance, modesty, and frugality in all things pertaining to our dwellings, table, dress, furniture, and mode of living. All should work and eat their own bread." The agreements still barred "all plays, sports, and games" as "improper, dangerous, and pernicious." As harsh as this mandate seemed, the passage was toned down from eighteenth-century agreements that condemned everything from horse racing to spinning and cotton picking.[87]

Wachovia's boards and congregational committees did not enforce the Brotherly Agreements as rigidly as in the eighteenth century. Indeed, Bahnson was quite cynical about the whole thing. In July 1837, he attended a conference at Salem that discussed how to enforce the revised agreement of 1836. "After much talk, it was for all found impracticable to insist upon the significance of each member's name upon the Brotherly Agreement, of which there would not be much use anyhow, for they observe or violate it no matter whether they have signed it or not." A month later, the pastor went ahead and distributed copies of the agreement to members. The brethren were glad to receive them, Bahnson reported, but he added: "Whether they [the agreements] will be strictly observed is another thing."[88] Nevertheless, congregation committees and the Land Arbeiter Conferenz did monitor behavior, albeit not as closely as in earlier periods. And as in the eighteenth century, these overseers of morals were kept quite busy. Drunkenness in the later antebellum period was especially a problem, and rowdy cornhuskings remained a concern—and worry—of settlement committees. As late as 1857, Friedberg's committee could be found declaring, "Brother Charles Crouch is to be spoken with in regard to a disagreeable occurrence at his corn husking. Several young men became very drunk, and made disturbance and it is said that Brother Crouch furnished the liquor. The committee hope [sic] it is not true."[89]

Most of all, the *Lebenslaufs* demonstrate that the brethren still struggled with a lifelong conversion cycle that saw them dedicate their lives to the Savior and their church, only to stray and to return again. The experiences of Johanna Gertrude Kearney were typical. She was born in 1792 in Bethania, the daughter of an old Moravian family, the Hausers. Her life was a difficult one. She married John Kearney, a shoemaker, in 1817 and bore him two sons and a daughter. He died in 1824, leaving Johanna destitute. "Those were the days of trial," her memoir recalled, and she was forced to rely on the kindness and help of Jesus, "who said, 'I will be the husband of the widow and the father of the fatherless.'" Here was a familiar lesson that someone in the 1780s would have quickly grasped and easily recognized: those in need turn to Jesus. Johanna's chronicler made this conclusion explicit: "She was poor, and often in want for the common necessities of life, but was wonderfully helped by Him." The church was thus her anchor that helped her through a searing life experience—the loss of her husband and subsequent poverty. But as in earlier generations, Johanna wandered from the church for a number of years for reasons her memoir did not explain. She, in other words, turned her back on Jesus after he helped her cope with her husband's passing. Her life then took a familiar turn: Johanna returned to the fold in 1837, when she was confirmed as a full member in Bethania's *Gemeine*. This joyful return did not end her trials, however. Her father died, and Johanna came down with a fever and the "flux." All of this, her chronicler noted with some satisfaction, drew "her nearer and in close bonds with her Savior." The familiar death scene followed: Johanna's health deteriorated, and she became more fearful about the state of her soul. As her memoir put it, "She became very distressed about her soul, fearing she had deceived herself, as she could not realize the presence and nearness of her friend." This former wanderer responded by praying harder for her salvation until "these clouds passed away, her faith again beamed forth brightly," and she again wanted the Lord "to come and take her home." Hence, a familiar conclusion: Johanna had "acquiesced in the will of her Savior, saying, 'Not as I will but let His will be done.'" Death thus became something joyful—Jesus would protect his faithful followers. In presenting a story of devotion and turmoil, Johanna Kearney's memoir was strikingly similar to those of the eighteenth century. These *Lebenslaufs* remained cautionary tales for the devout.[90]

Nothing better represented the changes—and continuities—from eighteenth-century life than the founding of new congregations in the antebellum period. There were only four: Muddy Creek in the 1820s; New Philadelphia in 1846; Mount Bethel in 1851; and Macedonia in 1856. Society members from Maryland and the northern colonies who founded the three *Landgemeinen* in the 1760s and 1770s traveled hundreds of miles and endured great hardships to join the Moravian community in North Carolina. Most were products of the society movement up north, where they had forged a strong Moravian identity in their home colonies before venturing south, and most came with explicit plans to found congregations in their new homes. Congregational formation worked differently in the late antebellum period. Founders were not society members from the north but residents of North Carolina and Virginia. New Philadelphia, for instance, was a community about six miles west of Salem that was visited by the Reverends Samuel Renatus Huebner and Edwin T. Senseman, the pastor of Friedberg. As in the eighteenth century, settlers in the area were responding to Moravian missionary efforts. And as in the eighteenth century, these settlers had the option of remaining members of their home churches while enjoying the occasional sermons of a visiting Moravian, or requesting a closer affiliation with the brethren. Zinzendorf's Diaspora, in other words, lived on. The Diaspora, though, was now called the Home Missionary Society, which concentrated its efforts on the mountains in Virginia to the north and west of Wachovia and on African-Americans in the area. In the mid-1830s, these Diaspora efforts were led by Van Neman Zevilly. Salem's diarist summed up Zevilly's efforts in words that could have been uttered in Pennsylvania in 1750: he "urged them to give themselves to the Savior and to be built up in His word, but in no ways to persuade them to become Moravians, but lovers of the Savior and children of God."[91]

Led by ten families, Philadelphia's settlers chose to become a congregation, and on May 31, 1846, the new congregation formally received its first five communicant members. Huebner served as pastor. This was an English-speaking congregation that did not have to go through an elaborate probationary period, as did the three *Landgemeinen* in the eighteenth century. The brethren welcomed newcomers, seeing growth as an opportunity to win over additional converts to Jesus Christ. In its early years, the congregation met in the home of Martin Rominger and at the Philadelphia schoolhouse. Despite the congregation's tiny size—it had only fifty-four members in 1856, and twenty-eight of them were children—New Philadelphia managed to build a church in 1851.[92]

The record of these new congregations was mixed. Muddy Creek, which bordered Friedberg, did not survive as a congregation, but the other three did. These three congregations, however, remained tiny. The Sunday school at New Philadelphia languished. The new congregations embraced the evangelical and readily used that new Moravian tool, the protracted meeting. This allowed them to survive during a period of explosive Methodist and Baptist growth. Macedonia, which was in Davie County near Hall's Ferry, used "an evangelical meeting" to build membership, gaining eighteen new members alone from one such meeting held in October 1857. The congregation was so enthusiastic about protracted meetings that the Provincial Elders Conference rebuked the minister and his flock for their "loud and disorderly carryings-on." The board reminded them that such behavior could not be introduced without the permission of the synod and that loudness was frowned upon anyway. The congregation was unhappy with the rebuke, and fifteen to twenty members left over their inability to change the services more to their liking.[93] The paradoxes, then, of Moravianism in the 1850s were fully felt in these new congregations. Moravian missionary efforts led to their founding; the embracing of protracted meetings enabled them to gain a foothold in evangelical terrain; but the persistence of German fears of "disorder" constrained their growth.

✝

Thus was the world of North Carolina's Moravians in the antebellum period: evangelical, and quite American and southern. Devotion to heart religion and the new birth had produced such a state of affairs. Zinzendorf's ecumenical vision resulted in a Wachovia inhabited by a multitude of ethnic groups (Irish, English, Danish, German) and numerous faiths (Anglican, Presbyterian, Methodist, Lutheran Reformed). The new birth and an evangelical religion allowed these diverse groups to find common ground and form close friendships. Acculturation then proceeded in two overlapping stages, with intermixing leading to the creation of an Anglo-German world centered on religion. Energetic and outward looking, this religious world evolved further under the impact of intermixing among the brethren and with outsiders. By 1860, Wachovia was a community of paradoxes: a community emphasizing discipline and hard work but readily engaging the marketplace and a material culture that saw them purchase some of the finer things in life, including black slaves. A community stressing inward piety and devotion to Jesus but allowing different levels of membership. A community embracing protracted meetings but condemning exuberance and shouting. A community welcoming outsiders but fearing outside influences. A community that saw itself as part of a worldwide church but that sent soldiers—including a son of George Frederic Bahnson—to fight for the Confederacy in the Civil War.[94]

Piety very much remained in 1860, but the nature of the brethrens' piety had changed. Hope, as always, was representative of this confusing state of affairs. The congregation did not grow in the late antebellum period—quite the contrary, its membership fell. The remaining members, however, did not abandon their church or their faith. They could be found Sundays at their meetinghouse, paying homage to their Savior. Hope, the congregation, endured, and so did its promise of a multiethnic evangelical world.

Notes

In citing works in the notes, shortened forms have generally been used. Full publication data are available in the bibliography. Frequently cited works have been abbreviated as follows:

LAC	Land Arbeiter Conferenz
MA-NP	Moravian Archives, Northern Province
MA-SP	Moravian Archives, Southern Province
MR	*Records of the Moravians in North Carolina*
JER	*Journal of the Early Republic*
NCHR	*North Carolina Historical Review*
WMQ	*William and Mary Quarterly*

Introduction

1. Population figures are from Harry Roy Merrens, *Colonial North Carolina in the Eighteenth Century: A Study in Historical Geography* (Chapel Hill, N.C., 1964), 53; and A. Roger Ekirch, *"Poor Carolina": Politics and Society in Colonial North Carolina, 1729–1776* (Chapel Hill, N.C., 1981), 6–8. Quote is from Richard J. Hooker, ed., *The Carolina Backcountry on the Eve of the Revolution: The Journal and Other Writings of Charles Woodmason, Anglican Itinerant* (Chapel Hill, N.C., 1953), 6–7.

2. For more on this religious migration, see S. Scott Rohrer, "Searching for Land and God: The Pietist Migration to North Carolina in the Late Colonial Period," *NCHR* 79 (October 2002): 409–39. Also see Susanne Mostelle Rolland, "From the Rhine to the Catawba: A Study of Eighteenth Century Germanic Migration and Adaptation" (Ph.D. diss., Emory University, 1991).

3. For a good recent look at the importance of evangelism to the backcountry, see Marjoleine Kars, *Breaking Loose Together: The Regulator Rebellion in Pre-Revolutionary North Carolina* (Chapel Hill, N.C., 2002). For an excellent study that shows how evangelism came to dominate the South, see Christine Leigh Heyrman, *Southern Cross: The Beginnings of the Bible Belt* (New York, 1997). For broader looks at evangelism and the South, see Donald G. Mathews, *Religion in the Old South* (Chicago, 1997); Dee E.

Andrews, *The Methodists and Revolutionary America, 1760–1800: The Shaping of an Evangelical Culture* (Princeton, 2000); Anne C. Loveland, *Southern Evangelicals and the Social Order, 1800–1860* (Baton Rouge, 1980); and Robert M. Calhoon, *Evangelicals and Conservatives in the Early South, 1740–1861* (Columbia, S.C., 1988). And for another view of religion's impact on the South, see Donald G. Mathews, "Religion and the South: Authenticity and Purity—Pulling Us Together, Tearing Us Apart," in *Religious Diversity and American Religious History: Studies in Traditions and Cultures,* ed. Walter H. Conser Jr. and Sumner B. Twiss, 72–101 (Athens, Ga., 1997).

4. See, for example, Philip N. Mulder, *A Controversial Spirit: Evangelical Awakenings in the South* (New York, 2002); Rhys Isaac, *The Transformation of Virginia, 1740–1790* (Chapel Hill, N.C., 1982); and Robert Alexander Armour, "The Opposition to the Methodists in Eighteenth-Century Virginia" (Ph.D. diss., University of Georgia, 1968).

5. For an interesting look at this nontraditional evangelical world that existed outside church walls, see Timothy D. Hall, *Contested Boundaries: Itinerancy and the Reshaping of the Colonial American Religious World* (Durham, N.C., 1994).

6. The best examination of Wachovia's early years is Daniel B. Thorp, *The Moravian Community in Colonial North Carolina: Pluralism on the Southern Frontier* (Knoxville, Tenn., 1989).

7. Elisabeth W. Sommer, *Serving Two Masters: Moravian Brethren in Germany and North Carolina, 1727–1801* (Lexington, Ky., 2000); Thorp, *Moravian Community,* 12. Also see J. Taylor Hamilton and Kenneth G. Hamilton, *History of the Moravian Church: The Renewed Unitas Fratrum, 1722–1957* (Bethlehem, Pa., 1967).

8. Sommer, *Serving Two Masters,* 1–3.

9. Moravian Church historians do not agree on whether these refugees were direct descendants of the Unitas Fratrum. For more on the Moravian Church in the early years and Zinzendorf's role, see A. J. Lewis, *Zinzendorf, the Ecumenical Pioneer: A Study in the Moravian Contribution to Christian Mission and Unity* (Philadelphia, 1962); and F. Ernest Stoeffler, *German Pietism during the Eighteenth Century* (Leiden, 1973), ch. 4.

10. Stoeffler, *German Pietism during the Eighteenth Century,* 131–138. For more on the pietist movement and the Moravians, see W. R. Ward, *The Protestant Evangelical Awakening* (Cambridge, U.K., 1992); Stephen L. Longenecker, *Piety and Tolerance: Pennsylvania German Religion, 1700–1850* (Metuchen, N.J., 1994); and Dale W. Brown, *Understanding Pietism* (Grand Rapids, Mich., 1978).

11. Stoeffler, *German Pietism during the Eighteenth Century,* 146.

12. Beverly Prior Smaby, *The Transformation of Moravian Bethlehem: From Communal Mission to Family Economy* (Philadelphia, 1988), 9. Also see Gillian Lindt Gollin, *Moravians in Two Worlds: A Study of Changing Communities* (New York, 1967).

13. Thorp, *Moravian Community,* 20–24.

14. *MR* 1, 59.

15. Thorp, *Moravian Community,* 11–33.

16. For a good overview of the development of the congregation town, see Sommer, *Serving Two Masters,* ch. 1.

17. Population estimate is for the year 1800 and is based on several primary sources,

including the Wachovia Memorabilia for 1800. Ethnicity was determined by examining family histories compiled from biographical cards at the Museum of Early Southern Decorative Arts (MESDA) research library at Old Salem Inc., and from various church records. For a detailed look at the *Landgemeinen* and its settlers, see S. Scott Rohrer, "Planting Pietism: Religion and Community in the Moravian Settlements of North Carolina, 1750–1830" (Ph.D. diss., University of Virginia, 1999).

18. All six congregations survive today, although not necessarily as geographical communities but as religious units. With more than twenty churches in the Winston-Salem area, the Moravians maintain a strong presence in Forsyth County, North Carolina.

19. For another look at this three-stage model, see S. Scott Rohrer, "Evangelism and Acculturation in the Southern Backcountry: The Case of Wachovia, N.C., 1753–1830," *JER* 21 (Summer 2001): 199–229.

20. The term "triple melting pot" refers to three groups producing three separate melting pots—Catholics of various nationalities marrying fellow Catholics, Jews marrying other Jews, and Protestants marrying Protestants. See Ruby Jo Reeves Kennedy, "Single or Triple Melting Pot? Intermarriage Trends in New Haven, 1870–1940," *American Journal of Sociology* 49, no. 4 (January 1944): 331–39. Also see Harold J. Abramson, "Assimilation and Pluralism," in *Harvard Encyclopedia of American Ethnic Groups,* ed. Stephan Thernstrom, 150–58 (Cambridge, Mass., 1980).

21. In addition to Isaac, *Transformation of Virginia,* see Isaac, "Evangelical Revolt: The Nature of the Baptists' Challenge to the Traditional Order in Virginia, 1765 to 1775," *WMQ* 31 (July 1974): 345–68.

22. Nathan O. Hatch, *The Democratization of American Christianity* (New Haven, Conn., 1989).

23. For an example of a local study portraying the Methodists' arrival as an invasion, see Larry E. Tise, *The Yadkin Melting Pot: Methodism and Moravians in the Yadkin Valley, 1750–1850, and Mount Tabor Church, 1845–1966* (Winston-Salem, N.C., 1967).

24. For an example of the former—a new study that shows the radicalism of religion—see Kars, *Breaking Loose Together.* She demonstrates how evangelism helped fuel the Regulator movement, maintaining that "radical and evangelical Protestantism's emphasis on the priesthood of all believers, on the authority of the Bible, and on the divine spark within created in common people a willingness to question received wisdom," 99. For an example of the latter—a historian who shows how radical evangelicals made accommodations with the gentry power structure in the nineteenth century—see Heyrman, *Southern Cross.* Her thesis modifies the work of Isaac in *Transformation of Virginia* in important ways but still falls within the cultural-conflict paradigm. Some of the newest works on Methodism interpret this movement largely through the lens of Nathan Hatch. See, for example, John H. Wigger, *Taking Heaven by Storm: Methodism and the Rise of Popular Christianity in America* (New York, 1998); and Cynthia Lynn Lyerly, *Methodism and the Southern Mind, 1770–1810* (New York, 1998).

25. For an interesting contrast to my approach, see Stephen L. Longenecker, *Shenandoah Religion: Outsiders and the Mainstream, 1716–1865* (Waco, Tex., 2002). The author

notes that studies of evangelism have stressed how the movement became more conformist and mainstream. He takes a different tack, asking why some groups drifted back to the mainstream and others did not.

26. Steven M. Nolt, *Foreigners in Their Own Land: Pennsylvania Germans in the Early Republic* (University Park, Pa., 2002). For studies on how religion and ethnicity reinforce each other, see Harold J. Abramson, "Religion," in *Harvard Encyclopedia*, ed. Thernstrom, 869–75; Milton M. Gordon, *Assimilation in American Life: The Role of Race, Religion, and National Origins* (New York, 1964); Jonathan D. Sarna, "From Immigrants to Ethnics: Toward a New Theory of 'Ethnicization,'" *Ethnicity* 5 (1978): 370–78; and Henry S. Stout, "Ethnicity: The Vital Center of Religion in America," *Ethnicity* 2 (June 1975): 204–24. For a different view, see Sally Schwartz, *"A Mixed Multitude": The Struggle for Toleration in Colonial Pennsylvania* (New York, 1987), who argues that colonists identified primarily by religion and not ethnicity. Also see Joyce D. Goodfriend, *Before the Melting Pot: Society and Culture in Colonial New York City, 1664–1730* (Princeton, 1992). Many scholars agree that "ethnicity" itself is a modern construct that, nevertheless, can be a useful tool in analyzing society in the early modern period. For a broader look at ethnicity and American history, see Kathleen Neils Conzen et al., "The Invention of Ethnicity: A Perspective From the U.S.A.," *Journal of American Ethnic History* (Fall 1992): 3–41; Werner Sollors, "Introduction: The Invention of Ethnicity," in *The Invention of Ethnicity*, ed. Werner Sollors (New York, 1989); and Kathleen Neils Conzen, *Making Their Own America: Assimilation Theory and the German Peasant Pioneer* (New York, 1990).

27. See, for example, Patrick Griffin, *The People with No Name: Ireland's Ulster Scots, America's Scots Irish, and the Creation of a British Atlantic World, 1689–1764* (Princeton, 2001), and Royden K. Loewen, *Family, Church, and Market: A Mennonite Community in the Old and New Worlds, 1850–1930* (Urbana, Ill., 1993).

28. Jerry Lee Surratt, "From Theocracy to Voluntary Church and Secularized Community: A Study of the Moravians in Salem, North Carolina, 1772–1860" (Ph.D. diss., Emory University, 1968).

29. Besides Surratt, see Michael Shirley, *From Congregation Town to Industrial City: Cultural and Social Change in a Southern Community* (New York, 1994) for a more recent example. More broadly, older traditional studies of ethnic groups see assimilation in generational terms: children of immigrant parents born in a new country become Americanized. For background on assimilation studies and their theoretical constructs, see Abramson, "Assimilation and Pluralism," 150–60.

30. Sommer, *Serving Two Masters*.

31. Daniel B. Thorp, "Assimilation in North Carolina's Moravian Community," *Journal of Southern History* 52 (February 1986): 19–42.

32. Thorp, *Moravian Community*, 4.

33. Ibid., 3; and Fredrik Barth, *Ethnic Groups and Boundaries: The Social Organization of Cultural Difference* (Prospect Heights, Ill., 1998). I want to stress that Professor Thorp's work does recognize that Moravianism attracted a diverse following. But in his article and book, he has not explored what this diversity meant to Wachovia's evolution.

I also want to stress that I agree with his overall thesis that Moravian leaders sought to selectively accommodate to American conditions. However, what Moravian leaders wanted and what happened in practice were two different things.

34. This conclusion is based not only on a reading of the general literature, which tends to portray the Moravians as utopians, but also on countless comments by referees of my journal submissions and by participants at conferences and graduate seminars.

35. Studies of the Moravians in Pennsylvania share the same failing—they focus almost exclusively on Bethlehem, with the society movement receiving very little attention. As a result, general studies of multiethnic Pennsylvania lump the Moravians with other "utopian" groups such as Ephrata. See, for example, Wayne Bodle, "Themes and Directions in Middle Colonies Historiography, 1980–1994," *WMQ* 51 (July 1994): 372. Also see James T. Lemon, *The Best Poor Man's Country: A Geographical Study of Early Southeastern Pennsylvania* (Baltimore, 1972), 109.

36. Hooker, *Carolina Backcountry on the Eve of the Revolution,* 78.

37. See, for example, J. C. S. Mason, *The Moravian Church and the Missionary Awakening in England* (Suffolk, U.K., 2001), and Colin Podmore, *The Moravian Church in England, 1728–1760* (New York, 1998).

38. See, for example, Mulder, *Controversial Spirit,* which stresses the differences and rivalries among evangelicals.

39. For more on some of the hostility generated by the Moravians, see Aaron Spencer Fogleman, "Jesus Is Female: The Moravian Challenge in the German Communities of British North America," *WMQ* 60 (April 2003): 295–332; Aaron Spencer Fogleman, "Shadow Boxing in Georgia: The Beginnings of the Moravian-Lutheran Conflict in British North America," *Georgia Historical Quarterly* (Winter 1999): 629–59; and Aaron Spencer Fogleman, "'Jesus ist weiblich': Die herrnhutische Herausforderung in den deutschen Gemeinden Nordamerikas im 18. Jahrhundert," *Historische Anthropologie* 2 (2001): 167–94. Also see Schwartz, *"Mixed Multitude,"* ch. 5.

40. See, for example, Andrews, *Methodists and Revolutionary America,* 18–26, and Frederick Dreyer, *The Genesis of Methodism* (Bethlehem, Pa., 1999).

1. Prelude: The Northern Years

1. It is unclear exactly why Nathan gave up his tavern, but the debts owed to him from this period were fairly substantial. See Mary Clement Jeske, "Autonomy and Opportunity: Carrollton Manor Tenants, 1734–1790" (Ph.D. dissertation, University of Maryland, 1999), 116, 129–30.

2. Jeske, "Autonomy and Opportunity," 109, 129–30.

3. Conclusion is based on the *Lebenslauf* of William Barton Peddycoard, MA-SP, and the research of Jeske, "Autonomy and Opportunity," into the general religious scene at the manor, 118–23.

4. "An Account of the beginning to Preach the Gospel on Esq. Carroll's Manor by the Brethren United Fratrum and the Baptism of Children There," in MyA: Carroll's

Manor, MA-NP. Also see "The Work of Our Church on Carroll's Manor, 1758–(circ.) 1790," in *Transactions of the Moravian Historical Society* (Nazareth, Pa., 1913), 301–5.

5. Ronald Hoffman, *Princes of Ireland, Planters of Maryland: A Carroll Saga, 1500–1782* (Chapel Hill, N.C., 2000), 100–18.

6. Elizabeth Augusta Kessel, "Germans on the Maryland Frontier: A Social History of Frederick County, Maryland, 1730–1800, vols. 1 and 2" (Ph.D. diss., Rice University, 1981), 31–32.

7. Jeske, "Autonomy and Opportunity," 10.

8. Kessel, "Germans on the Maryland Frontier," 3; Jeske, "Autonomy and Opportunity," 167–69.

9. Jeske, "Carrollton Manor Tenants," 84.

10. Ibid., 120–21.

11. *Lebenslauf* of Mary Padgett, MA-SP. (Other primary sources spell this name Padget, and that is the spelling I am using in text.)

12. Hoffman, *Princes of Ireland,* 344.

13. "An Account of the beginning to Preach the Gospel on Esq. Carroll's Manor," in MyA: Carroll's Manor, MA-NP.

14. Taken from "Observation" that is included in "Account of the beginnings to Preach the Gospel on Esq. Carroll's Manor," in MyA: Carroll's Manor, MA-NP.

15. Letter of the Reverend Joseph Powell to Nathaniel Seidel, undated but 1770 in MyA: Maryland: II, MA-NP.

16. *Lebenslauf* of William Barton Peddycoard, MA-SP.

17. Joseph Powell's Diary of Carroll's Manor, July 27, 1766, MyA: Maryland, folder 6, MA-NP.

18. Ibid., Aug. 20, 1766, MA-NP.

19. Ibid., Sept. 7, 1766, MA-NP.

20. Jeske, "Autonomy and Opportunity," 121.

21. See, for example, Powell Diary entry of Nov. 2, 1766, MA-NP.

22. Ibid., Aug. 7, Aug. 11, and Aug. 12, 1766, MA-NP. Also see "Work of Our Church on Carroll's Manor," 302.

23. Powell Diary, Sept. 5–Dec. 3, 1768, MA-NP.

24. Powell letter of Jan. 18, 1769, to Nathaniel Seidel, MyA V:1, MA-NP.

25. Powell Diary, May 19, 1772, MA-NP.

26. Ibid., Feb. 2, 1767, and Nov. 29, 1768, MA-NP; Powell letter of Jan. 18, 1769, to Nathaniel Seidel. Powell also attributed the effort of the county to collect taxes from him to the mischief caused by the Unity's enemies. See diary entries of March 21 and Oct. 26, 1770, for examples.

27. Powell Diary, Jan. 18, 1767, and March 4, 1768, MA-NP; memoir of Sophia Elisabeth Peddycoart, MA-SP. (Primary sources spell the Peddycoards' name several ways; I have chosen to use "Peddycoard" and not "Peddycoart.")

28. Powell Diary, July 27, 1766, and Jan. 27, 1767, MA-NP.

29. Ibid., July 10, 1768, and Nov. 15, 1770, MA-NP.

30. Alan Taylor, *Liberty Men and Great Proprietors: The Revolutionary Settlement on the Maine Frontier, 1760–1820* (Chapel Hill, N.C., 1990), 75.

31. *Lebenslauf* of George Hahn, MA-SP.

32. *Historicher Bericht vom Anfange und fortgange des Bruder=Establishments in der Wachau;* and *Kurzen Historiche Nachricht von dem Hauflein in Broadbay vom Anfang an bis jezt,* MA-NP.

33. John Rudolph Weinlick, "The Moravian Diaspora: A Study of the Societies of the Moravian Church within the Protestant State Churches of Europe" (Ph.D. diss., Columbia University, 1951), 29.

34. Ibid., 32.

35. Hamilton and Hamilton, *History of the Moravian Church,* 139–40.

36. This discussion of Pietism is based partly on the following works: Stoeffler, *German Pietism during the Eighteenth Century;* Longenecker, *Piety and Tolerance;* Brown, *Understanding Pietism;* and Howard Albert Snyder, "Pietism, Moravianism, and Methodism as Renewal Movements: A Comparative and Thematic Study" (Ph.D. diss., University of Notre Dame, 1983).

37. Dietmar Rothermund, *The Layman's Progress: Religious and Political Experience in Colonial Pennsylvania, 1740–1770* (Philadelphia, 1961), 31.

38. Hamilton and Hamilton, *History of the Moravian Church,* 132.

39. Hall, *Contested Boundaries,* 34–35, 79; also see Patricia U. Bonomi, *Under the Cope of Heaven: Religion, Society, and Politics in Colonial America* (New York, 1986).

40. Rothermund, *Layman's Progress,* 31.

41. Hamilton and Hamilton, *History of the Moravian Church,* 133–34, and 1759 Memorabilia, listed in Lititz records, *Bericht der Stadt u. Land Gemeinen,* MA-NP.

42. J. Max Hark, "The Beginnings of the Moravian Church in Lancaster, Pa.," *Proceedings of the Moravian Historical Society,* vol. 11 (Nazareth, Pa., 1936), 174–88; Henry Muhlenberg Journals I, Dec. 12, 1745, 109; and Schwartz, *"Mixed Multitude,"* 140–42.

43. Leonard Schnell's missionary diaries and *Lischy's und Rauch's Relation von ihrer Visitations reise und Predigten in den Reformierten Gemeinden in Pennsylvania, 1745,* MA-NP.

44. *Historiche Nachricht von dem Anfang u. Fortgang der Evangelischen Bruder Gemeinlein in Heidelberg township, Berks County, in der Provinz Pensilvania,* MA-NP.

45. "Copy of a Letter to our Friends at Carroll's Manor on the Patomik, concerning the Introduction of Brother and Sister Powells," July 2, 1766, MyA: Maryland, MA-NP.

46. Stoeffler, *German Pietism,* 144–46.

47. Craig D. Atwood, ed., *A Collection of Sermons from Zinzendorf's Pennsylvania Journey,* trans. Julie Tomberlin Weber (Bethlehem, Pa., 2001), 65–67.

48. *Lebenslauf* of John Padget, MA-SP.

49. Letter from Daniel and Catherine Smith to "Mister Siddle," Oct. 17, 1770, MyA V:2, MA-NP.

50. *Testimonium von dem Geschwistern u. Famillien in Heidelberg,* April 18, 1745, MA-NP.

51. *Lebenslauf* of Peter Pfaff Sr., MA-SP.

52. See, for example, the York congregation diary entries of April 24, 1759, March 17, 1757, and Oct. 13, 1771, MA-NP.

53. The movements of the Frey family are derived from the *Lebenslaufs* of sons Christian and Valentine, as well as the death notice of Peter in the church register of Friedberg, MA-SP. See also the church book for the Heidelberg congregation, MA-NP.

54. For more on this migration to the *Landgemeinen,* see Rohrer, "Searching for Land and God," 409–39.

55. For examples of entries on German attendance, see Powell Diary, June 3, Aug. 5, and Aug. 23, 1770, MA-NP.

56. The Rev. Joseph Powell to Nathanael Seidel, May 7, 1772, MyA V:2, MA-NP.

57. Powell Diary, Feb. 3, 1772, MA-NP.

58. Daniel Smith's lease-purchase indenture with Frederick Marshall is in Notebook D, MA-SP.

59. Jeske, "Autonomy and Opportunity," 21–24, 57, 90.

60. Oct. 17, 1775, lease-purchase agreement of William Barton Peddycoard for 150 acres, D153:5, MA-SP.

61. *Lebenslauf* of John Jacob Peddycoard, and two lease-purchases of Jan. 1, 1781, D153:5, MA-SP.

62. Powell Diary, Aug. 2, 1772, MA-NP.

63. Congregational address to Bethlehem, Aug. 26, 1772, MA-NP.

64. *Lebenslauf* of John Padget, MA-SP.

65. Figures on arriving families are from the 1774 and 1775 Wachovia Memorabilias. For another example of a family moving reluctantly to join other kin, see the Chittys, Hope Church Book, Register A, Burials at Hope, MA-SP.

66. *MR* 4, 1895.

67. Correspondence of George Soelle in box NeA IV and *Kurze Historiche . . . Broadbay,* MA-NP.

68. *Kurze Historiche . . . Broadbay,* MA-NP.

69. *MR* 2, 611.

70. *Kurze Historiche . . . Broadbay,* MA-NP.

71. *Lebenslauf* of Catharine Lanius, maiden name Rominger, MA-SP.

72. *MR* 2, 610.

73. It should be noted that the earliest arrivals to the settlement that became Friedberg were German speakers from Maryland. This tiny migration was unaffiliated with the brethren; these migrants learned of the brethren during the French and Indian War, and some decided to affiliate with the Unity.

74. Baptismal record in *Catalogue Aller zu der Gemeine in Heidelberg; Extract aus den Diariis der Stadt und Land-Gemeinen: 1765–1770;* deeds of April 29, 1765, Berks County, Pa.; and *Heidelberg Bericht,* MA-NP.

75. Merrens, *Colonial North Carolina,* 53; and Ekirch, *"Poor Carolina,"* 6–8.

76. This characterization of "extraordinary" is from Bernard Bailyn, *Voyagers to the West: A Passage in the Peopling of America on the Eve of the Revolution* (New York, 1986), 7.

77. Lemon, *Best Poor Man's Country,* 70–75.

78. Robert W. Ramsey, *Carolina Cradle: Settlement of the Northwest Carolina Frontier, 1747–1762* (Chapel Hill, N.C., 1964), 10–21.

79. *Lebenslauf* of Matthias Wesner, MA-SP.

80. Advertisement of March 1763, MA-NP. For more on the original plans for Wachovia and the decision to abandon them, see Thorp, "Assimilation in North Carolina's Moravian Community," 19–42.

81. Stokes County Deed Books, Forsyth County Library, Winston-Salem, North Carolina. For more on landholding practices, see Rohrer, "Planting Pietism," ch. 5.

82. Aaron Spencer Fogleman, "Moravian Immigration and Settlement in British North America, 1734–1775," *Transactions of the Moravian Historical Society* 29 (1996): 30.

83. Thorp, *Moravian Community,* 36.

84. Ibid., 36–48.

85. Ibid. Also see Sommer, *Serving Two Masters,* 33–58.

86. Thorp, *Moravian Community;* Thorp, "Assimilation in North Carolina's Moravian Community"; Aaron Spencer Fogleman, *Hopeful Journeys: German Immigration, Settlement, and Political Culture, 1717–1775* (Philadelphia, 1996), 123; Sommer, *Serving Two Masters.*

87. Fogleman, *Hopeful Journeys,* 123.

88. *MR* 1, 303; *Extract aus den Diariis der Stadt und Land-Gemeinen,* May 10, 1765, MA-NP.

89. May 10, 1765, *Heidelberg Bericht,* MA-NP.

90. *Historiche Nachricht von dem Anfang, in Kurchen Buch fur Heidelberg,* MA-NP.

91. *MR* 4, 1839; and Diary of L. C. Bachhof, Aug. 1, 1773, Donald J. Lineback translation, H278:5, MA-SP.

92. "Diary of a Journey of Moravians from Bethlehem, Pa., to Bethabara, N.C., 1753," in *Travels in the American Colonies,* ed. Newton D. Mereness, 328 (New York, 1961).

93. *MR* 1, 383 and 393.

94. Ibid.

95. Fogleman, *Hopeful Journeys,* 12. Fogleman stresses that migrants followed a collective strategy, and he does not use the term "cultural broker." That term is from the work of A. G. Roeber. See Roeber, "'The Origin of Whatever Is Not English among Us': The Dutch-Speaking and the German-Speaking Peoples of Colonial British America," in *Strangers within the Realm: Cultural Margins of the First British Empire,* ed. Bernard Bailyn and Philip D. Morgan, 265–66 (Chapel Hill, N.C., 1991), and A. G. Roeber, *Palatines, Liberty, and Property: German Lutherans in Colonial British America* (Baltimore, 1993).

2. A Community of Believers

1. *Lebenslauf* of George Soelle, reprinted in *MR* 2, 804–7.

2. John B. Boles, *The Great Revival: Beginnings of the Bible Belt* (Lexington, Ky.,

1996), 129. Standard works on southern evangelism and the camp-meeting movement include Heyrman, *Southern Cross;* Loveland, *Southern Evangelicals and the Social Order;* Paul Conkin, *Cane Ridge: America's Pentecost* (Madison, Wis., 1990); and Calhoon, *Evangelicals and Conservatives in the Early South.*

3. *Lebenslauf* of Soelle.

4. In early evangelism, dreams often played an important role in the conversion experience. See, for instance, Jon Butler, *Awash in a Sea of Faith: Christianizing the American People* (Cambridge, Mass., 1990), 222 and 238–39.

5. *Lebenslauf* of Soelle.

6. Andrews, *Methodists and Revolutionary America,* 74–75.

7. Boles, *Great Revival,* 129.

8. Andrews, *Methodists and Revolutionary America,* 32.

9. *Lebenslauf* of Soelle.

10. Ibid.

11. Diary of the Reverend George Soelle, July 24, 1771, translation by Bishop Kenneth G. Hamilton, F228:3, MA-SP.

12. Ibid., Feb. 7, 1773. "Spark of light" quote is from May 9, 1772, entry.

13. Bachhof Diary, March 5, 1770, Lineback translation, MA-SP.

14. Ibid., June 13, 1771, MA-SP.

15. Lewis, *Zinzendorf, the Ecumenical Pioneer;* Stoeffler, *German Pietism during the Eighteenth Century,* ch. 4; and Ward, *Protestant Evangelical Awakening,* 136–39.

16. Ibid.

17. Atwood, ed., *Collection of Sermons,* 32–33; Stoeffler, *German Pietism,* 143–50; and Martin Brecht, "Der Hallische Pietismus in der Mitte des 18. Jahrhunderts—seine Ausstrahlung und sein Niedergang," in *Geschichte des Pietismus* 2, ed. Brecht and Deppermann, 319–57 (Gottingen, 1993).

18. Atwood, ed., *Collection of Sermons,* 45–47.

19. Quoted in Hamilton and Hamilton, *History of the Moravian Church,* 170.

20. Soelle Diary, April 17, 1772, and May 12, 1771, Hamilton translation, MA-SP.

21. Atwood, ed., *Zinzendorf's Pennsylvania Journey,* xvii.

22. Craig D. Atwood, "Deep in the Side of Jesus: Zinzendorfian Piety in Colonial America" (conference paper presented at the "German Moravians in the Atlantic World" symposium, Wake Forest University, April 2002), 11. Also see Craig D. Atwood, "Blood, Sex, and Death: Life and Liturgy in Zinzendorf's Bethlehem" (Ph.D. diss., Princeton Theological Seminary, 1995).

23. Fogleman, "Jesus Is Female," 295–332. For more on the Unity's critics, see Fogleman, "Shadow Boxing in Georgia," 629–59; and Fogleman, "'Jesus ist weiblich,'" 167–94.

24. Ward, *Protestant Evangelical Awakening,* 136–39.

25. *Lebenslauf* of Cornelius Schneider, MA-SP.

26. *Lebenslauf* of Valentine Frey, MA-SP.

27. Soelle Diary, Feb. 18, 1772, Hamilton translation, MA-SP.

28. Percentages are derived from congregational church books in MA-SP and Wachovia Memorabilias reprinted in *MR*.

29. Ibid.

30. "Brotherly Agreement about Rules and Orders for the Brethren's Congregation in and about Hope settlement, made in the year 1785," MA-SP.

31. Ibid.

32. Ibid.

33. Soelle Diary, May 17, 1772, Hamilton translation, MA-SP.

34. Ibid., Sept. 7, 1771, MA-SP.

35. Bachhof Diary, Aug. 27, 1771, Lineback translation, MA-SP.

36. Ibid., March 21, 1773; Feb. 26, 1773; May 4, 1771; and Sept. 2, 1770.

37. Ibid., Sept. 10, 1772, and April 2, 1773.

38. 1818 Results of General Synod, MA-SP.

39. David Warren Sabean, *Power in the Blood: Popular Culture and Village Discourse in Early Modern German* (New York, 1984).

40. Bachhof Diary, June 28, 1772, Lineback translation, MA-SP.

41. *MR* 1, 200.

42. See, for example, Bachhof Diary, Dec. 19, 1771, Lineback translation, MA-SP. Friedberg held its first communion service on Jan. 16, 1772.

43. Ibid., Jan. 16, 1772, and April 18, 1773.

44. Sabean, *Power in the Blood,* 53.

45. "History of the Unity," by Bishop August Spangenberg, 1772, *MR* 3, 1014.

46. 1818 Synod, MA-SP.

47. *Lebenslauf* of Christian Zimmerman, MA-SP.

48. *MR* 4, 1738.

49. Bachhof Diary, April 18, 1773, Lineback translation, MA-SP.

50. For overviews of Puritanism and Roger Williams, see two dated but still classic works: Perry Miller, *Errand into the Wilderness* (Cambridge, Mass., 1956), and Edmund S. Morgan, *The Puritan Dilemma: The Story of John Winthrop,* ed. Oscar Handlin (Boston, 1958).

51. Bachhof Diary, May 19, 1773, Lineback translation, MA-SP.

52. Ibid.

53. Ibid., May 1, 1773.

54. Ibid.

55. C. Daniel Crews, "Moravian Worship: The *Why* of Moravian Music" (conference paper presented at the "German Moravians in the Atlantic World" symposium, Wake Forest University, April 2002), 10–11. Also see Atwood, "Blood, Sex, and Death," 177.

56. "Conclusion of the United Brethren assembled at Herrnhut in the year 1818 as addressed to the Country Congregations in Wachovia," MA-SP.

57. Conclusions based on an examination of congregational records in MA-SP.

58. The following discussion of the *Gemeine* and *Ortsgemeine* is based on my own research, as well as the following works on the *Ortsgemeinen:* Sommer, *Serving Two Mas-*

ters; Surratt, "From Theocracy to Voluntary Church and Secularized Community"; Thorp, *Moravian Community;* and Smaby, *Transformation of Moravian Bethlehem.*

59. Atwood, *Collection of Sermons,* 26.

60. Sommer, *Serving Two Masters,* 12–17.

61. *MR* 4, 1897.

62. Sommer, *Serving Two Masters,* 41.

63. LAC minutes, Sept. 15, 1780, Frances Cumnock translation, MA-SP.

64. Ibid., Sept. 15, 1781, and Nov. 14, 1785, Cumnock translation, MA-SP.

65. *MR* 2, 665, 690; *MR* 1, 266.

66. For the story of Friedberg's early years, see *MR* 1, especially 213–14, 266, and 330–31. Also see Bachhof Diary, Lineback translation, MA-SP.

67. Bachhof Diary, entry for 1759, Lineback translation, MA-SP.

68. *MR* 1, 213.

69. For more on the Friedberg migration, see Rohrer, "Searching for Land and God," 409–39.

70. Friedberg School Papers, H279:9, MA-SP, and *MR* 1, 352.

71. *MR* 1, 330–31, 408, 436

72. Provincial Elders Conference minutes, Nov. 13, 1769, MA-SP. Translations are available at MESDA's research library.

73. Ibid., Oct. 19, 1770.

74. Ibid., Nov. 20, 1770.

75. *MR* 1, 448–49; Provincial Elders Conference minutes, Nov. 20, 1770, MA-SP.

76. Salem Diary, Aug. 23, 1780.

77. *MR* 2, 742.

78. Ibid., 810.

79. Agreement with Simon Peter, April 30, 1787, H280:9:D, MA-SP.

80. *Beytrage zum Sustentation der Arbeiter in Hope . . . 1805, 1806, 1807.* For Friedland, see Friedland Church Subscription to the Sustentation of the Ministers, 1801–1823, H282:4, and *Subscribtion der mitglied der Gemeine u. Societat in Friedland sum Unterhalt der Arbeiters,* H282:3, MA-SP.

81. See, for example, descriptions of construction of the Friedland *gemeine Haus, MR* 1, 449.

82. *MR* 1, 394. In this reference, the Wachovia Diary notes that Richard Utley preached in "the little Saal in the second story of the school-house. The living rooms on the first floor are furnished." Friedberg possibly followed the Pennsylvania model, where the Saal was often on the second floor.

83. "Inventory of all the household goods, moveables, books, and belongings to the congregation house at Hope in the month of December 1819," MA-SP. For a comparison to Friedberg, see *Inventarium der zum Friedberger Gemeinhaus gehorenden Sacher den 4 Merz 1804,* H276:10, MA-SP.

84. Bachhof Diary, Sept. 29, 1771, and Dec. 31, 1770, Lineback translation, MA-SP.

85. "Personal Diary of George Frederic Bahnson," May 10, 1837; original is in MA-SP; translated copies by Alice North Henderson are available at MESDA.

86. *MR* 4, 1833.

87. See, for example, Friedland Diary entries of Feb. 10 and March 3, 1799, MA-SP.

88. Sommer, *Serving Two Masters,* 30.

89. *MR* 4, 1832.

90. Ibid., 2466–67, 1792 Memorabilia.

91. *MR* 1, 418.

92. For examples, see Bachhof Diary, March 4 and March 18, 1770, Lineback translation, MA-SP.

93. *Berichts von Friedland vom June 1783,* MA-SP.

94. *MR* 1, 202.

95. Ibid. Also see Crews, "Moravian Worship"; Maurer Maurer, "Music in Wachovia, 1753–1800," *WMQ* 8 (April 1951): 214–27; and Jeannine S. Ingram, "Music in Moravian Communities: Transplanted Traditions in Indigenous Practices," *Communal Societies* 2 (1982): 39–52.

96. Soelle Diary, Dec. 25, 1772, Hamilton translation, MA-SP.

3. An Anglo-German World

1. *Lebenslauf* of Adam Elrod Sr., MA-SP.

2. Ibid.

3. *MR* 2, 742, 776.

4. 1804 map of Wachovia; copy is on file at MESDA research library.

5. Bachhof Diary, Sept. 10, Oct. 14, Oct. 15, and Oct. 19, 1770, Lineback translation, MA-SP.

6. Roeber, *Palatines, Liberty, and Property,* 113–17. Also see Fogleman, *Hopeful Journeys,* ch. 3.

7. These five farms belonged to the Tesches, Hausers, Eberts, Hahns, and Hohners. See May 10, 1780, Friedberg Diary in *MR* 4, 1649.

8. *MR* 1, 817; *MR* 4, 1649; and 1804 map of Wachovia by Frederick Meinung.

9. *MR* 1, 294.

10. *MR* 2, 742.

11. Bishop Spangenberg to Bethania's brethren, June 29, 1755, MA-SP.

12. 1804 map of Wachovia.

13. Lemon, *Best Poor Man's Country,* 42 and 18.

14. Bachhof Diary, entries of Sept. 10, Oct. 14, Oct. 15, and Oct. 19, 1770, Lineback translation, MA-SP.

15. *MR* 2, 616; for a description of the village, see *MR* 1, 436.

16. Quote is from Resolutions of the 1775 Synod, MA-SP.

17. Ibid.

18. LAC minutes of October 1780, Cumnock translation, MA-SP.

19. Ibid., Sept. 15, 1780.

20. Ibid., November 1780.

21. Quote is from LAC minutes of Sept. 15, 1780, Cumnock translation, MA-SP.

22. LAC minutes of October 1780, Cumnock translation, MA-SP.

23. Some standard works on Puritan families include Philip J. Greven Jr., "Family Structure in Seventeenth-Century Andover, Massachusetts," *WMQ* 55 (April 1966): 234–56; Philip J. Greven Jr., *Four Generations: Population, Land and Family in Colonial Andover, Massachusetts* (Ithaca, N.Y., 1970); and Edmund S. Morgan, *The Puritan Family: Religion and Domestic Relations in Seventeenth-Century New England* (Westport, Conn., 1980).

24. Soelle Diary, April 20, 1771, Hamilton translation, MA-SP.

25. Ibid., Dec. 30, 1773.

26. Term is from Resolutions of the 1775 Synod, MA-SP.

27. Jon F. Sensbach, *A Separate Canaan: The Making of an Afro-Moravian World in North Carolina, 1763–1840* (Chapel Hill, N.C., 1998), has an excellent discussion of godparenthood. It also offers a good comparison of the differences and similarities between white and black godparenthood; see 415–38. Also see John Bossy, "Blood and Baptism: Kinship, Community and Christianity in Western Europe from the Fourteenth to the Seventeenth Centuries," in *Sanctity and Secularity: The Church and the World,* Studies in Church History 10, ed. Derek Baker, 129–43 (Oxford, 1973); and David Warren Sabean, "Aspects of Kinship Behavior and Property in Rural Western Europe before 1800," in *Family and Inheritance: Rural Society in Western Europe, 1200–1800,* ed. Jack Goody, Joan Thirsk, and E. P. Thompson, 96–111 (Cambridge, U.K., 1976), 96–111.

28. Friedberg Register A, 1774–1792, No. 6, MA-SP. Family relationships are derived from biographical cards at MESDA research library.

29. Ibid., No. 42.

30. See, for instance, No. 3 in Register 1 for Eva Rothrock, MA-SP.

31. Sensbach, *Separate Canaan,* 416.

32. *Lebenslauf* of Martin Walk and Friedberg Register A, No. 8, MA-SP.

33. Friedberg, Register A, No. 38, MA-SP.

34. See, for example, Nos. 2, 3, 9, and 54 in Register A, MA-SP.

35. There is considerable agreement among social historians that people in the early modern period married later than earlier generations of historians believed. See, for example, Keith Wrightson, *English Society, 1580–1680* (New Brunswick, N.J., 1982), ch. 3, who finds that the average age for first marriages for men was 27.1 in the seventeenth century. Also see George Huppert, *After the Black Death: A Social History of Early Modern Europe* (Bloomington, Ind., 1986), 126. Numerous studies of early America have echoed these conclusions as well. The average marrying age of twenty-seven for men and twenty-five for women means that marriages in the *Landgemeinen* were slightly younger than the norm.

36. Jo Ellen Patterson, "Church Control and Family Structure in a Moravian Community of North Carolina, 1753–1857" (Ph.D. diss., University of North Carolina at Greensboro, 1991), 64.

37. "First generation" is defined as those Moravians who were of marrying age when Hope was founded in 1772 or were the first in their family to join the Moravian Church. "Second generation" is defined as those members who were born into Moravianism.

38. *MR* 6, 2535, and *Lebenslauf* of Valentine Frey, MA-SP.

39. For the importance of intermarriage in acculturation, see Richard M. Bernard, *The Melting Pot and the Altar: Marital Assimilation in Early Twentieth-Century Wisconsin* (Minneapolis, 1980), and Gordon, *Assimilation in American Life.*

40. Laura Becker, "Diversity and Its Significance in an Eighteenth-Century Pennsylvania Town," in *Friends and Neighbors: Group Life in America's First Plural Society,* ed. Michael Zuckerman, 196–221 (Philadelphia, 1982); the figure is on page 203. For a broader look at German immigrants' endogamy rates, see Fogleman, *Hopeful Journeys,* 150–52. He argues that few Germans married non-Germans.

41. Stephanie Grauman Wolf, *Urban Village: Population, Community, and Family Structure in Germantown, Pennsylvania, 1683–1800* (Princeton, 1976), 132.

42. Warren R. Hofstra, "Land, Ethnicity, and Community at the Opequon Settlement, Virginia, 1730–1800," *Virginia Magazine of History and Biography* 98 (July 1990): 423. For more on Presbyterianism and its importance to ethnic identity, see Maldwyn A. Jones, "The Scotch-Irish in British America," in *Strangers within the Realm,* ed. Bailyn and Morgan, 284–313, and Griffin, *People with No Name.*

43. See chart on intermixing for sources.

44. Gollin, *Moravians in Two Worlds,* 117. For more on marriage and Herrnhut, see Sommer, *Serving Two Masters,* esp. chs. 2 and 4.

45. LAC minutes of Nov. 14, 1785, Cumnock translation, MA-SP.

46. *Lebenslauf* of Adam Spach Jr., MA-SP.

47. Ibid.

48. Ibid.

49. Deed Books 2:196 and 4:196, Stokes County, Forsyth County Library.

50. The activities of the Douthits are reconstructed from the memoirs of John, Mary, Isaac, and Sarah in MA-SP; biographical cards at MESDA; deed books at Forsyth County library; and the Rowan County will of John Douthit, C148.

51. *MR* 4, 1717–18.

52. *MR* 2, 592. There were exceptions, of course. For example, George Bahnson equated the decline of German's use in Wachovia with a religious declension. See Bahnson Diary, Aug. 1, Aug. 15, and Sept. 3, 1835, MA-SP.

53. *MR* 6, 2722.

54. Soelle Diary, March 31, 1771, Hamilton translation, MA-SP.

55. Ibid., May 12, 1771.

56. Ibid., Dec. 20, 1772.

57. Ibid., Aug. 8, 1772.

58. LAC minutes, June 19, 1788, MA-SP.

59. See, for example, the Salem Diary entry of Nov. 12, 1808, in *MR* 6, 2923; and Hope committee minutes of Aug. 16, 1801, in folder 2, MA-SP.

60. LAC minutes of Nov. 14 and Dec. 3, 1789, Cumnock translation, MA-SP.

61. *MR* 6, 2796 and 2833.

62. Quoted in William H. Gehrke, "The Transition from German to the English Language in North Carolina," *NCHR* 11 (January 1935): 1–2.

63. Stout, "Ethnicity," 207. For a comparison with the Presbyterian Scots-Irish and Scots, see Hofstra, "Land, Ethnicity, and Community," and Longenecker, *Shenandoah Religion*.

64. Marion L. Huffines, "Language-Maintenance Efforts among German Immigrants and their Descendants in the United States," in *America and the Germans: An Assessment of a Three-Hundred Year History*, vol. 1, ed. Frank Trommler and Joseph McVeigh, 241–42 (Philadelphia, 1985). For more on the German language, see Jurgen Eichhoff, "The German Language in America," in *America and the Germans*, ed. Trommler and McVeigh, 230–40.

65. Nolt, *Foreigners in Their Own Land*, 57, 141–43.

66. Stephanie Grauman Wolf, "Hyphenated America: The Creation of an Eighteenth-Century German American Culture," in *America and the Germans*, ed. Trommler and McVeigh, 69. Not all historians agree that ethnic identity among eighteenth-century immigrant groups was important. See, for example, Schwartz, *"Mixed Multitude,"* who argues that colonists identified by religion and not ethnicity. Also see Herman Wellenreuther, "Image and Counterimage, Tradition and Expectation: The German Immigrants in English Colonial Society in Pennsylvania, 1700–1765," in *America and the Germans*, ed. Trommler and McVeigh, 85–89, who argues like many other historians that Germans arrived with little self-awareness of their differentness but developed an ethnic identity as they became acclimated to an Anglo-American society. Yet others argue that German-speaking immigrants assimilated quickly into American society, largely because of economic pressures. See Wolf, *Urban Village*, and Lemon, *Best Poor Man's Country*.

67. Lorenz Bagge to Nathanael Seidel, Nov. 21, 1766, MA-NP, reel 1. Translated copy available at MESDA research library.

68. Daniel Snydacker, "Kinship and Community in Rural Pennsylvania, 1749–1820," *Journal of Interdisciplinary History* 13 (Summer 1982): 41–61. For more on the German approach to land and family, see Kathleen Neils Conzen, "Peasant Pioneers: Generational Succession among German Farmers in Frontier Minnesota," in *The Countryside in the Age of Capitalist Transformation: Essays in the Social History of Rural America*, ed. Steven Hahn and Jonathan Prude, 259–92 (Chapel Hill, N.C., 1985).

69. Barry Levy, "The Birth of the 'Modern Family' in Early America: Quaker and Anglican Families in the Delaware Valley, Pennsylvania, 1681–1750," in *Friends and Neighbors*, ed. Zuckerman, 26–63. For testate practices in the Chesapeake, see Lois Green Carr and Lorena S. Walsh, "The Planter's Wife: The Experience of White Women in Seventeenth-Century Maryland," *WMQ* 34 (Oct. 1977): 542–71.

70. Roeber, "'Origin of Whatever Is Not English Among Us,'" 265–66.

71. Roeber, *Palatines, Liberty, and Property*, 157.

72. Pro Memoria Concerning Bethania, April 17, 1766, MA-SP.

73. Barry J. Levy, "'Tender Plants': Quaker Farmers and Children in the Delaware Valley, 1681–1735," in *Colonial America: Essays in Politics and Social Development*, 3rd ed., ed. Stanley N. Katz and John M. Murrin, 177 and 192 (New York, 1983).

74. Stokes Deed Book 3:328; also see Stokes Will Book 3:42.

75. Stokes Deed Book 5:615 and 5:616. Jacob later bought Timothy's share and turned around and sold it to his oldest brother, Abraham Jr., Books 5:730 and 6:228.

76. Stokes Deed Books 5:7 and 5:253.

77. Stokes Will Book 2:80.

78. For other examples of childless couples forgoing the land market, see deed indexes for Lorenz Sides, Philip Lagenauer, and David Rominger.

79. Lutz K. Berkner, "Inheritance, Land Tenure and Peasant Family Structure: A German Regional Comparison," in *Family and Inheritance,* ed. Goody, Thirsk, and Thompson, 71–95, esp. 82. For more on inheritance practices, see Margaret Spufford, "Peasant Inheritance Customs and Land Distribution in Cambridgeshire from the Sixteenth to the Eighteenth Centuries," in *Family and Inheritance,* ed. Goody, Thirsk, and Thompson, 156–76; Joan Thirsk, "The European Debate on Customs of Inheritance, 1500–1700," in *Family and Inheritance,* ed. Goody, Thirsk, and Thompson, 177–91; Snydacker, "Kinship and Community," 41–61; Toby L. Ditz, *Property and Kinship: Inheritance in Early Connecticut, 1750–1820* (Princeton, 1986); and Bruce R. Penner, "Landholding and Testate Patterns: Acculturation and Adaptation in an 18th-Century Backcountry Swiss Settlement" (paper presented at the conference on the southern backcountry, Staunton, Virginia, October 1996).

80. Conzen, "Peasant Pioneers," esp. 266.

81. Roeber, *Palatines, Liberty, and Property,* 50–53, 109–10; 149–57.

82. This conclusion is based on examination of 215 wills.

83. This stability contrasted with other settlers on the frontier. For examples of this mobility, see William C. Davis, *A Way through the Wilderness: The Natchez Trace and the Civilization of the Southern Frontier* (New York, 1995), 821; Bernard Bailyn, *The Peopling of British North America: An Introduction* (New York, 1986), 20–48; and Richard R. Beeman, *The Evolution of the Southern Backcountry: A Case Study of Lunenburg County, Virginia, 1746–1832* (Philadelphia, 1984).

84. Stokes Will Book 1:104.

85. Will of Lazarus Hege, C141A, MA-SP.

86. Will of Peter Frey Jr., C141A, MA-SP.

87. Lois Green Carr, "Inheritance in the Colonial Chesapeake," in *Women in the Age of the American Revolution,* ed. Ronald Hoffman and Peter J. Albert, 155–97 (Charlottesville, Va., 1989).

88. Will of Matthew Markland, Book 1:81½, Stokes County Will Book; listing of land titled "The Land in Wachovia Amounts to 98,985 Acres Given in the Year 1795," S742:2, MA-SP; lease-purchase between Frederick Marshall and Matthew Markland, May 14, 1774, D153:4, MA-SP; and Stokes County Deed Books, 2:113.

89. The figures are derived from an examination of fifty-eight wills in the two settlements. Friedberg is included because of its extremely close relations with Hope and to increase the sample among German speakers; only six wills among German speakers in Hope are extant. Several German-speaking families had members in both congregations, and yet others switched congregations.

90. For these characterizations of Anglo and German testate practices, I am drawing

mainly on Levy, "Birth of the 'Modern Family,'" and Conzen, "Peasant Pioneers." Among the English Moravians in the 1772 to 1800 period, no wills indicate that fathers gave land to sons while they were alive, and six wills decreed that sons get land after their passing. From 1800 to 1830, six of sixteen wills show that fathers gave land while they were alive, and five bequeathed land after their death. For Germans in Hope and Friedberg, four of fourteen gave land before their decease in the early period; six gave land after. This percentage who bequeathed land before their deaths is lower than the rest of Wachovia—further evidence of intermixing's impact on the first generation in Hope. In the later period, six of twenty-eight gave land before their deaths and fifteen after. The total sample of wills includes five women who owned no land and men who were either childless or unclear as to how land was distributed, so all percentages are understated.

91. *MR* 1, 618.

92. *MR* 2, 859.

93. Thorp, "Assimilation in North Carolina's Moravian Community," 19–42.

94. Report of Bishop Spangenberg, in C. Daniel Crews, ed., "Bethania: A Fresh Look at Its Birth," undated church pamphlet printed by MA-SP, 21.

95. Pro Memoria Concerning Bethania, April 17, 1766, MA-SP.

96. *MR* 1, 38–39.

97. Gottlieb Reuter's "Recapitulation of the *Puncta* settled or suggested for Bethania," Cumnock translation, MA-SP.

98. Report of Bishop Spangenberg, Sept. 10, 1759, in Crews, ed., "Bethania," 20–21.

99. Thorp, "Assimilation in North Carolina's Moravian Community," 30.

100. Merrens, *Colonial North Carolina,* 211.

101. For more on German agriculture, see Alan Mayhew, *Rural Settlement and Farming in Germany* (London, 1973); Jorn Sieglerschmidt, "Social and Economic Landscapes," in *Germany: A New Social and Economic History, 1630–1800,* vol. 2, ed. Sheilagh Ogilvie, 1–38 (New York, 1996); and Terry G. Jordan, *German Seed in Texas Soil: Immigrant Farmers in Nineteenth-Century Texas* (Austin, 1966).

102. *MR* 4, 1501.

103. The signers of the 1759 letter seeking to affiliate with the Moravians were Martin Hauser, George Hauser, Michael Hauser, Peter Hauser, Daniel Hauser, Heinrich Spainhouer, Johannes Strub, Heinrich Schol, Phillip Schauss, Johannes Schor, and Johannes Spainhouer. A translated version of the letter is in Crews, ed., "Bethania," 17–18.

104. Bethania Committee Protocoll, March 18, 1768, Frances Cumnock translation, H269:1, MA-SP. Also see H265:3a, MA-SP.

105. "History of the General Lease," MA-SP.

106. Bethania was the first *Ortsgemeine* to allow society and *Gemeine* members to live in one congregation town; Zinzendorf himself condemned the practice and had harsh words for Spangenberg. Sommer, *Serving Two Masters,* 41.

107. *Lebenslauf* of Heinrich Schor, MA-SP.

108. Ibid.

109. "Letter from 6 Bethanians to Frederick Marshall," April 2, 1768, MA-SP.

110. *MR* 5, 2352.

111. *MR* 7, 3099.

112. *MR* 6, 2833.

113. Sommer, *Serving Two Masters,* 160.

4. Becoming "American": The Revolutionary Years

1. Friedberg Diary, 1780, *MR* 4, 1649 and 1775. Battlefield figures are from Craig L. Symonds, *A Battlefield Atlas of the American Revolution* (Mt. Pleasant, S.C., 1986), 83.

2. For some recent studies that probe the rise of nationalism from a variety of angles, see Joyce Appleby, *Inheriting the Revolution: The First Generation of Americans* (Cambridge, Mass., 2000); Joyce Appleby, *Capitalism and a New Social Order: The Republican Vision of the 1790s* (New York, 1984); and Robert H. Wiebe, *The Opening of American Society: From the Adoption of the Constitution to the Eve of Disunion* (New York, 1984). For the formation of an American culture in an earlier period, see Jack P. Greene, *Pursuits of Happiness: The Social Development of Early Modern British Colonies and the Formation of American Culture* (Chapel Hill, N.C., 1988), and Jon Butler, *Becoming America: The Revolution before 1776* (Cambridge, Mass., 2000). Also see Joseph J. Ellis, *After the Revolution: Profiles of Early American Culture* (New York, 1979). For a look at a later period and the meaning of nationalism to immigrants, see John Higham, *Send These to Me: Immigrants in Urban America* (Baltimore, 1984).

3. Fogleman, *Hopeful Journeys,* 152–53. Also see Nolt, *Foreigners in Their Own Land.*

4. Friedberg Diary 1776, *MR* 3, 1117.

5. Ibid., *MR* 3, 1110–11.

6. Hunter James, *The Quiet People of the Land: A Story of the North Carolina Moravians in Revolutionary Times* (Chapel Hill, N.C., 1976), 36–37; Thorp, *Moravian Community,* 168.

7. Memorabilia of Salem, 1776, *MR* 3, 1039.

8. Ibid., *MR* 3, 1040.

9. Gordon S. Wood, *The Radicalism of the American Revolution* (New York, 1993), 215.

10. *MR* 2, 851, 944.

11. *MR* 2, 1044–45. Also see "Declaration of the Moravians in North Carolina claiming exemption from military service," P602:11:89, MA-SP, which reiterated that "we are loyal and faithful subjects to his Majesty King George the third." This document is undated but was probably issued in 1776.

12. *MR* 2, 1087.

13. Friedberg Diary, 1776, *MR* 3, 1119.

14. Salem Diary, 1777, *MR* 3, 1168.

15. *MR* 4, 1710–11.

16. Salem Diary, 1777, *MR* 3, 1168.

17. Salem Diary, 1776, *MR* 3, 1073.

18. Salem Diary, 1778, *MR* 3, 1235.

19. Andrews, *Methodists and Revolutionary America,* 51. Also see Lyerly, *Methodism and the Southern Mind;* Wigger, *Taking Heaven by Storm;* and Keith Mason, "Localism, Evangelicalism, and Loyalism: The Sources of Discontent in the Revolutionary Chesapeake," *Journal of Southern History* (February 1990): 23–54.

20. Letter, Johannes Ettwein to Graff, Nov. 16, 1778, *MR* 3, 1424–25.

21. Ibid.

22. C. Daniel Crews, "Through Fiery Trials: The Revolutionary War and the Moravians" (church pamphlet published by MA-SP, 1996), 32–33.

23. Bagge Manuscript, 1778, *MR* 3, 1205–6.

24. Salem Memorabilia, 1779, *MR* 3, 1285; Salem Diary, 1779, *MR* 3, 1289–90; Crews, "Through Fiery Trials," 35–36.

25. Friedberg Diary, 1776, *MR* 3, 1117.

26. LAC minutes, Sept. 21, 1781, MA-SP. Also see *MR* 4, 1730.

27. Friedberg Diary, 1781, *MR* 4, 1778.

28. Salem Diary, 1776, *MR* 3, 1069. The reputation of North Carolina's militia was not a good one. When Nathanael Greene took over command of southern forces in 1780, he concluded that the state's militia was more interested in plundering than fighting and that its behavior was nearly as bad as the Tories. See Robert Middlekauf, *The Glorious Cause: The American Revolution, 1763–1789* (New York, 1982), 467.

29. *MR* 3, 1069–70.

30. Ibid., 1070.

31. Hope Brotherly Agreement for 1780, MA-SP.

32. Salem Diary, 1776, *MR* 3, 1052–53.

33. Friedberg Diary, 1776, *MR* 3, 1110–11.

34. Salem Diary, 1777, *MR* 3, 1165.

35. Hope Diary, 1780, *MR* 4, 1655.

36. Salem Diary, 1780, *MR* 4, 1575–76; Hope Diary, 1780, *MR* 4, 1655.

37. Friedberg Diary, 1776, *MR* 3, 1118.

38. Minutes, Unity Elders Conference, 1782, vol. 1, 400ff.; cited in Sommer, *Serving Two Masters,* 137.

39. Bagge Manuscript, 1777, *MR* 3, 1129.

40. In addition to *MR,* especially volumes 3 and 4, MA-SP has extensive documentation of these demands for supplies. See, for instance, P602:8:71–79 and P602:11:89–92.

41. Symonds, *Battlefield Atlas,* 89; Middlekauf, *Glorious Cause,* 458–62.

42. Bethabara Diary, 1780, *MR* 4, 1630–31.

43. Salem Diary, 1780, *MR* 4, 1562–63.

44. Middlekauff, *Glorious Cause,* 469–478; and Symonds, *Battlefield Atlas,* 93.

45. Salem Diary, 1781, *MR* 4, 1676–77.

46. Ibid., *MR* 4, 1675; Bethania Diary, 1781, *MR* 4, 1765–66.

47. Salem Diary, 1781, *MR* 4, 1666; Bethania Diary, 1781, *MR* 4, 1783.

48. Salem Diary, 1781, *MR* 4, 1678–79.

49. See, for example, P602:8:78 and P602:8:79, MA-SP.

50. Friedberg Diary, 1776, *MR* 3, 1111.

51. Bethabara Diary, 1780, *MR* 4, 1623.

52. Salem Diary, 1777, *MR* 3, 1145; Salem Memorabilia, 1779, *MR* 3, 1286.

53. See, for example, Salem Memorabilia, 1776, *MR* 3, 1039.

54. Thorp, *Moravian Community,* 155.

55. Ibid., 160.

56. "Offering of Praise and Thanksgiving of the Congregations in Wachovia for the Protection of God during the North American disturbances, from the Year 1774 to the Year 1783," reprinted in *MR* 4, 1879; also see Salem Memorabilia, 1778, *MR* 3, 1215.

57. Bagge Manuscript, 1776, *MR* 3, 1025.

58. Salem Diary, 1777, *MR* 3, 1143.

59. Bethania Diary, 1776, *MR* 3, 1108.

60. Salem Diary, 1777, *MR* 3, 1144.

61. Bethania Diary, 1776, *MR* 3, 1108; Bethania Diary, 1778, *MR* 3, 1271.

62. Salem Diary, 1776, *MR* 3, 1078.

63. Ibid., 1780, *MR* 4, 1529.

64. Congregation Council minutes, March 6, 1783, *MR* 4, 1848.

65. LAC minutes, March 7, 1783, MA-SP.

66. Salem Diary, 1782, *MR* 4, 1790.

67. Sommer, *Serving Two Masters,* 110–13; also see Gollin, *Moravians in Two Worlds;* Richard L. Gawthrop, *Pietism and the Making of Eighteenth-Century Prussia* (New York, 1993); Roeber, *Palatines, Liberty, and Property.*

68. Sommer, *Serving Two Masters,* 124.

69. Wood, *Radicalism of the American Revolution,* 146.

70. The literature on the coming of the Revolution is, of course, voluminous. Good starting points, though, are Jack P. Greene, *Peripheries and Center: Constitutional Development in the Extended Politics of the British Empire and the United States, 1607–1788* (New York, 1986); Jack P. Greene, *The Quest for Power: The Lower Houses of Assembly in the Southern Royal Colonies, 1689–1776* (Chapel Hill, N.C., 1963); Pauline Maier, *From Resistance to Revolution: Colonial Radicals and the Development of American Opposition to Britain, 1765–1776* (New York, 1972); and Gordon S. Wood, *The Creation of the American Republic, 1776–1787* (New York, 1972).

71. See, for example, Surratt, "From Theocracy to Voluntary Church and Secularized Community," and Sommer, *Serving Two Masters.* It should be stressed, though, that Sommer sees far more than a generational aspect at work in the assimilation of North Carolina's Moravians.

72. LAC minutes, Nov. 14, 1780, MA-SP; also see *MR* 4, 1609, and LAC minutes, April 28, 1792, MA-SP.

73. For more on the Revolution's impact on patriarchy, see Wood, *Radicalism of the American Revolution,* 183–84.

74. *MR* 6, 2833.

75. LAC minutes, Oct. 16, 1780, MA-SP.

76. LAC minutes, Sept. 15, 1780, Cumnock translation, MA-SP.

77. *MR* 4, 1774, 1778; *MR* 5, 2064, 2113–14; *MR* 6, 2833.

78. Sommer, *Serving Two Masters,* 63–64. Also see Daniel B. Thorp, "Yankee Doodle Dutchmen: North Carolina's Moravian Community and the New Nation" (conference paper presented at the "German Moravians in the Atlantic World" symposium, Wake Forest University, April 2002).

79. Krause's early years were reconstructed from his *Lebenslauf,* available at MA-SP, and from the file of translated primary sources on Krause available at MESDA research library, Winston-Salem, North Carolina. Also see S. Scott Rohrer, "Gottlob Krause: Master Builder," *Three Forks of Muddy Creek* 14 (1990): 14–23.

80. Salem Diary, 1777, *MR* 3, 1139–40.

81. Aufseher Collegium minutes, March 9, 1773, April 3, 1781, June 2, 1773, and Sept. 12, 1783; translations available at MESDA research library. Also see John Bivins Jr., *The Moravian Potters in North Carolina* (Chapel Hill, N.C., 1972), 24–30.

82. "Old Salem Official Guidebook," (Winston-Salem, N.C., 1987), 93–94. For Krause's importance to North Carolina architecture, see Catherine W. Bishir, *North Carolina Architecture* (Chapel Hill, N.C., 1990).

83. *Lebenslauf* of Johann Gottlob Krause, MA-SP. Krause also built some important public buildings, including the 1784 Salem Tavern and the Boys School.

84. Elders Conference minutes, June 15 and July 6, 1785; Aufseher Collegium minutes, June 29, 1785; and Sommer, *Serving Two Masters,* 133–34.

85. Boles, *Great Revival,* 139. Also see Heyrman, *Southern Cross.*

86. Wood, *Creation of the American Republic;* also see Maier, *From Resistance to Revolution.*

87. For an interesting look at the link between evangelical fervor and political resistance, see Kars, *Breaking Loose Together.*

88. Wood, *Radicalism of the American Revolution,* 229; John Shy, *A People Numerous and Armed: Reflections on the Military Struggle for American Independence* (Oxford, 1976); and Charles Royster, *A Revolutionary People at War: The Continental Army and American Character, 1775–1783* (New York, 1979).

89. Wood, *Radicalism of the American Revolution,* 230, 296. Because of space limitations, I have simplified Professor Wood's sophisticated argument on the changes in virtue. For more on the meaning of virtue and democracy, see Terence Ball and J. G. A. Pocock, eds., *Conceptual Change and the Constitution* (Lawrence, Kan., 1991), especially the essay by Lance Banning, "Second Thoughts on Virtue and Revolutionary Thinking."

90. Hatch, *Democratization of American Christianity,* 6, 9. For other treatments of religion and the new nation, see James H. Hutson, *Religion and the Founding of the American Republic* (Washington, D.C., 1998) and James H. Huston, ed., *Religion and the New Republic: Faith in the Founding of America* (Lanham, Md., 2000).

91. Report of Bishop Spangenberg, Sept. 14, 1759; reprinted in Crews, ed., "Bethania."

92. For a look at the battles in Salem between the "old" and the "new," see Surratt, "From Theocracy to Voluntary Church," and Shirley, *From Congregation Town,* especially ch. 1.

93. Conclusion is based on my readings of congregational diaries and conference board minutes in both the *Landgemeinen* and *Ortsgemeinen.*

94. Friedberg Diary, 1780, *MR* 4, 1651.

95. Boles, *Great Revival,* 171–81.

5. Becoming "Southern": The Slaveholding Years

1. For more on Salem, see Daniel B. Thorp, "The City That Never Was: Count von Zinzendorf's Original Plan for Salem," *NCHR* 61 (January 1984): 36–58. Also see Surratt, "From Theocracy to Voluntary Church and Secularized Community," and Johanna Miller Lewis, "A Social and Architectural History of the Girls' Boarding School Building at Salem, North Carolina," *NCHR* 66 (April 1989): 125–48.

2. "Survey and division of a Plantation lying on the Southside of the Middle Fork of Muddy Creek, resurveyed December 11, 1838," D151:2:E, MA-SP.

3. The story of the farm's early years was reconstructed from an examination of the file labeled the "Farm South of Salem" at MESDA's research library. The file contains key references from minutes of the Aufseher Collegium and other church boards.

4. Elder's Conference minutes, Dec. 12, 1815, and May 22, 1816; translations available at MESDA's research library.

5. For more on this debate, see Shirley, *From Congregation Town,* 49–53. Also see C. Daniel Crews, "Neither Slave nor Free: Moravians, Slavery, and a Church That Endures" (church pamphlet printed by MA-SP, 1998), 5–7, and Sensbach, *Separate Canaan,* 209–10.

6. Biographical information, including birthdate, is from the file on Friedrich Schumann at MESDA's research library. Benzien quote of Feb. 12, 1810, is from letter 213, BA3, Benzien to Loskiel, and is included in the Schumann file.

7. Bethania Diary, July 4, 1812, MESDA research library.

8. Relevant references on Schumann's request to move to Salem and the initial negotiations over his slaves include Nov. 20, 1813; June 21, 1814; and July 19, 1814, Aufseher Collegium minutes.

9. I am relying on Sensbach, *Separate Canaan,* and Shirley, *From Congregation Town,* for this discussion of slavery in Salem.

10. Aufseher Collegium minutes, July 19, 1814.

11. Shirley, *From Congregation Town,* 49, and Crews, "Neither Slave nor Free," 6.

12. Aufseher Collegium minutes, Aug. 16, 1814.

13. Ibid., Aug. 30, 1814.

14. Ibid., Oct. 20 and Nov. 14, 1817, March 11, 1819, March 7, 1825, May 5, 1829.

15. The holdings of Schumann's slave force were reconstructed from the List of Taxables, Salem District, Stokes County for the years 1816 through 1836 and from the 1820 and 1830 censuses. Both are available on microfilm at the Forsyth County Library, Winston-Salem, North Carolina. Ten of his slaves were worth $2,705.77 in 1817. See Inventory of Salem Plantation, May 31, 1817, *MR* 7, 3557.

16. Dell Upton, "White and Black Landscapes in Eighteenth-Century Virginia," in *Material Life in America, 1600–1860,* ed. Robert Blair St. George, 360–62 (Boston, 1988). For more on the gentry and architecture, see Isaac, *Transformation of Virginia,*

34–42; and Dell Upton, "Anglican Parish Churches in Eighteenth-Century Virginia," in *Perspectives in Vernacular Architecture II,* ed. Camille Wells, 90–101 (Columbia, Mo., 1986).

17. "Inventory of the Plantation as George Holder left it and as Peter Rose will now take it over, November 25, 1774," Reel A-31, Accounts and Inventories, MA-SP. Copy available at MESDA in "Farm South of Salem" file. For a brief look at the farm's early years, see S. Scott Rohrer, "Dr. Schumann and His Slaves: Portrait of a Plantation" (research report prepared for Old Salem Inc., 1990) and the file on the "Farm South of Salem" at MESDA.

18. Elders Conference minutes, May 22, 1816.

19. The farmhouse is visible in an 1830s painting by Daniel Welfare and a late nineteenth-century photograph; copies of both are available at the MESDA research library. Welfare moved into the house in 1839 after Schumann had moved out. Schumann, tired of fighting with Salem's boards over the plantation's management, had decided to sell his slaves and move into town with his new bride (his first wife had died years earlier). He freed his slaves and sent them to Liberia. For more on this period, see Rohrer, "Dr. Schumann and His Slaves." In 1999, Maggie Tyler, a graduate student in anthropology at the University of South Carolina, conducted digs at the site of Schumann's house. She suspects, based on the young ages of the slave force and the small size of Schumann's family, that Schumann housed his slaves in the barn and upper floors of his house, so it needs to be stressed that my portrayal of the plantation's layout is conjecture. The outbuildings visible in the 1838 plat, titled "Survey and division of a Plantation lying on the Southside of the Middle Fork of Muddy Creek," are unmarked, and Welfare's painting does not show any outbuildings near the house. I strongly suspect, however, that Schumann's large holdings, despite the demographics, necessitated the use of slave cabins and that these cabins were likely the buildings visible in the 1838 plat. Ms. Tyler does agree that Schumann purposely placed his house on a high hill so that it would look down on Salem. I am grateful to her for sharing her findings on the Schumann dig.

20. Sensbach, *Separate Canaan,* 66–68.

21. All figures on landholdings, including Bagge's, are derived from an examination of deeds for Surry County and Stokes County from 1780 to 1830 that are on microfilm at the Forsyth County Library.

22. *MR* 3, 1195.

23. *MR* 4, 1808.

24. For more on the mills and economy of Wachovia, see Johanna Carlson Miller, "Mills on the Wachovia Tract, 1753–1849" (master's thesis, Wake Forest University, 1985).

25. *Lebenslauf* of Christian Conrad, MA-SP.

26. *Lebenslauf* of Jacob Conrad, MA-SP; Surry County and Stokes County deeds, Forsyth County Library.

27. *MR* 5, 2135–36.

28. "Inventory of sundry Articles delivered by Christian Lash to Chr. L. Benzien," April 30, 1804, H270:4, MA-SP.

29. Percentages are derived from charts on land values in chapter 3.

30. Ibid.

31. Soelle Diary, Sept. 4, 1771, and March 4, 1772, Hamilton translation, MA-SP.

32. Bethabara Diacony Accounts, from 1772–1801, G259:9, C140:16, MA-SP.

33. Ibid.

34. Thorp, *Moravian Community,* 129.

35. *MR* 5, 2096–2097.

36. Merrens, *Colonial North Carolina,* 145, and Johanna Miller Lewis, *Artisans in the North Carolina Backcountry* (Lexington, Ky., 1995).

37. Alan D. Watson, "North Carolina and Internal Improvements, 1783–1861: The Case of Inland Navigation," *NCHR* 74 (January 1997): 37; and Merrens, *Colonial North Carolina,* 151–53.

38. Inventories for the Salem gristmill, R705:1, R705:2, MA-SP. The figures are compiled from the following years: 1774, 1786–87, 1789–90, 1796–97, 1799–1800, and 1804-5. Figures are available through 1807.

39. Carville Earle and Ronald Hoffman, "Staple Crops and Urban Development in the Eighteenth-Century South," *Perspectives in American History* 10 (1976): 7–78.

40. *Compendium of the Sixth Census, 1840; Compendium of the Seventh Census, 1850, Report of the United States in 1860;* Shirley, *From Congregation Town,* 32.

41. Shirley, *From Congregation Town,* 28–30.

42. Figure is from Robert D. Mitchell, *Commercialism and Frontier: Perspectives on the Early Shenandoah Valley* (Charlottesville, Va., 1977), 141.

43. Records of the Salem gristmill, MA-SP.

44. *MR* 5, 2313.

45. 1768 List of Jacob Laesch, reprinted in Jo White Linn, *Rowan County, N.C. Tax Lists, 1757–1800: Annotated Transcriptions* (Salisbury, N.C., 1995).

46. Stokes County tax lists, available on microfilm, Forsyth County Library.

47. 1790 and 1820 U.S. Censuses for Stokes County. North Carolina's population in 1820 stood at 638,829.

48. Percentages are derived from above chart.

49. Many studies have looked at the transformation from subsistence farming to slave-manned plantations. For three examples in different parts of the South, see Christopher Morris, *Becoming Southern: The Evolution of a Way of Life, Warren County and Vicksburg, Mississippi, 1770–1860* (New York, 1995); Allan Kulikoff, *Tobacco and Slaves: The Development of Southern Cultures in the Chesapeake, 1680–1800* (Chapel Hill, N.C., 1986); and Lois Green Carr, Russell R. Menard, and Lorena S. Walsh, *Robert Cole's World: Agriculture and Society in Early Maryland* (Chapel Hill, N.C., 1991).

50. Sensbach, *Separate Canaan,* 60–64. For other works on Moravian slavery, see Jon F. Sensbach, "Culture and Conflict in the Early Black Church: A Moravian Mission Congregation in Antebellum North Carolina," *NCHR* (October 1994): 401–29; Philip Africa, "Slaveholding in the Salem Community, 1771–1851," *NCHR* (July 1977): 271–307; and Daniel B. Thorp, "Buying Men and Saving Souls: The Moravians' Response to Slavery in Eighteenth-Century North Carolina" (unpublished paper, n.d.).

51. Jon Frederiksen Sensbach, "A Separate Canaan: The Making of an Afro-Moravian World in North Carolina, 1763–1856" (Ph.D. diss., Duke University, 1991), 144.

52. 1790 Census for North Carolina.

53. Figures are from Sensbach, "Separate Canaan," 351.

54. It should be noted that Wachovia's median slaveholding was typical for the South in the antebellum period. In 1850, half of the South's slaveholders owned five bondsmen or fewer. See James Oakes, *The Ruling Race: A History of American Slaveholders* (New York, 1982), 39.

55. 1830 Census for North Carolina.

56. 1790 Census for North Carolina.

57. See, for example, *MR* 3, 1332 and 1333, and *MR* 5, 2159 and 2573.

58. *MR* 5, 2047.

59. Ibid., 2201.

60. Bachhof Diary, Oct. 14, 1772, Lineback translation, MA-SP.

61. *MR* 3, 1262.

62. *MR* 5, 2275.

63. Lemon, *Best Poor Man's Country*, 125–34.

64. For an overview of Philadelphia's role as the center of German-American life, see Roeber, "'The Origin of Whatever Is Not English Among Us,'" especially 252–53, as well as Roeber, *Palatines, Liberty, and Property.*

65. *MR* 6, 2792–93.

66. Bachhof Diary, May 24, 1774, Lineback translation, MA-SP; also see *MR* 2, 837.

67. Jordan Trade Letters, C9:1; Godfrey Haga Letters, C22:1–5, MA-SP. For more on this so-called consumer revolution, see T. H. Breen, "'Baubles of Britain': The American and Consumer Revolutions of the Eighteenth Century," *Past and Present* 119 (1988): 73–104, and Neil McKendrick et al., *The Birth of a Consumer Society: The Commercialization of Eighteenth-Century England* (Bloomington, Ind., 1982).

68. Petersburg Trade Letters, C21:1, MA-SP.

69. Earle and Hoffman, "Staple Crops and Urban Development," 28.

70. Trade Letter of Sept. 1, 1828, from Henderson and Simmons, C21:5, and C21:1–4, MA-SP.

71. Charleston Trade Papers, C20:1, MA-SP.

72. Inventories of Peter Yarrell, C140:16, MA-SP.

73. Charleston Trade Papers, C20:1–6, MA-SP.

74. Earle and Hoffman, "Staple Crops and Urban Development," 17.

75. *MR* 1, 338–39.

76. Wilmington Trade Letters, C20:5, and Cross Creek Trade Letters, C23:1–5, MA-SP. Also see Merrens, *Colonial North Carolina,* 163–64, and Lewis, *Artisans,* especially 69, for Cross Creek's ties with Rowan County.

77. Population figures are from Merrens, *Colonial North Carolina,* 53.

78. Cross Creek Trade Letters, C23:1–5, MA-SP; quote is from Robert Cochran to Samuel Stotz, March 23, 1782, C23:1, MA-SP.

79. Cross Creek Trade Letters, C23:1, MA-SP.

80. Ibid.; and April 30, 1806, inventory of the Bethania store, H270:4, MA-SP.

81. Store inventories for Bethania, H270:4; for Friedberg, R705A:1; for Salem, S740:2; and for Bethabara, Ledgers 1–3, MA-SP.

82. Max Weber, *The Protestant Ethic and the Spirit of Capitalism*, trans. Talcott Parsons (Los Angeles, 1996). This definition of the Protestant dilemma is from Stephen Innes, *Creating the Commonwealth: The Economic Culture of Puritan New England* (New York, 1995), 25. For another view of the Puritan dilemma, see Morgan, *Puritan Dilemma.*

83. Some basic works on Anabaptism include Cornelius J. Dyck, ed., *An Introduction to Mennonite History* (Scottdale, Pa., 1981); Loewen, *Family, Church and Markets*; Richard K. MacMaster, *Land, Piety, Peoplehood: The Establishment of Mennonite Communities in America, 1683–1790* (Scottdale, Pa., 1985); Steven D. Reschly, *The Amish on the Iowa Prairie, 1840 to 1910* (Baltimore, 2000); and Victor Peters, *All Things Common: The Hutterian Way of Life* (Minneapolis, 1965).

84. Peter C. Erb, ed., *Pietists: Selected Writings* (New York, 1983), 305–6.

85. Quote is from Lewis, *Zinzendorf, the Ecumenical Pioneer,* 75.

86. Gollin, *Moravians in Two Worlds,* 145.

87. *MR* 5, 2140.

88. The great concern with behavior and proper work habits should be seen within the context of European social history and Christianity's efforts to reform behavior. This so-called civilizing effort was aimed at reforming popular culture. For more on this civilizing offensive, see Pieter Spierenburg, *The Broken Spell: A Cultural and Anthropological History of Preindustrial Europe* (New Brunswick, 1991); Thomas Robisheaux, *Rural Society and the Search for Order in Early Modern Europe* (Cambridge, U.K., 1989); Lyndal Roeper, *Oedipus and the Devil: Witchcraft, Sexuality, and Religion in Early Modern Europe* (London, 1994); and Peter Burke, *Popular Culture in Early Modern Europe* (New York, 1978).

89. *MR* 5, 2144.

90. *MR* 4, 1803. For more on Moravian fashion, see Elisabeth W. Sommer, "Fashion Passion: The Battle over Dress within the Moravian Brethren" (conference paper presented at the "German Moravians in the Atlantic World" symposium, Wake Forest University, April 2002).

91. *MR* 5, 2176–78.

92. *MR* 4, 1498–1501.

93. *MR* 5, 2184.

94. *MR* 6, 2504.

95. "Agreement between Christian Lewis Benzien and Herman Buttner concerning the Distillery at Bethabara," May 1, 1802, MA-SP. Also see "Agreement between Conrad Kreuser and Gottlb. Strehle concerning the Store at Bethabara," April 22, 1801, MA-SP.

96. Oakes, *Ruling Race,* 123. Oakes, in a later work, repudiated his view that master and slave formed a market relationship, but his earlier point about the materialism involved with the purchase of a slave remains valid. See James Oakes, *Slavery and Freedom: An Interpretation of the Old South* (New York, 1990), especially 54.

97. Peter Kolchin, *American Slavery, 1619–1877* (New York, 1993), 93. The literature on slavery in the South is vast and defies easy categorization. Starting points for students and general readers should be Eugene D. Genovese, *Roll, Jordan, Roll: The World the Slaves Made Together* (New York, 1974), and Oakes, *Ruling Race;* for those interested in slave religion, see Albert J. Raboteau, *Slave Religion: The "Invisible Institution" in the Antebellum South* (New York, 1978); and John B. Boles, ed., *Masters and Slaves in the House of the Lord: Race and Religion in the American South, 1740–1870* (Lexington, Ky., 1988).

98. Sensbach, *Separate Canaan*, 149.

99. Kolchin, *American Slavery*, 192.

100. Sensbach, *Separate Canaan*, 51.

101. Daniel Vickers, "Competency and Competition: Economic Culture in Early America," *WMQ* 47 (January 1990): 3–29. Also see Daniel Vickers, *Farmers and Fishermen: Two Centuries of Work in Essex County, Massachusetts, 1630–1850* (Chapel Hill, N.C., 1994).

102. See Joan M. Jensen, *Loosening the Bonds: Mid-Atlantic Farm Women, 1750–1850* (New Haven, Conn., 1986), who offers one of the more interesting variations in the capitalism in early America debate—that families engaged the market for preindustrial purposes. A variant of this theme is the thesis of Richard Lyman Bushman that farmers practiced "composite farming"—they "simultaneously produced for the farm family and for the market." Bushman, "Markets and Composite Farms in Early America," *WMQ* 55 (July 1998): 351–74; quote is from 364.

103. Roeber, *Palatines, Liberty, and Property*, 221–26.

104. Oakes, *Ruling Race*, 103.

105. Earle and Hoffman, "Staple Crops and Urban Development," 71–73.

106. These prices are based on my examination of Stokes County bills of sale in deed books, Forsyth County Library.

107. Bill of sale, Aug. 1, 1830, Stokes Deed Book 9:307.

108. Sensbach, *Separate Canaan*, 274.

109. Morris, *Becoming Southern*, 28.

110. John Patrick Daley, *When Slavery Was Called Freedom: Evangelicalism, Proslavery, and the Causes of the Civil War* (Lexington, Ky., 2002); Heyrman, *Southern Cross;* Oakes, *Ruling Race*, ch. 4.

111. Sensbach, *Separate Canaan*, 80.

112. Ibid., 82, 105.

113. Ibid., 126 and 120–21. Spangenberg quote is on 121.

114. Ibid., 121.

115. Elders Conference minutes, May 3, 1797; LAC minutes, June 1, 1797, MA-SP. Also see Sensbach, *Separate Canaan*, 183–84.

116. Hope Committee minutes, Oct. 11, 1801, MA-SP.

117. LAC minutes, June 25, 1802, MA-SP.

118. Sensbach, *Separate Canaan*, 192.

119. Oakes, *Ruling Race*, 96–97.

120. For more on the black congregation in the late antebellum period and the post–Civil War years, see S. Scott Rohrer, "The 1823 African-American Log Church: An Assessment" (research report prepared for Old Salem Inc., Summer 1995); S. Scott Rohrer, "Freedman of the Lord: The Black Moravian Congregation of Salem, N.C., and Its Struggle for Survival, 1856–1890" (research report prepared for Old Salem Inc., Summer 1993); and S. Scott Rohrer, "A Mission among the People: The World of St. Philip's Church from 1890 to 1952" (research report prepared for Old Salem Inc., Summer 1993).

121. Sensbach, *Separate Canaan,* 191–92; also see Gary B. Nash and Jean R. Soderlund, *Freedom by Degrees: Emancipation in Pennsylvania and Its Aftermath* (New York, 1991).

6. The New World of the 1830s and Beyond

1. Bahnson Diary, June 29, 1834, Henderson translation, MESDA research library.

2. *Lebenslauf* of George Frederic Bahnson, MA-SP.

3. Bahnson Diary, July 16, 1834, Henderson translation.

4. Ibid., June 29, 1834.

5. The 1785 membership total is from Wachovia Memorabilia for that year; the 1834 figure is from Bahnson Diary, Henderson translation.

6. Bahnson Diary, July 12, 1834, Henderson translation.

7. Ibid., July 11, 1834.

8. In 1838, Bahnson went to Bethlehem as an assistant minister and a professor at the theological seminary. In 1849, he returned to Wachovia. See his memoir in MA-SP and Bahnson Diary, Henderson translation.

9. Membership figures are from *MR* 5, 2355; *MR* 7, 3497; *MR* 8, 4220; and *MR* 12, 6669.

10. Bahnson Diary, Aug. 3, 1834, Henderson translation.

11. Ibid., June 27, 1837.

12. Ibid., Nov. 26, 1834, and May 9, 1837.

13. Ibid., July 14, 1834.

14. Ibid., July 13 and July 2, 1834.

15. *Lebenslauf* of Johanna Gertrude Kearney, MA-SP.

16. Because of the fluidity of the society movement and the stresses of the evangelical experience, it is extremely difficult to measure with mathematical precision the retention rates of Moravianism. Members came and went, and so did their offspring. Obviously, the strong membership growth of the Methodists and Baptists, when combined with the lagging rates of the Moravians, provides the strongest evidence that not all members of the later generation were joining the Unity.

17. Nancy F. Cott, *The Bonds of Womanhood: "Women's Sphere" in New England, 1780–1835* (New Haven, 1977), 3.

18. Source is above charts.

19. For background on the 1818 Synod, see Hamilton and Hamilton, *History of the Moravian Church,* 233–34.

20. Historian Beverly Prior Smaby found a similar process at work in Bethlehem; after 1818, the brethren married younger and had larger families because of the looser church controls. See Smaby, *Transformation of Moravian Bethlehem,* 51–65.

21. These general statements on farm sizes and land prices are based on a detailed analysis of deed books from 1750 to 1830.

22. Kulikoff, *Tobacco and Slaves,* 57.

23. Levy, "'Tender Plants,'" 177–203, and Levy, "Birth of the 'Modern Family,'" 26–64.

24. Bahnson Diary, Nov. 15, 1837, Henderson translation.

25. Laurel Thatcher Ulrich, *Good Wives: Image and Reality in the Lives of Women in Northern New England, 1650–1750* (New York, 1982), and Mary Beth Norton challenged the earlier view that the colonial period was a golden one for women and their work. See Norton, *Liberty's Daughters: The Revolutionary Experience of American Women, 1750–1800* (Ithaca, N.Y., 1996). Johanna Miller Lewis, in her examination of women in the North Carolina backcountry, agrees with this view. See Lewis, *Artisans,* ch. 6. For examples of studies challenging this view, see Jeanne Boydston, *Home and Work: Housework, Wages, and the Ideology of Labor in the Early Republic* (New York, 1980), and Mary P. Ryan, *Cradle of the Middle Class: The Family in Oneida County, New York, 1790–1865* (Cambridge, U.K., 1981).

26. Figures are derived from an examination of 215 wills in the six settlements, including 125 wills in the first period.

27. Suzanne Lebsock, *The Free Women of Petersburg: Status and Culture in a Southern Town, 1784–1860* (New York, 1984).

28. See, for example, Linda K. Kerber, *Women of the Republic: Intellect and Ideology in Revolutionary America* (Chapel Hill, N.C., 1980); Jan Lewis, *The Pursuit of Happiness: Family and Values in Jefferson's America* (New York, 1983); Cott, *Bonds of Womanhood;* and Merrill D. Smith, *Breaking the Bonds: Marital Discord in Pennsylvania, 1730–1830* (New York, 1991). For a more recent look at this debate, see Larry D. Eldridge, ed., *Women and Freedom in Early America* (New York, 1997).

29. Mary Ryan finds a similar process at work among early nineteenth-century evangelicals, that is, the conversion experience tended to undermine patriarchy with tangible benefits for women. See Ryan, *Cradle of the Middle Class.* Also see Hatch, *Democratization of American Christianity,* for a similar theme.

30. Nolt, *Foreigners in Their Own Land,* 49.

31. The activities of these societies can be found in S731:4–8 and S736:1, MA-SP. Bahnson quote is from Bahnson Diary, Oct. 7, 1835, Henderson translation.

32. Sensbach, *Separate Canaan,* 114–15.

33. Hamilton and Hamilton, *History of the Moravian Church,* 183.

34. This move toward the religious "middle" also occurred elsewhere in the Unity, including in Bethlehem. See, for example, Smaby, *Transformation of Moravian Bethlehem.*

35. Nolt, *Foreigners in Their Own Land,* 102.

36. *MR* 7, 3307. The secondary literature on the Sunday school movement is relatively slim. Jerry L. Surratt, *Gottlieb Schober of Salem: Discipleship and Ecumenical Vision*

in an Early Moravian Town (Macon, Ga., 1983) discusses Sunday schools in Wachovia and Stokes County. Also see Anne M. Boylan, *Sunday Schools: The Formation of an American Institution, 1790–1880* (New Haven, 1988); Edwin Wilbur Rice, *The Sunday School Movement 1780–1917 and the American Sunday-School Union 1817–1917* (New York, 1971); and Gerald E. Knoff, *The World Sunday School Movement: The Story of a Broadening Mission* (New York, 1979). For an older work, see Warren A. Candler, *The History of Sunday-Schools: A Brief Historical Treatise, with Special Reference to the Sunday-Schools of America* (Macon, Ga., 1881).

37. *MR* 7, 3327.

38. Ibid., 3394, 3404, and 3416.

39. See, for example, *MR* 7, 3394 and 3470.

40. Quoted in Rice, *Sunday School Movement,* 80; also see Surratt, *Gottlieb Schober of Salem,* 212.

41. *MR* 8, 3769, 3831, and 3848.

42. Ibid., 3934.

43. Ibid., 3869–70. Later meetings drew even larger crowds. See, for example, *MR* 8, 3915.

44. Boles, *Great Revival,* 76.

45. The literature on the camp-meeting movement is vast. Besides Boles's *Great Revival,* some of the best works include Hatch, *Democratization of American Christianity;* Heyrman, *Southern Cross;* Loveland, *Southern Evangelicals and the Social Order;* William G. McLoughlin, *Revivals, Awakenings, and Reform: An Essay on Religion and Social Change in America, 1607–1977* (Chicago, 1978); and Conkin, *Cane Ridge.* For a comparison with the North, see Paul E. Johnson, *A Shopkeeper's Millennium: Society and Revivals in Rochester, New York, 1815–1837* (New York, 1978). For the impact of revivalism on Pennsylvania Germans in the late eighteenth and early nineteenth centuries, see Longenecker, *Piety and Tolerance.*

46. Wachovia Memorabilia for 1801, *MR* 6, 2663 and 2676.

47. Aufseher Collegium minutes of Sept. 21 and Sept. 28, 1802, MA-SP; translations available at MESDA research library.

48. *MR* 6, 2830. Also see Lorenzo Dow's journals titled "History of Cosmopolite; or the Four Volumes of Lorenzo's Journal, concentrated in one . . . " that was printed in Philadelphia in 1815. Available on Early American Imprints, 2nd Series, S34591. On page 219 of the journal, Dow briefly described his visit to Salem and "Bethany" on February 9, 1805.

49. Weinlick, "Moravian Diaspora," 31.

50. *MR* 6, 2702–3.

51. For more on Wachovia's embracing of revivals, see Surratt, "From Theocracy to Voluntary Church and Secularized Community," 154–55. African American slaves were one of the first Moravian groups to push for more-emotional services. See Sensbach, *Separate Canaan;* Rohrer, "Freedman of the Lord"; and Rohrer, "A Mission among the People."

52. For good insights into the pietist conversion experience, see Martin H. Schrag,

"The Impact of Pietism upon the Mennonites in Early American Christianity," in F. Ernest Stoeffler, ed., *Continental Pietism and Early American Christianity* (Grand Rapids, Mich., 1976), esp. 98.

53. Lyerly, *Methodism and the Southern Mind,* 187.

54. Tise, *Yadkin Melting Pot,* 34.

55. *MR* 8, 3925.

56. Bahnson Diary, Aug. 10 and Oct. 5, 1834, Henderson translation.

57. Ibid., Sept. 19, 1837.

58. Dow Journal, 219, Early American Imprints, 2nd Series, S34591.

59. *MR* 7, 3260.

60. Ibid., 3136.

61. Ibid., 3368.

62. Conclusion is based on an examination of correspondence, diaries, and committee minutes for the *Landgemeinen,* as well as a survey of LAC records and relevant documents for the *Ortsgemeinen* in MA-SP.

63. *MR* 7, 3295.

64. Snyder, "Pietism, Moravianism, and Methodism as Renewal Movements," 5 and 142–48.

65. This is not to say that there was no rivalry between Methodism and Moravianism in North Carolina but that the similarities tended to mute it. For more on this rivalry, see Tise, *Yadkin Melting Pot.*

66. Bahnson Diary, Aug. 17, 1834, Henderson translation.

67. Ibid., Nov. 2, 1834. It should be noted that Bahnson recognized that there were many other causes of Bethania's languishing membership. One notable cause in his view was the burden of membership dues; members' inability to pay them caused many to leave the congregation.

68. Bahnson Diary, May 6, 1837, Henderson translation.

69. Ibid., June 11, 1835.

70. Ibid., Oct. 10 and Nov. 5, 1837.

71. Diary for Friedberg, Hope, Muddy Creek, and Macedonia, Aug. 15, 1858, H277:11, MA-SP.

72. Heyrman, *Southern Cross,* 211–14. Also see David L. Kimbrough, *Reverend Joseph Tarkington, Methodist Circuit Rider: From Frontier Evangelism to Refined Religion* (Knoxville, Tenn., 1997).

73. Heyrman, *Southern Cross.*

74. Sensbach, *Separate Canaan,* 114–15.

75. Bethania's Brotherly Agreement of April 2, 1780, is reprinted in *MR* 4, 1498. Quote is on 1501.

76. *Lebenslaufs* of Johanna Gertrude Kearney and Jacob Frey, MA-SP.

77. For an example of an exception, see Bahnson Diary, July 1, 1837, Henderson translation. Pastors for each congregation kept diaries of their activities; they also filed reports to LAC. All are available at MA-SP.

78. Roeber, *Palatines, Liberty, and Property,* 150, 226.

79. Quote is from the will of Hans Nagel of New Windsor; I am grateful to Bruce R. Penner for sharing his research on pietist testate practices with me in a personal communication of Feb. 27, 1997. I am also grateful to him for sharing a copy of his unpublished paper, "Landholding and Testate Patterns."

80. Quotes are from Roeber, *Palatines, Liberty, and Property,* 53.

81. Will of Peter Binkley, March 3, 1791, C141A, MA-SP.

82. Will of Samuel Miller, Sept. 17, 1772, Rowan County Will Book 1:91.

83. Will of George Hartman, Sept. 4, 1788, Rowan Will Book 3:107.

84. Will of Michael Spainhouer, March 4, 1827, Stokes Will Book 3:157.

85. Will of Joseph Pfaff, Feb. 16, 1815, Stokes Will Book 2:162.

86. Will of Catherina Frey, Dec. 26, 1821, C141A, MA-SP.

87. "A Brotherly Agreement adopted by the Congregations of Bethabara, Bethania, Friedland, Friedberg, and Hope in North Carolina as revised after the Synod of the United Brethren's Church in the Year of our Lord, 1836," R698:7, MA-SP.

88. Bahnson Diary, July 5 and Aug. 19, 1837, Henderson translation.

89. Friedberg Committee minutes, Feb. 18, 1857, MA-SP.

90. *Lebenslauf* of Johanna Gertrude Kearney, MA-SP.

91. Salem Diary, Nov. 11, 1835; reprinted in *MR* 8, 4175–77. Also see C. Daniel Crews, "Mountain Gospel: Moravian Church Evangelism in Virginia, 1835–36" (undated church pamphlet prepared by MA-SP).

92. "A History of New Philadelphia Church, 1846–1993," box 19, MA-SP.

93. Diary and *Berichte* for 1854–1859, H277:10–11; and "A History of Macedonia Moravian Church," box 3, MA-SP.

94. Sarah Bahnson Chapman, ed., *Bright and Gloomy Days: The Civil War Correspondence of Captain Charles Frederic Bahnson, a Moravian Confederate* (Knoxville, Tenn., 2003).

Glossary of Religious and German Terms

Abendmahl	holy communion; literally means evening meal
Aeltesten Conferenz	Board of Elders
Aufseher Collegium	Board of Supervisors
Auswartige	congregation members living outside of an *Ortsgemeine*
Brudergemeine	informal name for the Moravian Church; literally means a congregation of brethren; contemporaries used it to symbolize that they belonged to a community of believers
Diaspora	Moravian missionary effort to convert the unsaved to heart religion
Eigenland	land free of manorial control
Evangelism	broad reform movement in western Europe and America that included revivalists, Pietists, and others; it is based on a belief in salvation by faith in Jesus Christ
Gemeine	a congregation; on a deeper level, consisted of the reborn who belonged to a community of believers
Gemeine Rath	Congregation Council
Gemeinschaft	community
Gesellschaft	society and association
Kuppeleien	matchmakings

Land Arbeiter Conferenz	Conference of Country Congregation Ministers that oversaw the *Landgemeinen*
Landgemeine	farm congregation
Lebenslauf	life story, or memoir
Losungen	biblical daily texts used in worship services
Meirrecht	hereditary tenure
Nachrichten	church reports
Ortsgemeine	congregation town
Pietism	German-based reform movement that sought to spark a new Protestant reformation by leading people to a new birth
Pilgergemeine	missionary town
Saal	main hall, or sanctuary, in a meetinghouse where worship services were conducted
Sprechens	speakings held to determine whether a congregation member could take communion
Stunde	hour
Synodal *Verlaß*	synodal report
Unitas Fratrum	Unity of Brethren; another name for Moravian Church
Unterhalt	maintenance

Selected Bibliography

Primary Sources

Berks County Courthouse, Reading, Pennsylvania
    Deed Books for Berks County
Duke University Manuscript Collection, Durham, North Carolina
    Conrad Family Papers
Forsyth County Library, Winston-Salem, North Carolina
    Census Records
    Deed Books for Rowan, Stokes, and Forsyth Counties
    List of Taxables for Stokes and Forsyth Counties
    Marriage Records
    Will Books for Rowan, Stokes, and Forsyth Counties
Moravian Archives, Northern Province, Bethlehem, Pennsylvania
    Heidelberg:
        HeA, Catalogs, Varia, and Letters, 1743–1792
        HeB, Heidelberg and Tulpehoken, 1740–1760
        Heidelberg Varia: 1742–1792
            York, Pennsylvania: seven boxes containing diaries, varia, correspondence, conference minutes
    Kirchen-Buch for Pennsylvania, Maryland, and Maine congregations
    Maryland congregations:
        MyA: Monocacy, Carroll's Manor, Graceham. Includes correspondence, diaries, historical accounts
        MyB: includes catalogues, more diaries, and correspondence
    New England congregations:
        NeA IV, Brother Soelle's letters from New England
        NeA V, Broadbay Varia
    "Wachovia: Salem, Bethabara . . . " Letter Boxes:
        Wachovia I, Diaries, Memorabilia, Memoirs
        Wachovia III, Correspondence, 1761–1768
        Wachovia IV, Journey Journals, 1752–1852

Moravian Archives, Southern Province, Winston-Salem, North Carolina
    Board Minutes:
        Aeltesten Conferenz (Elders Conference)
        Aufseher Collegium (Board of Overseers)
        Land Arbeiter Conferenz (Conference of Country Congregation Ministers)
    General Church Records:
        Congregational Agreements with Pastors
        Diacony Journals
        Farm Rental Agreements
        Financial Records for Mills, Stores, Taverns
        Lease Agreements for Wachovia's Land
        Lebenslaufs (Memoirs) for Congregation Members
        Marriage Register for Wachovia
        Oeconomie Accounts
        Salem Diary
        Synodal Records for 1775 and 1818
        Trade Papers for Baltimore, Charleston, Cross Creek, Petersburg, Philadelphia, and Wilmington
        Wachau Kirchen Buch
    Settlement Records for Bethabara, Bethania, Friedberg, Friedland, Hope:
        Brotherly Agreements
        Committee Minutes
        Correspondence
        Diacony Journal
        Diacony Ledger
        Diarium (Diary)
        Friedberg School Papers
        Hausvater Conferenz (Housefathers Conference)
        Kirchen-buch (Church-Book)
Museum of Early Southern Decorative Arts (MESDA), Winston-Salem, North Carolina
    Files on Wachovia Residents
    Map Files
North Carolina Department of Archives and History, Raleigh, North Carolina
    Minute Dockets, Stokes County Superior Court
    Minutes, Stokes County Court of Pleas and Quarter Sessions
    Stokes County List of Taxables
York County Courthouse, York, Pennsylvania
    Deed Books for York County

Published Primary Sources

Absher, Mrs. W. O. *Stokes County Will Abstracts, Vols. 1–4, 1790–1864.* Easley, S.C.: Southern Historical Press, 1985.

Atwood, Craig D., ed. *A Collection of Sermons from Zinzendorf's Pennsylvania Journey.* Translated by Julie Tomberlin Weber. Bethlehem, Pa.: Interprovincial Board of Communication, Moravian Church in North America, 2001.

Clark, Walter, ed. *The State Records of North Carolina.* 16 vols. Raleigh: P. M. Hale, 1895–1907.

Cranz, David. *The Ancient and Modern History of the Brethren.* Translated by Benjamin LaTrobe. London: W. and A. Strahan, 1780.

Erb, Peter C., ed. *Pietists: Selected Writings.* New York: Paulist Press, 1983.

Fries, Adelaide et al., eds. *Records of the Moravians in North Carolina.* 11 vols. Raleigh: North Carolina Historical Commission, 1922–1969.

Hamilton, Kenneth G., ed. *Bethlehem Diary, 1742–44.* Bethlehem, Pa.: Archives of the Moravian Church, 1971.

Muhlenberg, Henry Melchior. *The Journals of Henry Melchior Muhlenberg.* 3 vols. Translated by Theodore G. Tappert and John W. Doberstein. Philadelphia: Muhlenberg Press, 1942–58.

Saunders, William, ed. *The Colonial Records of North Carolina.* 10 vols. Raleigh: P. M. Hale, 1886–90.

Spangenberg, August Gottlieb. *Idea Fidei Fratrum, an Exposition of Christian Doctrine as Taught in the Protestant Church of the United Brethren.* Translated and edited by Benjamin LaTrobe. Winston-Salem, N.C.: Moravian Church, 1959. First published 1778; first English edition 1779.

Spener, Philip Jacob. *Pia Desideria.* Translated and edited by Theodore G. Tappert. Philadelphia: Fortress Press, 1964.

Urlsperger, Samuel. *Detailed Reports on the Salzburger Emigrants Who Settled in America.* 16 vols. Translated by Hermann J. Lacher. Edited by George Fenwick Jones. Athens: University of Georgia Press, 1966–91.

Zinzendorf, Nicholas Ludwig von. *Nine Public Lectures on Important Subjects in Religion . . . 1746.* Translated and edited by George W. Forrell. Iowa City: University of Iowa Press, 1973.

Secondary Sources

Abramson, Harold J. "Assimilation and Pluralism." In *Harvard Encyclopedia of American Ethnic Groups,* edited by Stephan Thernstrom, 150–60. Cambridge, Mass.: Belknap Press, 1980.

Addison, William George. *The Renewed Church of the United Brethren, 1722–1930.* London: Macmillan, 1932.

Ahlstrom, Sydney E. *A Religious History of the American People.* New Haven, Conn.: Yale University Press, 1972.

Albright, S. C. *The Story of the Moravian Congregation of York, Pennsylvania.* York, Pa.: Maple Press Co., 1927.

Andrews, Dee E. *The Methodists and Revolutionary America, 1760–1800: The Shaping of an Evangelical Culture.* Princeton, N.J.: Princeton University Press, 2000.

Armour, Robert Alexander. "The Opposition to the Methodists in Eighteenth-Century Virginia." Ph.D. diss., University of Georgia, 1968.

Atwood, Craig D. "Blood, Sex, and Death: Life and Liturgy in Zinzendorf's Bethlehem." Ph.D. diss., Princeton Theological Seminary, 1995.

Bailyn, Bernard. *The Peopling of British North America: An Introduction.* New York: Alfred A. Knopf, 1986.

———. *Voyagers to the West: A Passage in the Peopling of America on the Eve of the Revolution.* New York: Alfred A. Knopf, 1986.

Bailyn, Bernard, and Philip D. Morgan, eds. *Strangers within the Realm: Cultural Margins of the First British Empire.* Chapel Hill: University of North Carolina Press, 1991.

Ball, D. E., and G. M. Walton. "Agricultural Productivity Change in Eighteenth-Century Pennsylvania." *Journal of Economic History* 36 (March 1976): 102–17.

Barth, Fredrik. *Ethnic Groups and Boundaries: The Social Organization of Cultural Difference.* Prospect Heights, Ill.: Waveland Press, 1998.

Becker, Laura. "Diversity and Its Significance in an Eighteenth-Century Pennsylvania Town." In *Friends and Neighbors: Group Life in America's First Plural Society,* edited by Michael Zuckerman, 196–221. Philadelphia: Temple University Press, 1982.

Beeman, Richard R. *The Evolution of the Southern Backcountry: A Case Study of Lunenburg County, Virginia, 1746–1832.* Philadelphia: University of Pennsylvania Press, 1984.

Bernard, Richard M. *The Melting Pot and the Altar: Marital Assimilation in Early Twentieth-Century Wisconsin.* Minneapolis: University of Minnesota Press, 1980.

Beyreuther, Erich. "Die Paradoxie des Glaubens: Zinzendorfs Verhaltnis zu Pierre und zur Aufklarung." In *Studien zur Theologie Zinzendorfs.* Verlage der Buchhandlung des Erziehungsvereins Neukirchen-Uluym, 1962.

———. *Frommigkeit und Theologie: Gesammelte Aufsatze zum Pietmus und zur Erweckungsbewegung.* Hildesheim: G. Olms, 1980.

———. *Geschichte des Pietmus.* Stuttgart: Steinkopf, 1978.

Boles, John B. *The Great Revival: Beginnings of the Bible Belt.* 2nd ed. Lexington: University Press of Kentucky, 1996.

Bonomi, Patricia U. *Under the Cope of Heaven: Religion, Society, and Politics in Colonial America.* New York: Oxford University Press, 1986.

Bowman, Carl F. *Brethren Society: The Cultural Transformation of a "Peculiar People."* Baltimore: Johns Hopkins University Press, 1995.

Brown, Dale W. *Understanding Pietism.* Grand Rapids, Mich.: William B. Eerdmans Publishing Co., 1978.

Bruce, Dickson D., Jr. *And They All Sang Hallelujah: Plain Folk Camp Meeting Religion, 1800–1845.* Knoxville: University of Tennessee Press, 1974.

Brunner, Daniel L. *Halle Pietists in England: Anthony William Boehm and the Society for Promoting Christian Knowledge.* Gottingen, Germany: Vandenhoeck and Ruprecht, 1993.

Bushman, Richard L. "Markets and Composite Farms in Early America." *William and Mary Quarterly* 55 (July 1998): 351–74.

———. *The Refinement of America: Persons, Houses, Cities.* New York: Vintage Books, 1992.

Butler, Jon. *Awash in a Sea of Faith: Christianizing the American People.* Cambridge, Mass.: Harvard University Press, 1990.

———. *The Huguenots in America: A Refugee People in New World Society.* Cambridge, Mass.: Harvard University Press, 1983.

Calhoon, Robert M. *Evangelicals and Conservatives in the Early South, 1740–1861.* Columbia: University of South Carolina Press, 1988.

Campbell, Theodore. *Religion of the Heart: A Study of European Religious Life in the Seventeenth and Eighteenth Centuries.* Columbia: University of South Carolina Press, 1991.

Carr, Lois Green, Russell R. Menard, and Lorena S. Walsh. *Robert Cole's World: Agriculture and Society in Early Maryland.* Chapel Hill: University of North Carolina Press, 1991.

Clark, Elmer T. *Methodism in Western North Carolina.* Nashville, Tenn.: Western North Carolina Conference, Methodist Church, 1966.

Coburn, Carol K. *Life at Four Corners: Religion, Gender, and Education in a German-Lutheran Community, 1848–1945.* Lawrence: University Press of Kansas, 1992.

Conkin, Paul K. *Cane Ridge: America's Pentecost.* Madison: University of Wisconsin Press, 1990.

Conzen, Kathleen Neils. *Making Their Own America: Assimilation Theory and the German Peasant Pioneer.* New York: Berg, 1990.

———. "Peasant Pioneers: Generational Succession among German Farmers in Frontier Minnesota." In *The Countryside in the Age of Capitalist Transformation: Essays in the Social History of Rural America,* edited by Steven Hahn and Jonathan Prude, 259–92. Chapel Hill: University of North Carolina Press, 1985.

Cott, Nancy F. *The Bonds of Womanhood: "Women's Sphere" in New England, 1780–1835.* New Haven, Conn.: Yale University Press, 1977.

Cross, Whitney R. *The Burned-Over District: The Social and Intellectual History of Enthusiastic Religion in Western New York.* Ithaca: Cornell University Press, 1950.

Daley, John Patrick. *When Slavery Was Called Freedom: Evangelicalism, Proslavery, and the Causes of the Civil War.* Lexington: University Press of Kentucky, 2002.

Davis, William C. *A Way through the Wilderness: The Natchez Trace and the Civilization of the Southern Frontier.* New York: HarperCollins, 1995.

Demos, John. *A Little Commonwealth: Family Life in Plymouth Colony.* New York: Oxford University Press, 1970.

Ditz, Toby L. *Property and Kinship: Inheritance in Early Connecticut, 1750–1820.* Princeton, N.J.: Princeton University Press, 1986.

Doggett, Coleman. "The Moravian Foresters." *Journal of Forest History* 31 (1987): 19–24.

Dreyer, Frederick. *The Genesis of Methodism.* Bethlehem, Pa.: Lehigh University Press, 1999.

Dunaway, Wilma. *The First American Frontier: Transition to Capitalism in Southern Appalachia, 1700–1860.* Chapel Hill: University of North Carolina Press, 1996.

Dyck, Cornelius J., ed. *An Introduction to Mennonite History.* Scottdale, Pa.: Herald Press, 1981.

Earle, Carville, and Ronald Hoffman. "Staple Crops and Urban Development in the Eighteenth-Century South." *Perspectives in American History* 10 (1976): 7–78.

Eighmy, John Lee. *Churches in Cultural Captivity: A History of the Social Attitudes of the Southern Baptists.* Knoxville: University of Tennessee Press, 1972.

Ekirch, Roger. *"Poor Carolina": Politics and Society in North Carolina, 1729–1776.* Chapel Hill: University of North Carolina Press, 1992.

Eldridge, Larry D., ed. *Women and Freedom in Early America.* New York: New York University Press, 1997.

Ensminger, Robert F. *The Pennsylvania Barn: Its Origin, Evolution, and Distribution in North America.* Baltimore: Johns Hopkins University Press, 1982.

Epstein, Barbara Leslie. *The Politics of Domesticity: Women, Evangelism, and Temperance in Nineteenth-Century America.* Middletown, Conn.: Wesleyan University Press, 1981.

Erbe, Hans Walther. "Zinzendorf und der fromme hohe Adel seiner Zeit." Ph.D. diss., Universitat Leipzig, 1928.

Farmer, Charles J. *In the Absence of Towns: Settlement and Country Trade in Southside Virginia, 1730–1800.* Lanham, Md.: Scarecrow Press, 1993.

Fischer, David Hackett. *Albion's Seed: Four British Folkways in America.* New York: Oxford University Press, 1989.

Fogleman, Aaron Spencer. *Hopeful Journeys: German Immigration, Settlement, and Political Culture in Colonial America, 1717–1775.* Philadelphia: University of Pennsylvania Press, 1996.

———. "Jesus Is Female: The Moravian Challenge in the German Communities of British North America." *William and Mary Quarterly* 60 (April 2003): 295–332.

———. "Moravian Immigration and Settlement in British North America, 1734–1775." *Transactions of the Moravian Historical Society* 29 (1996): 30.

———. "Shadow Boxing in Georgia: The Beginnings of the Moravian-Lutheran Conflict in British North America." *Georgia Historical Quarterly* (Winter 1999): 629–59.

Friedman, Jean E. *The Enclosed Garden: Women and Community in the Evangelical South, 1830–1900.* Chapel Hill: University of North Carolina Press, 1988.

Frost, William J., and John M. Moore, eds. *Seeking the Light: Essays in Quaker History.* Wallingford, Pa.: Pendle Hill Publications and Friends Historical Association, 1986.

Fulbrook, Mary. *Piety and Politics: Religion and the Rise of Absolutism in England, Wurttemberg, and Prussia.* New York: Cambridge University Press, 1983.

Games, Alison. *Migration and the Origins of the English Atlantic World.* Cambridge, Mass.: Harvard University Press, 1999.

Gawthrop, Richard L. *Pietism and the Making of Eighteenth-Century Prussia.* New York: Cambridge University Press, 1993.

Gehrke, William H. "Antebellum Agriculture of the Germans in North Carolina." *Agricultural History* 9 (January 1935): 143–60.

Gollin, Gillian Lindt. *Moravians in Two Worlds: A Study of Changing Communities.* New York: Columbia University Press, 1967.

Goodfriend, Joyce D. *Before the Melting Pot: Society and Culture in Colonial New York City, 1664–1730.* Princeton, N.J.: Princeton University Press, 1992.

Goody, Jack, Joan Thirsk, and E. P. Thompson, eds. *Family and Inheritance: Rural Society in Western Europe, 1200–1800.* Cambridge: Cambridge University Press, 1976.

Gordon, Milton M. *Assimilation in American Life: The Role of Race, Religion, and National Origins.* New York: Oxford University Press, 1964.

Gray, Lewis Cecil. *History of Agriculture in the Southern United States to 1860.* New York: Peter Smith, 1941.

Greene, Jack P., and J. R. Pole, eds. *Colonial British America: Essays in the New History of the Early Modern Era.* Baltimore: Johns Hopkins University Press, 1984.

Greven, Philip J., Jr. *The Protestant Temperament: Patterns of Child-Rearing, Religious Experience, and the Self in Early America.* New York: Alfred A. Knopf, 1977.

Griffin, Patrick. *The People with No Name: Ireland's Ulster Scots, America's Scots Irish, and the Creation of a British Atlantic World, 1689–1764.* Princeton, N.J.: Princeton University Press, 2001.

Hall, Timothy D. *Contested Boundaries: Itinerancy and the Reshaping of the Colonial American Religious World.* Durham, N.C.: Duke University Press, 1994.

Haller, Mabel. "Early Moravian Education in Pennsylvania." Ph.D. diss., University of Pennsylvania, 1953.

Hamilton, Taylor J., and Kenneth G. Hamilton. *History of the Moravian Church: The Renewed Unitas Fratrum, 1722–1957.* Bethlehem, Pa.: Interprovincial Board of Christian Education, Moravian Church in America, 1967.

Harrell, David Edwin, Jr., ed. *The Varieties of Southern Evangelicalism.* Macon, Ga.: Mercer University Press, 1981.

Hatch, Nathan O. *The Democratization of American Christianity.* New Haven, Conn.: Yale University Press, 1989.

Heer, David M. "Intermarriage." In *Harvard Encyclopedia of American Ethnic Groups,* edited by Stephan Thernstrom, 513–20. Cambridge, Mass.: Belknap Press, 1980.

Heyrman, Christine Leigh. *Commerce and Culture: The Maritime Communities of Colonial Massachusetts, 1690–1750.* New York: W. W. Norton, 1984.

———. *Southern Cross: The Beginnings of the Bible Belt.* New York: Alfred A. Knopf, 1997.

Hoffman, Ronald. *Princes of Ireland, Planters of Maryland: A Carroll Saga, 1500–1782.* Chapel Hill: University of North Carolina Press, 2000.

Hoffman, Ronald, and Peter J. Albert, eds. *Religion in a Revolutionary Age.* Charlottesville: University Press of Virginia, 1994.

Hoffman, Ronald, Thad W. Tate, and Peter J. Albert, eds. *An Uncivil War: The Southern Backcountry during the American Revolution.* Charlottesville: University Press of Virginia, 1985.

Hofstra, Warren R. "Land, Ethnicity, and Community at the Opequon Settlement, Virginia, 1730–1800." *Virginia Magazine of History and Biography* 98 (July 1990).

Hood, Adrienne D. "The Material World of Cloth: Production and Use in Eighteenth-Century Pennsylvania." *William and Mary Quarterly* 53 (January 1996): 43–66.

Hooker, Richard J., ed. *The Carolina Backcountry on the Eve of the Revolution: The Journal and Other Writings of Charles Woodmason, Anglican Itinerant.* Chapel Hill: University of North Carolina Press, 1953.

Hostetler, Beulah Stauffer. *American Mennonite and Protestant Movements: A Community Paradigm.* Scottdale, Pa.: Herald Press, 1987.

Hunter, James. *The Quiet People of the Land: A Study of the North Carolina Moravians in Revolutionary Times.* Chapel Hill: University of North Carolina Press, 1976.

Innes, Stephen. *Creating the Commonwealth: The Economic Culture of Puritan New England.* New York: W. W. Norton, 1995.

———, ed. *Work and Labor in Early America.* Chapel Hill: University of North Carolina Press, 1988.

Isaac, Rhys. *The Transformation of Virginia, 1740–1790.* Chapel Hill: University of North Carolina Press, 1982.

Jeske, Mary Clement. "Autonomy and Opportunity: Carrollton Manor Tenants, 1734–1790." Ph.D. diss., University of Maryland, 1999.

Johnson, Paul E. *A Shopkeeper's Millennium: Society and Revivals in Rochester, New York, 1815–1837.* New York: Hill and Wang, 1978.

Jordan, Terry G. *German Seed in Texas Soil: Immigrant Farmers in Nineteenth-Century Texas.* Austin: University of Texas Press, 1966.

Jou, Do-Hong. *Theodor Undereyck und die Anfange des Reformierten Pietmus.* Bochum, Germany: Brockmeyer, 1994.

Kars, Marjoleine. *Breaking Loose Together: The Regulator Rebellion in Pre-Revolutionary North Carolina.* Chapel Hill: North Carolina University Press, 2002.

Keever, Homer M. "A Lutheran Preacher's Account of the 1801–02 Revival in North Carolina." *Methodist History* 7 (October 1968): 38–55.

Kelly, Joseph J., Jr. *Pennsylvania: The Colonial Years, 1681–1776.* Garden City, N.Y.: Doubleday and Co., 1980.

Kennedy, Ruby Jo Reeves. "Single or Triple Melting Pot? Intermarriage Trends in New Haven, 1870–1940." *American Journal of Sociology* 49, no. 4 (January 1944): 331–39.

Kimbrough, David L. *Reverend Joseph Tarkington, Methodist Circuit Rider: From Frontier Evangelism to Refined Religion.* Knoxville: University of Tennessee Press, 1997.

Klassen, Walter, ed. *Anabaptism Revisited: Essays on Anabaptist/Mennonite Studies in Honor of C. J. Dyck.* Scottdale, Pa.: Herald Press, 1992.

Klein, Rachel N. "Frontier Planters and the American Revolution: The Southern Backcountry, 1775–1782." In *An Uncivil War: The Southern Backcountry during the American Revolution,* edited by Ronald Hoffman, Thad W. Tate, and Peter J. Albert, 37–69. Charlottesville: University Press of Virginia, 1985.

———. *Unification of a Slave State: The Rise of the Planter Class in the South Carolina Backcountry, 1760–1808.* Chapel Hill: University of North Carolina Press, 1990.

Kniss, Fred Lamar. *Disquiet in the Land: Cultural Conflict in American Mennonite Communities.* New Brunswick, N.J.: Rutgers University Press, 1997.

Knowles, Anne Kelly. *Calvinists Incorporated: Welsh Immigrants on Ohio's Industrial Frontier.* Chicago: University of Chicago Press, 1997.

Kraybill, Donald B. *The Riddle of Amish Culture.* Baltimore: Johns Hopkins University Press, 1989.

Kuenning, Paul B. *The Rise and Fall of American Lutheran Pietism: The Rejection of an Activist Heritage.* Macon, Ga.: Mercer University Press, 1988.

Kulikoff, Allan. *The Agrarian Origins of American Capitalism.* Charlottesville: University Press of Virginia, 1992.

———. *From British Peasants to American Farmers.* Chapel Hill: University of North Carolina Press, 2000.

———. *Tobacco and Slaves: The Development of Southern Cultures in the Chesapeake, 1680–1800.* Chapel Hill: University of North Carolina Press, 1986.

Lambert, Frank. *Inventing the "Great Awakening."* Princeton, N.J.: Princeton University Press, 1999.

———. *"Pedlar in Divinity": George Whitefield and the Transatlantic Revivals, 1737–1770.* Princeton, N.J.: Princeton University Press, 1994.

Langton, Edward. *History of the Moravian Church.* London: Allen and Unwin, 1956.

Lebsock, Suzanne. *The Free Women of Petersburg: Status and Culture in a Southern Town, 1784–1860.* New York: W. W. Norton, 1984.

Ledgerwood, Mikle Dave. "Ethnic Groups on the Frontier in Rowan County, North Carolina, 1750–1778." Master's thesis, Vanderbilt University, 1977.

Lehmann, Hartmut, Hermann Wellenreuther, and Renate Wilson, eds. *In Search of Peace and Prosperity: New German Settlements in Eighteenth-Century Europe and America.* University Park: Pennsylvania State Press, 2000.

Lemon, James T. *The Best Poor Man's Country: A Geographical Study of Early Southeastern Pennsylvania.* Baltimore: Johns Hopkins University Press, 1972.

Levy, Barry J. "The Birth of the 'Modern Family' in Early America: Quaker and Anglican Families in the Delaware Valley, Pennsylvania, 1681–1750." In *Friends and Neighbors,* edited by Michael Zuckerman, 26–63. Philadelphia: Temple University Press, 1982.

———. *Quakers and the American Family: British Settlement in the Delaware Valley.* New York: Oxford University Press, 1988.

———. "'Tender Plants': Quaker Farmers and Children in the Delaware Valley, 1681–1735." In *Colonial America: Essays in Politics and Social Development,* 3rd ed., edited by Stanley N. Katz and John M. Murrin, 177–203. New York: Alfred A. Knopf, 1983.

Lewis, A. J. *Zinzendorf, the Ecumenical Pioneer: A Study in the Moravian Contribution to Christian Mission and Unity.* Philadelphia: Westminster Press, 1962.

Lewis, Johanna Miller. *Artisans in the North Carolina Backcountry.* Lexington: University Press of Kentucky, 1995.

———. "A Social and Architectural History of the Girls' Boarding School Building at Salem, North Carolina." *North Carolina Historical Review* 66 (April 1989): 125–48.

Loewen, Royden K. *Family, Church, and Market: A Mennonite Community in the Old and the New Worlds, 1850–1930.* Urbana: University of Illinois Press, 1993.

Long, Ronald W. "Religious Revivalism in the Carolinas and Georgia, 1740–1805." Ph.D. diss., University of Georgia, 1968.

Longenecker, Stephen L. *Piety and Tolerance: Pennsylvania German Religion, 1700–1850.* Metuchen, N.J.: Scarecrow Press, 1994.

———. *Shenandoah Religion: Outsiders and the Mainstream, 1716–1865.* Waco, Tex.: Baylor University Press, 2002.

Loveland, Anne C. *Southern Evangelicals and the Social Order, 1800–1860.* Baton Rouge: Louisiana State University Press, 1980.

Luebke, Frederick C. *Germans in the New World: Essays in the History of Immigration.* Urbana: University of Illinois Press, 1990.

Lyerly, Cynthia Lynn. *Methodism and the Southern Mind, 1770–1810.* New York: Oxford University Press, 1998.

Macchia, Frank D. *Spirituality and Social Liberation: The Message of the Blumharts in the Light of Wurttemberg Pietism.* Metuchen, N.J.: Scarecrow Press, 1993.

MacMaster, Richard K. *Land, Piety, Peoplehood: The Establishment of Mennonite Communities in America, 1683–1790.* Scottdale, Pa.: Herald Press, 1985.

Maier, Pauline. *From Resistance to Revolution: Colonial Radicals and the Development of American Opposition to Britain, 1765–1776.* New York: Alfred A. Knopf, 1972.

Marietta, Jack D. *The Reformation of American Quakerism, 1748–1783.* Philadelphia: University of Pennsylvania Press, 1984.

Mason, J. C. S. *The Moravian Church and the Missionary Awakening in England, 1760–1800.* Suffolk, U.K.: Royal Historical Society, 2001.

Mathews, Donald G. "Religion and the South: Authenticity and Purity—Pulling Us Together, Tearing Us Apart." In *Religious Diversity and American Religious History: Studies in Traditions and Cultures,* edited by Walter H. Conser Jr. and Sumner B. Twiss, 72–101. Athens: University of Georgia Press, 1997.

———. *Religion in the Old South.* Chicago: University of Chicago Press, 1977.

Mayhew, Alan. *Rural Settlement and Farming in Germany.* London: Batsford, 1973.

McCardle, Arthur W. *Friedrich Schiller and Swabian Pietism.* New York: P. Lang, 1986.

McCusker, John J., and Russell R. Menard. *The Economy of British America, 1607–1789.* Chapel Hill: University of North Carolina Press, 1985.

McGiffert, Michael, ed. *God's Plot: The Paradoxes of Puritan Piety, Being the Autobiography and Journal of Thomas Shepard.* Amherst: University of Massachusetts Press, 1978.

McLoughlin, Willam G. *Revivals, Awakenings, and Reform: An Essay on Religion and Social Change in America, 1607–1977.* Chicago: University of Chicago Press, 1978.

McMurry, Sally. *Families and Farmhouses in Nineteenth-Century America: Vernacular Design and Social Change.* Knoxville: University of Tennessee Press, 1997.

Merrens, Harry Roy. *Colonial North Carolina in the Eighteenth Century: A Study in Historical Geography.* Chapel Hill: University of North Carolina Press, 1964.

Middlekauf, Robert. *The Glorious Cause: The American Revolution, 1763–1789.* New York: Oxford University Press, 1982.

Mitchell, Robert D. *Commercialism and Frontier: Perspectives on the Early Shenandoah Valley.* Charlottesville: University Press of Virginia, 1977.

Moore, R. Laurence. *Religious Outsiders and the Making of Americans.* New York: Oxford University Press, 1986.

Morgan, Edmund S. *The Puritan Dilemma: The Story of John Winthrop.* Edited by Oscar Handlin. Boston: Little, Brown, 1958.

———. *The Puritan Family: Religion and Domestic Relations in Seventeenth-Century New England.* Westport, Conn.: Greenwood Press, 1980.

Morris, Christopher. *Becoming Southern: The Evolution of a Way of Life, Warren County and Vicksburg, Mississippi, 1770–1860.* New York: Oxford University Press, 1995.

Mulder, Philip N. *A Controversial Spirit: Evangelical Awakenings in the South.* New York: Oxford University Press, 2002.

Nelson, Clifford E., ed. *The Lutherans in North America.* Philadelphia: Fortress Press, 1975.

Nobles, Gregory H. *American Frontiers: Cultural Encounters and Continental Conquest.* New York: Hill and Wang, 1997.

———. "Breaking into the Backcountry: New Approaches to the Early American Frontier." *William and Mary Quarterly* 46 (October 1989): 641–70.

Nolt, Steven M. *Foreigners in Their Own Land: Pennsylvania Germans in the Early Republic.* University Park: Pennsylvania State University Press, 2002.

Oakes, James. *The Ruling Race: A History of American Slaveholders.* New York: Alfred A. Knopf, 1982.

———. *Slavery and Freedom: An Interpretation of the Old South.* New York: Alfred A. Knopf, 1990.

Ogilvie, Sheilagh. "Coming of Age in a Corporate Society: Capitalism, Pietism, and Family Authority in Rural Wurttemberg, 1590–1740." *Continuity and Change* 1:3 (1986): 279–331.

———, ed. *Germany: A New Social and Economic History, 1630–1800.* Vol. 2. New York: St. Martin's Press, 1996.

O'Malley, Steven J. *Early German-American Evangelicalism: Pietist Sources on Discipleship and Sanctification.* Lanham, Md.: Scarecrow Press, 1995.

Otto, John Solomon. "The Migration of the Southern Plain Folk: An Interdisciplinary Synthesis." *Journal of Southern History* 51 (May 1985): 183–200.

Parsons, William T. *The Pennsylvania Dutch: A Persistent Minority.* Boston: Twayne Publishers, 1976.

Patterson, Jo Ellen. "Church Control and Family Structure in a Moravian Community of North Carolina, 1753–1857." Ph.D. diss., University of North Carolina at Greensboro, 1991.

Peters, Victor. *All Things Common: The Hutterian Way of Life.* Minneapolis: University of Minnesota Press, 1965.

Pitzer, Donald E., ed. *America's Communal Utopias.* Chapel Hill: University of North Carolina Press, 1997.

Podmore, Colin. *The Moravian Church in England, 1728–1760.* New York: Oxford University Press, 1998.

Puglisi, Michael J., ed. *Diversity and Accommodation: Essays on the Cultural Composition of the Virginia Frontier.* Knoxville: University of Tennessee Press, 1997.

Ramsey, Robert W. *Carolina Cradle: Settlement of the Northwest Carolina Frontier, 1747–1762.* Chapel Hill: University of North Carolina Press, 1964.

Redekop, Calvin. *Mennonite Society.* Baltimore: Johns Hopkins University Press, 1989.

Redekop, Calvin, Stephen C. Ainlay, and Robert Siemens. *Mennonite Entrepreneurs.* Baltimore: Johns Hopkins University Press, 1995.

Reschly, Steven D. *The Amish on the Iowa Prairie, 1840 to 1910.* Baltimore: Johns Hopkins University Press, 2000.

Rice, Edwin Wilbur. *The Sunday School Movement 1780–1917 and the American Sunday-School Union 1817–1917.* New York: Arno Press, 1971.

Richey, Russell E. *Early American Methodism.* Bloomington: Indiana University Press, 1991.

Roeber, A. G. "'The Origin of Whatever Is Not English among Us': The Dutch-speaking and German-speaking Peoples of Colonial British America." In *Strangers within the Realm: Cultural Margins of the First British Empire,* edited by Bernard Bailyn and Philip D. Morgan. Chapel Hill: University of North Carolina Press, 1991.

———. *Palatines, Liberty, and Property: German Lutherans in Colonial British America.* Baltimore: Johns Hopkins University Press, 1993.

Rohrer, S. Scott. "Evangelism and Acculturation in the Southern Backcountry: The Case of Wachovia, N.C., 1753–1830." *Journal of the Early Republic* 21 (Summer 2001): 199–229.

———. "Planting Pietism: Religion and Community in the Moravian Settlements of North Carolina, 1750–1830." Ph.D. diss., University of Virginia, 1999.

———. "Searching for Land and God: The Pietist Migration to North Carolina in the Late Colonial Period." *North Carolina Historical Review* 79 (October 2002): 409–39.

Rolland, Susanne Mostelle. "From the Rhine to the Catawba: A Study of Eighteenth Century Germanic Migration and Adaptation." Ph.D. diss., Emory University, 1991.

Rothermund, Dietmar. *The Layman's Progress: Religious and Political Experience in Colonial Pennsylvania, 1740–1770.* Philadelphia: University of Pennsylvania Press, 1961.

Roy-Hayden, Priscilla A. *A Foretaste of Heaven: Friedrich Holderlin in the Context of Wurttemberg Pietism.* Amsterdam: Rodopi, 1994.

Rutman, Darrett B., and Anita H. Rutman. *A Place in Time: Middlesex County, Virginia, 1650–1750.* New York: W. W. Norton, 1984.

Ryan, Mary P. *Cradle of the Middle Class: The Family in Oneida County, New York, 1790–1865.* Cambridge, U.K.: Cambridge University Press, 1981.

Sabean, David Warren. *Power in the Blood: Popular Culture and Village Discourse in Early Modern Germany.* New York: Cambridge University Press, 1984.

———. *Property, Production, and Family in Neckarhausen, 1700–1870.* New York: Cambridge University Press, 1991.

Sarna, Jonathan D. "From Immigrants to Ethnics: Toward a New Theory of 'Ethnicization.'" *Ethnicity* 5 (1978): 370–78.

———, ed. *Minority Faiths and the American Protestant Mainstream.* Urbana: University of Illinois Press, 1998.

Schlabach, Theron F. *Peace, Faith, Nation: Mennonites and Amish in Nineteenth-Century America.* Scottdale, Pa.: Herald Press, 1988.

Schwartz, Sally. *"A Mixed Multitude": The Struggle for Toleration in Colonial Pennsylvania.* New York: New York University Press, 1987.

Semmel, Bernard. *The Methodist Revolution.* New York: Basic Books, 1973.

Sensbach, Jon F. *A Separate Canaan: The Making of an Afro-Moravian World in North Carolina, 1763–1840.* Chapel Hill: University of North Carolina Press, 1998.

Sessler, Jacob John. *Communal Pietism among Early American Moravians.* New York: Henry Holt and Co., 1933.

Shirley, Michael. *From Congregation Town to Industrial City: Cultural and Social Change in a Southern Community.* New York: New York University Press, 1994.

Simler, Lucy. "Tenancy in Colonial Pennsylvania: The Case of Chester County." *William and Mary Quarterly* 43 (1986): 542–69.

Smaby, Beverly Prior. *The Transformation of Moravian Bethlehem: From Communal Mission to Family Economy.* Philadelphia: University of Pennsylvania Press, 1988.

Small, Nora Pat. "The Search for a New Rural Order: Farmhouses in Sutton, Massachusetts, 1790–1830." *William and Mary Quarterly* 53 (January 1996): 67–86.

Smith, Daniel Scott. "A Perspective on Demographic Methods and Effects in Social History." *William and Mary Quarterly* 39 (1982): 442–68.

Smith, Timothy L. *Revivalism and Social Reform in Mid-Nineteenth-Century America.* New York: Abingdon Press, 1957.

———. *Whitefield and Wesley on the New Birth.* Grand Rapids, Mich.: Francis Asbury Press, 1986.

Snydacker, Daniel. "Kinship and Community in Rural Pennsylvania, 1749–1820." *Journal of Interdisciplinary History* 13 (Summer 1982): 41–61.

Snyder, Howard Albert. "Pietism, Moravianism, and Methodism as Renewal Movements: A Comparative and Thematic Study." Ph.D. diss., University of Notre Dame, 1983.

Sollors, Werner, ed. *The Invention of Ethnicity.* New York: Oxford University Press, 1989.

Sommer, Elisabeth W. "Serving Two Masters: Authority, Faith, and Community among the Moravian Brethren in Germany and North Carolina in the 18th Century." Ph.D. diss., University of Virginia, 1991.

———. *Serving Two Masters: Moravian Brethren in Germany and North Carolina, 1727–1801.* Lexington: University Press of Kentucky, 2000.

Stein, K. James. *Philipp Jakob Spener: Pietist Patriarch.* Chicago: Covenant Press, 1986.

Stoeffler, F. Ernest. *German Pietism during the Eighteenth Century.* Leiden: E. J. Brill, 1973.

———. *The Rise of Evangelical Pietism.* Leiden: E. J. Brill, 1965.

——, ed. *Continental Pietism and Early American Christianity*. Grand Rapids, Mich.: William B. Eerdmans Publishing Co., 1976.

Stoever, William K. B. *"A Faire and Easie Way to Heaven": Covenant Theology and Antinomianism in Early Massachusetts*. Middletown, Conn.: Wesleyan University Press, 1978.

Stout, Harry S. "Ethnicity: The Vital Center of Religion in America." *Ethnicity* 2 (June 1975): 204–24.

Surratt, Jerry Lee. "From Theocracy to Voluntary Church and Secularized Community: A Study of the Moravians in Salem, North Carolina, 1772–1860." Ph.D. diss., Emory University, 1968.

——. *Gottlieb Schober of Salem: Discipleship and Ecumenical Vision in an Early Moravian Town*. Macon, Ga.: Mercer University Press, 1983.

Symonds, Craig L. *A Battlefield Atlas of the American Revolution*. Mt. Pleasant, S.C.: Nautical and Aviation Publishing, 1986.

Taylor, Alan. *Liberty Men and Great Proprietors: The Revolutionary Settlement on the Maine Frontier, 1760–1820*. Chapel Hill: University of North Carolina Press, 1990.

——. *William Cooper's Town: Power and Persuasion on the Frontier of the Early American Republic*. New York: Alfred A. Knopf, 1995.

Taylor, Gwynne Stephens. *From Frontier to Factory: An Architectural History of Forsyth County*. Raleigh: North Carolina Department of Cultural Resources, 1981.

Theibault, John C. *German Villages in Crisis: Rural Life in Hesse-Kassel and the Thirty Years' War, 1580–1720*. Highlands, N.J.: Humanities Press International, 1995.

Thernstrom, Stephan, ed. *Harvard Encyclopedia of American Ethnic Groups*. Cambridge, Mass.: Belknap Press, 1980.

Thorp, Daniel B. "Assimilation in North Carolina's Moravian Community." *Journal of Southern History* 52 (February 1986): 19–42.

——. *The Moravian Community in Colonial North Carolina: Pluralism on the Southern Frontier*. Knoxville: University of Tennessee Press, 1989.

——. "Taverns and Tavern Culture on the Southern Colonial Frontier: Rowan County, North Carolina, 1753–1776." *Journal of Southern History* 62 (November 1996): 661–88.

——. "Transplanting a Land Use System: Moravian Efforts to Transfer Agricultural Technology from Germany to North Carolina." *Journal of Forest History* 31 (1987): 25.

Tillson, Albert H., Jr. "The Southern Backcountry: A Survey of Current Research." *Virginia Magazine of History and Biography* 48 (July 1990): 387–422.

Tise, Larry E. *The Yadkin Melting Pot: Methodism and the Moravians in the Yadkin Valley, 1750–1850, and Mount Tabor Church, 1845–1966*. Winston-Salem, N.C.: Clay Printing Co., 1967.

Toews, Paul. *Mennonites in American Society, 1930–1970: Modernity and the Persistence of Religious Community*. Scottdale, Pa.: Herald Press, 1996.

Tolles, Frederick B. *Meeting House and Counting House: The Quaker Merchants of Colonial Philadelphia, 1682–1763*. Chapel Hill: University of North Carolina Press, 1948.

Trommler, Frank, and Joseph McVeigh, eds. *America and the Germans: An Assessment of a Three-Hundred Year History.* Vol. 1. Philadelphia: University of Pennsylvania Press, 1985.

Tuttle, Robert G. *John Wesley: His Life and Theology.* Grand Rapids. Mich.: Zondervan Publishing House, 1978.

Ulrich, Laurel Thatcher. *Good Wives: Image and Reality in the Lives of Women in Northern New England, 1650–1750.* New York: Alfred A. Knopf, 1982.

Vogt, Peter. "Zinzendorf and the 'Pennsylvania Synods' of 1742: The First Ecumenical Conferences of the North American Continent." Religion thesis, Moravian College, 1992.

Wall, Helena M. *Fierce Communion: Family and Community in Early America.* Cambridge, Mass.: Harvard University Press, 1990.

Ward, W. R. *The Protestant Evangelical Awakening.* Cambridge, U.K.: Cambridge University Press, 1992.

Watson, Alan D. "North Carolina and Internal Improvements, 1783–1861: The Case of Inland Navigation." *North Carolina Historical Review* 74 (January 1997): 37–73.

Weber, Max. *The Protestant Ethic and the Spirit of Capitalism.* Translated by Talcott Parsons. Los Angeles: Roxbury Publishing Co., 1996.

Weinlick, John R. *Count Zinzendorf.* New York: Abingdon Press, 1956.

———. "The Moravian Diaspora: A Study of the Societies of the Moravian Church within the Protestant State Churches of Europe." Ph.D. diss., Columbia University, 1951.

Westerkamp, Marilyn J. *Triumph of the Laity: Scots-Irish Piety and the Great Awakening, 1625–1760.* New York: Oxford University Press, 1988.

Wigger, John H. *Taking Heaven by Storm: Methodism and the Rise of Popular Christianity in America.* New York: Oxford University Press, 1998.

Wills, Gregory A. *Democratic Religion: Freedom, Authority, and Church Discipline in the Baptist South, 1785–1900.* New York: Oxford University Press, 1997.

Wilson, Charles Reagan, ed. *Religion in the South: Essays.* Jackson: University Press of Mississippi, 1985.

Wokeck, Marianne S. "The Flow and the Composition of German Immigration to Philadelphia, 1727–1775." *Pennsylvania Magazine of History and Biography* 105 (1981): 249–78.

———. *Trade in Strangers: The Beginnings of Mass Migration to North America.* University Park: Pennsylvania State University Press, 1999.

Wolf, Stephanie Grauman. *Urban Village: Population, Community, and Family Structure in Germantown, Pennsylvania, 1683–1800.* Princeton, N.J.: Princeton University Press, 1976.

Wood, Gordon S. *The Creation of the American Republic, 1776–1787.* New York: W. W. Norton, 1972.

———. *The Radicalism of the American Revolution.* New York: Vintage, 1993.

Wood, Jerome H., Jr. *Conestoga Crossroads: Lancaster, Pennsylvania, 1730–1790.* Harrisburg, Pa.: Pennsylvania Historical and Museum Commission, 1979.

Wust, Klaus. *The Virginia Germans.* Charlottesville: University Press of Virginia, 1969.

Yoder, Paton. *Tradition and Transition: Amish Mennonites and Old Order Amish, 1800–1900.* Scottdale, Pa.: Herald Press, 1991.

Zuckerman, Michael, ed. *Friends and Neighbors: Group Life in America's First Plural Society.* Philadelphia: Temple University Press, 1982.

Index

wills. *See* inheritance practices
Wilmington, N.C., 32, 147, 156
Witherspoon, Reverend, 186
Wolf, Stephanie Grauman, 80
women: arrival in Wachovia, 29; as execu-
    tors, 181; companionate ideal, 182; do-
    mesticity, 180; dowries, 182; economic
    roles, 181, 182; inheritance, 90–91;
    life span, 76; marrying age, 76, 179;
    membership on church boards, 134,
    182; missionary work, 185; position in
    antebellum period, 180–83; religious
    education, 176; role as "helpmaids," 73
Wood, Gordon S., 106, 124, 132
Woodmason, Charles, xx, xxxii
Wurttemberg, Germany, 71

Yadkin River, 29, 84, 189, 190
Yarrell, Peter, 155
York County, Pa., 16
Yorktown, Pa., 18, 68, 74, 154

Zahn, J. M., 6
Zevilly, Van Neman, 202
Zimmerman, Christian, 49
Zinzendorf, Nicholas von, xxii, xxxii, 166;
    blood-wounds theology, 41–42, 199;
    ecumenical vision, 12–13, 191, 202;
    links with Lutherans, 15; sermons,
    40–41; views of Great Awakening,
    188; views of heart religion, 16–17,
    39; views of slavery, 161; views of
    work, 158